Class No. _941.506_   Acc No. _C/134170_

Author: _WHEELER J.S._ Loc: 1 - MAY 2003

LEABHARLANN
CHONDAE AN CHABHAIN

1. This book may be kept three weeks. It is to be returned on / before the last date stamped below.
2. A fine of 25c will be charged for every week or part of week a book is overdue.

Cromwell
in Ireland

Cromwell
in Ireland

James Scott Wheeler

Gill & Macmillan

Gill & Macmillan Ltd
Goldenbridge
Dublin 8
with associated companies throughout the world
www.gillmacmillan.ie
© James Scott Wheeler 1999
0 7171 2884 9
Print origination by Carole Lynch
Printed by ColourBooks Ltd, Dublin

This book is typeset in 11/13 pt Bembo

A CIP catalogue record for this book is available
from the British Library.

1 3 5 4 2

Dedicated to Rose Katherine, Iree, and Dean Ennis

Contents

Maps

Preface

I owe a great deal of thanks to many people for their help and counsel during the writing of this sad tale. Special thanks are due to Edith Loe and Professors Linda Frey, Cliff Rogers, Dennis Showalter, Brad Gericke and Pilar Ryan. These wonderful scholars have read the drafts and made many useful recommendations. My wife Jane has served brilliantly as my research assistant and adviser. Frank Martini, the Cartographer of the Department of History at the United States Military Academy, and my associates Bob Doughty and Lee Wyatt have given me a great deal of support and encouragement in the preparation of the book. I am also in debt for their assistance in my research to the staffs of the Bodleian Library of Oxford University, the National Library of Ireland, the Public Record Office in London, and the Interlibrary Loan Office of the Library at the United States Military Academy. Fergal Tobin of Gill & Macmillan and Colm Croker, my copy-editor, have done a terrific job in guiding this project, and I deeply appreciate their help. All mistakes in this work are my own.

All placenames have been given in their modern spelling whenever possible. The calendar year beginning on 1 January has been used throughout, although the day and month of all documents remains as written on those documents in the 1640s and 1650s.

Introduction

> The object of this work is to give an account in full detail, as far as
> is possible, of Cromwell's Irish campaign, which began in August,
> 1649, and ended in May, 1650. It is a portion of history but little
> known. It lies for the most part in a few books, some of them
> difficult of access by reason of their scarcity, others written in a
> language not intelligible to the greater number of readers.
>
> Denis Murphy, *Cromwell in Ireland* (1883)[1]

It is fitting and timely to publish a new account of the Cromwellian conquest of Ireland four hundred years after Cromwell's birth (25 April
1599) and three hundred and fifty years after his arrival in Ireland at the
head of an invasion force of 12,000 soldiers (15 August 1649). During the
following nine months this army overran most of Ulster, Leinster and
Munster. In the process, Cromwell earned the reputation as the most evil
conqueror in Irish history. In the words of one historian, Cromwell was 'a
great, bad man'.[2]

While much has been written about Cromwell's conquest of Ireland
since Denis Murphy published his *Cromwell in Ireland* in 1883, his work
remains the best narrative of Cromwell's campaign of 1649–50. Murphy
provided an in-depth account of Cromwell's campaigns that was based on
extensive research in the available documents, memoirs and contemporary
records of the English conquest. Few historians have exceeded Murphy's
attention to detail. But his book is now out of print and is, in any case,
marred by his heavy reliance on the highly biased source known as the
Aphorismical Discovery, a contemporary Gaelic Irish source that avoided
no opportunity to denigrate anyone in Ireland who did not adhere to the
position of the papal nuncio, Rinuccini.[3] Because of Murphy's natural sympathy with the Roman Catholic Church and the Irish people, his *Cromwell
in Ireland* also tends to reflect a distinct anti-English and anti-Cromwellian
bias that is not fully justified by the sources readily available today.

Shortly after Murphy's account of the Cromwellian conquest was published, Samuel Rawson Gardiner produced a superb eight-volume history of Britain and Ireland in the 1640s and 1650s.[4] Gardiner's books remain an invaluable resource for the study of seventeenth-century Britain and Ireland because they provide an extensive narrative of the history of all three Stuart kingdoms that is based on a thorough use of the primary documents. No other comprehensive history of the three kingdoms has since been published. However, Gardiner's chapters on Ireland are scattered throughout his eight volumes, and he did not discuss important aspects of the Irish war of 1641–52. Moreover, Gardiner's Whiggish view of British history predisposed him to rationalise the English conquest of Ireland in general, and Cromwell's role in that conquest in particular.

No one in this century has published a satisfactory comprehensive military history of the Irish war and Cromwellian conquest. Although Patrick J. Corish's three chapters in Volume III of *A New History of Ireland* (1976) deal superbly with the period 1641–52, the author did not have the space to discuss many of the military and political aspects of the Irish war.[5] More recently Ian Gentles included an excellent chapter describing the Cromwellian conquest in his book *The New Model Army* (1992), but his narrative focuses primarily on the first six months of the Cromwellian conquest of 1649–52. Surprisingly, even the recently published *A Military History of Ireland* (1996) fails to discuss in any detail the military operations and battles in Ireland during this decisive period of Irish history.[6]

Historians now are attempting to integrate the histories of Scotland, Ireland and England into a new history that provides a cohesive account of the three Stuart kingdoms. This approach is an attempt to provide an analysis that is much more than the history of England with the Scots and Irish appended as afterthoughts. One result of this trend in historiography has been to show how much more politically and militarily successful the Catholic Confederates in Ireland were in the war of the 1640s, and how close they came to achieving autonomy within a tripartite Stuart monarchy.[7] Such work highlights the need for a thorough military history of Cromwell's conquest of Ireland which integrates that conquest into the Irish war of 1641–52 and the British wars of the same period.

This book provides a military history of the Irish war of 1641–52 and the Cromwellian conquest of 1649–52. This narrative is based on the extensive body of primary sources that document the dramatic events of this critical period in Irish and British history. The work of earlier historians has also contributed to the analysis. Major emphasis is placed on the Cromwellian conquest of 1649–52. However, since the course and outcome of that conquest cannot be explained adequately without an understanding of the military and political history of Ireland in the previous eight years, the first two chapters provide a summary of the Catholic struggle for religious toleration in a Stuart kingdom from 1641 to 1649. Chapters 3–6 deal extensively with Cromwell's role in the English conquest from August 1649 to May 1650. The last three chapters discuss the completion of the Cromwellian conquest by Cromwell's subordinates from 1650 to 1652, while he went on to lead the English conquest of Scotland.

The defeat of royalism and Catholicism in Ireland owed as much to the disunity of the Catholic and royalist factions in Ireland as it did to English power and Cromwellian military prowess. The deep-rooted splits within Catholic Ireland between the Gaelic Irish and the Old English were never closed completely, badly weakening their military efforts at critical junctures in the long war from 1642 to 1652. This weakness becomes painfully evident as the account and analysis of the Irish war and the Cromwellian conquest unfolds.

Deep internal political and ethnic divisions debilitated the Catholic cause in Ireland in the 1640s, and especially in 1648–9. These divisions exerted their disruptive influence just when the Catholics and royalists had a golden opportunity to expel all parliamentarians from Ireland. They failed to do so because of their disunity. Even when the execution of Charles I drove most royalists and Catholics into the Ormond coalition of 1649, the major Gaelic Irish army under Owen Roe O'Neill stayed out, enabling the last two parliamentarian garrisons in Ireland to hold out in Derry and Dublin. This made it possible for the English to reinforce their bridgehead in Dublin sufficiently so that in August, before Cromwell arrived, Michael Jones could win the decisive battle of the Cromwellian conquest at Baggotsrath/Rathmines. After that defeat the disunity in the Catholic ranks repeatedly weakened Ormond's military response to the English onslaught. 'God's Englishman' Oliver Cromwell played a crucial role in the military defeat of the Irish cause. But he would not have had the opportunity to defeat the royalist and Catholic causes in Ireland had the Catholics and royalists worked wholeheartedly together to defeat the parliamentarians before Cromwell and his army arrived.

Accounts of Cromwell's part in the conquest and his impact on Ireland have been strongly politicised for centuries, as is reflected in Murphy's and Gardiner's works. So much that has gone wrong in Anglo-Irish history has been blamed on Cromwell. Some of this blame is appropriate; much of it is not. Cromwell certainly played a critical role in the English conquest. Militarily, he demonstrated a mastery of the logistical aspects of warfare. His skill in manoeuvring his forces during the autumn and winter campaigns of 1649–50 produced decisive results. Politically, he exploited the fissures within the royalist cause to detach the Protestants of Munster and Ulster from Ormond's military alliance. As a result of his energetic leadership, by the time he departed for England the royalist cause had been defeated and the Catholic coalition's forces had been driven from most of Ulster, Leinster and Munster. However, a darker side to Cromwell's military prowess is evident in his campaigns in Ireland.

Cromwell's army committed appalling atrocities at Drogheda and Wexford, blackening his and his soldiers' reputations. Further, after his departure from Ireland the English resorted to a scorched-earth policy against the tory-infested areas of Ireland. English punitive expeditions and tory raids devastated those parts of Ireland that had been spared the ravages of war before 1650. As a result, by the nineteenth century Cromwell had become the 'personification of English violence in Ireland' for some, and the hero of Protestant and Whiggish England for others.[8] He had become the symbol of English oppression in Ireland and of the atrocities evident in warfare in the seventeenth century. But atrocities were not new when Cromwell arrived in Ireland, nor were they committed only by English Protestants.

Cromwell was typically English in his anti-Catholicism. However, he did not create English prejudice towards Catholics, nor did he wage genocidal warfare. He used all available force and resources to defeat his enemies swiftly, and his army committed two of the worst atrocities in a war noted for the brutality perpetrated by all combatants. But his overall treatment of civilians was lenient. Recognising the need to conciliate the Irish people for logistical purposes, he understood that he had to win the hearts and minds, or at least the passive acceptance, of the Irish population to English rule if the conquest was to succeed.

Oliver Cromwell never fought a pitched battle in Ireland. His progress through Leinster and Munster was marked by sieges and manoeuvres which stripped the initiative from his enemies and demoralised them. He did not win every tactical engagement nor capture every town he besieged. He was defeated at the first siege of Waterford, and his army suffered the worst losses ever inflicted on the famous New Model Army at the siege of Clonmel in May 1650. Cromwell's logistical organisation of his campaigns and his skilful use of tactical manoeuvre to force his foe into untenable positions contributed greatly to the steady progress of the English conquest. By the time he left Ireland in May 1650 the royalist coalition had been shattered. His soldiers had driven the last organised Irish forces into Kerry and Connacht, and English preparations for the final defeat of Catholic Ireland were well under way.

After Cromwell's departure another two years of hard fighting and costly sieges faced the English Puritans. This part of the story is not told in Murphy's *Cromwell in Ireland*, and is discussed only briefly in modern accounts. Particular attention is therefore paid to the military operations after Cromwell's departure. During this final period of Ireland's mid-century ordeal the English policy towards the Irish population living outside the English-held towns changed dramatically from Cromwell's original conciliatory approach. English frustration with the dogged persistence of the

Catholic forces in Connacht and the tory guerrilla bands throughout Ireland resulted in the promulgation of English edicts that declared wide swaths of Ireland to be 'free-fire' zones in which any living thing and any habitation could be destroyed by government forces. This savage war of peace only ended after a better way was found to get the tory bands out of the island — shipment overseas to serve in foreign armies.

Others in addition to Cromwell played a large role in the conquest of Ireland. His son-in-law Henry Ireton commanded the English forces until his death in November 1651. He was ably assisted by veteran professionals of the New Model Army. Second- and third-generation Anglo-Irish Protestants like Roger Boyle, Lord Broghill, and Sir Charles Coote also commanded major forces in the war. Broghill rallied the Protestant royalists of Munster and Ulster to the Cromwellian cause in 1649, when it became clear that the English regicides were their best hope of defeating the then triumphant Catholics in Ireland. Commanders such as Sir Charles Coote, whose families had arrived in Ireland in the Elizabethan era and were thus known as 'New English', conducted the most brutal operations against the Catholic forces. They, far more than Cromwell, made the conquest an ethnic war. The accounts of their operations show that they often appeared willing to exterminate the Irish population. Yet, amazingly, they are seldom singled out by historians today as the major perpetrators of the Protestant atrocities in the conquest.

When the war was over, Broghill, later created Earl of Orrery by Charles II, and men like him became the chief beneficiaries of the massive redistribution of Irish Catholic lands to Protestant hands. They were the backbone of the Protestant Ascendancy that emerged between 1652 and 1691. This account of the Irish war of 1641–52 illustrates their role in the atrocities generally described as Cromwellian. It also demonstrates how brutality was not a Protestant monopoly. From beginning to end, Catholic forces butchered Protestants, just as Protestants butchered Catholics, making the war at least as costly to Ireland as the Thirty Years' War was to Germany.

1

The War of the Three Kingdoms, 1641–8

My Lords,
  The miseries of distracted Ireland are so many in all corners of it, that it would require a just volume, rather than a letter to represent them.

A True Copy of Two Letters . . . from my Lord Forbes from Ireland
(12 Oct. 1642)[1]

Seventeenth-century Ireland was a troubled land, and an underlying cause of many of its troubles was its uneasy relationship with its larger neighbour, the island of Great Britain. Both islands were under the political control of an English Protestant monarchy which had no sympathy with, and little understanding of, the Catholic majority of the Irish population. The Irish political situation in 1641 seemed calm, in spite of the disturbances across the Irish Sea caused by the successful Scottish invasion of England.[2] The calm was deceiving, as the distracted Lords Justices in Dublin found out to their horror when a Catholic insurrection irrupted in Ulster.

The Irish rebellion of October 1641 opened one of the most tragic periods in Irish history. For the next eleven years Ireland suffered the effects of a war as destructive as the Thirty Years' War in Germany. Economic devastation was widespread. Military operations directly caused over 100,000 casualties, including civilians, while the total population of roughly 2 million declined by as much as one-third.[3] Like the German war, the outcome of the Irish conflict subordinated the interests of the native population to the will of a foreign power for hundreds of years. Worse, the Irish found themselves permanently subordinated to a foreign ruling class and denied the economic, political and religious rights granted to their fellow-subjects in the British kingdoms. As a result, generations of Irish fighting men chose

6

to leave Ireland, preferring to serve as mercenaries, or 'wild geese', in Spanish or French employ, rather than to remain under English rule.[4]

THE LOST OPPORTUNITY

The rising of 1641 did not lead inevitably to Irish military disaster and the shattering defeat of Irish religious and political aspirations. Some form of Catholic victory was possible. The Presbyterian Scots' successes during the Bishops' Wars in 1639 and 1640 against the poorly led and ill-supplied forces of the more powerful English state demonstrated that Scotland could defend itself against the tyranny of the English church and Charles I. Many of the leaders of the Irish rebellion hoped to emulate Scottish success and to win greater autonomy for a Catholic Ireland by rising against their oppressors. Although initially the odds for military success were heavily against the Irish, fissures soon opened within the English ruling classes as dispute arose over whether or not parliament could trust the king with command of the army which was to be sent to crush the Irish revolt. This debate helped ignite the English Civil War in 1642, evening the odds for the Irish insurgents substantially by diverting English resources and energy away from Ireland for the next four years.[5] Consequently, the Catholic Confederation, which was formed in May 1642, had a reasonable chance to achieve Catholic autonomy within a Stuart kingdom.

During the long war from 1641 to 1652 Catholics had several opportunities to drive their Protestant foes out of Ireland, while also contributing directly to a royalist victory in the English and Scottish civil wars. Both of these objectives needed to be accomplished so that the English parliamentarians would not conquer Ireland once they had concluded their struggles against Charles I. The failure of the Catholic Confederates and their royalist allies to achieve either of these goals by 1649 set up the situation in which Oliver Cromwell and the New Model Army were able to crush all opposition to English rule in Ireland.

From 1641 to 1648 the Irish Catholics and royalists failed to exploit their military advantages and, thereby, to achieve their military and political goals. The nature and course of the initial rising in 1641–2 and of the Irish war in the years before Cromwell arrived set a precedent for the violent and brutal conduct of the Cromwellian conquest.[6] The leaders of the anti-parliamentarian forces — such as the Marquis of Ormond, the Earl of Clanricarde, Owen Roe O'Neill, Archbishop Rinuccini, and Lord Inchiquin — made tactical and strategic mistakes which greatly facilitated the eventual English victory. Conversely, once Thomas Fairfax and the New Model Army secured their Independent allies' control of the Westminster government with Pride's Purge in December 1648, the Rump Parliament unleashed the total military effort of the English Commonwealth against Ireland in the hands of Oliver Cromwell and his veteran officers. These men and their powerful military machine exploited the opportunities given them by their Catholic and royalist opponents, bringing to an end the only period in her history when Ireland has been close to being fully united and independent.

THE RISING OF 1641

The initial uprising of 1641 was concentrated in the province of Ulster, where the Gaelic Irish leaders were strongest, as well as most threatened by British colonisation. The Gaelic Irish, also known as Old Irish and by the English as 'mere [i.e. pure] Irish', were families of Celtic origin whose ancestors had lived in Ireland before the arrival of the Norman invaders in the twelfth century. Many of their chief leaders had been defeated by Charles Blount, Lord Mountjoy, in the Elizabethan war and had later fled abroad.[7] Ulster Catholics had plenty of legitimate grievances against the English and Scots, in addition to their fear of aggressive Protestantism.[8] Their most pressing fear was that further colonial plantation by British settlers in Ireland would lead to their final and complete dispossession. The success of the Puritan movement in the English parliament in 1641 had heightened this fear, especially after John Pym and his followers passed a virulently anti-Catholic proclamation in March 1641 and continued to hound the king about his alleged sympathies with Catholicism.[9] By the summer of 1641 a conspiracy to revolt was under way in Ulster, although it was apparently limited to the Old Irish elements of the population.[10]

The Irish conspirators were seeking protection from further expropriation of their lands, guarantees of toleration for their Catholic faith, and the right to full citizenship within the Stuart kingdom of Ireland. Some of these goals had been expressed in the 'Graces' of 1628, an agreement negotiated with the government as a result of Old English lobbying and whose main points provided for loyal Catholic subjects to be able to practise law, to hold secure title to their land, to be safe from further expropriation by English colonists, and to be able to swear a simple oath of allegiance to the crown rather than the oath of supremacy.[11] The goal of full toleration for the Catholic Church, including the freedom of its hierarchy to exist in Ireland, was a major additional demand of the Ulster insurgents in 1641 and one which the Catholic Confederates later adopted.[12] By 1641 it seemed to many that these goals could only be attained through the use of violence. The conspirators, however, never explained how their violent uprising would achieve their goals.

The timing of the outbreak of the rebellion was partly determined by the progress of events in Britain, where the king's government had collapsed. The Scots' success in winning a remarkable amount of autonomy through armed resistance to the king gave the Irish hope of similar success. At the same time, the increasing power of the aggressive Puritans in the

Westminster parliament threatened Catholics throughout Britain and Ireland, and especially in Ulster, with further persecution.[13] It was not surprising that the rebellion began in Ulster.

Throughout the 1640s warfare in northern Ireland had some distinctive characteristics. It was only in the province of Ulster that a Scottish army operated, thereby imposing a unique pattern on the political, religious and military struggles there. A Protestant settler identity had emerged in the province as the English and Scottish colonists increasingly identified themselves as 'British'. The Catholic insurgents who operated against the British Protestants in Ulster were Old Irish, whereas in the other three provinces Old English, Old Irish and New English royalists all played major roles in the anti-parliamentarian struggles. Finally, the Gaelic Irish insurgents failed to capture a single major port or city in Ulster, forcing them to operate from the rural interior of the province, poorly supported by a population of migratory cattle-herders known as creaghts.

Sir Phelim O'Neill and Conor, Lord Maguire, were the most important insurgent leaders in 1641.[14] O'Neill, who considered himself the heir to the traditional power of the Earl of Tyrone, planned and led the rising in Ulster. Maguire was to have co-ordinated the seizure of Dublin, including Dublin Castle, where arms for 10,000 men reportedly were stored. However, Maguire's efforts were foiled by the discovery of the plot on 22 October 1641 by the Lords Justices in Dublin, who moved swiftly to secure the town, castle and arms.[15] The Lords Justices arrested Maguire, while most of his men fled to the countryside.

O'Neill achieved much greater results in Ulster, as his forces seized many surprised and undefended English farmsteads, villages and castles. Bloodshed was unavoidable, especially in those cases where the Protestants tried to defend their homes or when the insurgents suspected that their victims had hidden money and valuables. Local bands of Irish tortured English settlers to extract information about suspected caches of loot. They made short work of those English who resisted.[16] Phelim O'Neill tried to limit the military efforts of his forces to actions against the English settlements and towns and away from the Scottish areas, hoping that the Scots would support the rising. This strategy failed as the news of atrocities against English Protestants spread and a mass of refugees descended on the Ulster ports in flight from what they saw as bloodthirsty Irish.[17]

The Scots rallied to defend their fellow-Protestants, making sectarian differences the fault-line in the military and political struggle in Ulster. Although the number of settlers killed in the first flush of the rising was far smaller than the 154,000 claimed by English propagandists, thousands undoubtedly perished. Jane Ohlmeyer has estimated that somewhere between 10 and 25 per cent of the settler population of Ulster died in the first months of the war.[18] These deaths helped erect a permanent barrier between the Protestant settlers and the Irish, embittering all relations and leading to a vicious cycle of atrocities committed against innocent country people and prisoners of war alike over the next eleven years.

By mid-November 1641 most of central Ulster was in Irish control, with a majority of the English settler population forcibly expelled. During this process of expropriation and expulsion at least 4,000 Protestants were killed outright, and several hundred men, women and children were killed in major massacres.[19] In addition, many settlers died from hardships and exposure to the weather as they trekked to the coastal enclaves still held by Protestant garrisons.

The number of victims killed in the initial rising is unknown, although it is far fewer than contemporary Protestant observers claimed. As James Touchet, the English Catholic Earl of Castlehaven, noted in his memoirs, ''Tis very certain that there have been cruelties committed upon the English, though I believe not the twentieth part of what is generally reported.'[20] Lurid accounts of the thousands of dispossessed survivors were quickly published in England, creating an anti-Catholic hysteria which had much to do with the political crisis leading to the outbreak of the English Civil War.[21] Furthermore, these tales created in the minds of English Puritans like Oliver Cromwell and Henry Ireton the idea that Irish Catholics must pay a price in blood some day for the massacres of 1641. An outpouring of sympathy for the Protestant refugees was evident throughout England. Thousands of Englishmen contributed small sums to the relief fund for the settlers. Nicholas Canny has commented that 'This remarkable breadth of support that the fund enjoyed . . . makes it clear that whichever army prevailed in the English contest between king and parliament would be compelled by the sheer force of English (as well as Scottish) public opinion to take revenge on those who were known to have engaged in the insurrection.'[22]

The Irish insurgents experienced early successes with the capture of Charlemont, Newry and Dungannon, but they soon met effective resistance from better-armed settler armies. In western Ulster, in the counties of Donegal, Londonderry, and parts of Tyrone, Sir Robert Stewart and Sir William Stewart organised an army known as the Laggan force. Its garrisons of over 1,000 men each defended Derry and Coleraine, while a marching army of 3,785 soldiers protected the farms and settlements in the Foyle river valley and western Londonderry.[23] The Irish insurgents in the area outnumbered these Laggan forces, but they lacked the discipline, equipment and cannon needed to destroy the defences established by the Stewart brothers. Warfare in western Ulster consisted, consequently, of a series of cattle-raids and punitive expeditions by the British, and halfhearted sieges of Protestant strongholds by the Irish. The Laggan force routinely won the skirmishes and minor battles, preventing the Irish from establishing a major base in the western counties.[24]

As news of the rebellion spread, the settlers of eastern Ulster formed regiments to defend Belfast, Carrickfergus and Coleraine. These regiments were known by the names of their colonels, who were the leading gentry and lords of the region (Lords Clandeboye, Montgomery, Conway and Chichester, and Sir John Clotworthy). Their total strength fluctuated between 2,000 and 3,000 men when mustered for field duty, with a number of additional garrison companies guarding the towns.[25]

These Protestant forces, with ready access to arms and supplies from Britain, were far better armed than the Irish. Consequently, they easily repulsed most of the insurgents' attempts to capture the major towns of the province. For example, on 10 November, when Phelim O'Neill tried to take advantage of the initial turmoil of the revolt by assaulting Lisnagarvey, County Down, a regiment of east Ulster settlers, raised by Lord Conway and commanded by Sir George Rawdon, drove O'Neill's poorly armed troops away. O'Neill then moved south and seized Dundalk, where he established his headquarters for the winter.[26] Irish prospects looked bleak and were soon to deteriorate even further with the arrival of a third Protestant army in Ulster.

PROTESTANT REACTION

News of the insurrection spread quickly, reaching Edinburgh by 29 October and London on 1 November.[27] The Scottish and English governments quickly agreed in principle that a Scottish army of at least 2,500 men should be sent to Ulster to crush the rebellion.[28] The English were to pay and equip this army and the Scots were to provide the manpower and leadership. By early 1642 the number of Scottish soldiers to be dispatched had increased to 10,000 men, organised into ten regiments. On 15 April the first 2,500 Scots, commanded by the veteran professional soldier Major-General Robert Monro, arrived in Carrickfergus, where they joined Lord Conway's settler regiment of 1,500 men. By August 10,000 Scottish soldiers were in eastern Ulster.[29]

The organisation of the British settler forces and the arrival of the Scottish army doomed Irish military efforts in eastern Ulster in 1642. The Scots recaptured Newry and Dundalk while the British settlers drove O'Neill's men out of Dungannon in May.[30] Another force from the Laggan army relieved Coleraine from a six months' siege in June, thus opening, in conjunction with the British forces to the east, communications overland from Derry to Belfast. The Protestant forces drove most of the organised bands of Irish troops out of Counties Antrim, Down and Armagh, with the notable exception of Phelim O'Neill's garrison in Charlemont.[31] These actions were characterised by the brutal treatment and summary execution of Irish prisoners.[32] O'Neill's soldiers retreated west, forced to depend on the nomadic cattle herds of the Ulster creaghts for their sustenance.

As the Irish retreated into western Londonderry and Tyrone they encountered the Laggan forces. In June Sir Robert Stewart and the entire Laggan army trapped Phelim O'Neill and a force of 2,000 Irishmen at Glemaquin, near Raphoe, County Donegal. Stewart's cavalry and infantry overwhelmed the Irish infantry with successive attacks, forcing the survivors to flee into the bogs and mountains. The Laggan force then captured Strabane, putting the Catholic garrison to the sword.[33]

The Irish insurgents had been successful in Ulster only where they achieved surprise and found their Protestant enemies unprepared for the onslaught. They remained short of arms, money and experienced leadership. Their infantry was poorly trained and their horsemen too few and too poorly mounted to be an effective cavalry force. In every engagement where the settler armies or Scots deployed troops of cavalry, they routed the Irish. Even if the Irish could have stood toe to toe with the British forces in the field, they lacked a political organisation to direct their war effort and to develop a political strategy which might help to define and achieve their goals. By June 1642 the Irish rebellion in Ulster was reduced to a guerrilla campaign in a countryside which both the insurgents and British settlers had burned and looted bare. Only a miracle could have saved the Irish cause in Ulster. It was most unlikely that a *deus ex machina* would come from the Old English Catholics fighting desperately to survive to the south in Leinster and Munster.

Meanwhile, as the war commenced in Ulster, the Lords Justices in Dublin, Sir William Parsons and Sir John Borlase, secured the capital, raised three regiments of foot, and called upon James Butler, Earl of Ormond, to serve as Lieutenant-General. They also garrisoned Drogheda with an infantry regiment under the command of Sir Henry Tichborne, thus denying the Ulster insurgents easy access to north-eastern Leinster.

James Butler, twelfth Earl of Ormond, and later Marquis and then first Duke of Ormond, was one of the most influential figures in seventeenth-century Ireland. Heir to the Anglo-Norman earldom of Ormond and a member of the Catholic Butler family, James had been raised as a Protestant. By 1633 he was a protégé of Thomas Wentworth, Charles I's hated Lord Deputy of Ireland. Ormond began his military career as a cavalry captain in the king's army in Ireland in 1639–40. He was the natural choice to be Lieutenant-General of the English government's army in Ireland, owing to his Protestantism, his status as a major Irish landowner, and his immense social prestige.[34]

Charles I confirmed the appointment of Ormond as Lieutenant-General and agreed with the English and Scottish governments on the need for the dispatch of reinforcements to Ireland.[35] By late November Ormond, Sir Charles Coote and Henry Tichborne were leading punitive expeditions into the inland counties of Leinster in an effort to break up the rebels' supply and recruitment base. Reminiscent of the scorched-earth campaigns which Mountjoy had used in 1601 to defeat the Tyrone revolt, these raids established a pattern of warfare seldom broken until the arrival of Michael Jones in Dublin in 1647.

Further south, Protestants in Munster led by the ruthless professional soldier Murrough O'Brien, Lord Inchiquin, secured the important ports of Cork and Youghal. Protestant regiments from England and Wales, such as that under the command of Sir Charles Vavasour, soon joined the Munster Protestants in their efforts to crush the insurrection.[36] However, the initial uprising had far less impact on the Protestant positions in Munster and Leinster than it had in Ulster, owing to their distance from Ulster and the reluctance of many of the Old English Catholic landowners and townsmen in the southern provinces to join the rising.

In Connacht the dedicated royalist Catholic, Ulick Burke, Earl of Clanricarde, held Galway town and county for the king and against the Catholic insurgents. Clanricarde, known as the Earl of St Albans in the English peerage, maintained an uneasy understanding with the Catholic burghers of Galway, giving Connacht some relief from the warfare of the next three years. He remained loyal to Ormond throughout the 1640s and 1650s, while also generally remaining on good terms with the Old English lords of Leinster.[37]

Until December 1641 the Gaelic Irish insurgents stood alone against the English and Scottish forces. The Old English Catholic landowners of Leinster and Munster remained aloof, unwilling to commit themselves to a rebellion which promised to harm their economic interests along with those of the Protestant New English and Scottish colonists who had come to Ireland since the Elizabethan wars. However, events soon forced the Old English to abandon their neutrality and join the insurrection. This shift in policy by the Old English lords came about for several reasons. First, the English Puritans and the New English, best represented by Borlase and Parsons in their capacities as Lords Justices, seemed hell-bent to use the Ulster rebellion as an excuse to expropriate more Catholic lands throughout Ireland and to stiffen the enforcement of the recusancy laws against the Old English.[38] Second, the Catholic tenants of the Old English gentry began to take matters into their own hands and to attack their Protestant neighbours. Finally, ruthless Protestant commanders such as Sir Charles Coote led punitive military raids from Dublin into the surrounding counties which clearly seemed designed to destroy the homes and lives of the still loyal Catholic landowners. Consequently, the Old English lords joined the revolt in December in order to defend their lives, their political and economic interests, and their control of their tenants.[39] As the Earl of Castlehaven observed, 'Thus the contagion spread itself by degrees over the whole kingdom, and now there's no more looking back, for all are in arms, and full of indignation.'[40]

Although the Old English had decided to join the insurrection, the English and Scottish governments enjoyed significant military advantages over the Catholic insurgents during the winter and spring of 1642. The insurgents lacked sufficient arms, munitions and money to equip large armies, and they had not developed an effective political organisation to co-ordinate military operations in the north and the south. On the other hand, the Scottish and English governments had agreed upon the need to crush the Catholic revolt, and they possessed the military forces and munitions needed to do so. Protestant forces in Ireland held most of the key Irish ports such as Derry, Belfast, Dublin, Youghal and Cork. The Dublin government had weapons for the thousands of soldiers it had raised in Ireland in the autumn of 1641, and it had received reinforcements from England totalling at least 3,000 soldiers. Meanwhile an army of 10,000 Scottish soldiers was on its way to Ireland, with its last regiments arriving in Ulster by July 1642.[41]

As a result of these Protestant reinforcements and the weaknesses of the Irish forces, Tichborne and Ormond broke the Irish siege of Drogheda in March 1642, and Ormond defeated an Irish force, commanded by his uncle, Richard Butler, Viscount Mountgarret, near Kilrush, County Clare, in April.[42] Ormond and the virulently anti-Catholic commander Sir Charles Coote repeatedly marched forces of several thousand men unopposed into the inland counties of Leinster. While on these forays, Coote and Ormond destroyed rebel castles and the villages and farms in their vicinity which were so important for the supply of the insurgent forces.[43] The brutality of these raids both weakened the logistical resources of the Catholics and increased the level of hatred felt towards the Protestant government by the populace.

Few major engagements took place, primarily because Phelim O'Neill in Ulster and Lord Mountgarret in Leinster were unable to arm, pay, train or discipline their soldiers properly. While they heavily outnumbered the Protestant columns which were sweeping through the countryside, the insurgents were unable to stand up to their enemies' organised and well-armed regiments in open battle. For example, when Mountgarret attacked Ormond's outnumbered army near Kilrush on 15 April, as it was making its way back to Dublin with the loot of another raid into Catholic-held regions, Ormond's infantry, cavalry and artillery made short work of the Irish troops, killing as many as 500 in the rout that followed.[44]

In Ulster the story was the same. In late April the Scottish army and the forces raised by the settlers combined in an expedition of nearly 4,000 soldiers to clear the rebel garrisons from south-eastern Ulster, while another Scottish force lifted the siege of Coleraine and cleared the land route from Belfast to Derry.[45] This joint operation was completely successful. The Protestants captured Newry and Carlingford and seized large numbers of cattle from O'Neill's followers, driving the insurgents into the interior of the province. The entire coast from Derry to Dublin was again in Protestant hands. As a result, Henry Tichborne was able to make an overland visit from Drogheda via Dundalk to Newry in mid-May without fear of being intercepted. The Ulster revolt seemed to be broken as Phelim O'Neill prepared to disband the remnants of his army.[46] The Protestant victories in Ulster relieved the pressure on Ormond's position in northern Leinster as well, causing the Old English gentry to despair of reversing the tide of events against them.

THE FORMATION OF THE CATHOLIC CONFEDERATION

Beginning in May 1642, a dramatic series of events in Ireland and Britain changed the strategic and tactical situation in Ireland. The Old English lords and the Catholic hierarchy met in Kilkenny to form the Catholic Confederation. The Gaelic Irish readily joined. For the first time the Catholic forces in Ireland had a central political structure which could co-ordinate military strategy and articulate the political programme and goals without which the military struggle would mean little. The Confederates established a Supreme Council of twenty-four to serve as a executive body with the task of co-ordinating political and military operations. They also created provincial councils in the four provinces to raise the money and supplies needed to support four regional armies. In addition, they called for the selection of representatives from the four provinces to meet in a General Assembly of Catholics in September to ratify the actions taken by the Supreme Council. For the first time in history a united Catholic cause in Ireland had the political structure necessary to reach out diplomatically to the continental Catholic powers and the papacy in hopes of receiving financial and military aid.[47]

Concurrently, the political situation in England degenerated into the First Civil War. By midsummer Charles I and his parliamentarian foes were scrambling to assemble forces, munitions and money to fight one another. Consequently, the flow of troops, supplies and money to Ireland from England slowed to a trickle, severely hindering the operations of Ormond's forces in Leinster and Monro's Scottish troops in Ulster. In May English soldiers in Trim mutinied owing to lack of pay, refusing to go on campaign against the insurgents.[48] Ormond appealed to the king and to the English parliament to send money and supplies to Dublin to relieve an increasingly desperate situation.[49] Help was not available from England in the volume needed to allow Ormond and the other Protestant commanders to occupy the inland towns of Ireland, and only such a strategy could have ended the insurrection. As a result, by the end of July grim reports on the deteriorating condition of the government army were being received regularly in England. One of these described in graphic terms what the soldiers had to endure:

All this while our Army here doth nothing for want of money, our soldiers die very fast. God knows it is a hard case that poor sick men must (instead of some comfortable broths and other needful things for men in their case) be tied to eat nothing but bread, cheese, and salt beef; their case is bad enough and I am afraid that if this summer passeth over no otherwise then hitherto it hath done, that the next winter will be worse.[50]

The civil war in England soon siphoned off soldiers as well as supplies from the Irish war, as both the king and parliament diverted troops and equipment to their armies. Many Protestant soldiers serving in Leinster and Munster hoped to return to England, where they perceived that soldiers were better fed and paid than was the case in Ireland.[51]

As civil war loomed in England the town governments of Waterford and Limerick declared for the Confederation. This was a major addition to Confederate strength, because Waterford was one of the best seaports in Ireland and its accession to the rebellion gave the rebels reliable access to supplies and reinforcements from the continent. The adherence of Wexford had a similar effect. These ports were ideal locations from which the Catholics could launch privateering operations against the English commerce and supply lines to Ireland, and their fortifications mounted a significant number of cannon which could be used elsewhere by the insurgents.[52]

Even with these accessions of strength, the Confederates were unable to exploit fully the Protestant vulnerabilities in 1642–3 owing to the inadequate training of the Catholic armies. For example, when Lord Muskerry and his Catholic army in Munster attempted to stand against Lord Inchiquin's regiments at Liscarroll, County Cork, in August 1642, the inadequately trained Catholic levies were crushed by the better-disciplined Protestant soldiers.[53] However, Confederate weakness on the battlefield was about to change.

The most important military boost to the Catholic cause in 1642 came with the arrival of Irish professional soldiers from the Netherlands. These veterans of Spanish military service were led by Colonels Thomas Preston and Owen Roe O'Neill. The former was a member of the prominent Old English family of Viscount Gormanston, with many relatives in the Confederate forces in Leinster. During the late summer and autumn of 1642 Preston organised and trained the Confederate army of Leinster. This force of six regiments soon gave the Catholic confederacy a reliable military force in Leinster.[54] Because the Old English lords dominated the Supreme Council in Kilkenny, the lion's share of the financial resources of the Confederates were committed to the support of Preston's force. This army prevented Ormond from capturing the Catholic strongholds in western and southern Leinster. An equally dramatic change took place in the military situation in Ulster with the arrival of Owen Roe O'Neill.

THE ARRIVAL OF OWEN ROE O'NEILL, 1642

Help came to Ulster in the form of returning Irish soldiers who had served in the armies of Spain and France since the 'flight of the earls' in 1607. The most important and competent of these Irish 'wild geese' was Owen Roe O'Neill, a descendant of the Earl of Tyrone. Since the outbreak of the rebellion O'Neill had worked to get financial support from his Spanish employers and to receive their permission to take a number of his officers with him to Ulster. The Spanish government had been slow to approve his schemes, mainly because of concern that they would drive the English into the camp of their French enemy. However, once the English parliament began to talk of war against a Spanish-led Catholic conspiracy and about a possible alliance with the Dutch and French, the Spanish government allowed O'Neill to proceed. The Spanish also provided limited amounts of financial aid to O'Neill.[55]

O'Neill landed at Doe Castle in County Donegal in July 1642. He brought with him weapons, money, and three hundred commissioned and non-commissioned officers, veterans of Spanish service in Flanders.[56] Most of all, he and his experienced soldiers brought the kind of disciplined leadership and professional military expertise which the Irish insurgents in Ulster so desperately needed.

O'Neill arrived at an opportune time for the political fortunes of the Catholic cause throughout Ireland. The organisation of the Catholic Confederation had given the insurgents hope for greater political and material support from France, Spain and the papacy than that afforded to Phelim O'Neill.[57] When the Confederate Supreme Council organised its military structure of four provincial armies, it picked Owen Roe O'Neill to serve as the Lord General of Ulster, relegating Phelim O'Neill to the position of Lord President of the Council of Ulster.[58]

Owen Roe O'Neill and his officers forced much-needed discipline on the Ulster recruits. He tried, with some success, to suppress the wanton pillaging and slaughter of civilians which had characterised military operations in Ulster and to train his soldiers to fight modern warfare. However, he found it difficult to get his soldiers to submit to the drill and order of a professional military camp, making it hard to train them properly in the use of musket volley fire.

The use of volley fire and the 'countermarch' used in modern continental armies involved the difficult manoeuvre of passing the front rank of six ranks of musketeers back through the other five ranks of the formation to reload after it had fired its weapons, while succeeding ranks came forward one at a time to fire.[59] Theoretically, this drill allowed a unit of musketeers to fire three volleys per minute against the enemy. To make this possible, the soldiers needed to master the techniques of the drill and the skills of reloading their muskets within two minutes while marching rearward and then forward. This all had to occur while enemy infantry and cavalry returned fire. O'Neill, however, lacked sufficient powder to allow his soldiers to practise this drill with live ammunition, and he did not have enough money to pay and feed his troops in camp long enough for them to become proficient. Consequently, during the autumn and winter he avoided battle, even if this meant surrendering most of Ulster to the Scottish and local settler forces.[60]

For the next year the war in Ulster could best be characterised as a series of cattle-raids, although the killing continued. The Scottish army found itself in quarters too small to sustain its 10,000 soldiers with food and fuel. The counties of Antrim, Down and Armagh had been devastated by the first year of the war, and the Scots refused to venture very far south or west to increase their quarters. Their commander, Major-General Monro, refused to send units south to Leinster to serve with Ormond against the insurgents in that province, nullifying the impact their large numbers could have had on the overall war effort against the Catholics.

Since the Scots and English failed to co-ordinate their military efforts, O'Neill and Preston were able to develop effective armies. In the face of growing Confederate military power, the Protestant forces in Leinster and Munster found themselves increasingly confined to their coastal enclaves as Catholic units raided up to the town walls of places such as Newry, Dublin and Cork.[61] Although Ormond was able to inflict a sharp defeat on Preston's army near New Ross, County Wexford, on 18 March 1643, by May Preston had captured most of Ormond's garrisons in Queen's County and was moving towards Dublin with a force of 7,000 infantry and 700 cavalry.[62]

The promised flow of supplies and money from Scotland and England was intermittent at best, and the suffering of the Protestant soldiers and the local populations was horrific.[63] The Scots and English had established a logistical system to serve Leinster and Ulster. For example, John Davis served in Carrickfergus as the main contractor for the supply of bread, beef, cheese and butter for the Scottish and English garrisons in Antrim and Down. But the system broke down for want of money from Westminster, even before political conditions deteriorated in England in the summer and autumn of 1642.

The Laggan army and the east Ulster settler forces fared somewhat better logistically than the Scots. During most of the year the soldiers of the marching regiments dispersed to their homesteads and worked their fields. This work provided the basic provisions needed to sustain the garrisons of Derry and Coleraine and the settlers and their families. Thanks to their success in driving Phelim O'Neill's troops into the remoter regions of southern Ulster, and to the respite allowed them as Owen Roe O'Neill trained the nucleus of an army, the British of Ulster survived the winter of 1642–3.[64]

This situation began to change in the spring of 1643 as O'Neill's training bore fruit. In late May O'Neill started to make inroads into the territory defended by the Laggan army. However, while he was returning from one of these incursions, the Laggan field army of roughly 3,000 men caught up with and surprised O'Neill and 1,500 of his men, forcing him to fight a pitched battle. O'Neill placed his infantry in entrenchments on the south side of the River Finn, near the town of Clones, hoping that the river would offset Colonel Stewart's superiority in cavalry. The Laggan cavalry attacked directly across the river, followed closely by their infantry. The impact of their charge shattered the cohesion and resolve of O'Neill's men, who fled in terror from their positions. The Laggan cavalry pursued, cutting down stragglers for several miles. His defeat at Clones was nearly catastrophic for O'Neill. He lost 150 men and many of his professional officers and hundreds of weapons. His army was driven through the county of Cavan and out of Ulster to Portlester in Meath, where it remained for the rest of the year.[65] O'Neill, who blamed the defeat on his men's cowardice, vowed never again to fight a battle until his troops were properly trained and armed. Consequently, he left most of Ulster in Protestant hands for the next three years.

The only significant Confederate victory in Ulster in late 1643 was the capture of Dungannon in October after a five-week siege. Charlemont and Dungannon remained the only major Catholic strongholds in the province, although the rural Irish Catholic population of the western and southern counties remained independent of British control. None the less, the Scottish and settler armies could not exploit their military superiority owing to shortages of supplies, munitions and money.

THE CESSATION OF 1643

The growing effectiveness of the Confederate armies, coupled with the steady deterioration of the Protestant supply situation, led Ormond to seek a ceasefire with the Confederates in the spring of 1643.[66] Charles I had been encouraging Ormond to seek such a cessation and a treaty with the Confederation for months before he ordered Ormond to expedite the process in June. The king was desperate for reinforcements from Ireland for his military operations in England, where a stalemate had developed. He hoped to transfer many of Ormond's and Inchiquin's Protestant regiments to Wales and Bristol for use in his campaign against parliament in the summer of 1643.[67] While reluctant to offer religious concessions to the Confederates, Ormond was forced to give in to the military reality of his and the king's situations. The Cessation was accordingly signed on 15 September 1643.

The terms of the ceasefire allowed each side to keep garrisons in the places they controlled in September. Hostilities were suspended for one year. The Confederates promised to give £30,800 and food to the Protestant garrisons in return for the suspension of Protestant raids into the Irish countryside for provisions.[68]

The Cessation saved Ormond's and Inchiquin's positions in Leinster and Munster. They were joined in the ceasefire by the Old English Earl of Clanricarde, the king's strongest supporter in Connacht. Monro and the Ulster Scots refused to accede to the Cessation, believing that it gave the Catholics the opportunity to concentrate their forces against the Protestant garrisons in Ulster and that it would aid the royalist cause in Britain by releasing English regiments from Ireland to serve Charles I in England.[69] The Cessation, however, brought relative peace to Connacht, Munster and Leinster for the next year.

A stalemate of sorts fell on Ulster in late 1643 as well, as the civil war in England absorbed the energies of the Edinburgh and London governments. A better strategy for the Protestants in Ulster would have been to concentrate their resources to support a single effective field force while sending superfluous Scottish soldiers home to ease the logistical burden on the province. Owing to the Scots' reluctance to lessen their grip on eastern Ulster, the British allies did not adopt such as a strategy.

The cessation of hostilities in Ireland in September 1643 between Ormond and the Confederates also transformed the political situation in Ulster, forcing the anti-Catholic forces there to sort out whether or not they were royalist or parliamentarian in sympathies. Their choices ended the unity of the anti-Catholic front, as the Laggan army leaned toward the royalist cause represented by Ormond, and the Scots signed the Solemn League and Covenant with the English parliamentarians.

SQUANDERED CATHOLIC OPPORTUNITIES, 1643–5

Robert Monro, commander of the Scots army in Ulster, refused to accept the Cessation. He had pointed out to Ormond in July, as Ormond negotiated the final details of the Cessation with the Confederates, that a truce would favour the Catholic 'rebels' by allowing the Irish to concentrate their efforts on expelling the Scots.[70] Monro recognised that the Irish in Ulster could not support a concentrated army without help from the Confederate Supreme Council at Kilkenny. A cessation between them and Ormond would allow the Confederates in the southern provinces to send money and supplies to O'Neill's Ulster army and to quarter that army in the same areas from which the Scottish and settler forces drew their sustenance.[71] The Scots in Britain and Ireland also had decided to enter the civil war in England against the royalists, further souring relations between Monro and the royalist Ormond.

The Laggan army, with a far better logistical situation than Monro's Scots, favoured the royalist cause in England and wanted to accept Ormond's Cessation in Ireland. So, as Monro and the Ulster Scots accepted the Solemn League and Covenant with the English parliament and supported the Edinburgh government's policies, the Laggan forces attempted to rely on their own strength and to adhere to Ormond.[72]

The cold winter of 1643–4 and the horrible material conditions in war-ravaged Ulster soon drove all parties to extreme misery. In such circumstances, the trickle of supplies from Scotland looked a lot better to the eastern and western settler armies than did Ormond's fine words without money. By February most of the Ulster Protestants had accepted the Covenant and an alliance with the Scots.[73] This support was essential for places like Enniskillen, where Sir William Cole defended the town against a hostile hinterland.[74]

Monro was right in believing that the Cessation of 1643 provided the Catholic Confederates with the opportunity to drive the Scots out of Ireland and to send significant military aid to the royalists in the English Civil War. However, to exploit these opportunities, the Old Irish and Old English factions of the Catholic Confederation needed to co-operate fully in both endeavours. Such co-operation was not very likely, as the two factions were badly split over the issues of how much aid they should send to an heretical king before they received cast-iron guarantees from him that the Catholic gains achieved in the war in Ireland thus far would be secure.

The Old Irish, supported by most of the clergy and the papal representative Scarampi, insisted on such guarantees before they would sign a peace with the king and send him the 10,000 Confederate troops which he wanted for service in England.[75] The majority of the Old English, who dominated the Supreme Council, hoped to come to some interim treaty with Ormond on the king's behalf that would give them the substance of their demands without forcing the king openly to concede the religious terms. The king knew that if he made religious concessions to the Irish Catholics, he would alienate a significant number of his supporters in Protestant England and Scotland.

For the next three years the Catholics negotiated with Ormond and the king for a treaty which would allow them security while providing the king with substantial aid in his struggle against the English parliamentarians. In the meantime the Confederation determined to launch a campaign against the Ulster Scots and to send limited aid to the royalists in Scotland.

The military effects of the Cessation of 1643 were dramatic. Ormond sent at least 5,000 men to England by early 1644, reducing the royalist forces in all four provinces to a total of 6,700 soldiers.[76] This meant that there were not many more that 18,200 Protestant troops remaining in Ireland, including the Scots army of no more than 6,500 men and the various armed bodies of settlers, such as the Laggan army, totalling roughly 5,000 soldiers.[77] These forces were widely dispersed and perilously close to starvation. Monro's Scottish units in east Ulster were the most potent of these forces. Their defeat and expulsion was the Catholics' key to victory in Ireland.

The Confederates did eventually send some aid to the royalists in Britain. In November 1643 Randal MacDonnell, Earl of Antrim, secured

1,200 Ulster Catholic troops from the Confederation to be deployed to Scotland. These soldiers joined the Marquis of Montrose there in time for his campaign in the summer of 1644, forcing the Edinburgh government to divert thousands of soldiers from their main army in northern England.[78] Had these Irish reinforcements been larger, and had they arrived earlier, they might have deterred the Scottish army from playing its decisive role in the king's first major defeat at Marston Moor in July 1644. As it was, their campaign with Montrose forced Monro to send three of his ten regiments and most of his field artillery back from Ulster to Scotland in early 1644.[79] This move shifted the military balance against the Scots in Ulster.

The Confederate Supreme Council now saw the opportunity which the Cessation gave them of driving the Scots out of Ulster. In order to succeed, such a campaign would require the combined efforts of the Ulster and Leinster armies and the full co-operation of the commanders of those armies. Unfortunately for the Confederates, logistical and political difficulties delayed the campaign against north-eastern Ulster until June 1644. Furthermore, the Confederate Supreme Council had a great deal of difficulty resolving the issue of who was to command the combined army.

The Supreme Council's difficulties in selecting the commander for the Ulster campaign revealed the deep fissures within the Irish cause between the Old English and the Old Irish. Added to this were the problems created by the touchy pride of the three leading Confederate commanders. Owen Roe O'Neill expected to be chosen as the commander of the combined operation in Ulster, since he was the Confederation's Lord General in that province and had been senior to Thomas Preston in the Spanish army. Preston, however, was most reluctant to put himself and his Leinster regiments under O'Neill's command. Consequently, the Supreme Council alienated both officers by placing the Earl of Castlehaven in command of the oper- ation.[80] This was unfortunate for a number of reasons, not the least of which was that Castlehaven lacked the leadership skills needed to get his two col- leagues to work together in order to outmanoeuvre Monro's army of Scots.

Unfortunately for the Catholic cause, once the campaign was under way, O'Neill tended to sulk Achilles-like in his camp rather than to co-operate aggressively in the campaign. Jerrold Casway, O'Neill's biographer, correctly concludes that 'the incompatibility between the two leaders was at the root of the campaign's failure. . . . The jealousy and rivalry between the two commanders compounded the already basic racial and political differences troubling their two armies.'[81] The political problems in this campaign were a microcosm of the political problems which hamstrung the Catholic and royalist causes in Ireland throughout the decade.[82]

In May 1644 Monro, fearing further collusion between the royalists and the Irish, seized Ormond's garrison in Belfast and placed his own troops there. Consequently, Monro's forces were spread thin among the major towns of eastern Ulster, and he could not count on any help from the beleaguered Ormond. The Confederate Supreme Council, however, had delayed its acceptance of the Cessation until mid-September 1643, hoping to extract concrete religious concessions from Ormond. This delay was the most important reason for the failure of the Irish to campaign in force against the Scots in the autumn of 1643. By the time the Supreme Council decided to attack the Scots in Ulster, it was too late in the season for O'Neill's creaght-supported army to live off of Ulster's pastures. Since the Leinster forces had too few supplies on hand to support Preston's and O'Neill's forces together, the campaign was postponed until the following summer.[83] These setbacks ensured that not enough military pressure was put on the Scots before the summer of 1644 either to keep them out of the English war or to prevent them from expanding their hold on eastern Ulster.

The whole process of determining who was to command the combined forces delayed the start of the campaign until July 1644, by which time Inchiquin, the most important Protestant commander in Munster, had abandoned Ormond and the royalist cause and had declared for parliament.[84] Inchiquin's defection and renunciation of the Cessation posed a serious threat to the Kilkenny government from the south, requiring some of Preston's soldiers to remain in southern Leinster. Concurrently, the defeat of Charles I at Marston Moor by an Anglo-Scottish army raised the morale of the Ulster Scots, while also relieving Monro of the necessity of sending further reinforcements to Scotland.

At last O'Neill and Preston agreed to serve together in a northern campaign led by Castlehaven. However, Monro moved first with 6,000 men, hoping to sweep southern Ulster of Catholic forces and to prevent the juncture of the Irish armies. Monro rampaged through southern Ulster for twenty days in June, burning Kells, County Meath, and overwhelming a force of 1,000 Irish as he marched. He failed, however, to compel either O'Neill's or Preston's army to attack his force unilaterally. A shortage of supplies eventually forced him to return his troops to their Ulster garrisons.[85]

Castlehaven, O'Neill and Preston finally moved north in July with a combined strength of nearly 11,000 men. This was one of the largest Catholic armies gathered together for a campaign during the entire war. Such a formidable force should have achieved a great deal. By 26 July the Confederates had reached Armagh and halted to take in fresh supplies.[86] Swift action might have caught the Scots dispersed in their garrisons, giving the Irish overwhelming numerical superiority in a fight. At this critical point in the campaign O'Neill dispersed his troops and his herdsmen to take advantage of the grazing available in August, while Castlehaven built a fortified base at Tandragee, for his 5,000 men.[87] These defensive deployments by the Catholic commanders, in the face of an outnumbered and dispersed enemy, were a grave mistake which allowed Monro to recover the tactical initiative.

Monro, seeing the dispersal of Castlehaven's forces, rallied 6,000 soldiers from his garrisons and took the field in hopes of defeating the two Catholic forces separately. Protestant regiments from western Ulster joined Monro, creating an army of nearly 10,000 soldiers. Castlehaven, warned of the Protestant army's approach, evacuated his camp at Tandragee and retreated to a strong position near Charlemont, where O'Neill's 4,000 soldiers soon joined him.[88] The Scots followed Castlehaven's force 'over terrain littered by discarded carriages and baggage', coming to within five miles of the Irish entrenched position.[89] The two forces then faced each other in a seven-week stand-off near Charlemont. Neither side wanted to attack the other's entrenchments. Each hoped the other army would run out of supplies and withdraw first. Castlehaven was the first to give way, sending O'Neill's men to southern Ulster and north-western Leinster, and Preston's troops to Leinster for winter quarters.[90]

By refusing to risk a battle or to manoeuvre for a tactical advantage, Castlehaven threw away a chance to defeat the major Protestant armies in the north. His retreat gave the British settlers and Scots an important strategic advantage. For seven weeks the outnumbered Scots had faced the combined might of Catholic Ireland, but Castlehaven failed to seize the opportunity to fall on the Scots or to manoeuvre for a battle on open ground. The reported approach of additional Laggan units to reinforce Monro and the exhaustion of supplies and grazing for the Irish creaghts caused him to take counsel of his fears and to withdraw the Confederate forces.[91] As Castlehaven noted, 'Thus ended the Ulster expedition, like to be so fatal to the Confederate Catholics of Ireland.'[92]

In August 1644 the Catholics had a chance of winning a major victory which might have shifted the military balance in Ireland and Britain in the king's favour. O'Neill's victory at Benburb two years later would show that an Irish army could defeat the Scots in a pitched battle. Had the Confederates forced a battle and lost, things would not have been much worse than they were when they withdrew south in October. Monro's need to end his June foray after two weeks had shown that he lacked the logistical resources necessary to campaign long enough in the south to break the Confederation. Any battlefield losses suffered by the Scots would have been difficult to make up, since the Edinburgh government had its hands full with Montrose's army in the Highlands and with the need to support a large army in England. Catholic losses, on the other hand, could have been more easily replaced out of a larger population that was more directly concerned than Scotland's. An Irish victory in Ulster in 1644 would have provided major political and military opportunities to the Confederates, perhaps even leading to the expulsion of the Scots from Ulster. This development would have revolutionised the overall military balance in Ireland and made it much easier for them to send reinforcements to Montrose in Scotland.

O'Neill and Preston lacked the strategic vision to see the campaign in these terms. Castlehaven had even less military talent than these two officers. So while the Catholic armies of Ulster and Leinster had become organised and well-equipped military organisations by 1643, their effectiveness was severely limited for the rest of the war because their leaders did not possess the ability to turn tactical opportunities into strategic gains.

During the next year few significant Catholic forces operated in Ulster, except for the garrison at Charlemont. O'Neill's units remained in quarters in southern Ulster, unable to move owing to shortages of money and food.[93] Fortunately for O'Neill, the logistical situation of the Ulster Scots remained desperate and they made little effort to campaign against the Irish base areas. Furthermore, in 1645 the Edinburgh government ordered Monro to ship another 1,500 soldiers home to Scotland to help fight the army led by Montrose and Alasdair MacColkitto MacDonnell.[94] By April 1,400 Scots had embarked for Scotland from Lisnagarvey, and the remaining 5,100 Scots in Ulster feared that they also would be recalled from their safe billeting areas.[95]

To the west, the Laggan force under the command of Sir Robert Stewart and Sir William Stewart co-operated with Sir Charles Coote in his successful operations against Sligo in northern Connacht. In July 1645 Coote's capture of Sligo posed a serious threat to the Earl of Clanricarde in Connacht.[96] However, the Laggan soldiers, fearful of leaving their homes and farms undefended from any quick thrusts by O'Neill's forces, refused to campaign deep into Connacht for any length of time.

During the winter of 1644–5 the most pressing concern of all armies in Ireland was subsistence. The Irish economy was steadily contracting, making it harder and harder to raise taxes or monetary contributions in the towns. Some counties remained relatively unscathed by the war, but wherever the armies had been active, such as in the Pale, in eastern Ulster, or around Cork and Youghal, the farms had been picked clean, when not destroyed.[97] Now that they were unopposed in Ulster, the Scots took free quarter wherever they chose.[98] Ormond's poorly supplied garrison in Athlone remained his only base in western Leinster, while his commander in Newry, Edward Mitchell, reported in February that 'both inhabitants and soldiers would have eaten one another. . . . [The soldiers] have utterly beggared those few townsmen amongst us; especially the poor innkeeper.'[99] Similar problems plagued the Confederates as the armies dispersed for winter quarters.

THE CATHOLIC OFFENSIVES, 1645–6

The Confederates resumed military operations in March 1645 with a major campaign in Munster. Preston's army captured Inchiquin's garrison in Duncannon, County Wexford, while Castlehaven campaigned in western Munster with 5,000 men.[100] These armies put tremendous pressure on Inchiquin's position in Munster, but they lacked the siege artillery needed to

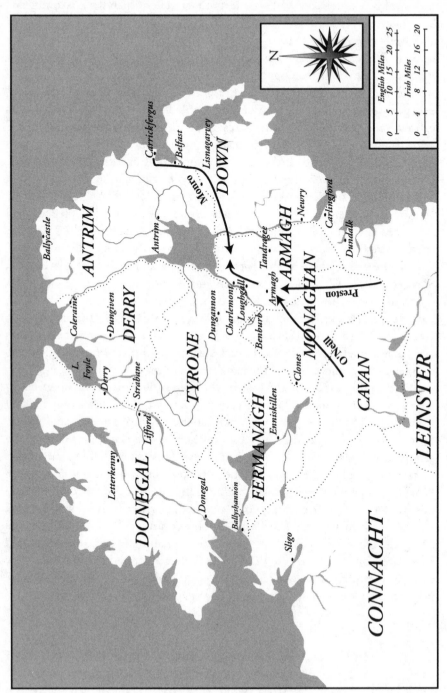

1. *Catholic Confederate Advance into Ulster, July–September 1644*

breach the defences and the logistical support needed to allow them to besiege and starve into submission fortified towns such as Cork. Furthermore, Preston refused to serve under Castlehaven again, thus allowing Inchiquin's deputy, Lord Broghill, to break Castlehaven's siege of Youghal in September. With little gained besides Duncannon, the Confederate forces again withdrew into winter quarters in early October.

In the north, O'Neill remained in quarters with his men dispersed during the summer and into the winter of 1645–6. Even the transfer of another Scottish regiment from Ulster to Scotland in April 1645 had no effect on his inactivity.[101] O'Neill's presence on the northern border of Leinster had as much political purpose as logistical. Unfortunately for the Catholic Confederation's military situation, the army of Ulster expended much of its energy during the next two years in support of the policies of the new papal representative, Giovanni Battista Rinuccini, rather than in combat against the Protestants in Ulster. Rinuccini, who had replaced Scarampi in October 1645, had the mission to 'restore and re-establish the public exercise of the Catholic religion in the island of Ireland'.[102] His way of attempting to do this fatally split the Catholic cause just as its opponents were at their weakest.

The long period of inactivity by O'Neill's army came to an end in March 1646, when the papal nuncio Rinuccini provided Ormond with sufficient money to arm and pay seven regiments of infantry for an extended campaign. By late May it had become clear that the objective of O'Neill's army was to be eastern Ulster, where he hoped to defeat Monro's Scots and capture a much-needed seaport.

O'Neill marched an army of 5,000 infantry and 400 cavalry into eastern Ulster in late May.[103] Monro, his main antagonist, had just received an additional infantry regiment from Scotland and knew that he could count on the support of the field armies of the Ulster settlers for help against O'Neill's advance. Consequently, Monro called for a rendezvous of the Protestant forces and marched with at least 3,500 Scots to meet O'Neill. Two thousand soldiers raised from among the British settlers in eastern Ulster joined him as he advanced.[104] Having located the advancing Irish on the hot afternoon of 5 June, Monro rushed his troops forward along the River Blackwater, hoping to force O'Neill to fight before he could withdraw, as the Irish forces had done for the past two years. This proved easier than expected. O'Neill remained in good defensive positions near Benburb, awaiting the Protestants' attack. But the results were not what Monro had expected. When the Protestant army launched its attack, the Irish held firm. O'Neill fought a skilful defensive battle until the Protestant soldiers, already suffering the effects of dehydration, were exhausted and disorganised from their assaults against his entrenched troops. Then, as Monro's men began to flag in their efforts, O'Neill launched a counter-stroke with a fresh infantry regiment. This attack caught the Scots completely by surprise, shattering their formations.

O'Neill's victory was complete once his enemies' ranks disintegrated. His troops routed the British, pursuing them for five miles. At least 1,800 Scots were killed, along with over a thousand men of the settler army.[105] The Irish captured significant amounts of ammunition and arms on the battlefield and during the pursuit as well, further improving their logistical situation. O'Neill's defeat of Monro at Benburb permanently crippled the Scottish army in Ulster. By December there were only 3,500 Scottish soldiers remaining in the province, just barely enough men to garrison Belfast and Carrickfergus, and too few to launch effective field campaigns. The heavy losses suffered by the east Ulster settler army at Benburb also meant that the Laggan army remained the only Protestant force in Ulster strong enough to conduct offensive operations.[106] Fortunately for the Protestants, however, O'Neill did not exploit his victory with a concerted attack against the Protestant towns in eastern Ulster. Instead, after conducting some foraging raids in Armagh, he marched his army south to Kilkenny to support Rinuccini in his struggle with those members of the Confederate Supreme Council who were seeking a compromise peace with Ormond.

The shift in the military balance in Ulster caused by O'Neill's victory at Benburb should have had a great impact on the political position of the Catholics in that province, but O'Neill's march south robbed his military victory of its political fruits and thereby saved the Protestant cause in Ulster. His decision to take his army to Kilkenny was partly due to Rinuccini's need for military assistance in his political struggle for control of Confederate policy. However, O'Neill could have delayed this march long enough to attempt a *coup de main* against Belfast.

His failure to exploit his victory with an admittedly risky immediate assault against a Protestant garrison may have been due also to his professional experiences of warfare. O'Neill had learned the art of war in the Netherlands during his service as an officer in the Spanish army. During their operations against the Dutch the Spanish experienced few battles. Instead the long Dutch war had been characterised by sieges which were usually won by starving the enemy into submission. A great premium was placed upon the preservation of one's trained soldiers rather than risking them in assaults against well-defended towns. Consequently, it was possibly alien to O'Neill to consider an assault against the Scottish-held towns because of the risks such attacks posed to his men. In any case, he marched south without reaping the full political or even military fruits of his only major victory.

A PEACE TREATY FOR IRELAND?

Since the Cessation of 1643 negotiations for a peace had been carried on intermittently between Ormond and the Supreme Council of the

Confederate Catholics. The major sticking-points were recusancy laws and the religious concessions to be granted to the Catholics by Charles I. An Irish delegation had waited upon the king in Oxford in the spring of 1644, asking for repeal of Poynings' Law, full toleration of Catholic worship, the calling of an independent Irish parliament, issuance of a general act of oblivion and pardon for all acts committed since August 1641, and annulment of all land forfeitures since 1634.[107] In return, the Confederates offered to send 10,000 soldiers to England to support the royalist war effort. Charles rejected these terms and delegated to Ormond the authority to negotiate a peace in Ireland that would not include any measure of religious liberty for Catholics.

By early 1645 the king's situation in England was desperate, and Ormond's in Ireland not much less so. In February Charles I ordered Ormond to conclude a peace which, while not openly including the public toleration of Catholic worship, would promise secretly to grant it after the king's victory in England.[108] Ormond, not believing that the Confederates would send much help to England in any case, strung the negotiations out, using the Earl of Clanricarde as a moderating influence on the Confederates in hopes of getting them to accept a secret undertaking of religious toleration.[109] Ormond clearly opposed the religious concessions, reminding Charles in a letter in April that he would concede everything except matters 'concerning religion, wherein your majesty is pleased to command there should be no ground given them'.[110] Ormond was reluctant to conclude matters by promising terms which he knew the king could not fulfil.[111] As a result of further delays, the king sent Edward Somerset, the Catholic Earl of Glamorgan, to Kilkenny to negotiate a separate treaty behind Ormond's back. This treaty granted far greater religious concessions to the Catholics than those contained in Ormond's proposals.[112]

Glamorgan concluded his secret treaty in August, after the king's disastrous defeat at Naseby on 14 June 1645 left the king little room to manoeuvre politically. This first Glamorgan treaty allowed Catholic worship in all churches held by Catholics at that time. It promised the revocation of Poynings' Law and the annulment of all land confiscation since 1634. In return, 10,000 Catholic troops were to be sent to aid the king.[113] The religious clauses were to be kept secret until after the king's victory. These terms were acceptable to the Old English, but not to the Old Irish and the nuncio Rinuccini.

As soon as he had arrived in Ireland Rinuccini had put the first Glamorgan treaty on hold. He correctly believed that neither Charles I nor Ormond had any intention of conceding more religious liberty to the Catholics than the military situation forced them to do, and that Charles was using Glamorgan duplicitously, with no intention of fulfilling the terms Glamorgan offered.[114] Rinuccini worked hard to prevent the Confederate General Assembly from accepting either the Glamorgan peace or the terms which Ormond offered because these postponed official recognition of Catholic religious liberty.

Rinuccini succeeded on both counts. He forced Glamorgan to renegotiate the treaty and to concede the open acceptance of the religious terms. Glamorgan also promised that the next viceroy of Ireland was to be a Catholic. This second Glamorgan treaty was signed on 20 December 1645. In the meantime a copy of the completed first Glamorgan treaty was found on the body of the Catholic Archbishop of Tuam at Sligo, where that prelate had been killed while taking part in a siege.[115] Ormond quickly arrested Glamorgan in Dublin, while the king disavowed the terms of the treaty when they were published in England. Ormond released Glamorgan in January 1646, evidently convinced that Glamorgan had negotiated the first treaty with the king's full connivance. Remarkably, Glamorgan still received permission in March from the Supreme Council to raise 3,000 Catholic soldiers to be sent to England. However, the parliamentarians' capture of Chester closed the last royalist port in England, ending all chances of Irish reinforcements.

The episodes of the Glamorgan peace mission and treaties revealed again the fissures within the Catholic Confederation. The Old English were willing to accept an 'Ormondist', or royalist, solution to the war. Such a settlement would have preserved the political and economic position of the Old English gentry, with limited personal religious toleration from the crown. The position of the Catholic clergy and church would still be ambiguous, with the hierarchy not officially recognised by the king and an English-dominated Irish parliament still subject to Poynings' Law. For the Old Irish, the Ormond treaty offered nothing of substance, since such a peace would not restore the lands of men such as Owen Roe O'Neill whose property had been confiscated when they or their fathers had fled Ulster in 1607.[116] The Old English were still hoping in 1646 that royalism and Catholicism were compatible. The Gaelic Irish and the Catholic clergy no longer trusted an heretical and obviously duplicitous monarch. Consequently, the Old English Ormondists on the Supreme Council who tried to conclude acceptable peace terms with Ormond were opposed, thwarted and finally excommunicated by Rinuccini and the Catholic hierarchy.

THE FIRST ORMOND PEACE, 1646

Because of parliament's victory at Naseby on 14 June 1645, and the Scots' victory against Montrose at Philiphaugh on 13 September, the only hope for the success of the Irish Catholic cause lay in a complete victory against all Protestant forces in Ireland.[117] The Scottish and settler armies in Ulster would have to be defeated and their garrisons captured; Ormond's garrison in Dublin would have to be seized; and Inchiquin's forces in Munster would have to be destroyed. The Confederates only had sufficient military forces to accomplish these ends if they could concentrate their efforts and find a way to supply their armies.

While Rinuccini's money and O'Neill's leadership were breathing new life into the Irish struggle in Ulster, Ormond and the Confederate Supreme Council continued to negotiate the terms of a peace treaty. Glamorgan's interference had, in Ormond's view, set the negotiations back, as the royalists' military situation went from disastrous to worse.[118] The royalists' loss of Chester in March cut the last communications link between Dublin and Oxford, making it impossible for major reinforcements to be sent to the king.[119] By February 1646 Ormond faced the choice of concluding a treaty with the Catholics or one with the Scottish and English commissioners in Carrickfergus.[120]

Ormond's inclinations were to settle with the Confederates, many of whom were his own relatives. Finally, in March, the Supreme Council agreed to accept a treaty which relieved the Catholics of political liabilities and left the religious question to be settled after the war by the king in a free Irish parliament. The terms of the settlement were signed on 28 March 1646, although the treaty was kept secret until August.[121] The terms of the treaty soon became meaningless as the king fled from Oxford to the Scottish army, becoming their prisoner in early May. Just before he left Oxford, Charles I wrote to Ormond, telling him to make the best deal that he could for the remaining Irish royalists. At the same time the king disavowed his previous undertakings with the Catholics.[122] The Ormond treaty of 1646 was the last chance to form a royalist coalition in Ireland that might possibly have driven the parliamentarians out before the Second English Civil War crushed royalism in Britain permanently. It failed miserably.

In August the publication of the Ormond Peace drew a negative response from the nuncio and the synod of the Catholic clergy, held at Waterford and presided over by Rinuccini. The synod condemned the peace, and the nuncio excommunicated anyone who accepted it. O'Neill's forces backed these moves and the nuncio's purge of the Supreme Council in September. Those Confederate 'Ormondists', like General Preston, who had accepted Ormond's terms, quickly found that the rank and file of the Leinster army and the populations of the major towns like Wexford and Waterford were fully behind the nuncio.[123] By October Rinuccini had a firm grip on the Kilkenny government and the armies of Leinster and Munster.

Rinuccini understood that the combined armies of O'Neill and Preston should seize Dublin quickly, before Protestant reinforcements could be sent to Ormond from England. Consequently, he ordered the Ulster and Leinster armies to begin operations against Ormond's remaining garrisons in Leinster. Again the combined campaign of the Confederate armies lacked a single commander, since both Preston and O'Neill refused to serve under anyone else.[124] By late October the Catholic forces, estimated by Ormond to total 13,000 soldiers, had advanced to within a few miles of Dublin. Preston and O'Neill, however, followed separate routes and failed to co-operate in any significant way.[125] Neither of them had brought the artillery needed to breach Dublin's fortifications and to cut the city's sea communications; and neither was willing to risk an assault. After a brief stay near Dublin, they withdrew their forces into winter quarters, ending another opportunity for the Catholic cause to clear Ireland of its Protestant enemies.

THE CALM BEFORE THE STORM: ULSTER, 1647–8

Rinuccini's political victory over the Ormondists in the Catholic Confederation in August and September 1646 directly affected the political and military situation in Ulster. Owen Roe O'Neill withdrew from Ulster without capturing any major Protestant strongholds and did not return until mid-1648. Consequently, the war in Ulster for the next two years was conducted at the level of cattle-raids and foraging. The Laggan force continued to support Sir Charles Coote's operations and garrisons in Connacht and to defend its own cantonment and logistical areas in Donegal and northern Tyrone. The east Ulster British defended Coleraine, northern Londonderry and Antrim, but were unable to contribute to Ormond's efforts against Owen Roe O'Neill in northern Leinster.[126] The Scots remained cooped up in the eastern Ulster seaports, unable and unwilling to co-operate in the field with Ormond.[127]

Owen Roe O'Neill maintained his army in Leinster, with occasional foraging operations into southern Ulster and eastern Connacht.[128] Phelim O'Neill held Charlemont and the areas immediately to its south. Neither the Protestant nor the Catholic forces in Ulster was strong enough to destroy the other. Consequently, the fate of Ulster was to be determined on the battlefields of England and southern Ireland.

In spite of Irish disunity, Ormond's situation was desperate. Rinuccini had crushed any hope for the immediate formation of a new royalist coalition shaped around the Ormond Peace, and Charles I had disavowed all agreements with Catholics. Consequently, Ormond opened negotiations with the English parliament for the surrender of Dublin.[129] At the same time, in November 1646, O'Neill and Preston offered Ormond new terms for a settlement with the Confederates. These terms would have allowed the practice of Catholicism in Dublin and the garrisoning of Dublin, Drogheda, Trim, Newry and Carlingford by Catholic troops.[130] Ormond refused to accept these terms, and the negotiations quickly broke down. But the season's campaigning had ended and a *de facto* truce settled on Leinster, giving Ormond time to come to an agreement with the London government.[131] The scarcity of supplies on both sides and bad weather also accounted for this lull in operations.

Ormond concluded his negotiations with the Westminster government for the surrender of Dublin in February 1647. Blaming the 'perfidy' of the Irish Catholics for the situation which forced him to treat with the king's enemies, he agreed to surrender the capital and his garrisons to the English parliament. In return, the English provided immediate logistical support and reinforcements to his garrisons, and promised £13,000 recompense to Ormond for the money which he had spent defending Dublin over the past six years.[132]

Ormond's surrender of Dublin to parliament in June 1647 brought new support from England for the settler armies in Ulster. Parliamentarian warships provided some protection from Irish privateers to the northern ports. The Westminster government sent arms, money, food, and a few soldiers to Derry in the summer, easing the supply situation of the Laggan force. Parliament also appointed Sir Charles Coote as commander of all Protestant troops in western Ulster and northern Connacht, thus combining the two strongest Protestant forces in that region. The Ulster British accepted this situation in return for the promise of further support from London.[133]

On 27 February 1647 the Derby House Committee, the parliamentarians' executive body, ordered that one cavalry and three infantry regiments be sent to Dublin.[134] These troops were to be the first major English reinforcements sent to Ireland since 1643. Parliament also appointed Colonel Michael Jones, a member of a prominent New English family, to serve as the commander of its forces in the Pale. The final transfer of Ormond's troops took place in June. Ormond, after receiving at least £5,000 for his expenses and the promise of another £5,000, left Dublin for England and ultimately France in July.[135] Without a shot, the parliamentarians had gained the most important city in Ireland.

Meanwhile, the Catholic forces remained inactive. Political divisions within the Confederation between the Old Irish and the Old English persisted. Rinuccini's position was secure only for as long as he could maintain O'Neill's army in Leinster. Its presence in Leinster, however, put increased pressure on the resources of that province. By April the Ormondists on the Supreme Council, i.e. those who were still willing to make a peace with Ormond, had grown stronger.

In June Rinuccini and O'Neill decided to send O'Neill's army into Connacht in an effort to clear the Protestant garrisons out of the northern counties and to provide a better logistical base for O'Neill's troops. The ultimate goal was to campaign against Sir Charles Coote's British units in western Ulster. But O'Neill's army exhausted the provisions and the patience of the people of Connacht, and the inhabitants responded by harrying the soldiers and killing many of O'Neill's camp-followers.[136] O'Neill moved too slowly to capture Sligo with a *coup de main*, and he had not brought along the artillery and logistical resources needed to conduct a siege. Failing in northern Connacht, he next turned towards western

Leinster. As he campaigned, the Old English consolidated their position on the Supreme Council, and in August they notified O'Neill that they could no longer support his army.[137] The political situation at this juncture has been succinctly described by Jerrold Casway: 'Irreconcilable differences now emerged among the Confederate Catholics. The Anglo-Irish feared that the extensive political-religious demands of their native brothers would jeopardise their own well-being. The Old Irish . . . believed Ormond's terms fell short of reconciling Irish-Catholic grievances. These differences were aggravated by the Ormondist faction, which was characterised by monarchists and Protestant affiliations.'[138] Rinuccini and the clerical party had contributed to the worsening of the Confederate position by forcing Ormond into a settlement with parliament. In the event, all of Catholic Ireland suffered.

THE DESTRUCTION OF THE CATHOLIC CONFEDERATION, 1647–8

After its victory in the First English Civil War the Westminster parliament turned its attention to the conquest of Ireland. The Derby House Committee offered lenient terms to Ormond. The English sent men, money and supplies to bolster the sagging spirits in the Protestant garrisons throughout Ireland.[139] Three fresh regiments arrived in Dublin by June 1647, and parliament called for an additional 6,500 additional troops to be sent.[140] It appeared that there was little hope for the badly divided Irish to defend themselves successfully from the victorious forces of English Puritanism.

The new parliamentary commander of Dublin, Michael Jones, arrived in June 1647. Events of the next three years would prove that Jones was one of the most talented commanders ever to serve in Ireland. A member of a prominent Protestant family in Ireland, Jones had travelled to England in 1644 to take part in the English Civil War as an officer in the parliamentary army. He served with distinction against the royalist forces in Wales and Cheshire, rising to the rank of colonel. Following the defeat of Charles I's main army at Naseby, Jones took part in the campaigns to subdue the remaining royalist strongholds in western England in 1645–6 and was appointed governor of Chester after its capture by parliamentarian troops in February 1646.[141] When the English government needed a successful military commander who had a good knowledge of Ireland to assume command of Dublin, they turned to Colonel Michael Jones.

By 1 August Jones was ready to campaign into the interior counties of Leinster with 4,300 soldiers and seven cannon (see Map 2). He co-ordinated his campaign with the garrisons in Drogheda and southern Ulster, raising his force to over 5,000 infantry and 1,500 cavalry.[142] Preston's Leinster army was the only Confederate force of any size in the area. Jones's goal was to force Preston to fight a pitched battle, hoping to annihilate his army.

Preston, who often had been timid in the face of favourable opportunities, now rose to the bait and accepted battle at a numerical disadvantage. After hastily gathering his regiments together from their quarters, he marched the Leinster army of 5,000 men to Portlester, south-west of Trim, hoping to cut Jones off from his Dublin supply base.[143] Preston placed his troops into good defensive positions on Dungan's Hill from which they could hinder Jones's march to Dublin. If Jones decided to attack, Preston knew that his soldiers would have the inherent advantage of defensive positions on the high ground against troops attacking uphill.

Jones learned of Preston's move on 7 August as his troops neared Trimlestown, several miles to the north-west of Trim. He quickly resolved to attack Preston's army in its positions on Dungan's Hill. On 8 August the battle opened with an exchange of artillery fire, followed by a mid-morning English attack. By noon Jones's cavalry had broken the Irish cavalry on both flanks of Preston's army, allowing the English infantry to attack the Irish centre. The impact of the English pikemen broke Preston's six infantry regiments, whose soldiers fled into a nearby bog. Jones surrounded the bog with his cavalry and methodically wiped out the Irish foot-soldiers in the bog with his infantry. The result was a complete disaster for the Leinster army. Over 3,000 Irish soldiers were killed. Many officers, including five of the six regimental commanders, were captured, along with Preston's correspondence and artillery. The English put to the sword all prisoners who were 'formerly of our side, and all English'. Jones's losses were minimal.[144] The army of Leinster was annihilated, while Preston himself barely escaped.

Jones sent his Ulster troops back to their garrisons on 10 August, while his Dublin units remained on campaign to clear eastern Leinster of enemy garrisons before returning to Dublin on 17 August. Jones had conducted a campaign focused on the destruction of the enemy army, and Preston, by accepting battle, had allowed him to succeed. This victory shifted the military balance against the Catholics in Leinster. Jones hoped to continue such campaigns and to receive reinforcements sufficient to allow him to garrison the towns of Ireland as he campaigned. This strategy was the one which Cromwell was to follow in 1649–50. However, it required massive support from England and the focused attention of the English government.

While Jones was destroying Preston's army, the already strained relations between the dominant Presbyterian interest in the English parliament and Independents of the New Model Army finally broke down altogether. Parliament's attempts to disband the army without paying the soldiers their arrears led to the army's first coup against the Westminster government in August 1647.[145] These political struggles in England between political Presbyterians and Independents split the parliamentarian cause, drove the Scots into an alliance with the remnants of the English royalist party and culminated in the Second Civil War. Consequently, Jones's and the other

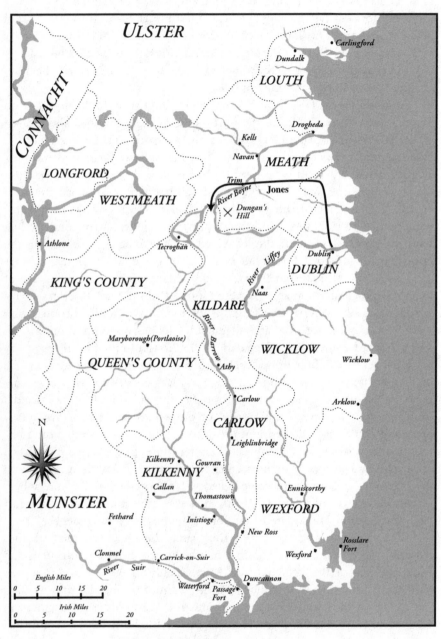

2. Michael Jones's Campaign, August 1647

Protestant garrisons in Ireland did not receive the support needed to carry out the conquest of Ireland in 1647 and 1648.

O'Neill, in the meantime, ravaged north-eastern Connacht. In August, however, his troops mutinied for lack of pay, and it was November before he restored order and was able to turn his attention again to Jones's threat in the Pale. Jones used this period to consolidate his hold on eastern Leinster. In October he took the field with 7,700 men to destroy Catholic garrisons in central and northern Leinster. On 7 October he attacked Portlester, using six cannon to blow down a tower in the wall before launching his assault. Part of O'Neill's garrison in the place escaped to Athy, but most of the defenders were put to the sword, 'having before refused conditions'.[146] This method of attack and the treatment meted out to the surviving defenders presaged the tactics of the Cromwellian conquest. Jones repeated this process to clear most of northern Leinster of Catholic garrisons, putting his own troops into the captured places before returning to Dublin on 19 October.

O'Neill could not move against Jones until he regained control of his army in early November. He then led 8,000 men to within seven miles of Dublin. The heavy rains turned the roads to mud, making it impossible for O'Neill to bring along the artillery needed to recapture his lost positions. When shortage of supplies forced O'Neill to withdraw, Jones made a sortie out of Dublin, hoping to force O'Neill to fight. O'Neill refused battle, retreating instead by forced marches to western Leinster.[147] After a futile pursuit Jones returned to Dublin.

Further bad news for the Catholic cause came from Munster in 1647. Inchiquin's Protestant garrisons there also had been supplied and reinforced from England in the summer of 1647. During the autumn Inchiquin led his army of 4,500 soldiers against Dungarvan and Cashel, taking both easily from their demoralised garrisons.[148]

On 13 November Inchiquin attacked and destroyed the Catholic Munster army under the command of Theobald, Lord Taaffe, at Knocknanuss, near Mallow, County Cork. In this battle Inchiquin's 5,000 infantrymen attacked uphill against a more numerous enemy, breaking the cohesion of the Confederate ranks with repeated cavalry charges against their flanks and the steady fire of two field guns. Eventually 'the rebels began . . . little by little, to descend from the top of the hill, and then the fight was very fierce, but lasted not long, for in half an hour they were routed and broken. And no quarter was given to the Irish rebels, nor to the Redshanks.'[149] The Confederates lost as many as 4,000 men killed, along with a considerable store of ammunition and arms. Inchiquin capped off his efforts with the capture of all of the major Munster towns except Waterford, Limerick and Clonmel.[150]

The battles of Dungan's Hill and Knocknanuss destroyed two of the three major Catholic armies in Ireland. Only the outbreak of the Second

Civil War in Britain diverted the English from exploiting these successes immediately. Consequently, in early 1648 the military tide again swung swiftly towards the Catholics as English aid dried up. Jones and Inchiquin found their garrisons starving as the Irish withdrew supplies from the reach of their foraging parties.

In February Inchiquin notified parliament that he would be compelled to take desperate action if food and money did not reach him.[151] He also was forced by the resumption of hostilities in England to take sides in the struggle between the Presbyterians and the Independents. As a moderate royalist, Inchiquin had no sympathy with the Independents and the New Model Army, both of whom were seeking to alter the English constitution. As he reached the end of his logistical tether a Catholic army moved nearer to his headquarters in Cork, preventing Inchiquin's soldiers from living off the land.[152] These logistical and military threats, along with his antipathy to the Independents in parliament, led Inchiquin again to change sides. In May he and the Confederate Supreme Council signed a ceasefire, opening the way for a new royalist coalition to form in Ireland.[153]

Rinuccini's reaction to the Supreme Council's treaty with Inchiquin split the Catholic Confederation. Rinuccini campaigned vigorously against an agreement with the heretical Inchiquin. In late April he forced the Irish prelates to form a committee of five bishops to decide on censure of the Supreme Council if an unsatisfactory agreement was signed with Inchiquin.[154] When the Council signed a truce with Inchiquin on 20 May, the nuncio precipitously issued a degree of excommunication, without support from the bishops.[155] This desperate move forced the bishops and the Old English to chose between loyalty to the legate and their own military survival. When the Confederate Supreme Council and Assembly stood by the decision to ally with Inchiquin against the parliamentary forces, O'Neill and the Gaelic Irish remained loyal to the nuncio. Rinuccini's use of excommunication to prevent an alliance with heretics failed, but 'it divided the Irish Catholics as no other event in the seventeenth century'.[156]

Because the Scottish government had joined the royalists in the Second Civil War, Jones was now isolated in Ireland. His position in Dublin was precarious, and only the outbreak of a civil war between the papal nuncio's supporters and the Confederate royalists in the summer of 1648 saved him from almost certain defeat. However, when the Anglo-Scottish war broke out in the spring of 1648, the Ulster Scots left Jones's parliamentarian garrisons in Leinster unmolested. Cromwell's defeat of the Scottish invasion force at Preston and the complete political shake-up in Edinburgh in August broke Scottish morale in Ulster as well as in Scotland.

In September, shortly after the Ulster Scots heard about the Scottish defeat at Preston, George Monck led a parliamentarian force from Leinster into eastern Ulster, capturing Belfast by surprise. Monck seized George

Monro, the son of Robert Monro and now the Scottish commander in Ireland, and disarmed his troops with little resistance. Monck then sent Monro to London and shipped back to Scotland any of his soldiers desiring repatriation. Monck's actions ended independent Scottish military action in Ulster for the remainder of the war. Henceforth all Scottish soldiers remaining in Ireland served under the command of others and as part of a combined British force.[157]

Equally dramatic events took place in western Ulster in the autumn of 1648. Sir Charles Coote, reinforced with a fresh regiment of English soldiers, seized the leaders of the Laggan army, who had recently begun to refuse to co-operate in his operations against Connacht. Coote sent Sir Robert Stewart and Colonel Mervyn to London as prisoners.[158] Pro-parliamentarian garrisons consequently held Derry, Enniskillen and Sligo. Coote also disbanded any Laggan units which refused to serve parliament. These actions forced the settler regiments in eastern Ulster to adhere to parliament for the time being. But the Ulster British settlers continued to harbour resentments against Coote and Monck, making their hold on the province dependent on the success of Jones and Inchiquin in the south.

Between 1643 and 1646 the Catholic Confederates missed several opportunities to bring about a royalist victory in Ireland and to help Charles I significantly in Britain. They failed to exploit their numerical superiority to drive the Protestant armies out of Ireland when the Protestants were at their most vulnerable in 1643–4. They failed to send sufficient aid to the Scottish royalists in 1644 to prevent the main Scottish army from entering northern England on its way to Marston Moor. And they failed to conclude a treaty with Ormond which could have united all royalists in Ireland, making the subsequent English conquest far more difficult. They failed in 1646 to exploit O'Neill's victory over the Scots at Benburb to its full military potential. Worst of all, by early 1648 the Gaelic Irish and Old English had come to see each other rather than Inchiquin's royalists in Munster or Jones's parliamentarians in Leinster as the more dangerous military threat. Consequently, while the English were distracted by their second civil war, the Catholics fought their own civil war in Ireland, further weakening themselves for the English onslaught that was to come.

2

The Catholic Civil War of 1648–9 and the Royalist Confederacy

Rinuccini's triumph over the Ormondists on the Catholic Supreme Council and his successful use of the threat of excommunication to bring the Old English military forces to heel in 1646 did not end the internecine struggles within the Catholic Confederation. Committed royalists like Ulick Burke, Earl of Clanricarde, and the majority of the Old English lords continued to believe that Ireland's only hope lay with an accommodation with Charles I and the defeat of the English parliamentarians. With the departure of Ormond from Ireland in July 1647, hopes of such an accommodation seemed less likely than ever.

The defeats inflicted on the Confederate armies at Dungan's Hill (August) and Knocknanuss (November) and Rinuccini's inability to make the Confederate armies co-operate effectively against either Jones in Dublin or Inchiquin in Munster in late 1647 showed many Confederates that new approaches were needed to achieve their goals. The occupation of western Leinster by O'Neill's Ulster army during the winter of 1647–8 only worsened the situation. The division within the confederacy between Old Irish and Old English was clear and would have been fatal for the Catholic cause in 1647–8 if the Westminster government had not been distracted by serious political dissension and the consequent Second Civil War in England and the Scottish invasion of the south on behalf of the king in July 1648.

The divisions within the Catholic Confederation did, however, provide an opportunity for the royalists to construct an Ormondist coalition within Ireland. Men such as Ormond and Clanricarde hoped that such a coalition would help to restore the monarch to the full enjoyment of his regal power in Britain. However, before the royalists could act on such hopes the divisions within the Confederation led to a Catholic civil war in Ireland between O'Neill and the nuncioists on one side and the Old English Ormondists on the other. This civil war prevented the royalists and Catholics from uniting in 1648 to expel the few remaining parliamentarian garrisons from Ireland and to consolidate royalist control of the island in preparation for resistance to the eventual Cromwellian assault.

THE INCHIQUIN TRUCE, 1648

In the spring of 1648 military control of the province of Munster was divided between the Protestant garrisons of Murrough O'Brien, Lord Inchiquin, and the Catholic forces commanded by Lord Taaffe. Inchiquin held the ports of Cork, Youghal and Kinsale, while the Catholics held Waterford and most of the hinterland. Inchiquin had been loyal to the Westminster parliament since the summer of 1644. He was strongly anti-Catholic, while also sympathetic to the mild royalism of the Presbyterian party in the English struggles in 1647–8. Inchiquin, whose brother was a Confederate, considered himself English rather than Irish, in the same manner as most Old English Catholics identified themselves as English. He, like Ormond, looked to the Old English Confederates as a welcome alternative to O'Neill's 'wild Gaels' of the north and the domineering papal nuncio.[1] The seizure of the king by the New Model Army in 1647 and the army's coup against parliament in August shocked Inchiquin. By early 1648 he was contemplating ways to resist the Independents' growing power in England.[2]

The outbreak of the Second Civil War in England coincided almost exactly with Inchiquin's decision to negotiate a ceasefire with the Supreme Council in Kilkenny. This decision was more palatable to Inchiquin because the Old English lords dominated the Supreme Council elected in December 1647.[3] In April Inchiquin

> with the advice of his officers [took] a resolution to oppose the present pretended Parliament in England . . . and to that purpose, was now putting himself into a posture of defence; And for the managing of this design, he had correspondency with the king, with the Scots, and generally all the Presbyterian party that were agreed with the king [and] who were resolved to endeavour to their utmost the re-enthroning the king, and restoring a free Parliament. . . . And for the better effecting and carrying on this design, he was resolved to join with the Lord Taaffe and the whole Irish of the province of Munster.[4]

The impact on the Catholic Confederacy of Inchiquin's overtures to the Supreme Council was divisive. The nuncio fought the conclusion of a ceasefire with the 'heretical' turncoat Inchiquin with all his might. He felt that the truce seriously threatened the Catholic religion in Ireland and that the Supreme Council had no right to reach an agreement with Inchiquin without the approval of the prelates of the Irish church led by the papal legate. He also believed that Inchiquin could not be trusted and that a truce would be neither helpful nor necessary to the Confederate cause.[5]

The Old English lords and a majority of the Catholic townsmen and prelates, however, favoured a truce and co-operation with Inchiquin as a means of self-defence against both the parliamentarians and against the unruly Ulstermen of O'Neill's army then occupying, and subsisting from, western Leinster.[6] The Old English were caught between O'Neill's powerful army and the evidently successful English Independents. Inchiquin's defection from the parliamentarian cause weakened the Protestant forces in Ireland and provided the Supreme Council with an effective military counter-weight to O'Neill's army.

The Confederate Supreme Council signed the truce with Inchiquin on 20 May 1648. An immediate cessation of hostilities was to be observed. Catholics were not to be molested in their religion, and Inchiquin was to receive supplies from the Confederates.[7] While Inchiquin refused to fight against other Protestants, he promised to provide military aid against O'Neill if that became necessary. The nuncio's excommunication of those who accepted the truce and his flight to O'Neill's camp near Maryborough (Portlaoise) split the Catholic Confederation, compelling all members to choose between the nuncio's hardline position or the *politique* royalism of the Supreme Council. Most Catholics stayed loyal to the Supreme Council. Bishops sympathetic to the Ormondist position resisted the nuncio's excommunication by launching an immediate appeal to Rome, and its effects were further mitigated by the decision of most of the Irish bishops not to enforce the ban.[8] 'The Old English and Rinuccini had reached a point of mutual incomprehension', and 'the Confederacy fell apart on what seemed inevitable lines of division'.[9]

The Inchiquin Truce opened the way for the creation of a royalist co-alition in Ireland. Ormond, still in exile in France, had been working to encourage the creation of such an alliance for months. He had remained in correspondence with his kinsmen and friends among the Old English, and he had the blessing and support of the queen and the Prince of Wales for his plans to return to Ireland as soon as the nuncioists had been defeated in the Catholic Confederation. He hoped to come to terms with O'Neill and the formerly hostile Scots in Ulster and Scotland, thus creating a powerful coalition that could effectively aid the English royalists in their planned uprising in England in the spring of 1648.

By April 1648 Ormond was making plans for his return to Ireland. In a memorandum entitled 'All that I conceive necessary to be done by way of preparation for the business of Ireland' he detailed how he intended to negotiate with the Confederates, making no open religious concessions, while gathering money, munitions and shipping for his return.[10] Then, 'if our hopes of the Scots, and my lord of Inchiquin, resolve into assurances of their declaring for the king, there may be no time lost in giving them those countenances of authority and assurance that they will in such case expect'.[11]

Ormond's plans for the revival of a royalist coalition in Ireland were part of a larger royalist strategy which encompassed the three Stuart kingdoms and the exiled royalist groups in France and Holland.[12] The conspirators hoped to trigger royalist uprisings in England, to be accompanied by a Scottish invasion of northern England and a royalist resurgence in Ireland which would drive the parliamentarians out of Dublin and Derry. Timing was important, since it was necessary for these events to occur simultaneously. As things turned out, the three component parts of the strategy took place, but at different times, robbing them of their potential combined effect. The risings in England and Wales started first, in April, but were crushed for the most part before the Scots began their invasion in late July. The Scottish army was decisively beaten by Cromwell at Preston on 17 August, over six weeks before Ormond was able to sail from France for Ireland.

Prominent Old English members of the Kilkenny government were in frequent correspondence with the royalists planners around the English queen in France. By mid-April they assured Ormond and the queen that the

> most considerable, both for numbers and quality, in this kingdom are very desirous of a settlement. . . . Only the clergy and Ulster are more inclined to an accommodation with Jones than Inchiquin. . . . But if the Marquis of Ormond come in any opportune time, it is the opinion of all [that] it will not be in the power of all his and His Majesty's enemies to hinder his design, especially if the Marquis of Ormond can come with aid sufficient or considerable money and other provisions and able and willing to give the papists, as well as Protestants, some reasonable content in religion.[13]

Ormond sent Inchiquin his commission as an officer of the crown shortly after he and the Confederates signed their truce in May.[14] By then Inchiquin's logistical situation was desperate, as he pointed out to Ormond: 'I have expended all I have or could borrow, or force in my quarters: yet divers of my men have died of hunger, after they had a while lived upon cats and dogs as many now do.'[15] Yet Inchiquin believed that the king's only chance of recovering his rightful influence lay with the success of a new royalist coalition. His views were shared by most royalists, especially after May 1648, when the New Model Army's officers determined 'that it was our duty, if ever the Lord brought us back again in peace, to call Charles Stuart, that man of blood, to an account for the blood he had shed and mischief he had done'.[16]

Inchiquin believed that many Old English lords could be counted upon to serve the king. Ulick Burke, Earl of Clanricarde, the chief royalist Catholic lord in Connacht, was a good example of those Old English who believed their loyalties to the crown and their Catholic faith were compatible. Such Catholics realised that the only hope of lasting religious toleration would come from the king, and not from the parliamentarians. They understood that without the help of royalists like Ormond and Inchiquin, the Catholics in Ireland had little hope of defeating the parliamentarians. Inchiquin considered Clanricarde to be 'very faithful to His Majesty' and a useful ally with his army of 3,000 men.[17]

The potential co-operation of Inchiquin's, Clanricarde's and Taaffe's forces against O'Neill's Ulster army would give the royalist coalition sufficient military strength to defeat O'Neill, unite with the Scots and British in the north, and drive the parliamentarians out of Ireland. However, these forces could not be united until Ormond returned to Ireland and negotiated a peace treaty with the Catholic Confederates. The longer he delayed his return, the worse things got for Inchiquin, and the more time Cromwell and Fairfax had to destroy the royalist uprisings in England.[18]

ORMOND'S RETURN AND THE SECOND ORMOND PEACE, 1649

Ormond's presence in Ireland was essential for the organisation of a royalist coalition. Only his prestige as the king's Lord Lieutenant of Ireland could be counted upon by the Catholics as a guarantee that the terms of any agreement they reached would be honoured by the king after the war.[19] His presence was just as important to Inchiquin as it was to the Old English, because by 13 August the Supreme Council had proclaimed that anyone who aided O'Neill's forces would be considered a traitor.[20] On 30 September the Confederate General Assembly went further, condemning O'Neill 'as a traitor and a rebel against the king and the fundamental laws of the land, a common disturber of peace, tranquillity, and quiet of the kingdom, and a manifest opposer of the government of the Confederates, contrary to his oath'.[21]

Ormond set sail from Le Havre on 30 September 1648. A shortage of money had prevented his departure in August, and unfavourable winds kept him in port until the end of September.[22] By that time he had received news of the disastrous defeat inflicted on the Scots by Cromwell at Preston on 17 August and of Fairfax's capture of the last major royalist stronghold in southern England. Ormond must have felt more than a little downhearted as well as grimly determined as he returned to Ireland to revive the royalist cause which had languished 'for want of the appearing [there] of some authority'.[23]

Ormond arrived in Cork by 3 October, after a swift voyage from Le Havre. He had come none too soon. Inchiquin's hold over his Protestant soldiers was precarious, partly because their pay was in arrears, and partly because of the adverse impact on them of the news of the New Model Army's victories in England. To steady the troops' wavering loyalties, Ormond gave Inchiquin enough money to pay his soldiers part of their arrears, while encouraging Prince Charles 'to send frequent and timely declarations of his confidence in the Munster troops, and to send as many ships as possible to Ireland'.[24] His next step was to negotiate peace with the Catholic Confederates as swiftly as possible.

Shortly after he arrived, Ormond, then at his house in Carrick-on-Suir, received thirty-eight propositions for a treaty from representatives of the Confederates.[25] The Confederate terms were unacceptable because they demanded full recognition of the Catholic clergy's jurisdiction in the parts of Ireland they currently controlled, as well as the repeal of Poynings' Law and the immediate convening of an Irish parliament which included full representation of Catholics. Ormond could never grant these terms and at the same time keep the Ulster Scots and Inchiquin's Protestants within the royalist coalition. Consequently, he stretched the negotiations out, hoping that the Catholics would see the futility of their position and the king's inability to submit to such terms, given his position as a captive in England.[26]

In the meantime Clanricarde and Inchiquin began to co-operate militarily to clear O'Neill's garrisons out of western Leinster. By 4 October Inchiquin's troops had captured Fort Falkland in King's County and handed it over to Clanricarde to garrison. During these operations Inchiquin's 4,000-man army was active in western Leinster and northern Munster, destroying stores of supplies that might be useful to O'Neill and constantly hoping that O'Neill would fight a pitched battle. O'Neill on several occasions tried to cut Inchiquin's force off from its bases in Munster, but the co-operation and logistical support provided to Inchiquin by Clanricarde from Connacht thwarted O'Neill's strategy.[27]

O'Neill kept his army in the field after Inchiquin returned to Munster in late October. Clanricarde was convinced that O'Neill meant to march across the county of 'Westmeath into Longford, and so over into Connacht at Ballyclare'. Such a move would have provided O'Neill a fresh logistical base and access to many recruits willing to join his army.[28] Ormond responded to Clanricarde's pleas for further military help by again dispatching Inchiquin and his army into western Leinster. This move deterred O'Neill, but Ormond saw these developments as diversions from the main effort which needed to be made against Jones in Dublin.

Jones used the Catholics' internal disputes in the spring and summer of 1648 as an opportunity to strengthen his position in the Pale. For example, in late September he conducted a campaign with 5,000 soldiers to clear out all Catholic garrisons within a fifty-mile radius of Dublin.[29] In this campaign Jones used artillery to blow breaches in the defences of a number of Confederate-held castles in preparation for a powerful infantry assault. This method of operation proved to be a successful way to deal with the obsolete curtain-wall fortifications that predominated in Ireland. The account of Jones's capture of the castle of Ballisonan provides a good example of his method and the results.

Ballisonan was a Catholic-held castle in Leinster, north-east of Carlow, which had never been captured by Ormond's forces during seven years of war. Its defences consisted of three rings. There was an outer wall with a ditch dug behind it which was also overlooked by a tower on the west end. The main defences were inside this outer wall, consisting of another wall overlooked by breastworks on a low hill. The castle itself was inside these works, surrounded by a moat and accessible only across a drawbridge. Three companies of infantry commanded by Captain St Leger garrisoned the place. These troops were encouraged in their work by the wife of the castle's owner, Pierce Fitzgerald, who had remained in the castle while her husband rode off to seek a relief force from either O'Neill or Preston.[30]

Jones arrived before the defences on 19 September and set up his three heavy battering pieces. He commenced firing the next morning after the garrison refused to discuss terms of surrender. After Jones's battery had fired about thirty-six shots the tower in the outer wall collapsed, allowing Jones's infantry to advance through a breach and up to the second defensive line. Jones next ordered an assault that seized the breastworks which dominated the second ring of defences, forcing the defenders back into the castle. At this point the garrison commander, St Leger, asked for a parley, hoping to gain time for a relief column to arrive. Jones accepted the parley, but limited it to a few hours, while also moving his cannon and a mortar into position to batter the remaining works.

On the afternoon of 21 September Jones ordered the bombardment to resume, with the mortar throwing shells into the castle while the cannon fired directly at the wall. After sixteen cannon-balls had struck the walls St Leger again requested, and was granted, a parley at which he offered to surrender the castle with the terms that the garrison could march away safely. Jones accepted, garrisoning the place with his own soldiers before moving on to the next Catholic strong point.[31] In this manner Jones cleared most of the Pale.

Sir Charles Coote, the parliamentarian commander in south-western Ulster, conducted similar operations in 1648, marching deep into Confederate territory, killing many people, and driving off cattle.[32] Such operations went mostly unchallenged by either Clanricarde or O'Neill, then fully engaged in fighting each other for control of western Leinster. This Catholic civil war was vicious, as the following report in the weekly news-book *The Moderate Intelligencer* makes clear:

> Owen Mac Art [O'Neill], about fourteen days since [15 December], sent Rory Maguire, with a strong body of horse and foot to take Jamestown, and Drumrusk, from Clanricarde's party. Jamestown was surrendered upon composition. Drumrusk was most furiously stormed and carried by Rory Maguire, but himself and several officers slain with 4 or 500 men. They put all, both in town and castle to the sword. . . .

From thence they marched to the [town of] Boyle where they burnt the town, and killed all they met, of what age or sex, and are destroying all before them in the county of Roscommon.[33]

Negotiations between Ormond and the Confederate Supreme Council dragged on through the autumn, while the king's position became more desperate in England. The delay in reaching a settlement and the continued uneasiness of Inchiquin's Protestant troops with the idea of allying with the Catholics triggered a mutiny in Inchiquin's garrisons in early November.[34] Ormond and Inchiquin moved swiftly to quell the mutineers by reassuring them that they had no intention of giving the Catholics religious concessions which would jeopardise the Protestants' privileged position in Munster. This mutiny was dangerous because, as Inchiquin told his soldiers, it could 'extinguish that small spark of hope that is left for his Majesty's restitution, without which we can never hope for a freedom of Parliament (for no king, no Parliament)'.[35] The two royalist leaders brought the troops back to their allegiance through tact and persuasion, although Inchiquin made it clear to Ormond that the soldiers would remain loyal only if the treaty with the Supreme Council omitted concessions upon the issues of Catholic jurisdiction and control of those churches not yet in Catholic hands.[36]

After this diversion of his energy to quell the mutiny, Ormond resumed the peace negotiations with the Confederates, seemingly with little chance of success. However, a series of events in England transformed the Irish situation, beginning with the New Model Army's 'Remonstrance' of 20 November, continuing with the army's purge of the House of Commons on 6 December, and culminating with the decision of the Rump Parliament to try Charles I as a traitor in early January 1649. The total victory of the English Independents meant that there was no hope of compromise between the Westminster government and the Catholics in Ireland. As a result, the Confederate Supreme Council decided to drop its demands for full religious liberty and jurisdiction and to accept Ormond's promise that Catholic religious concerns would be fairly dealt with by the king in a free parliament in Ireland once he was restored to his full power. The Catholics had little choice, realising, as Ormond observed to them, 'how miserable their condition is like to be under the servitude that seems in all hands to be prepared for them, if this treaty end not in a peace'.[37]

In spite of the desperate situation in December, the Confederates and Ormond still had difficulty coming to terms. Ormond promised them only freedom of worship, no jurisdiction, and only temporary possession of the churches they then held until a free parliament could meet with a restored king to sort the matter out. After realising that in these difficult times Ormond would not concede more, the Catholic Confederates finally gave in, accepting the terms on 28 December. Considering the king's proclamation of May 1647 disavowing Ormond's efforts and authority to reach an agreement with the Irish Catholics, it is not hard to understand why the Old English distrusted the promises which Ormond was making on the king's behalf in late 1648.[38] The truce with Inchiquin was extended on 1 January 1649, and the final peace between Ormond and the Confederates was signed on 17 January.[39]

The Ormond Peace of 1649 promised

> free exercise of the Roman Catholic religion. . . . And that . . . the said Roman Catholics or any of them shall not be questioned or molested in their goods or estates, for any matter or cause whatsoever for, concerning, or by reason of the free exercise of their religion. . . . And that the said Oath [of Supremacy] shall not be tendered unto them . . . they taking the Oath of Allegiance. . . . That they shall not be molested in the possession which they have of present of the churches and the church-livings, or the exercise of their respective jurisdictions as they now exercise . . . until such time as His Majesty upon the full consideration of the desires of the said Roman Catholics in a free Parliament to be held in this kingdom shall declare his further pleasure.[40]

The Catholic Confederates had to be satisfied with these assurances, which, however, meant nothing if the king was not restored to full power.

The articles of agreement of the new Ormond Peace included provisions for the governance of the coalition. Ormond was the chief executive as the king's Lord Lieutenant of Ireland. Twelve Catholic Commissioners of Trust were selected to meet regularly in Kilkenny to advise Ormond and to organise the efforts of the Catholic towns and forces in support of the combined war effort. This support included the levying of excise and customs taxes on the Irish towns and an assessment on the counties.[41] The new royalist confederacy was evidently able to raise enough money to pay its army through the month of May, allowing Ormond to put together an effective field force in the spring.[42]

The royalist Confederates also reorganised their military command. Gone were the independent provincial forces, at least in theory. In their place, a single army hierarchy was set up, with Ormond as the Lord General, Inchiquin and Castlehaven as Lieutenant-Generals of Horse, and Sir Patrick Purcell as Major-General of Foot. General Preston remained associated with the Lord General, but he was not given command of an independent force of any size. Total unity of command could not be achieved, however, because of the mutual distrust between the Catholics and Inchiquin. Throughout 1649 and 1650 it took all of Ormond's tact and sensitivity to keep these two components of the royalist confederacy together.

The realignment of forces in Ireland that started with Inchiquin's truce with the Supreme Council in May 1648 was furthered by Ormond's return to Ireland in the following September. This shift culminated with the

Ormond Peace and the creation of a royalist–Confederate alliance in January 1649. But Ormond's efforts to unite Protestant settlers with Old English Catholics against the parliamentarians would not have succeeded without the New Model Army's seizure of power in London in December and their momentous decision to bring Charles I to trial for his actions against the nation. These events in England drove the British in Ulster into Ormond's camp, just as they drove the majority of the Catholics on the Supreme Council to accept peace and an alliance with the representative of an heretical king.[43]

If these anti-parliamentarian forces could have captured the garrisons in Ulster and Leinster which were still loyal to the Westminster government before large numbers of reinforcements arrived from England, the history of the Cromwellian conquest of Ireland would have been very different. At the very least, Cromwell would have been denied Dublin as a logistical base. Ulster would have been united against him, and the various armies of Ulster and Connacht would have been available to serve with Ormond against Jones at Rathmines. Unfortunately for the royalists, Owen Roe O'Neill, the commander of the largest and most experienced Catholic army in Ireland, refused to join the royalist coalition.

ROYALIST STRATEGY IN 1649

The New Model Army's defeat of the Scots and royalists in Britain made the royalist and Catholic positions in Ireland precarious if not desperate. None the less, Ormond believed that now that peace had been concluded with the Catholic Confederates, 'if we can but receive moderate countenance and assistance from abroad, this kingdom will very speedily be in absolute subjection to the king's authority' and therefore able to assist in the restoration of the monarch to power.[44] The potential military power of the royalist coalition was considerable if all of their forces could be brought to play a part in the effort. The field armies of the various partners in the coalition totalled roughly 15,000 infantry and 3,000 cavalry, dispersed into six separate forces in the four provinces. This total included Clanricarde's forces in Connacht, Preston's in Leinster, Taaffe's in Munster, Inchiquin's in Munster, Monro's Scots in Ulster, and the Laggan army in Ulster.[45] If O'Neill could be won over, an additional four or five thousand soldiers would be available.

The challenges facing Ormond as he attempted to harness the military power of these armed forces were immense. O'Neill and his army either had to be destroyed or convinced to join the new royalist Confederation. Relations between the Catholic Confederates and the Protestant forces in Munster and Ulster had to be managed in such a way that they all felt the royalist coalition was preferable to adherence to the Westminster parliament. The parliamentarian garrisons in Sligo, Enniskillen, Derry and in the Pale had to be taken and Dublin captured so that Cromwell and his army would not have a base from which to launch their conquest.

To accomplish this strategy quickly, Ormond first hoped to win Owen Roe O'Neill over to the royalist cause. This became somewhat more feasible after Rinuccini, the papal nuncio and a fervent opponent of the Ormond Peace, left Ireland in February 1649. Ormond's hope was not unrealistic. In fact O'Neill suggested to Clanricarde that same month that he was interested in a rapprochement with Ormond. As Clanricarde observed to Ormond, 'it would be a great advantage to gain him', but if that failed, 'he ought to be prosecuted with all the forces that can with expedition be drawn together [since] . . . the working of a violent party of the clergy makes any delay dangerous'.[46] O'Neill's logistical situation was desperate, but his army was growing from the recruitment of men from disbanded Confederate units, giving him a total of at least 4,000 soldiers.[47] Such a force was a prize worth trying to attain through negotiation.

In late February Ormond instructed Francis Nugent, a Catholic Confederate trusted by O'Neill, to offer the Ulsterman an act of forgiveness and oblivion and all the benefits of the peace if he would join the royalist alliance.[48] Unfortunately for the royalist and Catholic causes, O'Neill demanded the restoration of the lands of six counties of Ulster to the native Irish, a demand which Ormond could not grant without dismantling the entire land settlement of Ireland. O'Neill therefore remained alienated and continued to operate against the Confederate-held areas in Leinster to improve his logistical base. The royalist forces thus found it necessary to move against him before they could move against the parliamentarian enclaves.

By the late autumn of 1648 the Confederates had captured most of Owen Roe O'Neill's garrisons and supply areas in Leinster and northern Connacht, forcing O'Neill and his army to retreat into south-eastern Ulster. O'Neill and his army were caught between the hostile forces of the Confederates, now including Phelim O'Neill and a number of Gaelic Irish regiments in central Ulster, and Monck's Protestant garrisons in eastern Ulster. Lacking sufficient arms and munitions to equip his troops for battle, Owen Roe O'Neill steadily had to give ground to Inchiquin's offensive from the south. These attacks pushed him to the point where he either had to give in to Ormond's continuing entreaties to join the royalist cause or find another source of munitions.[49]

O'Neill preferred to co-operate with Sir Charles Coote and George Monck in their defence of Derry and Dundalk rather than to join Ormond in an alliance supporting an 'heretical' monarch. O'Neill's absence from the Ormond alliance was due to the seemingly unbridgeable rift which had opened between the Old Irish and Old English during the past seven years of warfare. O'Neill was fighting in defence of total Catholic religious liberty, refusing to make a *politique* alliance with Protestants such as Inchiquin and

Ormond in January 1649.[50] By May, however, his shortage of gunpowder, arms and money caused him to decide to make temporary mutual defence pacts with the Parliamentarian commanders in Ulster in exchange for munitions. O'Neill's willingness to fulfil the terms of these pacts with Monck and Coote greatly aided their resistance to the royalists' armies, preventing the Ulster royalists and the Connacht forces under Clanricarde from coming to Ormond's aid in Leinster in the crucial campaign against Dublin in July.

ROYALIST NAVAL STRATEGY

While he was attempting to deal with O'Neill, Ormond devised a naval strategy to help in his efforts against Jones and his Dublin garrison. This naval strategy was possible because, for the first time in the 1640s, the royalists possessed an effective navy. The royalist cause had only recently acquired a significant naval force as a result of the mutiny which took place in the parliamentarian fleet in the Downs and the Thames in April 1648. When the Second Civil War was breaking out in England, the crews of seventeen major warships mutinied against the Independents then dominating the New Model Army and the city of London. Eleven of these ships escaped the counter-measures taken by the Earl of Warwick, the parliamentarian Lord Admiral, and sailed to Holland, where they joined the Prince of Wales.[51] In late July 1648 this fleet blockaded the mouth of the Thames for several weeks before returning to Holland to avoid a battle against their former comrades in the parliamentarian fleet. The royalist navy then lay idle in the Dutch port of Helvoetsluys until December.

Ormond readily understood the need to cut Dublin off from English supplies and reinforcements if he was going to be able to force Jones to surrender. He and the royalists in France planned to move the royalist navy from Holland to Ireland, where the fleet could support the only active royalist military operations. By December the fleet, consisting of four 'great ships', four frigates and some smaller vessels, was fitting out for sea. Prince Rupert was to serve as the commander of the fleet, since the Prince of Wales was intending to move to the Scilly Isles, from which he could easily go to Ireland when things there were most favourable. Rupert and the fleet sailed from Holland in late January, after the usual delays of weather and slow provisioning. Although rough weather dispersed the ships *en route*, a number of them arrived at Kinsale on 26 January, and Rupert arrived at a place he referred to as 'Broockehaven' (perhaps Oysterhaven) on the following day. On 28 January he joined the remainder of his fleet at Kinsale, giving the royalists an effective naval force in Irish waters and the chance to isolate Dublin.[52]

Rupert, however, arrived with a completely different strategic design from Ormond's, and with an under-manned fleet, short of money, food and drink. Rupert needed 400 seamen to fill his crews, quarters ashore for the families of many of his seamen, and at least £2,000 worth of naval supplies immediately to make all of his ships seaworthy. Instead of accepting Ormond's plan for the use of the fleet, Rupert suggested that he use his ships to ferry 1,000 Irish soldiers to Guernsey to support royalist operations in the Channel Islands. Ormond's response to this last suggestion is not known, but he did make his views clear to Rupert that the fleet was needed to cut Dublin off before the Westminster government could send additional regiments and food supplies to Jones.[53]

Rupert also requested the establishment of an Admiralty court in Ireland to adjudicate the disposition of vessels captured as prizes in Irish waters. Potentially, such a court could take a share of the lucrative profits enjoyed by the large Irish privateering fleet in Wexford, thus providing the money needed to support Rupert's squadron.[54] There is no complete record of how much money was raised by Ormond's Admiralty officers once he established the court, but it has been estimated that the privateers captured and sold 250 prizes in Ostend and Dunkirk between 3 March 1648 and 25 February 1649.[55] Certainly the Mayor of Waterford provided Ormond's agent in that port with £3,000 in cash and £4,000 worth of grain as a loan secured by the proceeds of the government's tenth of the value of prizes.[56]

The opportunity for Rupert's fleet to blockade Dublin was limited by the length of time before a superior parliamentarian fleet would arrive in Irish waters. In February 1649 two English frigates routinely patrolled Dublin Bay to protect the fishing boats of the capital and to keep communications open with England. Parliamentary squadrons also patrolled the Irish Sea 'for clearing the channel about Dublin of pirates and robbers'. On 7 February one such English squadron of five ships, under the command of Captain Peacock, encountered a royalist force of ten warships, 'five whereof belonging to the Prince's fleet, the rest Irish, who were designed against Dublin'. An hour-long battle ensued, during which the English claimed to have sunk two royalist vessels and captured one frigate armed with forty cannon.[57] The royalist ships withdrew after their vice-admiral's ship was captured.

The Westminster government readily understood the dangerous threats to Dublin's communications and English commerce offered by Rupert's fleet in Kinsale and the dozens of privateering vessels in Wexford. On 2 February parliament voted to send forty warships and thirty armed merchant ships to sea, manned by 6,000 sailors, 'for the dispersing the Prince's fleet, and encouragement of trade'.[58] At the same time the English government carried out a major reorganisation of its naval administration and appointed Robert Blake, Edward Popham and Richard Deane to serve as its 'Generals at Sea' to invigorate and command naval operations.[59] These commanders divided among themselves the responsibilities for dealing with Rupert's fleet in Kinsale, protecting Dublin's communications, and safeguarding English shipping in the Irish Sea. While the fruits of these actions took several months to reap, the results were to be fatal to royalist naval and privateering operations in Irish waters.

Although Ormond encouraged Rupert to be more active in February and March, Rupert failed to lead a major naval operation against Dublin. Instead he sent a steady stream of messages to Ormond complaining of his lack of money, supplies and seamen.[60] Inchiquin made Rupert's task of manning his ships harder when he refused to allow Rupert to impress sailors in Cork or Youghal, forcing him to rely on Waterford, Kinsale and Wexford for additional crewmen.[61] By May both Rupert and the young Charles Stuart, now calling himself Charles II, seemed to have come to the conclusion that the royalist fleet should leave Ireland and move to either the Scilly Isles or Lisbon, from where, Charles had been assured by the Portuguese government, his fleet would be allowed to operate as a major privateering force against English shipping.[62] However, on 22 May, before Rupert could move against Dublin or depart to Lisbon, a parliamentarian squadron of ten warships arrived at Kinsale, blockading that port and Rupert's fleet. This blockade was maintained until October, as was a similar operation at Wexford, paralysing royalist naval power and robbing Ormond of the ability to cut Dublin's supply lines with Britain.[63]

THE FINAL ROYALIST OFFENSIVE IN ULSTER

The royalists continued to try to clear Ulster of parliamentarian forces, especially that of the hated Sir Charles Coote. The final royalist campaign against Coote's garrisons in Sligo, Enniskillen and Derry commenced in the spring of 1649. However, Clanricarde's Connacht forces were slow to move north, and it was not until the Laggan army joined the royalist effort that real headway was made.

Sir Charles Coote had attempted to forestall these royalist operations by launching a campaign deep into Connacht in January to destroy the food supplies which would be essential for the support of a royalist campaign against Sligo and Derry. When he called on the Laggan army leaders for support, they had refused to co-operate.[64] Soon thereafter the remaining leaders of the Laggan forces decided to join the Ormond coalition opposing Coote, mostly because they associated Coote with the London regicides.[65] At about the same time, in mid-February, the Scottish Presbytery of Belfast declared that 'The sectaries [in London], and their abettors, do directly overturn the laws and liberties of the Kingdoms, root out lawful and supreme magistracy (the just privileges whereof we have sworn to maintain) and introduce a fearful confusion, and lawless anarchy.'[66] Consequently, they encouraged Scottish settlers in Ulster to refuse to support Monck in his efforts to hold Dundalk for parliament. By March most Scots had joined the royalist coalition.[67] Catholic Confederates were thus united with Protestant

British settlers in a war against Protestant parliamentarians who increasingly were in league with Owen Roe O'Neill's Catholic Gaelic army.[68]

This remarkable revolution of political affairs in northern Ireland in early 1649 was directly caused by the New Model Army's seizure of power in London in December 1648 and its decision to execute the king in January 1649. The king's execution brought the Scots into Ormond's coalition. In Ulster only Sir Charles Coote's and George Monck's garrisons remained loyal to the English regicide government in London. In February a report from Coote's garrison in Derry summarised the Ulster situation accurately when it noted that 'At present we see most opposition from Royal Protestants, which will be of the interest of Ormond, Inchiquin, etc., to carry on which George Monro is come to these parts with plenty of arms and ammunition . . . by which we shall be much prejudiced, unless a frightening power come over.'[69] Ormond had developed an argument which allowed Protestant royalists to join with Irish Catholics with a clearer conscience when he declared that the Catholic Confederates' 'real intentions and often protested principles were to subsist and live under the ancient rule and government of a king'.[70] Consequently, by early March 1649 the parliamentary garrisons in Ireland faced a formidable royalist alliance.

Most Ulster Protestants sided with Ormond, isolating Monck's garrison in Dundalk and Coote's troops in Sligo and Derry.[71] In late March the Laggan army began military operations against Sir Charles Coote when Sir Alexander Stewart's tenants refused to provide supplies for the Derry garrison and forcibly repulsed a foraging party from the city.[72] The siege of Derry soon followed.

Derry was a small but well-fortified city with defences too strong for an infantry assault to take without the support of a powerful artillery train to breach the walls. The Laggan army lacked heavy siege guns and consequently had to starve the garrison into surrender. However, Derry was a seaport connected to the ocean by the River Foyle and was thus able to receive succour by sea from England until the royalists found a way to cut its water communications. On 28 March the Laggan forces began building an artillery position, known as Charles-Fort, on the Foyle between Derry and the sea in order to cut the city off from supplies and reinforcements. They also cut off Derry from most local sources of food by tightening the landward ring of siege positions.[73]

Sir Charles Coote reacted aggressively to the tightening of the siege. On one occasion he sortied out with 800 men against Laggan soldiers operating near the city, capturing Lieutenant-Colonel James Galbraith and a number of Laggan officers and soldiers. He exchanged these prisoners for a considerable amount of oatmeal. Coote also had his soldiers level all buildings, hedges, orchards and gardens near the city which could be used by the besiegers to get close enough to his defences to fire at his soldiers.[74] Consequently, the besiegers were unable to make appreciable headway against Derry's defences in April or May.

Unfortunately for the Laggan army, Charles-Fort proved to be an ineffectual block to ship traffic into Derry along the River Foyle owing to its lack of heavy artillery. At least one supply ship was able to reach the town in late May, greatly easing Coote's logistical situation.[75] Coote was also able to launch foraging raids into County Londonderry by sending soldiers by boat across the Foyle. On one of these expeditions the raiders captured over 300 cows, far too many to feed in Derry, so the extra animals were sold back to the Laggan force for ten shillings each.[76]

The Laggan force received a major boost in morale and organisation in May when Sir Robert Stewart returned from London, where he had been a prisoner for a brief period. Sir Robert brought new energy to the efforts to tighten the siege of Derry, and he hindered Coote's efforts to disrupt the besiegers more effectively than had been the case earlier. By early June Coote's troops were feeling the sharp pinch of short rations and daily harassment from the besiegers, while the news from the rest of Ireland told of the fall of garrison after garrison to Inchiquin's and Ormond's columns.[77]

While the Laggan army was operating against Derry in western Ulster, the eastern settler garrisons joined the Scots in Ormond's royalist alliance. In early April a Presbyterian council of war at Belfast declared 'against the public enemies of our God, such as are now the prevalent party in England, who have overturned authority from which we might have accepted orders'.[78] The Scottish army and the British settlers called upon George Monck to join them and to open the arsenal of arms and ammunition in Dundalk to their forces. Monck refused, but he found himself isolated and his troops deserting in large numbers.[79]

Ormond meanwhile continued to try to win O'Neill over to the royalist cause.[80] O'Neill's refusal to accept Ormond's entreaties because of his loyalties to the ultra-papalist cause meant the continuation of the fatal split among Irish Catholics. This 'Old Irish intransigence came, again, at a point when royalists, the kirk party, the Ulster Scots, and many ex-Confederates seemed about to unite against the regicide parliament'.[81]

Once it was clear that O'Neill was still operating against the Confederates, Ormond ordered a rendezvous of the Munster forces to be held at Cashel. His intention was 'to disperse them toward the frontiers, and there put them in the best order I can' to protect the northern borders of Munster from an invasion by the Ulstermen.[82] On 14 March Inchiquin began to move an army of 4,000 infantry towards Athlone to provide a blocking force to prevent O'Neill from moving west into Connacht and to stop, in Ormond's words, 'the devouring caterpillar [O'Neill's army]'.[83] Simultaneously Clanricarde sent a force of roughly 1,000 men to Ballinasloe, west of the Shannon in County Galway, to prevent O'Neill from crossing to the west in that area.[84]

Castlehaven assumed command of an army of 5,000 to 6,000 soldiers gathered around Tuam. With this force and several artillery pieces, Castlehaven advanced into Queen's County 'to reduce Portlaoise, Athy and other garrisons possessed by O'Neill's people'. He captured these garrisons with little trouble and then encamped his army at Leighlinbridge, where he waited for Ormond to arrive with the main army.[85] O'Neill could do little to defeat Castlehaven's forces, as his army was almost out of gunpowder, short of food, and unpaid. Consequently, O'Neill began to withdraw towards Ulster.

The royalist cause received a major boost in strength at this time when the Ulster Scots and the Laggan force adhered to the coalition.[86] This development left only Coote's garrisons around Derry, Monck's garrisons in eastern Ulster, Jones's forces in the Pale, and O'Neill's Gaelic Irish opposed to the royalists' goal of a unified kingdom of Ireland.

In late March, as the noose tightened around Monck's garrison, he sought help from Owen Roe O'Neill, whose army, now quartered in southern Ulster, was being regularly harassed by Inchiquin's royalist troops.[87] O'Neill had approximately 4,000 infantry and 200 cavalry and was acquiring additional recruits from under-strength Confederate regiments which had been disbanded by Ormond and Castlehaven. O'Neill, however, had little gunpowder and too few arms to equip his recruits.[88] Refusing to join the royalists, O'Neill turned to Monck, seeking a peace treaty that would allow him and his soldiers to remain in Ulster in exchange for submission to the political authority of the Westminster parliament.

O'Neill sent his proposals for peace to Monck on 25 April. He sought complete religious toleration, a parliamentary act of oblivion and forgiveness for all hostile acts committed since 22 October 1641, and the restoration of all lands 'taken illegally' from the Irish Catholics, including the O'Neill lands. O'Neill's army was to be taken into parliament's service, and O'Neill was to continue as its commander. Monck responded to this proposal on the same day, telling O'Neill that he saw some merit in the terms and that he had sent them to parliament with some alterations. Monck further proposed that a three-month truce be observed between them, during which they would come to one another's aid if either were attacked by the royalists.[89] O'Neill accepted the proposed cessation of hostilities and the mutual defence pact, demonstrating both his and Monck's desperation and the deep division between O'Neill and the partners of the Ormondist coalition.

By 30 March Inchiquin's army had reached Athlone, where a supply depot was to have been established to support his operations against O'Neill. Inchiquin found, however, that the mayor had failed to follow Ormond's instructions to stockpile supplies, forcing Inchiquin to pause for several weeks while beer and grain could be brought up by boat along the Shannon.[90] The arrival of Inchiquin's army at Athlone and the rendezvous of Taaffe's troops with Castlehaven's in Queen's County threatened O'Neill with two armies on separate flanks, each larger than his own. Consequently, O'Neill moved his troops into central Ulster in early May.[91]

The presence of O'Neill's army near Dundalk protected Monck from the eastern Ulster royalists during May and June. In July, however, Monck was forced to call on O'Neill for help against Inchiquin's forces, which were then moving north against Dundalk. O'Neill responded by promising to come to Monck's aid with his army. However, he told Monck that he needed a supply of gunpowder before he could face Inchiquin. Monck agreed to provide the powder, and O'Neill sent Lieutenant-General Richard Farrell to Dundalk with 200 horse and 1,200 foot to escort the twenty barrels of powder back to his camp at Crossmaglen, seven miles from Dundalk. After Farrell's men had picked up the gunpowder, they tarried to drink the health of their new allies in Dundalk. They drank to excess, and when they were returning to O'Neill's camp in a state of intoxication, Inchiquin's cavalry attacked. Inchiquin's men killed hundreds of the Irish, captured the precious powder, and drove the remainder of Farrell's troops away in full retreat.[92]

This disaster had immediate repercussions in the struggle in eastern Ulster. O'Neill decided that he had to withdraw his army into western Ulster, out of Inchiquin's reach. This move left Monck completely over-matched. Monck's troops' morale fell drastically, and most of his Dundalk garrison deserted to Inchiquin before Inchiquin summoned Monck to surrender.[93] On 24 July Monck surrendered Dundalk and accepted a pass to return to England, where he subsequently faced inquiries about his agreement with O'Neill. As a result of Inchiquin's operations against Dundalk in late July, all of Ulster's major ports except for Derry had fallen to the royalist coalition.

Sir Charles Coote continued to defend Derry with fewer than 2,000 soldiers. William Cole commanded a small force also loyal to Coote in Enniskillen, but neither garrison could aid the other. The Laggan army around Derry had been joined in its siege by George Monro's eastern Ulster forces, composed of Scottish Highlanders, Ulster British, and a few Irish loyal to Phelim O'Neill.[94] Because of Inchiquin's capture of Dundalk and Ormond's and Clanricarde's successes in the southern provinces in June and July, it seemed only a matter of time before Coote would be forced to surrender Derry. However, the worst of times were nearly over for the parliamentarian garrisons.

MICHAEL JONES, ORMOND, AND THE CAMPAIGN AGAINST DUBLIN

In the spring and summer of 1649 the Westminster government's control of the sea-lanes around Ireland enabled the parliamentarians to supply and reinforce Derry. Since the Laggan army and its allies lacked a train of siege artillery with which to batter down Derry's walls, their only hope of capturing the town lay in starving Coote out. The arrival of an English supply ship in May had sustained Coote's troops for a month. On 21 June another vessel arrived, carrying 150 tons of wheat and 220 fresh soldiers.[95] Heartened by this relief, Coote continued to push his troops to improve the defences and to make sorties against work parties of their besiegers. His garrison was reinforced by over 400 cavalrymen and dragoons who had escaped from Sligo in Connacht before it fell to Clanricarde.[96] Consequently, the morale of the Derry defenders improved and the chances of a royalist victory diminished.

George Monro's arrival in the Laggan camp in early July with nearly 2,000 troops might have swung the tide of operations against Coote again. Monro brought twelve light field guns which could be used to fire on any parliamentarian supply ships trying to sail up the Foyle to Derry, even if the guns were too light to damage Derry's walls. On 12 July Monro's men built another fort blocking water access to the town, forcing Coote to react. Coote sent a small force under Captain Keyser to drive Monro's men out of the fort, but the royalists drove Keyser's men off and continued to interdict the sea route into Derry with their cannon.[97]

With less than two weeks of food left in Derry in mid-July, the situation of Coote's garrison looked desperate. In a letter to parliament Coote estimated that he needed another 4,000 men to break the siege. He further implied that if reinforcements did not arrive soon to break the royalists' hold on his supply lines, he might be forced to surrender. At this moment of despair Owen Roe O'Neill's army arrived on the scene, retreating from its humiliating defeat by Inchiquin near Dundalk.

Monro and the Stewarts reacted to the news that O'Neill was on his way to western Ulster by massing their forces in front of Derry, hoping to tempt Coote to attack. In this way they hoped for a chance to win by battle what they could no longer get by siege. Coote refused to be drawn into such a fight, outnumbered as he was, frustrating his enemies' plans.[98] O'Neill's 4,000 infantry and 300 cavalry arrived on 7 August. By 14 August the combined forces of Coote and O'Neill had captured Charles-Fort on the Foyle and most of the Laggan garrisons in the vicinity of Derry.

Unable to face O'Neill and Coote with equal numbers, Sir Robert Stewart withdrew the remnants of the Laggan army south to join Clanricarde in Connacht, while Monro's conglomerate force retreated to Coleraine and Belfast.[99] The twenty weeks' siege of Derry was over. Parliamentarian control of the sea had allowed the English to sustain Coote until O'Neill's arrival with overwhelming force broke the siege. The royalists forces in Ulster dispersed, leaving them vulnerable to defeat in detail by the Cromwellian columns that were soon to arrive.

Just as Jones's victory at Baggotsrath/Rathmines would prepare the way for Cromwell's smooth landing in Dublin, O'Neill's and Coote's efforts in Ulster opened that province to a swift conquest by Cromwell's well-supplied veterans. Coote's successful defence of Derry and his and Monck's agreements with O'Neill prevented the Ulster royalists from finishing their work in Ulster. Consequently, they could not join Ormond in front of Dublin in late July, when Ormond's chances of taking the city were greatest. O'Neill's refusal to join Ormond was a major, if not the decisive, factor in the royalist military defeat not only in Ulster and in Leinster, but also throughout Ireland.[100]

While the Confederate royalists were working to win over or defeat O'Neill and to implement a naval strategy with Rupert's fleet, Michael Jones, George Monck and Sir Charles Coote worked to preserve the few remaining parliamentarian enclaves in Ireland. Their strategy was to hold on until the expeditionary force expected from England could arrive and redeem the situation once and for all. They received regular reassurances from the Council of State in London that help was on its way, despite the delays attributable to a shortage of ready cash for the force and the mutinies in some of the New Model Army regiments that had been infected with Leveller sympathies.[101] Their hopes were buoyed by the news from England in February that Colonel Moore's infantry regiment had been ordered to recruit to full strength and move to Ireland.[102]

Ormond understood the royalists' need to capture Dublin before the 8,000 infantrymen and 4,000 cavalrymen promised by the Westminster government to Jones and Monck could be sent from England.[103] Hoping to avoid a military campaign to capture Dublin, Ormond wrote to Jones, asking him to join the royalist cause,

> now that the mask of hypocrisy (by which the Independent army hath ensnared and enslaved all estates and degrees of men) is laid aside, now that barefaced they evidently appear . . . having laid violent sacrilegious hands upon and murdered God's anointed and our king . . .[104]

Jones responded quickly. In accordance with his belief that the Westminster parliament was the sole legitimate political authority in Britain and Ireland, he rejected Ormond's authority as Lord Lieutenant of Ireland and refused to join the royalists.[105] By 8 April Ormond had given up hope of winning Jones's allegiance. Consequently, he prepared to set in motion a campaign to drive Jones and Monck out of their garrisons as soon as the growth of the spring grass would allow his cavalry units to campaign.[106]

Active campaigning by all of the royalist forces in Leinster resumed in late April. On 16 May Inchiquin captured the castle of Leix, giving quarter to the garrison, while Castlehaven moved the main army to Maryborough, where, on 18 May, he awaited the arrival of Clanricarde's contingents.[107] The two major problems faced by the advancing royalist forces were the continued distrust within the coalition between Inchiquin's Protestants and the Old English Catholics and the steady desertion of soldiers. Only military success could mitigate the first problem, while the second was connected to the first, rather than to the chronic problems of lack of pay and supplies.[108]

In spite of logistical difficulties, Castlehaven and Inchiquin continued to make progress. Castlehaven captured Athy from O'Neill's garrison on 21 May, and Inchiquin's cavalry joined Castlehaven's army there the next day, bringing royalist strength to roughly 10,000 foot and 3,000 horse. While O'Neill was contained in Ulster, Ormond understood the need to move swiftly against the Pale before Jones was reinforced.[109]

By 1 June the main royalist army, totalling at least 11,000 foot and 3,000 horse (not counting garrisons), was at Clogrennan, near Carlow, ready to conduct the final campaign to capture Dundalk, Drogheda, Trim and Dublin.[110] Clanricarde with an additional 3,000 men was preparing to march north from Connacht to join the Laggan force operating against Sir Charles Coote in Derry.

ORMOND'S OFFENSIVE AGAINST DUBLIN

The royalists had little time left to exploit their numerical superiority and their possession of the initiative in Ireland. The Rump Parliament and the Commonwealth's Council of State had resolved in February and March to make the conquest of Ireland its major priority.[111] In March the Commons ordered the Council of State to send 8,000 foot and 4,000 horse to Ireland under the command of Oliver Cromwell. The Commons also ordered the immediate dispatch to Dublin of three infantry and one cavalry regiments, along with £10,000 in cash and tons of supplies.[112] The supplies and money began to arrive in Dublin in April, unhindered by Rupert's ineffective fleet.

Ormond's forces resumed their advance in June. Their progress was remarkable. Many parliamentarian garrisons surrendered outright without even a whiff of gunpowder in the air. By 28 June the only major towns in Leinster still in parliamentarian control were Dublin, Drogheda and Dundalk. As Ormond reported to the king, 'I lie within two miles of Dublin, with 5,000 foot and 1,510 horse. The Lord Inchiquin with as many horse and 2,000 foot has blocked up Drogheda, and we are attempting to surprise Colonel Monck in Dundalk, where there is a considerable magazine of clothes, arms, and ammunition.'[113] In Ulster, Monro, with another 4,000 soldiers, was clearing Belfast and Carrickfergus and then was expected to campaign against Derry. But forward momentum was essential because the coalition 'is precarious, [and] will not stand strain; And the Catholic Confederates, and especially their clergy, will expect an Act of Parliament giving them their enlarged demands'.[114]

Clanricarde was equally successful in Connacht, capturing Sligo on 9 July. But the decisive theatre of royalist operations was in the Pale, against Jones and Monck. Success there was essential, and possible. At that point, in late June, Ormond had to decide whether to attempt a major assault against

Dublin immediately, or to first take Drogheda, Trim and Dundalk. A council of war was held. It was agreed that Dublin was so well fortified that an attempt to take it by assault would be hopeless, that the army was not sufficiently numerous to invest it wholly, especially as O'Neill and Monck, with garrisons at Drogheda and Trim, threatened to fall on the lines of the besiegers; that Ormond should continue encamped with 5,000 foot and 1,800 horse, to prevent supplies from entering and to support a revolt within the city.[115] Therefore, as Ormond had written to the king, Inchiquin was dispatched north to take Drogheda, Trim and Dundalk. The decision not to attack Dublin directly, but instead to divide the main force, was successful in the short term but fatal to the royalist army in the long run.

Inchiquin soon captured Drogheda, Trim and Dundalk. Significant portions of the garrisons in those places joined his Protestant force. Only Drogheda's garrison resisted, holding out from 23 June to 4 July and requiring Inchiquin to deploy four cannon to fire a hundred shots against the walls. After repulsing one assault, the garrison of 500 men ran out of ammunition and compelled the governor to capitulate before Inchiquin launched another assault with his 4,000 men.[116] Trim was abandoned, and Dundalk's garrison deserted *en masse*, forcing Monck to surrender. By mid-July Inchiquin could rejoin the main army in front of Dublin.

However, because the royalists did not cut Dublin off from supplies and reinforcements, they allowed the English to continue to strengthen Jones's position. In June Colonel Moore's infantry regiment arrived safely in Dublin, and it was joined by the regiments of Colonels Venables and Reynolds in early July.[117] Even before these troops arrived in Dublin Jones had demonstrated his tactical acumen by launching spoiling attacks against the royalists. On 14 June, for example, he attacked the advance guard of the approaching royalist army near Johnstown, near Naas, with 4,000 men and four field guns, forcing them to deploy and making it clear to the Confederate leaders that Dublin would not fall without a major campaign.[118] While he could not stop the royalists' advance, he easily eluded Ormond's efforts to isolate his field force on its return to Dublin.

Once Ormond's army was camped close to Dublin, Jones continued to sally forth to harry the Confederates and to prevent them from cutting the city off from Dublin Bay. For example, he sent his cavalry out on two occasions, on 23 and 24 June, to attack enemy work parties which were trying to set up fortifications close to the city walls. He also worked his men hard 'to fortify against them, [and] he hath given orders for the pulling down all the outhouses that may advantage their design, and hath set forth a proclamation for all the Irish papists, and other disaffected citizens, to depart the city within 12 hours'.[119] Jones continued to harass his enemies with small attacks throughout July, preventing them from seizing the initiative in front of the capital.[120] His sorties may have helped to convince the royalist council of war that his position was too strong to seize with a direct assault until the city had been isolated from further succour from England. Michael Jones's energy and leadership in this critical period before he received major re-inforcements did much to preserve the Dublin bridgehead for Cromwell. Many of his sallies failed, but the Dublin garrison 'was seldom out of action . . . [and Jones was] not in his bed these ten nights'.[121]

Ormond failed to match this level of aggressive and energetic leadership. His decision to delay the final assault on Dublin, whether or not it might have succeeded, gave Jones and the English time to gather forces strong enough to launch a major counter-attack to reclaim the strategic initiative in Ireland. This delay did allow Inchiquin to clear all parliamentarian garrisons from the Pale, but the longer Ormond had to maintain his forces concentrated in the field without decisive results, the worse his logistical situation got, as he recognised in his letter to the king on 18 July:

> That which only threatens any to our success is our wants which have been and are such that soldiers have actually starved by their arms, and many of less constancy have run home. . . . But I despair not [that we will] be able to keep them together and strong enough to reduce Ireland.[122]

Such a scenario required the quick capture of Dublin. Ormond and his council of war had taken counsel of their fears in June when they decided to split their forces and reduce the outlying garrisons before assaulting Dublin. They made a similar resolution to delay an assault in late July, even though their troops in the area totalled possibly as many as 15,000 men and had successfully repulsed Jones's sorties. They hesitated in spite of the evidence that they outnumbered Jones and that there was significant discord in Dublin, with parliamentarian troops deserting in large numbers.[123]

Ormond had worked miracles in pulling together a coalition of the Old English, Inchiquin's Protestants, Monro's Scots and the Ulster British. By June he somehow had found the means to pay and feed one of the largest field armies ever assembled in Ireland. But he could not bring himself to risk that army in an assault against Dublin, even when its chances for success were greatest. Part of this failure rests with him and his council of senior officers, and part of it rests with Owen Roe O'Neill, who had failed to join the only coalition that could possibly have achieved any positive results for the Catholics in Ireland. A large part of the credit for the defeat of the royalist strategy belongs to Michael Jones for his spirited and aggressive defence of the Pale and Dublin.

By late July things were at a standstill. Jones had been reinforced. Inchiquin had rejoined Ormond's main army. Before 'the forces employed under Inchiquin, etc., were disengaged, he could not block up the south of Dublin, not daring to divide his army, but now those at liberty might go upon that service: and now if the Lord Lieutenant [Cromwell] or governor get over [to Ireland], he is like to have one town for accommodation and security, which will much further him in gaining more'.[124] Ormond knew by then that Cromwell had left London to join a large Irish expeditionary force which was being assembled in Milford Haven. However, he under-estimated the military threat this entailed, as is demonstrated in his last letter to the king before Jones launched the parliamentarian offensive:

If Cromwell came over . . . I shall fear his money [more] than his force, and both much the less if Dublin be possessed by your majesty.[125]

The situation was ripe for Cromwell's arrival. Jones, however, did not wait for Cromwell to seize the initiative. His opportunity for decisive action came as a result of Ormond's hesitation in July to assault Dublin before Jones was reinforced.

3

Cromwell's Preparations, Arrival and Campaign from Dublin to Drogheda, August–September 1649

While the royalist cause prospered in Ireland during the first half of 1649, Cromwell and the Independents struggled desperately to consolidate their control over England. To control England, Cromwell and his fellow-revolutionaries had to contain a series of army mutinies and Leveller-inspired demonstrations which threatened the integrity of the New Model Army and the security of the regime. They also had to improve the precarious financial situation of the Westminster government and find a way to pay at least £1.5 million owed to its contractors and creditors, while simultaneously settling nearly as much in pay arrears owed to the Commonwealth's soldiers.[1] However, before any of these things could be done, they had to organise a republican government to replace the monarchy they had abolished in February. Their ultimate success in these efforts cleared the way for the English to launch the most powerful military assault made against Ireland to that date and thereby crush the most dangerous royalist threat to the fledgling English republic.

The Rump Parliament, so called after the army purged the House of Commons of members unsympathetic to the army and Independency in December 1648, established a Council of State to perform the executive duties of the Commonwealth. The Rump gave this body of forty-one members the power 'to order and direct all the militias and forces both by sea . . . and land' and to 'use all good ways and means for the reducing of Ireland'.[2] The Council of State retained Sir Thomas Fairfax as Lord General of the army and resolved to maintain the English army at a total of 44,000 men. The Council further resolved to send a force of 12,000 men out of this army to conquer Ireland as swiftly as possible.

One of the most important decisions which the Council of State faced was the selection of the commander of the Irish expedition. There were two logical choices: Sir Thomas Fairfax and Oliver Cromwell. Fairfax had commanded the New Model Army since 1645, leading it to victory at Naseby and in a string of victories in 1645–6 which ended royalist military resistance to parliament in the First Civil War. Fairfax enjoyed immense prestige with the soldiers and with most parliamentary political factions. During the Second Civil War in 1648 Fairfax swiftly crushed the royalist uprisings in Kent and successfully conducted the siege of Colchester. His decision to have the royalist commanders of Colchester tried and executed as traitors underscored his loyalty to the parliamentarian cause.

Fairfax also had led the New Model Army on its fateful march to London in November 1648 and acquiesced in Colonel Pride's purge of the House of Commons in December. Nominated as one of the judges for Charles I's trial, he had absented himself from the proceedings, but he accepted the verdict of the court and the execution of the king. He accepted the establishment of the Commonwealth and faithfully commanded the army in Britain until the summer of 1650. However, he was not the best choice for command of the Irish campaign for two reasons. First, his presence in England as Lord General of the army was essential to the security of the new regime. Most of the officers and the rank and file would follow him against threats to the regime from the royalists on one hand and the Levellers on the other. Second, Cromwell was a better choice for military reasons to serve as commander of the assault on Ireland.

While Fairfax had served competently as an army commander during the English Civil Wars, the flashes of violent tactical brilliance exhibited by the New Model Army at Naseby were due to the leadership of his Lieutenant-General of Horse, Oliver Cromwell. Cromwell conceived and executed the army's most daring operation in the Second Civil War when he swiftly deployed 5,000 men from south Wales to join John Lambert in the north in the summer of 1648, completely unhinging the Scottish–royalist invasion of England. Cromwell discerned the opportunity for a decisive battle offered by the Scots' ponderous march south into Lancashire in August. Instead of meeting the invaders' column head-on from the south, he shifted his army to Yorkshire, away from the Scots' line of march. Then, after crossing the Pennines, he launched a surprise attack into their flank at Preston. This manoeuvre, which risked allowing the enemy to march south unopposed, enabled Cromwell's troops to strike the Scots' army in the middle of its long marching formation, dividing its infantry from its cavalry. Cromwell then defeated the two parts of the Scots' army separately, inflicting thousands of casualties and capturing its entire artillery train.[3]

Cromwell's victory at Preston on 17 August 1648 shattered the Scots' army. His swift pursuit of the remnants of the Scottish forces to Edinburgh and his occupation of that city were extremely effective military operations which ended the Second Civil War. Once in possession of Edinburgh, Cromwell placed the government of Scotland in the hands of men who were unlikely soon to interfere in English matters, giving the Independents and the New Model Army time to settle affairs with the king, their Presbyterian foes in parliament, and the dangerous royalist coalition in Ireland. His effective exploitation of his military victories endeared him to his soldiers. Cromwell's combination of military and political skill in dealing swiftly and decisively with the Scots identified him as the perfect choice as the commander to settle Ireland once and for all and to crush the last organised royalist resistance to the English republic.

The Council of State nominated Oliver Cromwell to command the expeditionary force in part because it hoped that his reputation with the soldiers would help to calm the men's fears of ill-treatment on an overseas expedition. Cromwell himself harboured no doubts about the justice or necessity of the campaign. But he hesitated to accept the command because of his concerns about the practical problems of raising the money, material and men necessary for a swift conquest. Perhaps, as his biographer W. C. Abbott insinuates, Cromwell also was reluctant to be away from England for long, anticipating further royalist uprisings or Presbyterian intrigues in parliament and in London.[4] In any case, his correspondence and public utterances all stressed the need for an adequate and steady stream of financial and logistical support for the campaign. Consequently, he made it clear to the Council of State and parliament that he would not set out for Ireland with an army until the issues of logistical and financial support were resolved fully.

On 23 March 1649, after two weeks of deliberation, Cromwell agreed to command the expedition with the condition that the soldiers' pay arrears would be satisfactorily settled and that the government would provide the expedition with enough cash in advance to pay and feed the army for at least three months. On 30 March parliament confirmed Cromwell as the expedition's commander and, soon thereafter, as Lord Lieutenant of Ireland for three years.[5]

One of Fairfax's and Cromwell's most pressing challenges was to find enough soldiers willing to serve in the expedition. Many soldiers of the New Model Army had no desire to serve in Ireland, historically the grave-yard of English soldiers as well as of generals' reputations. Deaths from disease, hunger and the effects of the weather had always taken a large toll of any English force sent across the Irish Sea. Additionally, the rank and file of the New Model's regiments feared that if they went to Ireland they would never receive the large arrears of pay owed to them. They also knew that the soldiers already in Ireland were paid, fed and clothed only on an irregular basis. Parliament's earlier attempt, in 1647, to send soldiers involuntarily to Ireland without satisfactory settlement of their arrears and adequate logistical support had helped precipitate the army's coup against parliament in August of that year.[6] In 1649 the unresolved grievances of the soldiers and their fear of service in Ireland provided fertile soil for the Levellers to cultivate in their agitation against the army's leadership.

A favourable attitude by the army's rank and file towards service in Ireland was critical to the successful launch of the expedition. Veteran troops were needed to fight the war-hardened Irish forces under Ormond. Therefore impressment was an inadequate recruiting device to provide the large number of trained soldiers required in the spring of 1649, especially given the size of the force deemed necessary to carry out a swift conquest. And a swift victory over the royalists in Ireland was necessary if the republic was to survive.

Cromwell concluded that overwhelming force was necessary to achieve the vital objective of a speedy conquest. Accordingly, the expeditionary force was planned to consist of 12,000 men — 8,000 infantry and 4,000 cavalry — and a large train of artillery.[7] Michael Jones commanded at least another 7,000 soldiers in Dublin, including the four regiments that parliament already had ordered to be recruited to full strength and sent to Ireland. In addition, the Council of State had directed that £10,000 in cash and large amounts of food and munitions be sent immediately to Jones in Dublin.[8] As a result, reinforcements and supplies began to arrive in Dublin in May, providing Jones with the means to resist Ormond's advance aggressively. Jones successfully fended off Ormond's probing attacks against Dublin in July, deterring a concerted attempt by the royalists to assault the city when it was most vulnerable. Consequently, if the Commonwealth could raise the money needed to organise, pay and transport the expedition to Ireland, Cromwell would have a secure logistical base awaiting him from which to launch his conquest.

THE ARMY CRISIS AND ITS RESOLUTION

As planning proceeded for the Irish campaign, things were not going smoothly for the new republican government in England. In April Lord General Fairfax and the Council of the Army selected the regiments to serve with the expeditionary force by drawing lots. Four infantry and four cavalry regiments were chosen, along with five troops of dragoons, to join the one cavalry and three infantry regiments already selected to go.[9] Cromwell ordered the newly selected regiments to be recruited to full strength and to march to Milford Haven, which he had chosen as the main port of embarkation. But a severe shortage of money to pay for the expedition, coupled with unrest in the ranks of the army, complicated the tasks facing Cromwell and his officers.

The Council of State found it difficult to raise enough money to supply the expedition, settle the soldiers' arrears of pay, and to provide a treasury for the field army. The Commonwealth began life deeply in debt inherited from the earlier parliamentarian governments. Its credit was encumbered with £1.5 million in loans and unpaid charges for services and supplies, while the receipts of two of its main revenues, the excise and the customs taxes, were obligated for several years in advance. The collection of its third major source of regular revenue, the assessment tax on land, had also fallen deeply into arrears because taxpayers had refused to pay their assessments during the Second Civil War. Therefore, until the state's debts were paid off or secured with tangible assets, no one, including the Common Council of London, would loan the government the cash needed to settle the arrears of the expeditionary force and to provide £100,000 for its treasury.[10]

Exacerbating these financial problems was the fact that parliament owed the soldiers at least another £1.3 million in pay by early 1649. Parliament's decision to maintain an army totalling 44,000 men meant that an additional £1.2 million needed to be raised annually for the army's current pay and support. In addition, the Commonwealth needed to increase the size of its navy from forty-five to seventy-three warships, manned by 6,000 men, to support the army's operations in Ireland and simultaneously to contain Rupert's fleet in Kinsale and the Irish privateers in Wexford.[11] This expanded navy required an additional £500,000 per year.[12]

Parliament and the Council of State focused their energy on efforts to solve these financial problems. The assessment tax rate on property was raised to £90,000 per month. In April and May much of the parliamentarian government's debt to contractors and lenders was secured by the Rump's pledge to sell church lands worth an estimated £1.1 million and to use the proceeds to pay the debt.[13] Once the Rump made these commitments and passed the necessary legislation to carry them out, the Council of State was able to borrow money in London in anticipation of future revenue. This process took some time, and in the meantime the soldiers were ripe for Leveller agitation against the army's high command and the projected Irish campaign.

While the Council of State and the Rump were dealing with their financial problems, Cromwell and Fairfax had to face down a series of Leveller-inspired mutinies and demonstrations in the regiments selected to deploy to Ireland. In March and early April soldiers petitioned the Council of the Army demanding not only the satisfactory settlement of their material concerns, but also a more radical settlement of the government, to include new elections for all members of parliament. There was also some resistance among the Levellers to the conquest of Ireland itself. Although such opposition was not widespread, it made it more difficult to get the soldiers willingly to deploy to Ireland to conquer people who some Levellers thought deserved the same natural rights as Englishmen.[14] If such views had been more widely held, the subsequent course of Irish history — and of British history too — would have been very different.

In response to this interference with the leaders' plans for the army and state, Fairfax and the Council of the Army ordered the malcontents to be purged from the ranks. Attempts to carry out this purge triggered a serious mutiny, led by Robert Lockyer, in late April.[15] This mutiny threatened the cohesion of the army, the safety of the regime, and raised the hopes of the royalists everywhere.

Cromwell and Fairfax moved swiftly to crush the mutiny. They brought in a number of loyal regiments, with which they surrounded and disarmed the mutinous units. The ringleaders were court-martialled, and several, including Lockyer, were shot. Lockyer's funeral in London, however, provided another opportunity for many soldiers to show their sympathy for the Levellers' demands for a reformed Commonwealth and for thousands of Londoners to show their distaste for the Rump.[16]

The political unrest and the delays in the launching of the expedition to Ireland created a potentially even more dangerous situation for the republican government and its allies in the army's high command. In its earlier resolutions to send a large army to Ireland, the Council of State had promised that those soldiers who did not want to serve in Ireland could leave the army with six weeks of their arrears paid in cash. Many of the men in the regiments selected to go now decided to leave the army, and some attempted to connect their departure from the army with another mutiny. Consequently, many soldiers in Ireton's, Scrope's and Reynolds's regiments refused to go to Ireland until their rights and the 'nation's privileges' had been secured.[17] By early May at least three hundred of these soldiers had deserted and gathered near Oxford.

Cromwell and Fairfax now faced the most serious threat to their control of the army since the creation of the New Model Army in 1645. They reacted swiftly. Cromwell mustered his regiment of horse, the famous Ironsides, alongside Fairfax's regiment of horse in Hyde Park on 9 May. He addressed the assembled troops, telling them that any soldier who wanted to leave the army could do so with the promise of eventual payment of his arrears. He reminded the men of their years of service together and of the blood they had shed for the new political covenant. Cromwell promised that he personally would ensure that the Rump raised the money needed to pay their arrears and to pay them regularly in the future. It was one of Cromwell's most successful speeches. Only one soldier left the ranks, and the last Leveller symbols were pulled from the soldiers' hats.[18]

Although we do not have Cromwell's exact words, the force of his remarks and the trust held in him by his soldiers were clear. Cromwell was the general who had always led them to victory and who had taken part personally in the hottest actions on the battlefields. He had always shown a great interest in their material needs and had shared the hardships of the toughest campaigns. These veterans followed him to Ireland in large numbers.

Cromwell's concern for the material well-being of his troops was a critical factor in his success as a military commander. His understanding that the logistical aspects of warfare were crucial to tactical success on the battlefield mark him as one of the great generals in European history and explain why he took such great care to ensure that the expedition was so well provided for before it embarked for Ireland. To solve the short-term pay problems of his soldiers, he immediately wrote to the Council of State asking for the diversion of £10,000 from the pay of the navy to pay the army. The Council of State complied, ordering that an additional £50,000 be placed at the disposal of the Treasurers-at-War for the army's current pay.[19]

With money in hand and more promised, Cromwell and Fairfax led a large force of cavalry against the mutineers who had fled to Burford, west of Oxford. This force overwhelmed the disaffected soldiers, capturing most without resistance. The ringleaders were court-martialled. Four men were convicted, and three were shot in the Burford churchyard on 15 May.[20] The remaining pockets of resistance in the army to the Irish expedition, to its commanders and to the regime swiftly collapsed. By the end of May the regiments chosen to go to Ireland were marching to Milford Haven, Chester and Bristol. While isolated disruptions occurred during the deployment of the regiments going to Ireland, they were easily handled by the commanders on the scene.

The soldiers' arrears, however, had still not been paid, and there remained potential for disorder in the regiments gathering in the west. Consequently, on 10 July Cromwell departed from London for Bristol, where he could better control and mollify discontent in the ranks while also supervising the prepar-ations for the Irish expedition.[21] Once in Bristol, he continued to prod parliament with messages to resolve the issue of the soldiers' arrears and to provide the cash needed for a field treasury of at least £100,000 to accompany the army.[22]

Finally, on 4 and 16 July 1649, the Rump resolved to sell the possessions and lands of the exiled royal family and dedicate the proceeds from the sales to pay the soldiers their arrears.[23] The soldiers' pay accounts were audited and debentures issued to the veterans in payment for their £1.3 million arrears.[24] The soldiers could use these debentures to buy crown land, and it was further enacted that such land would not be available for purchase by civilians until all the debentures issued to soldiers had been honoured. In fact almost the entire £1,464,409 worth of crown lands which were sold by the Commonwealth were purchased with soldiers' debentures, although in many cases the enlisted men had sold their debentures to their officers at a steep discount.[25] In any case, the use of debentures secured by the proceeds of the sale of crown lands resolved the Commonwealth's debt to its soldiers, helping not only to remove the major cause of soldier disaffection in England, but also to clear the way for the expeditionary force to go to Ireland.

The Commonwealth resolved its financial crisis in 1649 by selling church and royal property to pay off its inherited debts to civilians and soldiers. Thereafter it raised tax rates and successfully enforced the collection of taxes to raise the money needed for its military forces' pay, munitions and supplies. Taxation in 1649–50 was at a rate more than seventeen times that of the pre-1640 period.[26] By July 1649 the resumption of effective tax collection allowed the government to borrow £120,000 in London to provide Cromwell with his army's field treasury. Consequently, the English government was able to pay for the first two years of the Cromwellian conquest with money raised mostly by taxes in England and Ireland, and not by the confiscation of Irish land.[27] The famous confiscations of the Cromwellian settlement were carried out to pay the soldiers for their service in Ireland after 1650, and not for their service in the decisive campaigns of 1649–50.

THE DESTINATION OF THE EXPEDITIONARY FORCE: CROMWELL'S OPTIONS AND DECISION

Cromwell prepared for the embarkation of the expeditionary force with the army under control and most of the Commonwealth's pressing financial issues resolved. By mid-July only Dublin and Derry remained in parliamentarian hands, making it imperative for Cromwell to decide quickly where to land his main force.

This decision was a very important one for the campaign's strategy. If the main force landed in Dublin, it would face directly the largest royalist army in Ireland, giving Cromwell the opportunity to seek a decisive battle. Such a battle, if successful, might open Ireland to conquest, just as the battle of Preston had done for Scotland the year before. On the other hand, if the main force landed in Munster, it would outflank Ormond's army, compelling Ormond either to divide his forces or to abandon the siege of Dublin. However, none of the towns and ports of Munster were in friendly hands, making a landing there very difficult. We do not know for certain where Cromwell intended the main body of the expedition to land, but the evidence does not support the theory that he gave priority to Munster.

A plan to land the main force in Dublin accords more with Cromwell's personality and military experience. Cromwell was a man who favoured direct action in the resolution of even the most difficult military problems.[28] He had learned during the English Civil Wars that the destruction of the enemy's main army rather than the seizure of his garrisons led to the greatest and quickest political and strategic results (as, for example, after the parliamentarian victories of Naseby and Preston). Landing the main force in Munster would have necessitated capturing hundreds of castles and towns from the royalists while Ormond's main army remained intact and able to threaten his logistical communications. Moreover, it would have exposed his army to a much more protracted effort in Ireland.

Cromwell had a third option. He could divide his invasion force, sending part of it to Munster in the hope that disaffected Protestants there would desert Inchiquin and open the ports to the invaders. At the same time Cromwell could lead the remainder of his army to Dublin to reinforce Jones. Ormond's army then would be caught between two large English forces, as a result of which Ormond would have to choose either to divide his army or to risk a desperate assault against a strongly reinforced Dublin garrison.

It is unclear which approach Cromwell initially intended to pursue. We know that the four regiments which had been sent to Dublin to reinforce Jones in July had embarked in Chester, the nearest major port to Dublin,[29] while the main body of the expedition was marched to Milford Haven, a port much closer to Munster. Gardiner and other historians interpret these troop movements to indicate that Cromwell intended to land all or most of the expeditionary force in Munster.[30] For example, Denis Murphy, in *Cromwell in Ireland*, notes that 'Cromwell's original design was that a part of the army under Ireton should effect a landing somewhere in Munster, for the Irish did account that province to be the key to the kingdom.'[31]

Gardiner further points out that Cromwell, who was in communication with some of Inchiquin's officers in Cork and Youghal in the spring of 1649, hoped that they would surrender those ports in return for £6,000. Cromwell's attempts to win or buy the loyalty of the Munster Protestants does not prove that Munster was his preferred destination for the main force. It only shows that Cromwell understood how to use political as well as military weapons to conquer Ireland. Cromwell had won the allegiance of Lord Broghill, the fifth son of the Protestant Earl of Cork, to the parliamentarian cause when Broghill was *en route* through London to the continent to offer his services to Charles II. Cromwell offered him a commission as Master of the Ordnance in the expedition if he would help defeat the Catholics in Ireland, or residence in the Tower of London if he refused.[32] Broghill accepted Cromwell's offer and the commission. Since his family's influence was strongest in Munster, this incident lends some weight to the view that Cromwell intended the bulk of the expedition to land in Munster. But other evidence does not support that conclusion.

On 5 July Cromwell sent his artillery train to Dublin. The train of heavy artillery was a central instrument of his intended method of crushing royalist resistance in Irish castles and fortified towns.[33] This was a critical decision which clearly indicates that he did not intend the main force to land in Munster. A force in Munster without an artillery train would have been unable to breach the defences of that province's walled towns and castles. Cromwell also had no assurances from anyone in authority in

Inchiquin's garrisons in Munster that they would allow him to land his troops in one of the province's ports. Since his force had no amphibious capability, it is unlikely that he intended to make his main effort in Munster. Most important, the major forces of the coalition facing his conquest were operating in the Pale and south-eastern Ulster. Cromwell needed to defeat these forces before he could begin the arduous process of reducing the royalist garrisons scattered throughout Ireland. Consequently, it made sense for Cromwell personally to lead the first part of the invasion force to Dublin, where it could then join the artillery train and Jones's force of 7,000 soldiers.

As the main force approached Dublin, Cromwell sent his son-in-law Henry Ireton to lead a substantial force to Munster to exploit any political opportunities that might have opened there. There had been many examples in the past eight years of garrisons in Ireland changing allegiance at the approach of an army of co-religionists, and several major ports in Munster were held by Inchiquin's Protestant troops. Cromwell would gladly have accepted the surrender of any town in Munster, but his shipment of the artillery and his part of the expedition to Dublin indicates that he saw the Pale and Ormond's army as the most important initial objective of his campaign strategy.

The other reason why Cromwell might have decided to go to Dublin with the first part of the expedition, even if he had hoped to land in Munster, was the fear that Dublin might fall to Ormond if he did not quickly reinforce it. However, by the end of July the English newspapers were publishing reports which indicated that the arrival of the four regiments, money and supplies sent earlier had minimised the danger that Ormond would be able to take Dublin with a quick assault.[34] Cromwell, who had already received Michael Jones's account of his decisive victory over Ormond's army at Baggotsrath/Rathmines on 2 August, knew this before he embarked his forces for Dublin.[35] As the *Perfect Weekly Account* reported, 'their intentions were to land at Dublin and likewise Drogheda if [it] surrendered'.[36]

Cromwell sailed from Milford Haven on the night of 13 August with thirty-five ships. Two days later Ireton set sail with about seventy ships, reportedly *en route* to Kinsale. They were followed several days later by a third flotilla of eighteen ships under the command of Colonel Horton.[37] Ireton arrived off the Munster coast by 20 August, but no ports were opened to him. After sailing in circles for several days, he changed course for Dublin, arriving there by 23 August.[38] These actions indicate that while Cromwell had planned that Ireton should indeed seize any opportunity that might arise to take a Munster port cheaply, Ireton's moves were diversionary to his main effort in Leinster.

ROYALIST ACTIONS AND STRATEGY, JULY 1649

As Cromwell and the Commonwealth scrambled to suppress mutinies and raise money in the spring of 1649, the royalist coalition had conquered most of Ireland. By 24 July Ormond and Inchiquin had captured all major towns in Ireland except Dublin and Derry. After his seizure of Drogheda and Trim in late July, Inchiquin had rejoined Ormond near Dublin, bringing Ormond's army up to a strength of nearly 11,000 soldiers.[39] The army was accompanied by a substantial artillery train, including at least 'one whole cannon, three demi-cannon, one long square gun [firing twelve-pound balls], one saker-drake, and one mortar piece (all of brass)', pulled by two hundred oxen.[40] The royalist strategy was to capture Dublin before Cromwell arrived, denying him the logistical base essential for the conquest of Ireland.

Michael Jones and the Dublin garrison were in a difficult situation in mid-July 'since the taking of the impregnable garrisons of Drogheda, Dundalk, and Trim', and with Ormond's outposts within one mile of the city's defences.[41] On 24 July royalist troops captured two small forts on Lowzey Hill, cutting off the streams supplying water for the mills which ground much of the city's flour.[42] Jones fought back aggressively with sallies, with the expulsion of all adult Catholic males from the city, and with ruthless reprisals against any officer who had switched to the royalist cause and was subsequently captured. For example, he executed his sister's son on 1 August because the young officer, who had defected to Ormond's forces, had been captured while serving with royalist cavalry attempting to run off some of the garrison's cattle.[43]

On 25 July the royalists tightened the siege of Dublin by moving the majority of their army south from Finglas across the Liffey, to a new camp at Rathmines. Lord Dillon was left with a force of 2,000 infantry and 500 cavalry in Finglas, three miles north of Dublin, to cut off the northern approaches to the city. Ormond's main force at Rathmines, two miles south of Dublin Castle, was then in a position from which it could block the Dublin garrison's access to the grazing lands south of the city, and also conveniently near a point where a battery of artillery could be placed to fire on ships coming into Dublin at Ringsend. Just as the royalist army made this move to Rathmines, Reynolds's and Venables's English regiments arrived in Dublin, protected by a naval squadron under the command of Sir George Ayscue, and false rumours were circulated that Cromwell intended to land in Munster.[44]

Ormond and the royalist commanders had been following the accounts of Cromwell's preparations closely, noting that Cromwell had ordered the major rendezvous of his expedition to be held at Milford Haven, opposite the Munster coast. They concluded that he might be planning to land in Munster, in large part because they knew of his efforts to suborn disaffected

Protestant garrisons in the south. On 27 July, therefore, a royalist council of war, which included Ormond, Lord Taaffe, Thomas Preston, Sir Arthur Aston, Sir William Vaughan and Major-General Patrick Purcell, decided to send Inchiquin with two cavalry regiments south to Munster to prevent defections which might open the way to an easy landing there for the English invasion force.[45]

The royalists' council of war also resolved to hold the main army at Rathmines until an English garrison at the small castle of Rathfarnham, three and a half miles south-east of Dublin, was captured. Then at that time, if things had not changed, the army would withdraw from Rathmines and await the arrival of Cromwell further inland.[46] Such a plan of action would have ended any hope of taking Dublin before Cromwell arrived, but it also would have reduced the risk of losing the army in a pitched battle against the English.

The dispatch of Inchiquin with two regiments to the south evidently did more to undermine Ormond's will to fight than it did to weaken the numerical strength of the royalist army. Throughout the campaign Inchiquin had been the most ruthless and efficient of the royalist commanders. He and his Protestant troops had captured Drogheda, Dundalk and Trim in July. They also had carried the brunt of the fighting against Owen Roe O'Neill's army earlier, allowing more faint-hearted commanders like Clanricarde to advance safely in their wake. With Inchiquin gone, the precariousness of Ormond's hold over his Catholic allies became more evident and his willingness to launch an aggressive attack against Jones declined even further.

On 28 July Confederate troops took the castle at Rathfarnham by storm, capturing 500 prisoners and a fair amount of money and supplies. This victory emboldened many of the Catholic officers to demand that the royalist army should not abandon the siege of Dublin. Under pressure from these officers, Ormond and his council met again and decided to continue operations against Dublin from the base at Rathmines.[47] Pursuant to this decision, they sent Colonel Thomas Armstrong with a cavalry regiment to drive the garrison's cattle and horses from the meadows south of Dublin. The next day, however, when Armstrong attempted this mission, Jones's troops drove his regiment away from the meadows with the loss of forty royalist soldiers.[48]

THE BATTLE OF RATHMINES, 2 AUGUST 1649

On 29 July Ormond and his council of officers decided to cut off Dublin from the sea by establishing a battery of artillery near the demolished castle of Baggotsrath overlooking Ringsend, thus threatening Dublin's lines of communications. Ormond expected that Jones would react to such a dangerous situation with a vigorous counter-attack. To protect this artillery position, the royalist council of war also planned to establish breastworks facing Dublin, running east to west from Baggotsrath Castle, across the meadows recently contested by Armstrong's and Jones's cavalry. This breast-work would face north, further constraining the parliamentarian garrison.[49]

On 31 July Castlehaven, Preston and Purcell reconnoitered Baggotsrath and the projected location for the entrenchments. Their reconnaissance confirmed that it was suitable ground on which to build the breastworks and the battery, although they also found Baggotsrath Castle indefensible in its present condition, having been demolished on Jones's orders earlier. Consequently, the first phase of the operation would be to send a work party to fortify Baggotsrath under the cover of darkness. Major-General Purcell was to lead a force of 1,500 infantry to protect this work detail.[50]

Purcell set out with his force from the royalist camp at Rathmines on the evening of 1 August. Ormond remained awake in the camp, awaiting word of the progress of Purcell's operation and working on a dispatch to Charles II. Somehow Purcell's unit got lost in the dark as it marched the one mile from Rathmines to Baggotsrath, arriving at its destination after sunrise on 2 August. When Ormond rode over to Baggotsrath to see the progress of the work, sometime before nine o'clock in the morning, he found that little had been accomplished in the way of fortifications. He also observed that troops from the Dublin garrison were assembling in the fields north-west of Baggotsrath, 'yet hiding themselves the best they could behind some houses at Lowsy-hill, in a hollow betwixt Baggotsrath and the Strand'.[51] Realising the danger posed to Purcell's troops by a parliamentarian attack, Ormond ordered Purcell and Major-General William Vaughan to bring the rest of the army from Rathmines to Baggotsrath to support Purcell's force in case Jones launched a major attack.[52] He then returned to his tent at Rathmines to rest.

Michael Jones had watched these royalist movements with interest. On 26 July he had received the last two regiments of his reinforcements from Chester, which brought his garrison's strength to roughly 8,000 men fit for duty.[53] Spoiling for a chance to inflict major damage on Ormond's army, Jones quickly saw his opportunity to strike a blow against Purcell's exposed troops at Baggotsrath.[54] On 2 August, therefore, Jones deployed 4,000 infantry and 1,200 cavalry into the meadows between Dublin and Baggotsrath, with the intention of beating up Purcell's detachment. At approximately nine in the morning he launched a co-ordinated attack with his 5,200 soldiers against the royalists in their unfinished works.[55]

Purcell and Vaughan had not yet had a chance to carry out Ormond's order to bring up reinforcements from the camp at Rathmines, less than a mile away. Ormond, after being awake all night, had retired to rest in his tent at Rathmines, just before Jones launched his attack.[56] Jones's assaulting infantry caught the royalists unprepared and with their senior officers absent. The attackers quickly entered the partially completed defensive works at

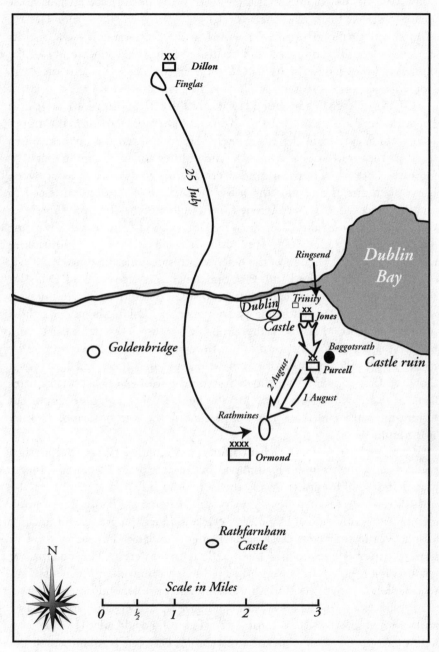

3. *Operations around Dublin, 25 July–2 August 1649*

Baggotsrath Castle, though, as Jones later wrote, 'not without strong dispute: Most of the enemy's foot there were slain and [or] taken, their horse having deserted them after the first charge.'[57] Vaughan, the Major-General of Horse in Ormond's army, was killed in the first assault as well, further weakening royalist command and control. Seizing the opportunity of the moment, Jones launched his entire force in an attack towards the main Confederate camp at Rathmines, hoping to expand his victory.

Ormond, who had been awakened by the sound of firing at Baggotsrath, rode to the battle and bravely attempted to rally the troops who were fleeing from the engagement. He found that the only organised force in the fight at that time was Inchiquin's infantry, commanded by Colonel Giffard. These soldiers were trying to form a line between Baggotsrath and the main camp at Rathmines. Jones's troops advanced so rapidly, however, that a coherent front could not be formed. Worse for Ormond, whenever the Confederate infantry stood to fight the advancing parliamentarians, Jones would send his unopposed cavalry into their flank or rear, breaking the cohesion of the defence and spreading the rout.

At this point in the battle Ormond sent a message to Lord Dillon at Finglas, asking Dillon to march his 2,500 soldiers south across the Liffey to attack the rear of the advancing parliamentarians. Dillon, however, refused to bring his troops into the battle, probably because it seemed clear to him by then that it was too late for his force to swing the tide of battle over to the royalists' favour.[58] Dillon also may have realised that Jones still had several thousand fresh troops in Dublin who would have been able to fall on his flank or rear as he moved south into the fight. In any case, his decision not to join the battle ended any hope of preventing the rout of Ormond's army at Rathmines.

Ormond, his brother Richard Butler and Colonel Giffard did all they could to rally the troops at Rathmines, but regiment after regiment disintegrated into flight south towards the Wicklow hills rather than face the onrushing torrent of Jones's cavalry and infantry. Finally, Inchiquin's infantry, still commanded by Giffard, cracked under the pressure of infantry assaults to the front and cavalry attacks in their flanks and rear.[59] Most of Giffard's men who had not been killed surrendered. The collapse of Giffard's force ended the last organised resistance against the parliamentarians, who rapidly overran the Rathmines camp and, as Ormond noted, 'routed' the royalist troops in the area.[60] Ormond gave up at this point and retreated south with his lifeguard and as many stragglers as he could rally. He caught up with precious few soldiers in the twelve miles between Rathmines and the small English–held castle of Ballisonan. Here Ormond achieved one of his last military successes in Ireland when he convinced Jones's garrison in that castle that Dublin had fallen to the royalists. As a result, the Ballisonan garrison surrendered. Ormond then continued on his way south to Kilkenny.

Jones won the most important battle of the Cromwellian conquest at Baggotsrath and Rathmines. He shattered the Confederate army before it was reinforced by Clanricarde from Connacht and George Monro from Ulster. He killed a large number of royalist soldiers (variously estimated between 600 and 4,000; the higher figure is more likely to be correct) and captured over 2,500 more.[61] He also captured Ormond's artillery train, papers, ciphers, supplies, money and baggage.[62]

This defeat grievously weakened royalist resistance to the Cromwellian conquest. While replacements could be found for the soldiers captured or killed, the loss of experienced company and regimental commanders was a major blow to the Confederate army which could not be repaired. Jones captured seventeen field-grade officers, including eight colonels and six lieutenant-colonels, and thirty-nine captains, crippling Ormond's efforts to rebuild his army.[63] The royalists' loss of firearms and cannon was an almost equally debilitating blow to their future war effort. While men could still be recruited for new regiments, the weapons needed to equip them and the experienced leaders needed to train and lead them were not available. The only way for the royalists to acquire large numbers of new weapons rapidly was to import them from the continent. But the Commonwealth's navy was blockading the major ports of Leinster and Munster and there was little money available to pay for arms and to ship them to Ireland.

Rathmines was the last major battle fought by the Old English forces of the Confederation. The remnant of the Leinster army once commanded by Thomas Preston was destroyed. Many of Inchiquin's Protestant troops from Munster were killed or captured, and the majority of the remainder were in his Munster garrisons. The Connacht army of 3,000 men under the command of the Earl of Clanricarde remained on the defensive in the west, while the British royalists in Ulster under Lord Montgomery and the Scots under George Monro remained reluctant to join Ormond and face Cromwell's main army. Only Owen Roe O'Neill's army of roughly 5,000 men seemed capable of reinforcing Ormond with sufficient strength to give him an army capable of fighting a battle. But O'Neill had agreed to support the royalists' cause only after his truce with Charles Coote in Derry expired in late August. As a result, Ormond was forced to disperse most of the remaining Confederate units into the major fortified towns of Leinster and Munster in an attempt to defeat the invaders.

ORMOND'S STRATEGY, AUGUST 1649

After Rathmines the royalist coalition held together precariously. The common danger of English conquest was the sole bond of the confederacy. The Catholics' increasing frustration with Ormond and Inchiquin remained a powerful solvent. Ormond understood that only a military victory against the invader could keep the unstable alliance together. But without a large field army he was forced initially to try to prevent the expansion of the parliamentarian bridgehead in the Pale through defensive means. He therefore adopted a Fabian strategy of delay and inactivity, carefully avoiding any direct engagement with the enemy, just as he had done against the Catholic Confederates in 1643–6, when he had managed to maintain his army intact in Dublin in spite of his foe's numerical superiority. Such a strategy against Cromwell in 1649 offered some hope of success, since no previous English expedition in the decade had been adequately financed and supplied for very long, and none had been able to capture swiftly the walled towns of Ireland. The precariousness of the Commonwealth government in London meant that time was on Ormond's side. His allies of hunger, disease and winter also promised to weaken the invaders to the point where they would either withdraw or could be defeated by a royalist army. With this in mind, Ormond set to work to rebuild his army and his fortunes while retaining the important towns.

After reaching Kilkenny on 4 August, Ormond immediately set to work to rebuild his army, reorganise his political structure, and redirect his strategy to deal with the drastically changed military situation.[64] Initially he hoped to gather the forces of Clanricarde, Lord Montgomery and George Monro into a single army with which to face Jones.[65] However, after sending a series of letters summoning these commanders to a rendezvous, Ormond realised that they were either unwilling or unable to combine forces with him in the near future. Clanricarde, for example, excused himself from marching to Leinster with his 3,000 men because of his chronic shortage of money and the potential threat to northern Connacht posed by Sir Charles Coote's Derry garrison.[66] Lord Montgomery likewise regretted the invitation to march south, alluding to the threat posed to his garrisons by O'Neill's Ulstermen who, until late August, remained in alliance with Coote.[67]

Ormond also increased his efforts to convince Owen Roe O'Neill to abandon his arrangement with Sir Charles Coote and to join the royalist cause as the only viable way to preserve any Catholic or Gaelic rights. This argument won over O'Neill, who was seeking to come to an accommodation with the royalist coalition. However, as always, negotiations with O'Neill progressed slowly, while Jones and Cromwell moved swiftly. Furthermore, even after an understanding was reached, shortages of money, food and munitions prevented O'Neill from proceeding southwards swiftly enough to affect the forthcoming operations around Drogheda.[68]

Operating first from Kilkenny and then from Tecroghan, a small place west of Trim and roughly thirty miles south-west of Drogheda, Ormond did all he could to find reinforcements and supplies for the crucially important town of Drogheda.[69] Drogheda was on the most direct road over the River Boyne from Dublin to Ulster, and it was a seaport capable of providing a logistical base for English operations in eastern Ulster. If Drogheda remained in royalist hands, Cromwell would find it difficult to support Derry's garrison while also trying to conquer southern Leinster and Munster, and Dublin would always be in danger from a royalist assault by the combined forces of Lord Montgomery, Monro and O'Neill. Thus the invaders would be compelled to leave substantial forces in the Pale to defend Dublin while they sent an army into southern Leinster or Munster. Cromwell's hopes for the speedy capture of the major towns of Ireland could be undermined from the outset of his campaign if Ormond could hold Drogheda.

Ormond's first task was to thwart Michael Jones's attempt in early August to capture Drogheda with a *coup de main* after his victory at Rathmines. Realising the importance of Drogheda, Jones led a force of 4,700 men and four field guns to Drogheda, hoping that the commander of that place, Colonel Moore, would surrender rather than face a siege. Ormond, however, relieved Moore of his command after Moore sent him a pessimistic letter, and replaced him with Colonel Thomas Armstrong, one of his most reliable commanders. He also moved his field force closer to Drogheda to a position from which he could harry Jones's communications with Dublin and keep open the supply route to Drogheda. Ormond's move forced Jones to withdraw to Dublin, since Jones was not prepared to carry out either a protracted siege or an assault of the town.[70]

Following Jones's withdrawal, Ormond entered Drogheda and reorganised the garrison. On 17 August he appointed Sir Arthur Aston, an English Catholic officer and veteran of the Thirty Years' War and the English Civil Wars, as governor. Aston had defended Reading and Oxford successfully in 1643 and 1644 respectively, and he was well known for his uncompromising hatred of the parliamentarians. Ormond reinforced Drogheda with his best regiments, including his own under the command of Sir Edmund Verney, bringing the garrison to a total of 2,871 men. At least two of the four complete foot regiments in the place were composed largely of Protestant soldiers, while the soldiers of the other two, under Colonels Wall and Warren, were mostly Catholic.[71] The garrison remained critically short of ammunition and food, but Aston was resolute and confident that he could hold the place while Ormond put together a new field army.

CROMWELL'S ARRIVAL AND THE START OF THE CAMPAIGN, AUGUST–SEPTEMBER 1649

Cromwell arrived in Dublin harbour with thirty-five ships on 15 August, followed by Ireton and seventy or eighty ships by the 23rd. The first task facing Cromwell was the reorganisation of the forces in Dublin. There was a pressing need to reduce six of Jones's small regiments into regular-sized regiments of 1,000 soldiers each and to purge the ranks of ill-disciplined soldiers who had never served in the New Model Army in England.[72] Many of these soldiers had served in Ireland for years and had become accustomed to supporting themselves with food and money exacted from the civilian population. This practice of 'free quarter' had been unavoidable as long as sufficient resources were not received from England. Now, however, Cromwell planned to hasten the progress of the conquest by winning over as many of the population as he could. An essential part of this strategy was to ensure that the troops paid for all food and supplies they received from the people. Accordingly, the regiments which came over in the summer of 1649 had received four to six weeks of their pay in advance, and tons of food were shipped to Dublin and Derry to sustain the troops and the population.[73]

As part of this strategy, Cromwell issued a proclamation to the people of Dublin promising that the soldiers' depredations would be ended and that any offences would 'be strictly proceeded against and punished according to the utmost severity and rigour of the law'.[74] Cromwell rapidly enforced this declaration, immediately improving the relationship of Dublin's population with the army. Ormond, in contrast, could not follow such a policy in his garrisons owing to lack of money, thereby further weakening the cohesion of the royalist cause.

Cromwell, in his capacity as Lord Lieutenant, also issued a general proclamation to the country people, Catholic and Protestant, which was going to have an immediate impact on the logistical operations of the English army:

> Whereas I am informed that, upon the marching out of the armies heretofore, or of parties from garrisons, a liberty hath been taken by the soldiery to abuse, rob and pillage, and too often to execute cruelties upon the country people: Being resolved, by the Grace of God, diligently and strictly to restrain such wickedness for the future, I do hereby warn and require all officers, soldiers, and others under my command, henceforth to forbear all such evil practices as aforesaid; . . . That it shall be free and lawful to and for all manner of persons dwelling in the country . . . to make their repair, and bring any provisions unto the army (while in march or camp) . . . Hereby assuring all such, that they shall not be troubled or molested in their persons or goods; but shall have the benefit of a free market, and receive ready money for goods and commodities they shall so bring and sell.[75]

The field treasury of £100,000 made it possible for Cromwell to enforce these declarations and to feed his army properly. For the next three months there is little indication that his units suffered serious shortages of food, although Cromwell's letters to parliament and the Council of State are full of reminders to keep the food, money, clothes and munitions flowing to Ireland. This attention to logistical details and the integration of psychological warfare into his campaign paid enormous dividends and explains, in part, the swift collapse of resistance in many towns in south-eastern Ulster.

After reorganising the army, Cromwell and newly promoted Lieutenant-General Michael Jones mustered the cavalry and infantry in two reviews in the meadows outside Dublin. While the troops practised their tactical skills, Cromwell and Jones selected eight infantry and six cavalry regiments to serve in the marching army.[76] Then, on 31 August, Jones led the advance guard from Dublin, followed by Cromwell and the main body the next day. After a night at Ballygarth (Ballyboghil?, thirteen miles north of Dublin) on 2 September, the army arrived on the southern side of Drogheda on the 3rd.[77]

Simultaneously a naval squadron commanded by Sir George Ayscue escorted transports carrying the artillery siege train and supplies by sea to the River Boyne, where they could sail up to Drogheda's walls with no impediments. The heavy guns and tons of ammunition arrived by 5 September and were put into position over the next four days. For the first time in the Irish wars a large train of artillery was available for the attack against a walled Irish town, thanks to the use of sea power. This use of naval power was to figure prominently in the Cromwellian conquest.

THE FALL OF DROGHEDA, SEPTEMBER 1649

Drogheda was, by Irish standards, a well-fortified town. The main part of the town was north of the River Boyne, with a smaller district south of the river and connected to the main town by a drawbridge (see Map 4). The town walls were four to six feet thick and twenty feet tall, with towers reinforcing each gate. Outworks, known as tenalia, covered the approaches to the gates as well. The large circumference of the walls made a siege difficult because it would have required large numbers of soldiers to block off the town completely from outside logistical support. If Cromwell had attempted to starve the place into submission, as the Irish had attempted to do unsuccessfully in 1641–2, he would have exposed his army to attack by Ormond's army at Tecroghan. Besides, such a siege would have taken a lot of time, and time was exactly what Ormond hoped could be gained by a prolonged defence, allowing weather and disease to take their tolls of an army exposed to the wet climate.

Cromwell, however, planned to take the town by storm after his heavy artillery blasted breaches in the obsolete curtain-wall defences. He therefore set up two batteries of guns on the south-eastern corner of the part of the town which was south of the river. The first battery was set up where it could fire north towards the wall between the Duleek Gate and St Mary's Church, whose tower was a prominent landmark and royalist observation-point in the south-eastern corner of the walls.[78] Cromwell sited the second battery to the east of St Mary's Church where it could fire across a ravine which ran along the eastern wall. This battery was on what was later known as Cromwell's Hill, an elevated position which allowed the guns to fire on a flat trajectory across the ravine to the eastern wall and the tower of

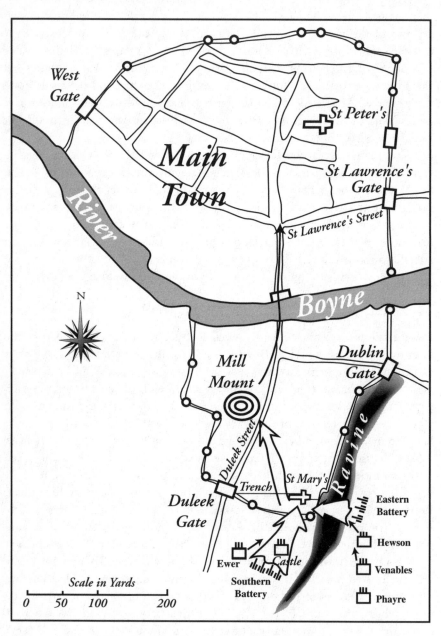

4. Assault on Drogheda, 11 September 1649

St Mary's.[79] The location of the eastern battery is clearly described by Cromwell and Colonel Hewson in their accounts written within eleven days of the assault. Nevertheless, Gardiner is convinced that they were mistaken as to its location, as he did not think that Cromwell would have planned for an assault against a breach in the eastern wall because the troops would have had to move down into the ravine and then charge uphill into the breach.[80]

However, that is exactly what Cromwell planned, and his scheme of manoeuvre for the assault made good sense militarily. By battering breaches in the southern and eastern walls near the south-eastern corner, Cromwell's guns could achieve converging fires and his assault columns would converge and be mutually supporting. By firing across the ravine to the east of the town wall, the eastern battery could fire on a flat trajectory, while the southern battery had to fire uphill. The assault troops crossing the ravine would not block or mask the fires of the artillery or supporting musketeers until the last moment in their attack, since they had to go down into and then up out of the ravine. The troops assaulting the southern breach masked their supporting fires when they started across the open ground to the south of the walls. For these reasons, Cromwell deployed two regiments in the southern attack and one regiment in the eastern attack. Once the breaches were cleared, the rubble from the demolished church tower would also serve as a defence against royalist cavalry as the assaulting infantry widened the breaches to allow their cavalry to enter the town.[81]

Aston recognised the danger to the south-eastern corner and ordered his troops to dig two sets of trenches to back up the two separate places where it was obvious that Cromwell was planning to blow a breach. He did so because he could see where Cromwell was aiming his two batteries. All accounts agree that one set of trenches ran from the Duleek Gate to St Mary's, while the second ran the fifty yards east from the church to the eastern wall which overlooked the ravine.

When the guns were ready, Cromwell summoned Aston to surrender:

Sir,

Having brought the army belonging to the Parliament of England before this place, to reduce it to obedience, to the end the effusion of blood may be prevented, I thought fit to summon you to deliver the same into my hands to their use. If this be refused you will have no cause to blame me,

I expect your answer and rest,

Your Servant,
O. Cromwell[82]

Aston refused, and the English artillery began to fire. By noon on 11 September the guns had fired 200 to 300 cannon-balls into the walls, creating the breaches in the 'east and south wall' and demolishing the steeple of St Mary's Church.[83] At about five o'clock Castle's and Ewer's infantry regiments attacked the tenalia and the southern breach, while Hewson's regiment charged across the ravine and into the eastern breach. The tenalia on the south fell swiftly, but the sally port from it into the town wall was choked with the bodies of defenders and attackers alike, preventing the attackers from using it. Castle's men got a foothold in the southern breach at the same time.

A vicious fight took place at the eastern breach as Aston's men fought tenaciously to repel Colonel Hewson's troops. Hewson later wrote that 'We entered the breach, but not so orderly as was appointed; [we] were stoutly resisted, and after a short dispute, did retreat disorderly, tumbling over the breach and down a steep hill that ascends up to the wall.' But Cromwell had planned for such a possibility and had additional regiments of foot ready to support the attack. As Hewson further related, 'Col. Venables's regiment and Col. Phayre's being both upon guard . . . did come down another hill [into the ravine] . . . so that before our men got half way down the hill upon their retreat, we got them faced about . . . that they fell on again, entered the breach, beat off the enemy, pursued him, entered their great mount, where was their governor, with almost 200 officers and soldiers, who were put to the sword.'[84]

Meanwhile Castle's and Ewer's soldiers met a withering fire of musketry and then were counter-attacked by the garrison at the breach in the south wall. Colonel Castle was shot in the head, dying instantly. Stunned and demoralised by their losses, the attacking infantrymen began to retreat. At this point in the battle Cromwell moved to the southern breach, rallied the faltering pikemen, and launched a second assault. This action turned the tide.[85] Colonel Wall, the royalist commander nearest the breaches, was killed, disheartening the defenders. The English troops poured through both breaches and drove Aston's exhausted men from the entrenchments behind the walls. While the final assaults were moving over the entrench- ments and towards the Mill Mount, Cromwell gave the fateful command to give no quarter.[86]

Aston and many of his officers had retreated to the defences on the Mill Mount. There is evidence that Lieutenant-Colonel Axtell offered quarter to Aston's men on the Mill Mount and that this offer was accepted and then reneged upon.[87] If this is so, the slaughter that ensued was cold-blooded murder. Hewson's men beat Aston to death with his wooden leg and slaughtered the 250 officers and men with him on the Mill Mount. The remainder of the royalists who had not died in the initial assaults or on the Mill Mount fled across the bridge to the northern part of town, pursued closely by the parliamentarian soldiers. They were unable to pull up the drawbridge before their pursuers were upon them, thus allowing Cromwell's troops to continue the slaughter up to the far end of town near

St Peter's Church. By this point in the struggle as many as 6,000 parliamentarian troops were in the town, overwhelming all attempts at resistance. At the same time an English cavalry screen outside the northern walls prevented retreat in that direction.

The final mass atrocities committed by the attackers took place at St Peter's Church and at the towers on the north wall. Fleeing royalist soldiers had taken refuge in the steeple of St Peter's and in the towers on the north wall. No quarter was offered these men by the attackers. Instead Cromwell gave the word to pile the church pews under the steeple and set fire to them so as to burn out the fugitives. The scheme worked: '50 of them got out of the church, but the enraged soldiers put them all to the sword, and 30 of them were burned in the fire, some of them cursing and crying out, God damn them. . . . Those in the towers [on the north wall] being about 200 did yield to the General's mercy.' All the officers were killed, and the great majority of the common soldiers were shipped to Barbados.[88] Over the next two days any remaining prisoners were murdered, closing the curtain on the blackest episode in Cromwell's career.

The loss of Drogheda, one of the best ports in north-eastern Ireland, was a major defeat for Ormond and the royalist coalition. More than two thousand of their very best soldiers were killed (at least half of whom were Protestant). The strategic gateway to Ulster was opened to Cromwell's columns. The strongest royalist position in Leinster was lost.[89] And the political tensions between Protestant and Catholic within the Confederate coalition were worsened, as the Catholics further lost confidence in Ormond as a military leader. His pleas for money and supplies were increasingly met with refusal or evasion.[90]

The fall of Drogheda and the massacre of its garrison struck fear into the hearts of Catholic and Protestant royalists alike. Ormond concluded that 'no place can resist his [Cromwell's] assault without help'.[91] Confederate garrisons knew in the future that resistance to the invaders after they had been summoned to surrender was likely to end in their massacre, since no fortifications in Ireland could stand up to the siege guns and English infantry assaults. Largely as a result, the royalists abandoned the remaining fortified towns in the Pale without a fight, and discipline broke down in the garrisons of Trim and Dundalk, preventing the retreating garrisons from destroying the defences or the guns in those places.[92]

It is easy to see from the immediate results of the slaughter at Drogheda why Cromwell was 'persuaded that this [was] a righteous judgment of God upon these barbarous wretches, who have imbrued their hands in so much innocent blood; and that it will tend to prevent the effusion of blood for the future'.[93] But there is no justification we can make today for a soldier, even in the violent seventeenth century, to have refused to accept the surrender of enemy soldiers. In the words of Gardiner, 'the deed of horror was all

Cromwell's own'.[94] Cromwell's apparent need to explain to Lenthall why he gave the fateful command to give no quarter suggests possible feelings of unease. The fact that Ormond and the Confederate leaders said little about the atrocities confirms for us the brutal nature of the Irish wars since October 1641, but even by the standards of that violent and merciless age the sack of Drogheda must be considered an appalling event.

Ormond withdrew southwards to Kilkenny after the loss of Drogheda, Trim and Dundalk, correctly anticipating that Cromwell would next march against Munster. The events at Drogheda may have shocked Owen Roe O'Neill into finally coming to terms with the Confederates. It certainly convinced the Old English and royalists that an alliance with O'Neill was their only hope of redressing the military balance. The Drogheda disaster also convinced Ormond, Prince Rupert and Charles II that it would be too risky for the king to come to Ireland, as they had earlier planned. Charles now turned towards Scotland and the Scots as his most promising potential base and supporters in his efforts to regain his throne. The ultimate price for Scottish help in the spring of 1650 would be Charles's unprincipled desertion and denunciation of his Irish Catholic subjects.

As Ormond and the Confederates recoiled and reassessed their strategy, Cromwell dispatched Venables with three regiments to move into Ulster to clear that province of all organised resistance and to open landward communications with Sir Charles Coote's garrison in Derry. As these operations commenced, Cromwell and the main body of his army returned to Dublin to replenish supplies and put their wounded and sick comrades into the two hospitals that had been established there by Mr Linne, the Apothecary-General of the army.[95] After less than a week's rest Cromwell and his troops renewed the campaign, moving south this time towards the heart of Catholic Ireland.

4

Cromwell's Southern Campaign, September–November 1649

The rebels are strong in their numbers, exalted with success, abundantly provided of all necessaries . . . On the other side, to withstand them our numbers are inferior, discouraged with misfortune, hardly and uncertainly provided for, the people weary of their burdens, wavering in their affections.

Ormond to Charles II, 27 September 1649[1]

Cromwell's victory at Drogheda altered the strategic situation in Ireland. It opened the gateway to Ulster, allowing Colonel Venables to lead a column rapidly north to join Sir Charles Coote in the total subjugation of the Irish and British forces in the northern province. The parliamentarians' capture of Drogheda, Trim and Dundalk secured the north-west approaches into the Pale, relieving the parliamentarians of the need to leave large forces in the area to defend against a major Confederate attack on Dublin while they were campaigning in northern and southern Ireland. Consequently, Cromwell was free to pursue his strategic plan of moving south to seize the ports of Leinster and Munster before winter's onset, thus cutting the royalists' most direct communications with their sympathisers in France and Spain.

Ormond faced a dismal situation with a sadly weakened army. The loss of four to six thousand of his best soldiers at Rathmines and Drogheda made it impossible for him to face Cromwell's army in a pitched battle. Therefore he had to continue a Fabian strategy, hoping that the effects of wet weather, disease and hunger would weaken the invaders to the point where they could be attacked and defeated in detail by the smaller forces available to the royalists. Pursuant to that strategy, Ormond led his remaining

89

regiments south to Kilkenny, from where, as he told Prince Rupert, 'we will look for an advantageous pass to fight him [Cromwell] at'.[2]

The Confederates faced immense problems in late September 1649. The Catholic burghers in towns such as Galway, Wexford and Waterford refused to send to the Kilkenny treasury the money which had been assessed on them by the Commissioners of Trust, in spite of Ormond's urgent pleas to them to do so.[3] In addition, the Confederates had not yet concluded a treaty of alliance with Owen Roe O'Neill in Ulster, although they desperately needed O'Neill's 4,000-man army to help stop Cromwell.[4] Clanricarde was writing regularly from Connacht to tell Ormond that he was unable to send troops or money to the king's Lord Lieutenant, partly because of the threat to Sligo from Coote's forces in Ulster, and partly because of a severe outbreak of the plague in Galway.[5] And Ormond could not convince Prince Rupert to use the royalist fleet in Kinsale aggressively to cut Cromwell's supply lines from Britain.[6]

The best that Ormond could do was to call for replacements for the infantrymen he had lost at Drogheda and try to rebuild a field army large enough to hinder the parliamentarians' operations in the south. He could only hope that the walled towns of the south could withstand Cromwell's assault until he was able to come to their aid. To help them in doing so, he planned to reinforce critical garrisons, such as those in Wexford and Waterford, with his few remaining reliable regiments and with some of O'Neill's troops.

CROMWELL'S SHIFT TO THE SOUTH, SEPTEMBER 1649

Following the fall of Trim and Dundalk, the majority of Cromwell's army marched to Dublin, arriving there by 17 September.[7] While the infantry and cavalrymen rested and refreshed themselves, the artillery train of eleven siege guns and twelve field pieces was loaded onto ships at Drogheda and shipped to Dublin in preparation for the southern campaign. With the detachment of Venables with three regiments into Ulster and Hewson with one regiment to garrison Drogheda, Cromwell's field army was reduced to a strength of roughly 9,000 men. Though reduced in size, this force was twice as large as the army Ormond could muster on a single battlefield, making it possible for Cromwell to go wherever he chose. Cromwell and the Council of State had discussed his plans for the next phase of the conquest several months earlier, as is indicated in Cromwell's letter to John Bradshaw from Dublin on 16 September:

> We are marching the army to Dublin, which we hope will be here tomorrow night, where we desire to recruit with victual, and then shall, God willing, advance towards the southern design — you know what — only we think Wexford will be our first undertaking in order to the other.[8]

Cromwell had three options for the initial direction of the campaign to conquer southern Leinster and Munster. First, he could embark his army on ships and move it by sea to Munster, forcing the Confederates to defend many places simultaneously until he made his landing. Second, he could march his army along the coastal road through Wicklow and Arklow to Wexford, using his fleet to support him logistically as he went and to carry his artillery train and supplies. Or, third, he could march his troops over the Wicklow mountains to the south-west, from Dublin to Kilkenny, making it necessary for Ormond to engage in battle in order to defend the Confederate capital.

The amphibious option was not as feasible as it might appear for the English in the autumn of 1649. There was not enough shipping available in the Irish Sea to carry the thousands of horses and men of the army, along with the tons of supplies, hundreds of wagons, and the heavy cannon of the artillery train which accompanied them.[9] An amphibious force also had no place to land, since none of the Munster ports had declared for parliament in mid-September. The need for a port of debarkation for a descent on the Munster coast had been made amply clear in August, when Ireton's contingent had been unable to land in the south and was obliged to disembark in Dublin.[10]

The second course of action of moving the army along the coastal route provided the easier overland journey, with less toil in moving guns and supplies than in the inland option over the Wicklow hills. An advance southward along the coast would allow the English to attack Wexford sooner than if they proceeded by the inland route. This was a very important consideration, since Wexford was the major port of the Irish privateers who had taken a heavy toll of English merchant shipping during the 1640s. Consequently, it was a priority objective of the Westminster government.[11]

The third course of action required the hardest march, but perhaps a better chance of forcing the Confederates to fight a final major battle, the prize of victory of which would be the destruction of the main and largest remaining royalist army. This course of action would have made the English army more vulnerable to the type of ambushes that Ormond had alluded to in his letter to Rupert in mid-September. A march inland would have been the hardest to support, and the most difficult one with which to move the all-important artillery train.

Cromwell chose the coastal operation, realising that Ormond would most likely avoid a major battle in any case. Even if such a battle were to occur, an English victory would leave the royalist garrisons intact in the Leinster and Munster ports as winter approached. Perhaps most importantly, this course of action promised to bring the ports of Munster into parliament's hands the quickest.[12]

Ormond knew that his forces could not stand successfully against the 9,000 soldiers in Cromwell's field army. He made no effort to resist the

English advance along the Leinster coast. Instead he reinforced the garrisons of Wexford and New Ross, since these were the first two fortified towns in Cromwell's path which were critical to English supply efforts. Ormond maintained a mobile field force of 3,000 foot and horse with which he hoped to crush isolated detachments of English troops, thereby wearing down Cromwell's tactical superiority.[13]

The English army departed from Dublin for Wexford on 23 September, anticipating little resistance along the way. Cromwell reissued his pledge to the Irish people that he would ensure that his troops paid cash for all the food that farmers brought in to his camp to sell. He soon hanged several of his soldiers who failed to obey his ban on looting. Such measures seemed to have had a positive affect, as the army was able to march from Dublin to the outskirts of Wexford in a week, making only one halt along the way for supplies from the supporting ships at Arklow.

The royalist garrisons in towns such as Arklow and Ferns either surrendered outright or fled before the English arrived. Each captured castle required the posting of a garrison, slowly reducing the strength of Cromwell's host as Ormond had hoped.[14] The only significant resistance to the English progress to Wexford was a small ambush set at a passage through the hills south of Arklow, where an Irish party commanded by Brian O'Byrne surprised the column, capturing some horses and, reportedly, Cromwell's camp furniture. By 30 September the town of Enniscorthy had surrendered to the threat of bombardment by a few English field guns. Cromwell's army was just twelve miles from Wexford, with a secure line of communications along the coastal road to Dublin and complete command of the sea.[15]

As his army moved south Cromwell redoubled his efforts to get the Westminster government to hasten the flow of supplies and replacements to Ireland. On 17 September, in his letter describing the taking of Drogheda, he told Speaker Lenthall that 'We keep the field much, our tents sheltering us from the wet and cold, but yet the country-sickness overtakes many, and therefore we desire recruits and some fresh regiments of foot, may be sent.'[16]

The invaders' continual need to garrison the castles and towns captured along their march drew troops from the main force, reducing Cromwell's field army to 6,000 men by mid-October. There were over 400 castles and towns throughout Ireland,[17] most of which had to be taken and garrisoned by the English if they were ever going to end the war in Ireland and hold the population in check. This meant that the size of the English forces in Ireland would have to grow eventually to 35,000 soldiers.[18] It was therefore critical to the success of the conquest that the English government find a way to send a steady stream of replacements to Ireland.

Continuous recruiting had to be carried out in England to prevent the field armies in Ireland from melting away. The response from the English

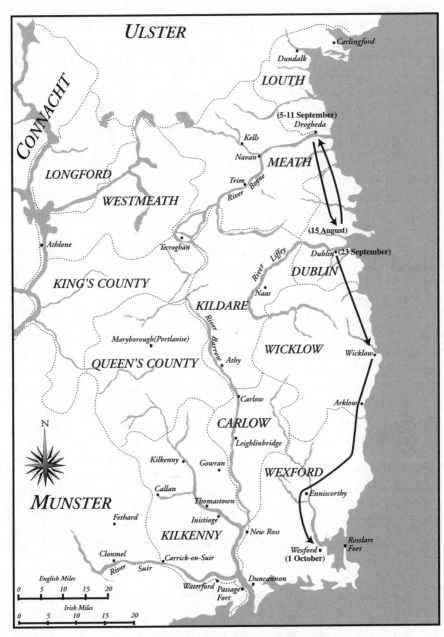

5. Cromwell's Campaign, September 1649

government initially was slow, owing to the difficulties in raising new recruits and moving them from England to Ireland. Recruiters could not simply impress new soldiers in the time-honoured English fashion. Political considerations, especially the endemic threat of popular riots by Levellers and other populist groups, made impressment a risky proposition. Instead the Council of State contracted with colonels and captains to raise companies and regiments of volunteers and to move them to the embarkation ports.

In 1649–50 English recruiting officers posted a cash bond for the raising of recruits and for the good conduct of these new soldiers while marching to the ports. In return, the recruiting officers received a cash bonus upon successful completion of their mission and command of the companies and regiments sent to Ireland.[19] With commission and contract in hand, the recruiting officers beat the drum and scoured the towns and villages of England looking for men willing to serve in Ireland in exchange for six weeks' pay in advance and a steady job. These efforts were successful. By October the English had raised 4,000 recruits and veterans to send to their armies in Ulster and Leinster, and nearly 9,000 men were raised and sent to Ireland by February 1650.[20]

The Westminster government also met the need for a steady supply of food for its forces in Ireland. For example, it sent 252,000 pounds of oats, 5,262,000 pounds of wheat, 1,565,000 pounds of rye, 300,000 pounds of biscuit and 513,000 pounds of cheese to Dublin in September, October and November.[21] These tonnages of victuals provided a very large portion of the 16,000 to 24,000 pounds of bread needed daily to feed the parliamentary troops in Leinster, Munster and Ulster.[22] The English shipped 45 tons of salmon and 133,000 gallons of beer to Ireland from England in this period to round out the soldiers' rations. In addition, Cromwell's men captured large amounts of food from the Confederates in Enniscorthy and Wexford, easing the supply situation further.[23] Consequently, Cromwell was able to keep his men on active operations uninterrupted for three months. The duration of Cromwell's first field campaign was much longer than that of any earlier campaign in Ireland from 1641 to 1649, where all armies routinely had been forced to return to base to replenish their supplies after one to three weeks in the field.[24]

THE FALL OF WEXFORD, OCTOBER 1649

On 1 October, when the English army approached Wexford, it found that a fleet under Richard Deane had already arrived off the outer banks of the harbour (see Map 6). The town of Wexford sits at the mouth of the River Slaney, with a large bay between it and St George's Channel, which was in turn sheltered by two fingers of land. Protecting the narrow mouth of Wexford harbour was Rosslare Fort, situated on the finger of land jutting from the south. Wexford was on the south side of the Slaney, making it very difficult

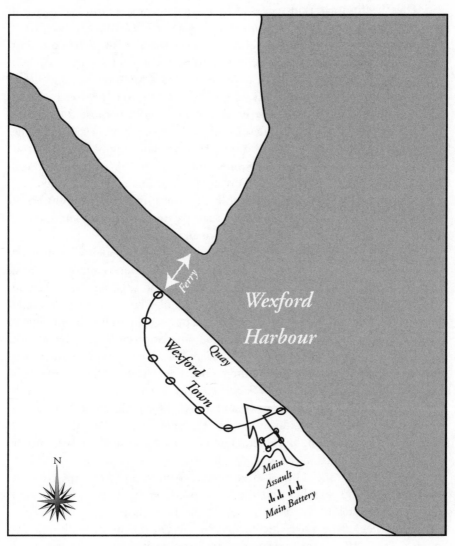

6. *Assault on Wexford, 11 October 1649*

for Cromwell to encircle the town without splitting his army. Cromwell moved his army to the south-western side of the Slaney and approached Wexford from the south, with the harbour to the army's eastern flank. This deployment facilitated the supply of the army from its supply ships.[25]

The Wexford garrison seems to have been surprised with the speed at which Cromwell and the Commonwealth navy had advanced. The townsmen had failed to put enough soldiers into Rosslare Fort for defence against determined land or sea attacks. On 2 October Lieutenant-General Michael Jones, now Cromwell's second-in-command, led a force of foot and horse towards the fort. When his advance guard of dragoons approached, the garrison fled.[26] This was a major break for the English because the capture of Rosslare Fort allowed Deane's warships and the supply vessels to enter the well-protected harbour and to land the siege train and supplies for the army. A contemporary news report identified the garrison's disarray as a crucial factor in the capture of the fort: 'This showed our enemies to be void of all council, for neither had we cannon to batter, nor provisions to subsist without our navy, nor could our fleet force their passage by that fort and the two frigates there riding, nor [was there] scarce any other way to supply us.'[27]

Ormond was appalled at this turn of events. He had just reinforced Wexford with 1,000 soldiers commanded by David Sinnott, and he believed that the town could hold out as long as it could be kept supplied. He had moved his field army to New Ross, twenty miles away, so that he could prevent the total investiture of Wexford and protect the town's supply line.[28] Ormond's relations with the Irish Catholic population of Wexford were not good, and it was only after the fall of Rosslare Fort that the leading townsmen had agreed to accept Sinnott as their governor.[29] Just as these difficulties were working against Ormond's Fabian strategy, some of Inchiquin's English officers in Youghal seized that town and declared for parliament. This forced Ormond to dispatch Inchiquin and a regiment of horse to the west to subdue this insurrection, weakening his ability either to succour Wexford or to attack English units in the area.

Meanwhile Deane's ships moved to the south side of Wexford Bay and landed the army's supplies and the heavy siege guns. This move allowed Cromwell to establish batteries aimed at the castle dominating the south-eastern corner of the town's defences. He selected this point for bombardment because the rest of the town's walls were backed up by 'a rampart of earth within the wall, near fifteen foot thick',[30] making it hard to blow a breach through the defences with the artillery. The castle overlooked a portion of the town wall and offered the chance, once it was taken, for English musketeers to shoot down on the defenders and to cover an assault over the walls by the pikemen at that point.

Cromwell summoned the town to surrender on 3 October. He offered favourable terms in hopes of securing Wexford undamaged so that he might use it for winter quarters and as a logistical base. An exchange of letters took place between Sinnott and Cromwell from 3 to 11 October, as Sinnott played for time.[31] During this interlude Ormond sent an additional 1,500 soldiers and ammunition into the town, hoping to strengthen the will and the ability of the garrison to resist.[32] The extended resistance by the Wexford garrison was a key component of Ormond's defensive strategy, which was based on the notion that the English army could be weakened if it were forced to live for an extended period in tents in the cold and rainy weather.

During the exchange of letters Cromwell moved his army to the south-east of the town, away from the swampy area in which it had initially camped. On 10 October the bombardment commenced. By the 11th it was obvious to the townsmen and Sinnott that Ormond's field army was in no position to attack Cromwell's army before his heavy guns breached the defences. Consequently, Sinnott and the town's aldermen decided to accept Cromwell's terms, which offered the soldiers 'quarter for life, and leave to go to their several habitations . . . to take up arms no more. . . . And the commissioned officers quarter for their lives, but to render themselves prisoners . . . and that I shall protect the town from plunder.'[33]

At this point, on 11 October, Wexford's population and garrison had a chance to survive, if they had accepted these terms. Sinnott dispatched two field-grade officers from the garrison and two aldermen to Cromwell to serve as security and to negotiate the final terms. Cromwell, in return, promised to cease his bombardment once they arrived. However, when this delegation met with Cromwell, it presented him with a list of ten new proposals for further negotiation. These included several provisions for the protection of the Catholic clergy in the town. Perhaps more irksome to Cromwell, the Irish proposed the withdrawal of the garrison intact to Ross with arms, ammunition and horses.[34] Sinnott also asked for permission for the townsmen to be free to leave the town with their goods and ships and to sail to wherever they saw fit.[35]

Much has been made of Cromwell's bigotry towards Catholicism during this campaign. The religious terms among the delegates' proposals certainly provoked a typically angry and dismissive response, but they did not cause the massacre at Wexford. Cromwell could not afford to allow a garrison of nearly 3,000 men to leave with all their arms and equipment and to march immediately to reinforce the main royalist army. Further, the idea of allowing the merchant privateers of Wexford to depart with their armed ships, at least three of which mounted twenty or more guns, was unacceptable. These privateers would have sailed to another Irish port from which they could continue to harry English commerce and logistics, a situation unthinkable to either Cromwell or the Commonwealth government. What followed is somewhat unclear, although Cromwell undoubtedly rejected further negotiations.[36]

During the meeting between the town's delegates and Cromwell on 11 October the English cannon continued to hammer away at the castle at the south-eastern end of town. In the afternoon the gunners succeeded in blowing two wide breaches in the wall, and the troops prepared for the assault. At the same time the English offered lenient terms to Captain Stafford, one of the town's negotiators and the commander of the castle outside the walls. When the negotiations broke down, Stafford agreed to surrender the castle. Shortly thereafter Cromwell's veterans poured through the castle and over the town's walls just to the north. This turn of events unnerved the defenders of the town. The garrison abandoned their defences, allowing the rest of the English army to scale the southern wall and seize the gates.[37]

Cromwell lost control of his soldiers once his troops scaled Wexford's walls. Worse, he made no efforts to regain control and enforce discipline until after the slaughter of at least 1,500 soldiers and townsmen in the town square. The panicking civilians in the town were caught in the crossfire as the garrison fled, and the English troops made little effort to spare them. Many townsmen attempted to cross to the north of the Slaney in boats to escape the slaughter. Hundreds of them drowned when the parliamentarian troops opened fire on them.[38] Therefore, instead of gaining a living town whose industries and population could have been used to sustain future operations, the English captured a desolate and ruined place incapable of logistically or financially supporting the future conquest. Unquestionably, and with no moral or military justification, hundreds of non-combatants were killed by the rampaging troops.

In his report to parliament Cromwell recorded no remorse for the slaughter of the unarmed civilians at Wexford. Perhaps because he had not given an order for no quarter, he did not feel responsible for the useless slaughter of the civilian population. He certainly was angry with Colonel Sinnott for the changes made by the defenders in the preliminary surrender terms. In any case, he made little effort to stop the slaughter. This was a military failure for several reasons. First, such conduct by soldiers hurts the discipline of an army, and disciplined behaviour was essential to the English logistical effort. Second, the example of Wexford possibly stiffened the resolve to resist of the garrisons of other Catholic towns, lengthening the war and increasing its costs.

The capture of Wexford was a major English tactical victory. Over 2,000 more of Ormond's best troops were killed or dispersed. These losses, when added to the 2,000–3,000 men lost at Drogheda and the 3,000–4,000 men lost at the battle of Rathmines, meant that over fifty per cent of the royalists' army had been destroyed by the English invaders in a little over two months. Once again, the victory demonstrated English tactical superiority, as only twenty or thirty English soldiers were killed in the fighting.

Wexford was one of Cromwell's most inglorious yet militarily important tactical victories. As a result, Ormond's field army had dwindled to fewer than 3,000 men. He continued to lack sufficient trained manpower to meet the English in a pitched battle with any real hope of achieving a reversal of the military situation.

Wexford's capture was a major logistical coup for the English, who captured seventy cannon and tons of supplies in the town and at least three warships in the harbour.[39] The possession of Wexford's harbour was equally important. Until Wexford's capture the English lacked a adequate port south of Dublin from which they could support the southern design. Now they could more easily supply Cromwell from southern England, and they had rooted out the nest of royalist privateers which had played such havoc among English merchant shipping.

The importance of the loss of Confederate naval resources in Wexford is seldom noted, but it was a major factor in ensuring English success during the remainder of the campaign. The Confederates lost one of the most important ports for their communications with continental friends and for sources of supply.[40] Nearly as important, the only credible royalist naval force remaining after Wexford's fall was Prince Rupert's fleet in Kinsale. However, this force remained short of victuals, munitions and manpower, hindering Rupert from following Ormond's instructions to launch sudden raids and disrupt the parliamentarians' communications.[41] The removal of these threats to English supply lines allowed the English to shift their naval units to other pressing tasks such as convoy protection and sea interdiction in the Channel and North Sea. Shortly after the fall of Wexford, Rupert was able to slip away from the English squadron blockading Kinsale with seven warships and to sail to Portugal. In the process he left three ships behind. He was no longer in a position to interfere with Blake's efforts to support Cromwell's seizure of the Munster ports in November.[42] This ended any credible royalist naval threat to the English enterprise in Ireland and Britain.

The swiftness of Wexford's capture was a major psychological blow to whatever taste the royalists might have had for a pitched battle against either Cromwell or Jones. Ormond, Inchiquin, Taaffe and Castlehaven were accustomed to fighting a war in which no one had been able to maintain the offensive for as long as Cromwell had done by mid-October.[43] In the Irish wars of 1641–8 no army had been able to capture by assault a well-defended town such as Drogheda and Wexford or able to maintain control over wide areas of the countryside. Consequently, the Confederate military leaders were disheartened when faced with the defeats inflicted upon them from August to October 1649.[44]

A sense of despair is increasingly evident in the correspondence between Ormond and the other royalist leaders after Wexford's fall. For example, Lieutenant-General Barry observed in a letter to Ormond that 'If Cromwell have not some speedy interruption given to his victories, I doubt you will not only find the English, but also the Irish will desert you.'[45] It was becoming increasingly difficult for Ormond to gather troops or support from the Catholic population, given his complete military failure to date.

The psychological effects of Wexford's fall also played a crucial part in Cromwell's eventual success in winning the allegiance of the Protestant garrisons in Munster by late November. The heart of Cromwell's strategy for the swift destruction of the royalist coalition in Ireland was the plan to convert the Protestants in Leinster and Munster, who had formerly served under the Earl of Inchiquin, to the Commonwealth's cause. Lord Broghill, a scion of a leading New English family in Munster, was at the centre of this conspiracy. In August, when Ireton's part of the invasion fleet approached the Munster coast, none of the Munster garrisons declared for parliament, forcing Ireton to sail north to join Cromwell in Dublin.[46] After the sack of Wexford the Protestant garrisons in Munster became ripe for the picking.

When Cromwell approached Wexford in early October, some of Inchiquin's officers in Youghal declared for parliament. But there were no English forces close enough to provide them with aid, and Inchiquin was able to quell the coup with promises of lenient forgiveness for the soldiers and imprisonment for the ringleaders (Colonels Townsend, Warden and Giffard).[47] However, serious tactical damage was done to Ormond's main army with the diversion of Inchiquin from the main force near Wexford. Later, in mid-October and early November, the Munster ports and towns fell to Broghill's design like ripe fruit. Ormond found that he could no longer trust Inchiquin's Protestant regiments to fight in the open or to defend places like New Ross, worsening his shortage of troops.[48]

THE SURRENDER OF NEW ROSS, OCTOBER 1649

Cromwell wasted little time before exploiting the momentum of his Wexford victory. Leaving Colonel Cook and his regiment as a garrison in Wexford, he marched to New Ross to seize a crossing over the River Barrow. Ormond was faced with the choice of either surrendering New Ross, 'which is a walled town, situate[d] upon the River Barrow, a very pleasant and commodious river, bearing vessels of a very considerable burthen',[49] or of risking the loss of the 2,000-man garrison of the place. He initially determined to delay Cromwell for as long as possible, hoping that the 'country disease' (probably dysentery) would so weaken Cromwell's field army that it would be unable to assault the town. The governor of New Ross, Lucas Taaffe, however, persuaded Ormond to allow him to surrender on terms if the English were able to bring up their siege guns and begin the process of blowing a breach in the town walls.

The English arrived on 17 October, accompanied by three siege guns drawn by teams of oxen. Commonwealth naval support arrived shortly

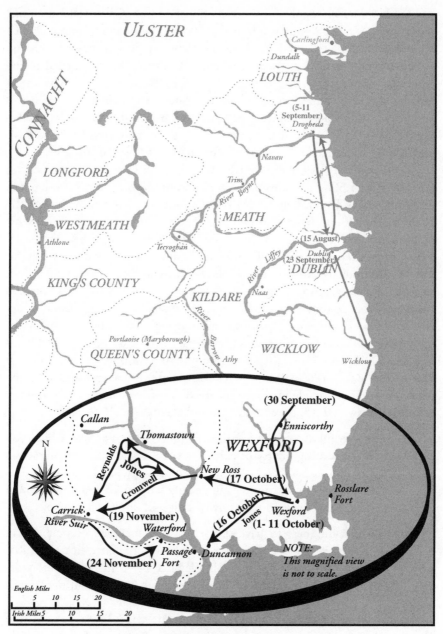

7. *Cromwell's Campaign, October–December 1649*

afterwards, escorting supply ships and additional cannon. Cromwell summoned Taaffe to surrender, reminding him that '[Since] my coming into Ireland I have endeavoured to avoid the effusion of blood, having been before no place to which terms have not been first sent, as might have turned to the good and preservation of those to whom they were offered.'[50] The threat and the promise were clear. The horrible fates of Drogheda and Wexford hung over Taaffe's head. Conversely, Cromwell hoped that the 'terrible effusion of blood' at those places might induce Taaffe to surrender New Ross undamaged and suitable for use as winter quarters for part of his army.

Taaffe did not answer the initial summons, and Ormond reinforced his garrison with 1,500 men. Cromwell deployed his guns on the following day, 18 October, and commenced his bombardment on the morning of the 19th. Just as Lieutenant-Colonel Ingoldsby was preparing the assault columns to storm the breach made by the artillery near the main gate, Taaffe responded to Cromwell's' message, asking the Lord Lieutenant for terms.[51] Anxious to gain the town intact and to show that he would grant lenient terms to garrisons which surrendered in a timely manner, Cromwell announced his readiness to allow Taaffe to 'march away with those under your command, with their arms, bag and baggage', while the townsmen, for their part, might remain unmolested or depart with their goods. He refused to allow Taaffe to remove the artillery and ammunition from the town. It was in this exchange of letters between Taaffe and Cromwell that the famous request was made by Taaffe for freedom of conscience in the town.[52] Cromwell answered this request directly and clearly:

> To what I formerly offered I shall make good. . . . For that which you mention concerning liberty of conscience, I meddle not with any man's conscience. But if by liberty of conscience you mean a liberty to exercise the mass, I judge it best to use plain dealing, and to let you know, where the Parliament of England have power, that will not be allowed of.[53]

Cromwell's unwillingness to have the state probe people's consciences in political or religious matters allowed a liberty of conscience not permitted in most parts of Europe in 1649. His intolerance of Roman Catholic worship mirrored the intolerance of Protestant worship encountered in all Catholic countries of his time.

Taaffe accepted the terms and marched out with 2,000 men to join Ormond's army on the west side of the Barrow. Cromwell scrupulously observed the terms, hoping to convince the occupants of the remaining Irish towns to surrender in the same manner in future sieges. As Taaffe's troops marched out of the town 500 soldiers in one of Inchiquin's Protestant regiments in New Ross refused to withdraw, opting instead to join Cromwell's army. Cromwell thus secured not only an excellent town for winter quarters, but also a welcome reinforcement to his field army.[54]

The capture of New Ross opened western Leinster and Munster to Cromwell's landward advance. He immediately ordered the construction of a boat bridge across the Barrow which would enable his army to cross and begin operations in the direction of either Waterford to the south or Clonmel to the west. The construction of such a bridge was a remarkable engineering feat. The Barrow is swift and nearly two hundred yards wide at New Ross. When swollen with autumn rains, the river fills its banks, making such an operation quite difficult. The English army, however, successfully carried it out, greatly surprising their enemies with this demonstration of engineering skill.

Meanwhile the fissures within Ormond's royalist coalition widened significantly as a result of his failure to find a way to prevent the fall of Wexford and New Ross. He had done all he could to garrison these places properly. However, the hostile attitude of the Catholic townsmen in Wexford towards Ormond and the Protestant royalists had hindered Ormond's and Castlehaven's efforts to put troops into that town before Cromwell attacked.[55] Ironically, the rising dissatisfaction of many Catholics with the Ormondist coalition took place at the same time as Owen Roe O'Neill finally agreed to join the royalist cause on 20 October.[56]

O'Neill's adherence was the only really favourable military news for Ormond that month. O'Neill's army numbered at least 4,000 foot and 800 horse and possessed a remarkable mobility owing to its reliance for sustenance on the mobile herds of cattle maintained by the Ulster creaghts. O'Neill's host was not tied down to the defence of any major towns, since it controlled none. Hence O'Neill was able immediately to send Lieutenant-General Richard Farrell to Kilkenny with a very welcome reinforcement of 2,000 men. These troops did not arrive in Kilkenny until the end of October, after the fall of Wexford and New Ross.

At the same time as Cromwell advanced to New Ross on 16 October the first fruits of the southern design of Cromwell and Broghill became apparent with the defection of the garrisons of Cork and Youghal to the parliamentarian cause.[57] The revolt against Inchiquin began when some Protestant officers in Cork, fearing that Catholic troops might be introduced into their garrison, freed Broghill's imprisoned agents, Colonels Townsend, Warden and Giffard. These three officers persuaded the rest of the garrison to declare their support for Broghill and Cromwell, promising that 'they would live and die with them'. On the following day Townsend ejected the few dissenting soldiers and Inchiquin's commander in Cork, Colonel Robert Starling, from the town. At the same time Inchiquin's garrison in Youghal seized their royalist governor, Sir Piercy Smith, and sent a message to Cork asking that Colonel Warden come to Youghal to assume command.[58]

Cromwell had dispatched Lord Broghill with Colonel Phayre's regiment from Wexford to Cork in Blake's ships with the mission of converting the

Protestants of the Cork area to parliament's cause and to recruit fresh troops for the campaign. Broghill diverted his ships to Youghal when he received news of its defection. Once Colonel Phayre had secured Youghal with a garrison of 200 infantrymen, he and Broghill led a force overland to Cork, where they joined Colonel Townsend's troops. The civilian governments of Cork and Youghal sought and received favourable terms of reconciliation from Cromwell in November, assuring their loyalty for the remainder of the war.[59]

Lord Broghill continued to do his work well. Within the next month Bandon and Kinsale surrendered without terms to Cromwell.[60] This stroke gave Cromwell control of all major ports in Leinster and Munster except for Limerick and Waterford, ending any realistic hope that the royalists could be supplied or reinforced from the continent except through Waterford or Galway. Denis Murphy, in his book *Cromwell in Ireland*, concluded that this series of defections to Cromwell 'decided the fate of Ireland, for it gave Cromwell's army excellent winter quarters . . . just when his forces were reduced by sickness and losses in the field from 12,000 to 6,000 men and demoralised by the repulses they had met with at Waterford and Duncannon'.[61] This assessment is not far off the mark, given the importance of logistics to Cromwell's strategy for the swift conquest of Ireland.

As Cromwell led the main campaign in Leinster in September and October his trusted subordinates Venables and Coote led the English offensive in Ulster. After the fall of Drogheda the gateway to Ulster was open, and the political fissures within the royalist coalition made it possible for the English columns to make short work of the anti-parliamentarian forces in the north.

THE CONQUEST OF ULSTER, SEPTEMBER–DECEMBER 1649

Derry was the only major town in Ulster held by parliamentarian troops when Cromwell landed in Dublin on 15 August. Cromwell's first concern was to secure the approaches to Dublin from royalist attacks. He accordingly concentrated his forces on the capture of Drogheda. His complete victory at Drogheda on 11 September and his swift seizure of Newry and Dundalk in the next few days shocked Ormond's coalition. Cromwell moved quickly to exploit this shock by sending Colonel Robert Venables with 5,000 soldiers into eastern Ulster to capture the ports and towns held by George Monro and his eastern Ulster allies.[62]

As Venables approached Carlingford, Captain Fern sailed his frigate into the harbour and engaged the fort overlooking it. This combined sea and land operation completely unnerved the defenders, who surrendered immediately. Venables thus captured Carlingford and the three castles and fort dominating that town without a fight. There he found 1,000 muskets, 500 pikes, seven cannon and forty barrels of gunpowder.[63]

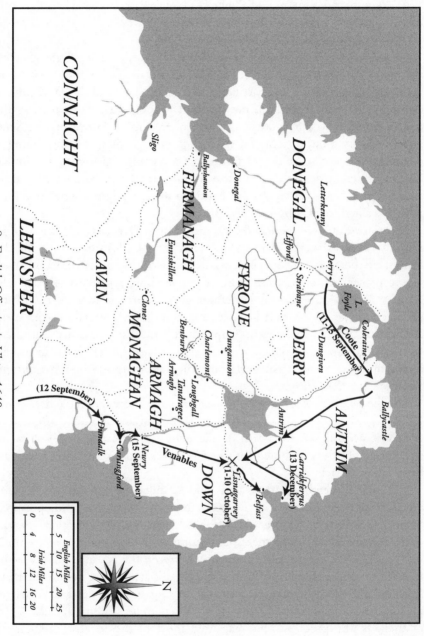

8. English Offensive in Ulster, 1649

CONNACHT

LEINSTER

DONEGAL

FERMANAGH

· Sligo

· Ballyshannon

· Donegal

Letterkenny

Lifford·

· Derry

Strabane·

TYRONE

DERRY

Coleraine·

L.
Foyle

·Dungiven

Coote
(11-15 September)

Ballycastle

ANTRIM

CAVAN

· Clones

Enniskillen·

Benburb·
Dungannon·
· Charlemont·

MONAGHAN

Loughgall·
Armagh· ·Tandragee

ARMAGH

(12 September)

· Dundalk

· Carlingford

Newry
(15 September)

Venables

DOWN

Antrim·

Carrickfergus
(13 December)

✗ Lisnagarvey
(1-10 October)

·Belfast

N

English Miles
0   5   10   15   20   25

Irish Miles
0   4   8   12   16   20

Venables next led a column of cavalry to Newry, which also surrendered without firing a shot. The eastern Ulster royalists under Monro failed to respond to Venables's advance. In fact the only concerted attempt to stop Venables was made by some of Phelim O'Neill's Irish troops when they surprised Venables's camp near Lisburn. Venables, however, rallied his surprised veterans and drove the Irish away.[64]

In early October Venables pushed further north, facing little effective resistance. He captured Lisnagarvey, Antrim and Belfast without having to conduct a siege or to land artillery. In Belfast the English found fifteen cannon and twelve barrels of powder which could have been used in the town's defence by the Scottish garrison of 800 men. However, the Scots surrendered without a fight, on the condition that they and their families would be allowed to settle on farms in the vicinity.[65] Most Protestants in eastern Ulster evidently decided to surrender to the parliamentarian army and accept its terms rather than to continue the struggle on behalf of a king who was allied to a Catholic coalition.[66]

Sir Charles Coote launched a campaign from Derry against the royalists in Coleraine as well. When he approached Coleraine, some of the Protestants betrayed the garrison by letting Coote's forces into the town. Coote proceeded to massacre most of the garrison, regardless of their religion.[67] Coote's atrocities at Coleraine were representative of his brutal approach to war. Coote and Venables linked up shortly afterwards and spent the rest of November mopping up isolated royalist garrisons. Although Carrickfergus and Enniskillen were the only major Ulster towns in royalist hands by then, small Irish garrisons still held outposts in Charlemont, Dromore and Castleleagh.[68]

In the face of these blows, the Laggan army disintegrated and Monro's force was reduced to 3,000 men with little food or ammunition.[69] Pushed to extremes, Monro was forced to decide either to retreat from Ulster or to stand and fight the combined forces of Venables and Coote. He choose the latter course of action.

In early December Monro and Lord Clandeboye marched their combined forces north towards Carrickfergus to protect that town from operations being undertaken by Coote and Venables. Learning of their approach, the Cromwellians advanced to meet the royalists near Lisnagarvey, twenty miles south of Carrickfergus. A brief skirmish between the advance guards of the two forces quickly became a rout of the royalist army, even before the main force of the English infantry was able to engage.[70] Coote and Venables pursued the fleeing royalists for eight to ten miles, killing at least 1,500 of them in the process. They captured most of the royalists' remaining ammunition, baggage, pack-horses and muskets, and 'they gave no quarter to any Irish'.[71] Monro fled to Charlemont and then on to Enniskillen, while Lord Clandeboye soon surrendered the remainder of his troops owing to lack of food supplies.[72] Most Ulster Protestants now joined Venables and Coote.

The fight at Lisnagarvey ended organised resistance to parliament in eastern Ulster. Coote took Carrickfergus on 13 December, turning the Scottish garrison and their families out into the winter cold.[73] In March the badly demoralised George Monro surrendered Enniskillen to Coote in exchange for £500 and a pass to Scotland.[74] Owen Roe O'Neill's army now constituted the only remaining opposition to English rule in western Ulster.

O'Neill's army, after helping Coote finish off the Laggan garrisons around Derry, had remained quiet until the news of Drogheda arrived. At that point O'Neill finally realised that an alliance with Ormond's royalists was his only hope, and so he resumed serious negotiations with Ormond. However, O'Neill did not sign final terms with Ormond until 20 October, at which time he received nearly every conceivable concession from the king's desperate Lord Lieutenant.[75]

During the negotiations O'Neill had started his army south, sending Lieutenant-General Farrell ahead with 2,000 picked soldiers to assist Ormond's defence of New Ross. By 12 October the rest of O'Neill's army was at Finea, County Longford, where it stopped because O'Neill was incapacitated by an illness which proved to be fatal. While some of his Ulstermen played an important role in the resistance to Cromwell in Munster, most of his soldiers withdrew to southern Ulster to select a new commander after O'Neill died in November. Thus, from August 1649 to early 1650, the largest Gaelic Irish army took little part in the struggle for Ulster, allowing Coote and Venables to complete most of the Cromwellian conquest of that province.

These successful English efforts in Ulster allowed Cromwell to continue his campaign in Munster into late November without concern for the security of Dublin. Venables's and Coote's victories also allowed them to prepare for a spring offensive against the Irish forces in western Ulster and northern Connacht.

THE DEFENCE OF DUNCANNON, OCTOBER–NOVEMBER 1649

In the south, meanwhile, Waterford remained the most important major port still in royalist hands and the main objective of Cromwell's southern design. Waterford was well defended and would require a major effort to capture. It was essential, however, that the Barrow estuary be opened to English ships before a siege commenced, so that supplies and siege artillery could be brought in for the besiegers. Two major defensive works mounting heavy cannon restrained ship movement into the Barrow. These defences were Passage Fort, on the western side of the estuary, and Duncannon Fort on the eastern side (see Map 7). Passage Fort could not be attempted by the English yet because the English did not control crossings over the Suir in

October. On the other side, Duncannon could be attacked from the east by forces marching overland from either Wexford or New Ross.

Since the boat bridge across the Barrow at New Ross was not completed until 6 November, Cromwell decided to clear the sea communications between New Ross and Waterford by taking the fortress of Duncannon. This would allow English supply ships unhindered access to the Barrow so that operations on both sides of the river could be supported logistically. On 15 October, after his capture of Wexford, Cromwell dispatched Major-General Henry Ireton with a force of several thousand men to the south-west to attempt to capture Duncannon Fort without a protracted siege, while he himself led the main force to New Ross.

Ormond understood the importance of Duncannon to the defence of Waterford, and he anticipated the threat to it. He sent his Lieutenant-General of Horse, the Earl of Castlehaven, to Duncannon with reinforcements, while he also asked the town council of Waterford to send gunpowder and food to the fortress. Although the town refused to provide much support, Castlehaven successfully reinforced the garrison by 21 October, reporting to Ormond that 'I must expect ammunition from you; without which the fort must need be soon in distress.'[76]

Ormond, while attempting to cope with the situation arising from the fall of New Ross, negotiating the treaty with O'Neill, and facing the task of confronting Cromwell's main force, did his best to provide relief for Duncannon. He sent money, powder and, most important, a new commander to replace Duncannon's governor, Thomas Roche. Roche was a soldier most likely to take counsel of his fears after the English sack of Wexford. By contrast, Colonel Edward Wogan, the new commander of Duncannon, brought vigour and resolution to the garrison. Wogan was a native of County Kildare who had been raised as a Protestant in Wales. He served parliament in the English Civil War, but changed sides in 1648.[77] He joined Ormond in 1649. Wogan was well aware that if he surrendered, he would be executed as a traitor. He was accompanied by 120 men of Ormond's lifeguard, a unit of former Protestant officers deeply loyal to Ormond and the royalist cause.[78]

Wogan successfully defended Duncannon, even though Cromwell reinforced Ireton's command with 2,000 additional soldiers commanded by Michael Jones. Wogan was one of few royalist leaders in Ireland who successfully led a mixed force of Protestant and Catholic soldiers in the tight confines of a besieged fort. He aggressively attacked English work parties and captured several field guns from Jones during one of his sorties. Even the presence of Cromwell failed to break the garrison's resolve. As a result, Duncannon was saved. The fort's modern ramparts were too strong for the few field guns accompanying Jones to blow a breach in, and the garrison was too strong for the English to defeat with an infantry assault against intact walls.[79] After loosing two guns to Wogan's sortie on 5 November, Jones ended the siege, withdrawing his and Ireton's men to rejoin the main army near New Ross.[80] Wogan's defence showed what resolute leadership could do to stem the tide of English victory. However, his garrison was fortunate in that the English were unable to get their ships past Duncannon to a point nearby where they could land the train of heavy siege artillery.

Wogan's successful defence of Duncannon denied the English navy the ability to sail into the Barrow to a suitable point at which to land the big siege guns carried by the transports. This, in turn, made it impossible for Cromwell to blow a breach in Waterford's walls in the same manner as he had done at Drogheda.

As a result of the string of English victories, only barely broken by Wogan's defence of Duncannon, Ormond and Charles II decided that the king should not sail to Ireland from the Scilly Isles, his base in October. This decision had immense long-term consequences for the royalist cause and coalition in Ireland. The king's next strategic decision, made by January 1650, was to begin the negotiations with the Scots which would result in Charles's opportunist abandonment of his subjects of all faiths in Ireland in April and May 1650.[81] But this was yet in the future.

THE MARCH TO WATERFORD, NOVEMBER 1649

Ormond, meanwhile, had not lost hope and continued to plan further action against the English army, although his appraisal of the situation was bleak:

> His Majesty's army . . . in the field and dispersed in garrison in the country amount to no less than 18,000 foot and 4,000 horse: Of these I had lately in the field 8,000 foot and 2,500 horse. . . . Sir George Monro hath 2,800 foot and 200 horse in the Lagan and the north; [he cannot] draw into the field without supplies, however. The rebels have most of Inchiquin's former garrisons; besides Dublin, Londonderry, Wexford, Ross and other lesser places garrisoned by them: Coleraine and Belfast and other dependent garrisons . . . have been surprised and betrayed to them.[82]

In another letter Ormond noted that Cromwell's field strength had fallen to 4,000 foot and 1,200 horse and that the enemy 'army is getting weaker'.[83] Thus the situation, while desperate, was not hopeless. The royalists' strategy continued to be to protract the war and wear Cromwell down while the spirits of their forces revived, and to avoid a major battle against the English army. As Ormond himself put it, 'If we can but protract this war and keep them weakening, we shall destroy them without either loss or hazard, especially if England be embroiled by the king's complying with the Scots.'[84]

As Wogan's defence of Duncannon successfully checked English progress, Ormond and Inchiquin prepared to take the first major offensive action attempted by the royalists in Leinster since the battle of Rathmines. At the end of October Ormond had received intelligence from Dublin that a column of English soldiers, who had recovered from wounds and illnesses in the English hospitals in Dublin, was going to march from Dublin to Wexford to rejoin Cromwell's force in the south.[85] These reinforcements were critical to replenish the English field army. Their march appeared to offer Ormond the chance to destroy a major detachment of the enemy without risking the entire royalist army in a battle against Cromwell's main force.

The first of the reinforcements from O'Neill's army in Ulster had arrived in Kilkenny in late October. Their arrival allowed Ormond to detach Inchiquin and Taaffe with a force of 1,000 cavalry and 1,500 infantry to attack the English column coming from Dublin to Wexford along the coast road through Arklow.[86] Inchiquin planned either to ambush the English troops south of Arklow, in a confined area where the Arklow hills come close to the sea, or to attack them at night as they rested. The intended victims, who numbered about 800 foot and 350 horse commanded by Major Nelson, were to have been met at Glascarrig by an escort of cavalry from Wexford. However, the escort failed to arrive. Major Nelson decided at this point, on 1 November, to push on to Wexford rather than spending the night in Glascarrig, having received a message that Inchiquin was intending to intercept the column. This decision threw Inchiquin's plan out of gear because his strong force of infantry could not catch up with the English column. Consequently, he decided to strike at Nelson's command with his cavalry alone, hoping to force the column to stand and fight long enough for the Irish infantry to come up and join the battle.[87]

The English spotted the advancing royalists in time to deploy into a battle formation. 'Whereupon' (as Cromwell later reported) 'they immedi-ately drew up in the best order they could upon the sands, the sea on the one hand, and the rocks on the other.'[88] The 350 horsemen were drawn up in several ranks in front of most of the infantry, with musketeers on their flanks, and they attacked the Irish as the latter deployed. The Irish cavalry, commanded by Sir Thomas Armstrong, repulsed two charges by the out-numbered English horse before driving them back to their infantry with a charge of their own. The English infantrymen, a large percentage of whom were veterans, allowed their own cavalry to retreat through their ranks and then raked the Confederate horse with a well-controlled volley of musket fire at close range. This spirited action shattered the Irish troops' cohesion and morale. At this point Major Nelson launched his reorganised cavalry against the demoralised Irish, driving them from the field at a gallop.[89] Nelson and his men then resumed their march to Wexford, seven miles to the south.

The engagement on the road to Wexford was not a major battle, but it demonstrated and increased the confidence of the English forces, while it further weakened the cohesion and morale within the Ormondist alliance.[90] The royalists not only outnumbered Nelson's command in this fight; they actually outnumbered the entire parliamentarian military presence in southern Ireland. However, they could not convert numerical superiority into battlefield supremacy. Garrisons refused to join Ormond in the field, and townsmen refused to provide the money and supplies needed to keep a large army together long enough for Ormond to fight a pitched battle.[91] This situation forced Ormond to continue to pursue a defensive strategy, even though it was clearly not working.

After receiving the sharp setback in front of Duncannon, Cromwell and Jones marched their forces back to New Ross and prepared for a direct effort against Ormond's main force which was located between the Nore and Suir rivers (see Map 7). Their first step was to complete the boat bridge over the Barrow so that troops, artillery and supplies could cross. This was accomplished by 15 November, with no opposition from Ormond's forces. Cromwell then split his outnumbered force into two brigades. Jones and Ireton crossed the Barrow on the 15th with most of army and marched north towards Kilkenny. Their task was to come into contact with Ormond's army, recently reinforced by the rest of O'Neill's Ulstermen, and engage it if possible. If that could not be accomplished, they were to try to continue on to Kilkenny, where the Confederate Commissioners of Trust were located. Cromwell remained at New Ross recovering from a bout of illness.

The English advance caught Ormond off guard as he was trying to gather his army for action at the bridgehead near New Ross. Jones and Ireton moved quickly, taking the small town of Inistioge, about ten miles northwest of New Ross, with a surprise night attack which met little resistance. They continued several miles further north towards Thomastown, a larger town with a bridge over the River Nore. The Confederates refused to fight, instead withdrawing north and east across the Nore. When the English arrived at Thomastown in pursuit, they found that the bridge over the river had been destroyed. Ormond had successfully avoided a major battle, and he had prevented the English from crossing the rain-swollen Nore and marching on to Kilkenny.[92] This was one of his better tactical manoeuvres.

Jones's movements north in November were designed to destroy the main enemy army in battle if at all possible. Cromwell was confident that his troops could defeat royalist field forces if given the chance, even when they were outnumbered by the royalists. He and Jones hoped that a battle against Ormond's force would end the Munster campaign in a single blow, bringing with it Waterford and Clonmel. Because Ormond foiled this plan by retreating, Jones and Ireton were compelled to withdraw their brigade to New Ross to replenish their food supplies.

As his infantry and artillery marched steadily south to New Ross on 18 November, Jones dispatched Colonel Reynolds with a large party of cavalry to capture Carrick, a fortified town on the River Suir. Reynolds moved quickly, arriving before Carrick early in the morning of 19 November. He split his force, and while one part attacked one gate, he led the remainder of his troops into the town through another, unmanned gate.[93] There is talk of treachery in royalist accounts of this action.[94] In any case, the garrison lost hope of successful resistance at this point and fled to the south-west. Without English losses, Reynolds had captured a fortified town full of provisions on a strategically important river crossing. Carrick, along with Inistioge and Thomastown, gave the English a string of fortified points between Ormond's forces and their army's rear during the coming siege of Waterford. The capture of Carrick also gave Cromwell an intact bridge over the Suir on the road running west from Waterford, greatly easing his logistical challenges.

The capture of Carrick with its bridge allowed Cromwell to lead his army from New Ross over the Suir from 21 to 23 November, arriving at the western side of Waterford on the 24th.[95] Land communications with Lord Broghill's garrisons to the west in Youghal, Cork and Kinsale were now open. Colonel Reynolds was left to secure Carrick with 150 infantry and the 600 troopers of his cavalry regiment.

Reynolds's capture of Carrick and Cromwell's advance towards Waterford put Ormond in a difficult situation. He needed to reinforce Waterford and, if possible, recapture Carrick with its strategically critical bridge. He reacted vigorously, leading his army south to attack Reynolds's small garrison, while also escorting infantry reinforcements into Waterford along the north side of the Suir. He arrived before Carrick on 23 November, accompanied by Castlehaven, Inchiquin and about 3,500 soldiers, including a large contingent of Ulster infantrymen. The royalist leaders were evidently divided in their council as to the best way to thwart Cromwell's design on Waterford. Ormond wanted to reinforce Waterford before an attempt was made against Carrick, while the Ulster officers wanted to attack Reynolds in Carrick before he could be reinforced.[96] In a poor compromise, Ormond decided to split his forces, leading in person the column which marched to Waterford to deliver reinforcements to that city. Castlehaven and Inchiquin remained at Carrick to supervise the assault on that town.

The royalists' assault against Carrick was made only by the Ulster troops, led by Major Charles Geoghegan. The Ulstermen had insisted upon an assault when Ormond seemed reluctant to order the attack. Heavy fighting continued for four hours as the Irish tried to burn the gates and to climb the walls. Reynolds's troops exhausted their ammunition and killed more Irish 'with sticks and staves than with powder and bullets'.[97] The Irish lacked both the artillery with which to blow a breach in the defences and pickaxes to break the gates down. In spite of their bravery, the Ulstermen had to give up their attack after losing 500 men killed in the assaults.

Ormond should have ordered the force at Carrick to await his return with his escort before attacking the town. The royalists' failure to launch a co-ordinated attack with all of their forces against Carrick allowed the defenders to concentrate on the repulse of the Ulstermen.[98] Reynolds's garrison was short of ammunition, and the defences of Carrick were not formidable. A concentrated effort by all available military strength might have delivered the important town into royalist hands, cutting Cromwell's communications with New Ross and adding another setback to the one that Cromwell had received at Duncannon. But Ormond failed to control his subordinates and was unable to influence events. This situation was another indicator of the internal rifts within the royalist coalition and an indicator of Ormond's weakness as a tactical commander.

At the same time as the Irish attempted to capture Carrick, Ormond was busy trying to strengthen Waterford for its resistance to Cromwell's siege. He sent Major Walsh and 200 infantrymen from Butler's regiment to the town on 23 November, promising to send more soon. Waterford's governor, John Lyvett, opened negotiations about a possible surrender with Cromwell on the same day. However, he told Ormond that these communications were a tactic to delay the English long enough for reinforcements and supplies to be sent into the town.[99] Lyvett asked Cromwell for fifteen days to negotiate, stipulating that during this time the English army was to come no closer. Cromwell consented to a four- or five-day cessation of hostilities, but he ordered his troops to move closer to the town walls, and he demanded that no Irish reinforcements be sent to Lyvett.[100]

Cromwell's field army had been reduced to roughly 3,000 soldiers by this point in the campaign. A very large portion of his total force was tied up in garrisons stretching from Dublin to Wexford and New Ross to Carrick. Additional large numbers were ill, including Michael Jones and, at times, Cromwell himself. Confederate possession of Duncannon prevented his heavy artillery train and much of his supply train from being brought into the estuary of the Barrow and landed to support the army. The weather also worsened, with rain making the camp an unhealthy quagmire. Without his guns there was little he could do to take Waterford by storm, and with so few healthy soldiers remaining it was unlikely that an attack would have succeeded in the face of Lyvett's vigorous defensive efforts.

In a last effort to force open the sea passage into the Barrow, Cromwell sent Jones, before the latter fell ill, to capture Passage Fort, 'a very large fort with a castle in the midst of it, having five guns planted in it, and commanding the river better than Duncannon'. Although the place was well manned, the garrison surrendered on terms, allowing the English to 'bring hither [to the camp near Waterford] ships of three hundred tons, without any danger from Duncannon'.[101] Even with this fortunate turn of events, the ground near the southern walls of Waterford proved too wet to support the heavy siege guns if they were landed, and Cromwell had no fresh troops ready to bring to his camp. His only hope of taking the town was for Lyvett to surrender, and the Irish were determined to prevent that from occurring.

Thanks to the arrival of O'Neill's contingents and reinforcements from Connacht, Ormond was able to draw over 5,000 infantry and 1,300 cavalrymen into his field army in his efforts to sustain Waterford. On 30 November he sent Lieutenant-General Richard Farrell with 1,500 Ulster troops and supplies into the town, demonstrating to Cromwell how unlikely it was that Waterford would fall without a determined assault. The talented and capable Farrell was appointed governor, since the majority of the garrison now was drawn from O'Neill's army, making it futile for Cromwell to think that the town would surrender on terms. Farrell wisely refused to move his troops out of their defensive works to fight a battle in the open, in spite of Cromwell's efforts to draw him out.[102] Consequently, in early December Cromwell retreated, leaving garrisons in Passage Fort and in a number of smaller castles his troops had captured near Waterford.

Ormond, Farrell, Castlehaven and Lyvett had saved Waterford. Their success showed what could be accomplished once Owen Roe O'Neill decided to join the Ormondist coalition. O'Neill died on 6 November, too soon to see the fruits of his decision to join the royalists. The treaty which he signed on 20 October with Ormond drove most of the remaining New English Protestants into the hands of Broghill and Cromwell because the terms of the alliance conceded total religious freedom to the Catholics and promised a radical adjustment in land claims going back to the plantations of the early seventeenth century.[103] The Protestants' defection, however, was well under way before the terms of the treaty were known. O'Neill's decision, if made in June or July, would have changed the dynamics of the campaign dramatically. As it was, the accession of the Ulster regiments to the Confederate forces in the south prevented Cromwell from ending the campaign against Kilkenny and Waterford before Christmas.

Cromwell moved west to Dungarvan after the Confederate success at Waterford. Here he met Lord Broghill, who had recently taken the town on terms. Cromwell now dispersed his exhausted soldiers into winter quarters in towns stretching from Cork to New Ross.[104] His setback at Waterford was accompanied by a second stroke of ill fortune — the death of Michael Jones, who succumbed to disease at Dungarvan on 10 December. Jones, the Lieutenant-General of Horse, was one of the best commanders on either side in the Irish wars. His victories in 1647 had preserved the parliamentarian position in the Pale, and his victory at Rathmines had opened Ireland to Cromwell's conquest. His ability to hold on to Dublin in the dark days of 1648 and early 1649 was equally remarkable and important. Jones had done more than anyone else to defeat the royalist coalition of 1649, and his death was undoubtedly a severe blow to the English war effort.

In spite of the setbacks that the English army suffered at Duncannon and Waterford, the parliamentarians had been more successful in 1649 than at any other time in the long Irish war since 1641. Cromwell's and Jones's campaign in the south had taken all major Irish seaports in Leinster and Munster by storm or defection, except for Waterford and Limerick. They had destroyed over half the veteran troops of the royalist armies, forcing Ormond to recruit untried levies and to give in to the religious terms of O'Neill. This, in turn, furthered defections by Protestant Scottish and English garrisons in the towns of Munster and Ulster. Cromwell's possession of these garrisons made it impossible for the Confederates to recruit in the richest parts of Ireland during the winter of 1649–50. The parliamentarian victories in Ulster in this same period were possible because Cromwell had pinned down the majority of the royalist and Irish regiments in the south. Finally, Ormond's generally ineffective tactical leadership and the continual unwillingness of all of the factions of the Ormondist coalition to work together prevented the numerically superior royalists from stopping the course of the English conquest of Ireland.

5

Cromwell's Winter Campaign: Waterford to Kilkenny, December 1649–March 1650

The breathing time which probably the enemy will give us this winter is like to be but a short reprieve unless good use be made of the season to make all sorts of provision for their attempts the next year which we expect will be both early and furious.

Ormond to Clanricarde, 5 December 1649[1]

Cromwell's conquest of Ireland had seemed unstoppable in the autumn of 1649. Royalist positions had fallen like bowling-pins after the English had taken out the head pin at Rathmines and Drogheda. In October and November Venables and Coote had overcome almost all organised resistance in Ulster, and in mid-December they went on to capture Carrickfergus, the last major royalist town in the province. No English armies had accomplished so much in such a short period of time in Irish history. No forces operating there had ever been as well supplied and as well led as the Cromwellian forces were. And no English commander in Ireland had ever combined the military, political, and social dimensions of strategy as effectively as Oliver Cromwell. However, his inability to capture Waterford without a prolonged siege meant that he had to put his forces into winter quarters and to regroup for the next phase of the conquest, with the enemy fortresses of Waterford and Duncannon to his rear.

WITHDRAWAL FROM WATERFORD, DECEMBER 1649

Waterford was the only town in Ireland able to defeat Cromwell's personal efforts to take it. Its successful defence was due to Ormond's and Castlehaven's determination to reinforce it with Farrell's Ulster troops and all available supplies, and to Cromwell's inability to bring to bear against the town the overwhelming force needed to breach and assault its defences.[2] Cromwell's shortage of troops, due to the attrition caused by disease and his need to garrison so many captured towns and castles, made it impossible for him to surround and isolate the town. Furthermore, the rain-soaked ground was too soft to allow the English to bring their heavy guns ashore and to establish a battery to blow a breach in the town's walls. The English soldiers also were exhausted after four months of strenuous campaigning. Cromwell, 'finding the indisposition in point of health increasing and our foot falling sick near ten of a company every night they were upon duty', had only 3,000 healthy soldiers left in his marching army. Cromwell himself had been ill in mid-November owing to the effects of fatigue and the wet climate. Taking all of these factors into consideration, and believing that the royalists still had over 12,000 men under arms throughout Ireland, Cromwell, Jones and Ireton decided at a council of war to end the siege and put their weary soldiers into winter quarters.[3]

Cromwell lifted the siege of Waterford on 2 December 1649. His tired troops marched west towards Cork and Youghal, where Cromwell, Jones and Broghill had decided the army would be quartered. The troops suffered horribly from the incessant rain: as Cromwell noted, 'it being as terrible a day as ever I marched in, in all my life'.[4] The army reached Kilmacthomas on the River Mahon on 3 December, and crossed the rain-swollen river and proceeded towards Dungarvan the next day. Lord Broghill, who had taken Dungarvan without resistance on the 2nd, met Cromwell there on the 4th, reporting that he had brought 1,300 soldiers to Whitechurch, a small town west of Dungarvan. This reinforcement and the news that the royalist garrisons of Kinsale, Mallow and Bandon had declared for parliament raised Cromwell's spirits and greatly eased the material problems facing his army.[5]

Sad news accompanied this short run of good luck, however. According to Cromwell,

> The noble Lieutenant General [Michael Jones] . . . fell sick (we doubt upon a cold taken upon our late wet march and ill accommodation) and went to Dungarvan, where (struggling some four or five days with a pestilent and contagious spotted fever) he died. . . . Before that, my poor kinsman, Major Cromwell (if I may name him) died before Waterford of a fever; since that, two persons, eminently faithful, godly and true to you, Lieutenant-Colonel Wolf and Scout-Master-General Rowe, are dead at Youghal.[6]

Rumours and accounts claiming that Cromwell poisoned Michael Jones are unsupported.[7] Cromwell knew that he had lost a commander of great resolution, courage and skill. He also lost a friend with whom he had worked harmoniously since they first met in August. Cromwell had entrusted

Jones with independent commands against Duncannon and Kilkenny. There is no hint in any reliable source that he had anything but respect for Jones. Judging from Jones's remarkable successes in 1647 and 1649, it is likely that, had he lived, the war in Ireland would have been carried on more effectively with him as commander than it was to be by Henry Ireton in the period after Cromwell's departure. The saddened Lord Lieutenant and his army carried Jones's body to Youghal, where Cromwell gave a moving eulogy for one of the most successful commanders of the war.[8]

CROMWELL'S WINTER QUARTERS, DECEMBER 1649–JANUARY 1650

Cromwell's decision to go into winter quarters was unavoidable. The average strength of his regiments had fallen to 300–500 men each, and he had detached large garrisons to secure Drogheda, Trim, Dublin, Arklow, Wexford, New Ross and Carrick-on-Suir. Although 5,000 fresh soldiers were on their way from England, the first major contingents did not arrive before January.[9] Consequently, recuperation in winter quarters was essential. This respite cut two ways. While it allowed the English troops to recuperate, it also gave Ormond a chance to pull his coalition together and to organise a field force that might be able to face the English army successfully in battle. Further, the delay in the campaign meant added costs for the English Commonwealth and postponed Cromwell's return to England, where the threat to the newly constituted republic posed by royalist Scotland weighed heavily on the leaders of the government in London. It was therefore essential that Cromwell spend as little time as necessary in quarters before he resumed his assault on Catholic Ireland.

In Munster the defections in October and November of Inchiquin's garrisons to the parliamentarian cause was crucial to the success of Cromwell's strategy. Several thousand royalist soldiers deserted Ormond and joined Cromwell when his field strength was at its weakest. The Munster towns from Kinsale to Youghal were ideal places for his army to recuperate, recruit and re-equip. To take advantage of the housing and supplies in the widest possible area, Cromwell dispersed his army into regimental-sized garrisons in Cork, Youghal, Bandon, Carrick and Kinsale. Additional smaller forces controlled a ring of posts around Waterford, cutting that town off from re-inforcements and supplies.[10]

For two months Cromwell rested his regiments and prepared for his next move by concentrating his efforts on financial and logistical matters. His letters to parliament and the Council of State show his attention to the sinews of war, and especially to the need for the Westminster government to send a steady supply of money for him to pay his troops. His constant theme was that 'If the money out of England allotted to this army be not continued to us, the army will no ways be able to subsist, nor to prosecute your business.'[11]

The Council of State heeded these pleas, as did the Rump Parliament. Money and supplies, worth a total of £435,562, were sent to Ireland from March 1649 to 16 February 1650.[12] Cromwell and his commanders levied local assessments on the areas of Ireland under their control as well, using this money to pay for the garrisons protecting these towns from attacks by the Irish forces. Support from England did not cease after Cromwell's departure in May. For example, during the period from March 1649 to March 1656 money and supplies worth a total of £1,606,851 were sent to Ireland by the English government to pay and support its army, while a further £1,902,545 in cash and supplies was raised in Ireland.[13]

A large supply of manpower was crucial to Cromwell's strategy, requiring as it did the occupation of every major town in the island. Consequently, efforts had to be made to preserve the health of the forces already in Ireland, even as fresh troops were sent over from England. One of the more innovative things the English did during the Cromwellian conquest of Ireland was to set up a number of army hospitals in which sick or wounded soldiers could recuperate. Such a step was generally not necessary in England during the Civil Wars because incapacitated soldiers could be quartered in local homes, whose owners were paid to care for the soldiers. This system could not be used in Ireland. Consequently, Mr Linne, the Apothecary-General of the army, established two army hospitals in Dublin in the summer, and Cromwell established additional hospitals in Munster in December.[14] A surgeon and his assistants with medical chests accompanied each regiment, and an extra wagon or cart was provided to transport both the supplies and the sick soldiers. These provisions paid off, as thousands of soldiers recuperated and rejoined their regiments in time for the winter campaign in February.[15]

The difficulties of reinforcing Cromwell in Ireland should not be minimised. The English *Calendars of State Papers* are full of references to the problems associated with recruiting soldiers and marching them to the ports of embarkation. There were also many cases of fraud associated with the process of paying off soldiers' pay arrears before they were shipped to Ireland.[16] Complicating the process further, the Commonwealth was beginning to spend time and money on the efforts needed to prepare regiments in the north to face the growing royalist threat from Scotland.

In addition to the problems of paying and recruiting troops in England, there was the problem of shipping them across the Irish Sea in the middle of winter. For example, five ships attempted to sail from Minehead to Cork on 15 January, but while in the middle of St George's Channel they ran into gale-force winds. The entire flotilla foundered, and over 150 soldiers drowned. Such a loss could not have been of much help to recruiting efforts, as the *Diurnall of the Armies* reported that 'there cannot be less than one hundred widows and fatherless children or more in Minehead'.[17] In spite of such setbacks, the Commonwealth found ways to raise and ship thousands of soldiers to Ireland. As a result, by late January 1650 Cromwell's average regimental strength had risen to nearly 900 men, and additional regiments under Sir Hardress Waller and Oliver Cromwell's son Henry had arrived safely in Munster.[18]

Clothing and munitions were equally important to the recuperation of Cromwell's forces. In December and January parliament contracted for 17,950 sets of clothing for the infantry, including shoes, stockings, shirts and breeches, worth £19,437.[19] The mounted troops received 2,000 pairs of boots and stockings and 1,950 pairs of breeches in the same period. The Westminster government also sent a steady supply of arms and ammunition to Ireland, including 800 barrels of gunpowder, 3,790 pikes, 2,200 matchlock muskets, 1,060 pairs of pistols, 8,000 bandoleers and 8,000 knap-sacks.[20] The impact of adequate shoes and clothing on a winter campaign in Ireland cannot be overestimated. These supplies were essential to Cromwell's subsequent successes.

Special attention was paid by Cromwell, Broghill and Ireton to the morale of their troops as well. Cromwell visited every garrison in Munster in December and January at least once. He reminded the soldiers of what they were fighting for and emphasised the need for strict discipline.[21] He issued another proclamation to his soldiers forbidding looting and com-manding 'all soldiers to forbear such like practices upon pain of death. . . . But that they content themselves with peas, oats, hay, and such other forage, as the country affords, paying or giving tickets at such reasonable rates for the same.'[22] Cromwell's attention to the details of logistics, soldier morale and the need to maintain harmonious relations with the civilian population are the attributes of a great commander. Battlefield success is of no avail if one's army disintegrates or if the rapacious actions of one's soldiers drive the local population to desperation and then to rebellion. This was especially the case when the long-term objective was the restoration of English rule.

ORMOND'S WINTER QUARTERS, 1649–50

Ormond understood that his strategy for the first half of 1649 had failed. He had attempted to unify Protestant royalists, British settlers and Scots with Catholic Old English royalists against the parliamentarian garrisons in Ireland. This coalition failed to give him sufficient power to drive the English out of Ireland before Cromwell could bring England's military strength to bear on the 'Irish problem'. His Fabian strategy against the English after the battle of Rathmines failed to wear down the invading army to the point where the royalist forces could achieve local superiority and defeat the Cromwellians in battle. The steady loss of garrisons and towns weakened his cause logistically and politically. Because the numerically superior royalist coalition lacked adequate logistical resources to sustain sieges and an adequate artillery train to breach fortifications, small English garrisons could defend themselves from royalist field forces until superior English units arrived on the scene. Thus it was nearly impossible for the royalists to recover fortified posts lost to Cromwell.

A steady diet of defeat helped split the royalist cause politically along religious lines. The defection of most of Inchiquin's garrisons in October and November and the destruction of the British settler and Scottish forces in Ulster in the same period left Ormond with no choice but increasingly to rely on Catholic Ireland. But Catholic religious and military leaders were deeply suspicious of him and his few remaining Protestant royalists and dissatisfied with his military leadership. For Ormond, going into winter quarters was a way to recuperate his military strength while finding a way to retain Catholic political and military co-operation in the royalist coalition.

Ormond dispersed his troops into winter quarters as soon as the English abandoned the siege of Waterford. His greatest military needs were to refresh and re-equip his troops and to find ways to sustain a field army capable of finally stopping the English advance when operations resumed. The crux of his difficulties was logistical. He wrote to Charles II, on 30 November, that 'While the 18,000 foot I mentioned in the last letter is correct [for the strength of his total forces], I can barely draw 5,000 foot and 1,300 horse into the field due to shortages of money and supplies.' Consequently, he had to 'disperse the army into garrisons and lesser bodies where there may be more probability of their subsistence'.[23]

His logistical problems, however, could only be solved if the Catholic towns of Munster were willing to provide quarters, pay and supplies for his troops. Unfortunately few towns were eager, or even willing, to help him. For example, the Mayor of Limerick wrote to Ormond on 4 December asking not to be forced to accept a troop of Ormond's cavalry on account of the city's poverty. Clanricarde reported to him that the citizens of Clonmel had treated Colonel Flaherty's Catholic regiment badly, and he threatened to withdraw the unit to Connacht if it was not treated better. Mayor Lyvett of Waterford wrote to Ormond asking that as few troops as possible be stationed in his town, even though it was ringed by Cromwellian garrisons.[24] Only the last of these towns was cut off from local markets by Cromwell, but the power of Cromwell's reputation also weighed heavily, as Ormond bitterly noted in his report to the king on 30 November:

> We are superior to Cromwell's army. Yet towns fifty miles from him are sending ambassadors to entreat him for terms to allow him to turn Roman Catholic churches into stables and hospitals.[25]

Clanricarde experienced the same problem of extraordinarily low morale in Connacht, where he was trying to rally the population to defend itself from the advance of Coote in the north and Cromwell in the south. He noted that officers clamoured for arrears and recruits wanted more pay, as if they are not interested in the danger of the kingdom. . . . Their stupidity in general [is] so incredible as that either they apprehend no danger near them or [are] so desperately dejected as scarce any will afford a helping hand to their own preservations; and for anything I can observe the clergy that ought to dispose them to better resolutions, are in dead silence.[26]

THE SYNOD OF CLONMACNOISE, DECEMBER 1649

The Catholic hierarchy manifested the same malaise. Recognising the dangerous military position of Catholic Ireland, the prelates held a synod in Clonmacnoise to search for ways to energise the Irish resistance to Puritan England. On 4 December they issued their first proclamation to the laity of Ireland telling them not to lose themselves 'with vain expectations of conditions to be had from that merciless enemy'.[27] However, they were not certain as to whether or not they wanted to continue the struggle under Ormond's command or to appoint a new leader.

During the synod the bishops and Ormond discussed the best ways to invigorate the coalition's military efforts. Ormond was aided by the Bishop of Clogher, Heber MacMahon, in his efforts to keep the coalition together and to retain his authority.[28] The bishops wanted Ormond to appoint more Catholic officers to command and to serve on his personal staff. They wanted assurances that their clergy could retain control of the churches then in their possession. Finally, they wanted greater influence in the formulation of Ormond's military plans. Ormond offered concessions where he could in appointments, naming, for example, the Catholic general Thomas Preston to assume command in Waterford. He refused to dilute his military authority, but promised clearer recognition by him, as the king's Lord Lieutenant, of the position of the Catholic clergy in Ireland. In return, the bishops declared it essential for Catholics to remain united with Ormond against the common and most dangerous enemy — Oliver Cromwell — who, they believed, was determined to extirpate the Catholic religion.[29]

The political results of the synod were favourable for the royalists and Ormond. The Commissioners of Trust continued to be his advisory council, and his military authority theoretically remained intact. The bishops made a strong pitch to the Catholic population to remain loyal to the king and to Ormond. However, the proclamations of the clergy could not pay, feed, arm or recruit Ormond's army. Catholic towns continued to be unwilling to shelter Ormond's troops, causing royalist commanders such as Inchiquin to garrison their troops forcibly on towns like Kilmallock.

The proclamations of the Clanmacnoise gathering reached Cromwell in January. The references to his desire to extirpate Catholicism particularly enraged him. He recognised the potential impact which a call for Catholic unity could have on his efforts to further divide the Old English from the Gaelic Irish. Cromwell took the trouble to write a long response to the bishops' message in a letter entitled 'For the Undeceiving of Deluded and Seduced People'. Cromwell presented his view of seventeenth-century Irish history in this letter. The Irish, he declared, had caused the current war because they had ungratefully risen against the English, who had brought the blessings of civilisation and religious light to Ireland: 'You, unprovoked, put the English to the most unheard-of and most barbarous massacre (without respect of sex or age).' He attacked everything from the Petrine doctrine to the clergy, ridiculing the bishops' notion that Charles Stuart stood for anything that anyone in Ireland should be fighting to defend.[30]

Cromwell's declaration shows that his view of the 1641 rising deeply affected his thoughts and actions towards all Catholics in Ireland during his campaign in 1649–50. It explains but does not excuse his actions at Drogheda and Wexford and his continued callousness on the execution of priests simply because they were priests.[31] Additionally, his response shows how aware he was of the importance of propaganda in a military campaign in a hostile country. Hence his attempt to convince the Old English to abandon the coalition with the Gaelic Irish and the Catholic hierarchy, even though his response could not have won Catholic hearts and minds. His complete rejection of the Roman Catholic faith indicates that the strategist and propagandist in Cromwell always gave way to the Puritan, even at the expense of driving the Old English Catholics further into union with the Old Irish.[32]

While Cromwell's response to the bishops may have helped unite Ormond's coalition, Ormond could not use such declarations to feed and pay his forces any more than he could the fine words of the bishops. He knew that time was against his efforts to prepare a field force that could defeat Cromwell's next moves, and without such a force the initiative would remain with the English.[33]

Cromwell, in a letter to parliament that is not published in Abbott's collection of his letters and speeches, estimated that Ormond and the Catholic clergy were resolved to continue the struggle together:

> The affairs of the enemy are much endeavoured to be brought under the inspection and government of the Roman Clergy. To which end they have had some meeting at Kilkenny and elsewhere to new model their armies, and indeed to unite themselves upon principles wherein they will give the precedence to their religion avowedly, and yet make use of the king of the Scots name that they may be able to say with others, they reject not, but are for their king's interest, and by declaring their interest as is before expressed, they expect cheerful assistance from a hearty conjunction amongst themselves: As also foreign Catholic aids against the spring.
>
> This enclosed book was the result of one of their late conventions. The war thus stated will have good harmony with Montrose and all his participants. I hope all honest men's minds will be opened.

I hear they have had disputes about their general. It is said Antrim was named and refused. They offer as I hear to pay 6,000 foot and 2,000 horse at the Church's charge.[34]

THE WINTER CAMPAIGN: CROMWELL'S PREPARATIONS, DECEMBER 1649–JANUARY 1650

Military operations did not cease completely while the main armies were in winter quarters and the Catholic clergy and Ormond worked to patch up their coalition. In Leinster the royalists captured Enniscorthy by bribing several members of the garrison to allow women and alcohol into the castle. Once the guards were incapacitated by drink, the Irish entered the gates, putting the garrison commander, Captain Todd, and five soldiers to the sword. The other twenty-five members of the garrison were taken as prisoners to Kilkenny and were later exchanged for a Major Rochford, held as an English prisoner.[35]

Further south, Colonel Edward Wogan and troops from the Waterford garrison made an attempt to capture Passage Fort, one of the critical posts astride Waterford's communications to the sea. Unfortunately for Wogan's men, in the midst of their approach march to the fort, Colonel Jerome Sankey and several troops of English cavalry surprised them while they were in the open and unprepared for combat, inflicting hundreds of casualties and capturing Wogan.[36] Cromwell also tightened the noose around Waterford in December by capturing several small castles north of the town, making it harder for the royalists to supply Waterford or to use its garrison to threaten his columns when they moved into Tipperary and Kilkenny.

Ormond knew that the winter respite would not last long. In late November he had correctly predicted the nature of Cromwell's strategy for the winter campaign that was about to open in January:

His design is evidently first to [take] the sea coast and then [to capture,] by degrees, the inland towns and counties wherein, though he be far advanced, yet if he meet any sign [of successful resistance] it will so much discourage his men and give life to the country.[37]

By late January Cromwell had received two fresh regiments from England and filled his other regiments with recruits and recuperated soldiers. He suspected that a message was coming from parliament requesting him to return to England to consult with the Council of State about the worsening situation in the north. It was becoming evident that Charles II was negotiating seriously with the Scots in the hope that he could return to Scotland and from there launch his attempt to claim his father's English throne.[38] None the less, Cromwell knew that the conquest of Ireland was incomplete. Until all of the Munster and Leinster towns had been captured and garrisoned, it would still be possible for Ormond to continue the war effort while the English Commonwealth had to face a war with the Scots. In such a situation, the royalists might be able to recapture the ground they had lost in Ireland. Therefore it was imperative for the English to launch the next phase of their conquest as soon as possible.

The unexpectedly mild weather made a winter campaign feasible because of the dryer than normal road conditions in January 1650.[39] The adequate logistical support sent from England by the Westminster government also helped to make it possible. In the previous years of war in Ireland, military operations had been constrained in winter by the amount of animal fodder available to feed the baggage and artillery draft animals. Extended campaigns had to wait for a sufficient growth of grass to feed the horses. Cromwell, however, could move his cavalry and artillery horses before the spring growth because large supplies of oats had been shipped for them from England to Munster in December and January, and because his troops had enough cash to purchase animal fodder and food from local stocks.[40] All the same, his decision to move out of winter quarters in late January took both his own government and Ormond by surprise.

Cromwell's campaign plan for his offensive was audacious and somewhat complex. He divided his army in Munster into three columns (see Map 9).[41] Two of these were to march north on separate routes from the Munster ports to overrun the counties of Limerick, Tipperary and Kilkenny. These columns were to capture all of the major crossing-points over the Blackwater and Suir rivers. Next they were to clear all enemy posts from the major towns along the roads from the southern ports to Cashel, Clonmel and Kilkenny. Then they would attack the largest royalist garrisons in the area, at Clonmel and Kilkenny. The third force, commanded by Lord Broghill, was to provide protection to the western flank of the columns moving north. Broghill's mission was to prevent royalist forces in western Limerick from moving through Mallow towards Cork and Youghal. Another small army, under the command of Colonel Hewson, was to move south-west from Dublin to link up near Kilkenny with the two columns advancing north.

The capture of the major towns and castles of the inland counties of Kildare, Kilkenny, Tipperary and Limerick would secure the resources of those counties for the English while denying them to the Catholic coalition. The royalists would then be confined to Connacht for support and recruitment, making it possible for Cromwell to hand over command in Ireland safely to Henry Ireton for the mopping-up operations. The columns moving north and the forces coming from Dublin would form a pincer movement intended to catch and destroy a royalist field army in the vicinity of Kilkenny.

THE WINTER CAMPAIGN, JANUARY–FEBRUARY 1650

Cromwell set his plan in motion on 29 January 1650, when he led fifteen troops of cavalry and 300 infantrymen from Youghal to Mallow. On 31 January he took the castle of Kilbeheny, leaving a thirty-man garrison, and continued on to Clogheen. Cromwell, with few infantry and no artillery, hoped by his rapid advance to take royalist castles and towns by surprise. This tactic worked well. At Clogheen Cromwell captured the fortified house of Sir Richard Everard without firing a shot, and his cavalry took Rehill Castle, on the Mallow road nine miles south-west of Cahir, simply by summoning its garrison of Ulster foot and horse to surrender on easy terms. The capture of these posts between Mallow and Cahir opened the route to the crossings over the River Suir near Cahir.[42]

On 29 January Lord Broghill set his force in motion from Cork to screen the western flank of the offensive. Accompanied by 700 cavalrymen, 500 infantrymen and two siege guns, he moved north to attack Old Castletown, near Kildorrery, north-east of Mallow. At first the castle refused to surrender, but after Broghill had blown a breach in its wall with ten cannon shots the Irish submitted. Broghill 'gave quarter for life and their wearing apparel to the private soldiers, but the officers to be at his discretion. That thereupon by advice, he caused all those [six] officers to be shot to death, to affright those little castles from so peremptorily standing out.'[43] With this bloody business out of the way, Broghill led his troops to Mallow, from where he could protect the western flank of the winter offensive. From that base he sent raiders west, over the mountains, to burn the home of Sir Edward Fitzharris at Cloughnosty, and another force well to the east to Newcastle, on the Suir.[44] By these moves, Broghill secured the flank, opened the crossings over the Blackwater from Mallow to Fermoy for the movement of supplies to Cromwell's and Reynolds's columns, and secured a crossing over the Suir at Newcastle, south of Clonmel. He now controlled a territory which also could pay £1,500 per month for the support of the parliamentarian forces.[45]

As Broghill worked in the west, Cromwell continued his advance to the north-east by fording the rain-swollen Suir near Rochestown, four miles south of Cahir, 'with very much difficulty, and from thence to Fethard' in County Tipperary.[46] Cromwell's men reached Fethard on the evening of 2 February, finding shelter from the rain in the ruins of an old abbey on the outskirts of town. Fethard had 'a very good wall with round and square bulwarks, after the old manner of fortification'. If its garrison had defended it resolutely, it would have been very difficult for Cromwell to capture with fewer than 1,200 men and no artillery.[47] However, Cromwell was able to convince the governor, Lieutenant-Colonel Pierce Butler, that his force was a strong advance guard of a well-equipped army. 'After almost the whole night spent in treaty, the town was delivered to me the next morning, upon

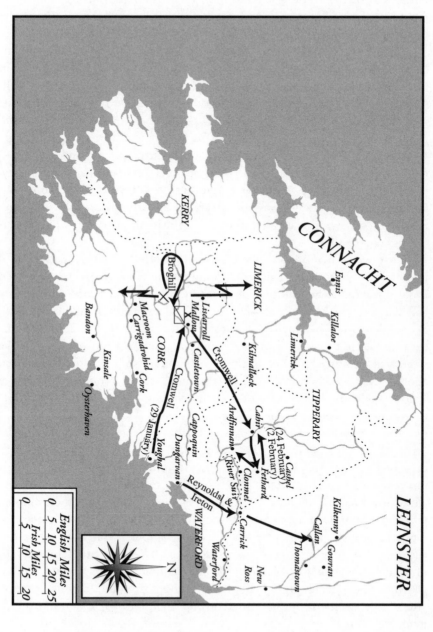

9. Cromwell's Winter Campaign, February 1650

terms we usually call honourable; which I was willinger to give, because I had little above two-hundred foot, and neither ladders nor guns . . . there being about seventeen companies of the Ulster foot in Cashel, about five miles from thence.' The fear induced in the Cashel garrison by Cromwell's reputation for ruthlessness may account for that force's hasty departure the next day and the surrender of Cashel without a formal summons.[48]

Cromwell's march from Youghal to Mallow (30–40 miles) and his advance into enemy-held territory from Mallow to Fethard (40–50 miles) in five days was a remarkable example of his audacity and military skill. Travelling light, his column took the castles essential to his forward thrust without being slowed by artillery or large numbers of infantry. Cromwell planned Broghill's activities to protect his advance and to seize the bridge over the Suir at Newcastle that would allow an artillery train and supplies to follow. He placed himself at the head of the most dangerous and critical prong of his offensive, ensuring a vigorous execution of the manoeuvre. Cromwell's risks paid off, as the surprised garrisons along the way surrendered, giving him a defensible bridgehead in County Tipperary at Fethard and Cashel.

Cromwell's manoeuvres were risky. If royalist garrisons had resisted resolutely at Fethard and Cahir, the timing of the offensive would have been badly disrupted. The vigorous defences by the Irish garrisons of Kilkenny and Clonmel in March and May showed what great damage could have been inflicted on the English attackers. Delays caused by the need to bombard and assault every major castle and garrison in Munster would have weakened Cromwell's columns, slowing the offensive just as the threat from Scotland increased in England. Furthermore, more protracted defensive actions might have given Ormond, Inchiquin and Clanricarde enough time to organise an effective counter-offensive in either Munster or Leinster.

The timing and speed of Cromwell's winter offensive, however, shocked Ormond and his generals. They recognised that Cromwell's goal was to capture Clonmel and Kilkenny, but they found it difficult to bring their forces out of winter quarters quickly enough to delay or engage with the advancing English columns. A shortage of money remained their chronic problem, as the remaining Irish-held towns refused to contribute money for forces to be used to defend other places or regions.[49] Garrisons refused to leave their winter quarters, perhaps fearing that some other unit might move into their comfortable quarters. For example, when Ormond tried to get Major-General Hugh O'Neill to unite troops from his Clonmel garrison with Castlehaven's troops near Kilkenny, O'Neill refused, asking instead for reinforcements.[50]

A serious outbreak of the plague made matters even more difficult for the Ormondist coalition. The bubonic plague had arrived in western Ireland in July 1649. Clanricarde soon reported to Ormond that the disease was decimating the population of Galway, the last major port in Catholic hands which was not blockaded by the Commonwealth's navy. Plague soon raged in Kilkenny, weakening the resolve to resist of soldier and civilian alike. Hugh O'Neill's garrison in Clonmel reported similar visitations of the disease.[51] The economic effects of the plague on the Catholic cause were nearly as bad as the demographic and psychological, further weakening Ormond's and Clanricarde's efforts to find money to pay their forces and the ability of large garrisons to subsist locally.[52] Cromwell's columns seem to have been less affected by the plague, possibly because they were operating in the field instead of being concentrated in quarters in towns.[53]

Amidst the ravages of the plague, Cromwell's moves, along with those of the other columns of his offensive, paralysed the royalist high command. No one knew for sure which garrison would be next. Ormond proved unable to impose his will upon the forces scattered in winter quarters throughout Limerick, Tipperary and Kilkenny. The work of Colonel Reynolds and Major-General Ireton, in command of the eastern column, made matters worse for the royalists.

Colonel Reynolds led the eastern pincer of the offensive from Youghal and Dungarvan on 29 January. He moved with sixteen troops of cavalry (about 900 men) and 2,000 infantry north-east to Carrick, where he crossed the Suir on the bridge held by the English garrison. Ireton followed with the reserve of infantry and a train of siege artillery.[54] These forces constituted the main thrust of Cromwell's offensive. They were equipped to carry out sieges against Clonmel and Kilkenny, both of which were well fortified and strongly garrisoned, once Cromwell's and Hewson's pincers had isolated these towns. Perhaps because Cromwell himself was with the forces to the west, Ormond failed to recognise the main thrust of the offensive until too late.

By 3 February Reynolds had reached Callan in County Kilkenny, where he drove off a force of royalist cavalry and invested the three castles which dominated the town. Reynolds offered terms to the two smaller castles, but their garrisons refused to accept, forcing Reynolds to order assaults supported by artillery placed within 200 yards of the defences. The assaults succeeded, with few casualties to the attackers. The 200 soldiers holding the castles were executed.[55]

Major-General Richard Butler surrendered the third castle at Callan on terms which allowed his garrison to march away without weapons. He remained as Cromwell's prisoner to be exchanged for officers held by Ormond. During these operations Cromwell, fresh from his capture of Fethard and Cashel, joined Reynolds at Callan, where a substantial supply of grain was reportedly captured as well.[56] After leaving a garrison of infantry and cavalry in Callan, Cromwell moved his main force back to Fethard and Cashel, 'where . . . [we are resting,] having good plenty of both horse meat and man's meat for a time; and being indeed, we may say, even almost in the heart and bowels of the enemy'.[57] At the same time he sent Reynolds to capture the castle at Knocktopher, twelve miles south of Kilkenny. The swift surrender of Knocktopher opened a good communications route between Callan and New Ross.

The English pincers were progressively isolating Kilkenny and Clonmel while securing Cromwell's communications between those places and his ports in Munster and Leinster. This meant that Cahir and Ardfinnan, both on major crossing-points over the River Suir, had to be taken, since the English had no bridges over the Suir west of Carrick. To gather enough soldiers to carry out these operations, Cromwell shifted troops from Mallow to Fermoy, freeing Colonel Ewer's regiment of cavalry there from garrison duty so that it could join the main force.[58] Broghill was expected to cover the western flank with fewer troops. At a council of war on 17 February, Cromwell, Ireton and Reynolds decided to continue the offensive against Clonmel and Kilkenny by completing their isolation and then by moving the reunited army, along with its siege artillery, against Kilkenny.

Ormond responded to the English moves against Kilkenny by evacuating the Confederate Commissioners of Trust and his own staff from the city in mid-February. He went to Limerick and Connacht to consult with the Catholic hierarchy and Clanricarde about the best way to fend off the English advance. He placed Castlehaven in command of the operations to defend Kilkenny in his absence. Castlehaven had between 3,000 and 4,000 men available to serve as a field force against the English columns, but he felt this force was too weak to attack Reynolds's column coming from the south or Hewson's approaching Kilkenny from the north-east.[59] As a result, English operations continued largely unhindered.

English attacks on Ardfinnan Castle and the town of Cahir followed soon thereafter. Ireton led the assault against the castle overlooking the Suir bridge at Ardfinnan at 4 a.m. on 10 February, killing thirteen men of the garrison before the place surrendered. This was an important triumph because, as Cromwell noted, Ardfinnan was 'a considerable pass [over the Suir], and the nearest to our pass at Cappoquin over the Blackwater, whither we can bring guns, ammunition, or other things from Youghal by water, and over this pass to the army'.[60] Cahir presented special difficulties to the attackers and was a harder nut to crack.

Cahir was the last major Catholic-held town in the vicinity of Clonmel. It controlled a crossing over the Suir between Cromwell's garrison at Fermoy and his advanced positions at Fethard and Callan. Its capture was important logistically for Cromwell; conversely, its defence was essential for royalist communications into Clonmel from Limerick. The castle of Cahir was situated on an island in the Suir accessible only across a drawbridge. The garrison's commander was Ormond's half-brother, Captain George

Mathews. Hugh O'Neill had recently reinforced Mathews's garrison with a company of Ulster infantry, giving Mathews a reliable force with which to face the coming onslaught.[61]

Cromwell moved his army from Fethard to Cahir on 24 February. He brought sufficient artillery and infantry to make a breach and carry out an assault if necessary. However, his first move was to offer generous terms of surrender to Mathews, in the hope that he could take Cahir quickly and intact.[62] Mathews ignored the summons, and Cromwell ordered an immediate assault by his infantry against the defences on the north side of the Suir, in front of the drawbridge. This position was defended by the company of O'Neill's Ulstermen which had joined the garrison. The Irish met Cromwell's first attack head-on, preventing the English from reaching the drawbridge. After repulsing the first assault, however, the Ulstermen asked Mathews to let them cross the drawbridge into the stronger confines of the castle, as he had promised to do. Mathews refused.

At this point in the action the English began to establish their artillery battery to blow a breach in the walls. Cahir, like most Irish castles, lacked the low, thick walls of the modern artillery fortress, known as the *trace italiene*, making it vulnerable to the same tactics which Cromwell had used at Drogheda. Observing the establishment of the siege battery, the Ulstermen prudently sought a parley with Cromwell. Mathews, seeing the futility of further defence against Cromwell's guns, decided to join the parley.[63] Cromwell granted generous terms to Mathews, similar to those he had granted the garrison at Callan. The troops and their priests were allowed to march away with horses, arms and baggage, while Mathews was allowed to keep his and his wife's personal property.[64]

Ormond was so furious at his brother's surrender of Cahir without a protracted struggle that he ordered him to appear before him and explain his failure.[65] Mathews did so, asserting that the castle was ill-provisioned with food and gunpowder, that its walls could not withstand the bombardment of modern cannon, that there were no modern breastworks or flankers, and that the local population had refused to pay their assessments to sustain the garrison and finance improvements. To top off this dismal list, he noted that both his Old Irish and Old English troops were preparing to desert or mutiny.[66]

The easy capture of Cahir was an important victory for Cromwell. Clonmel was cut off from direct access to Limerick. The English captured a large supply of grain in Cahir and a bridge over the River Suir. The Catholic troops from the Cahir garrison marched sixteen miles east to Clonmel, where they would have a chance to distinguish themselves against the English.[67] During the following week Cromwell sent a force commanded by Colonel Sankey to capture castles at Goldenbridge and Dundrum. Sankey met some resistance, receiving a wound in his hand at the assault against Dundrum. But both places fell quickly, allowing the English to complete the ring of strongholds which cut off the best avenues of approach for any Catholic forces trying to march from Limerick to relieve Clonmel.[68]

HEWSON'S ADVANCE FROM DUBLIN, FEBRUARY–MARCH 1650

While Cromwell's Munster columns were on the march from the south in February, another major force under the command of Colonel John Hewson was operating from Dublin in a drive to the south-west towards Carlow. Hewson's design was to expand the area to the west of Dublin held by the parliamentarian forces. Once that was done, his mission was to cut Kilkenny off from relief from the north and north-west and to meet Cromwell's main army somewhere near Kilkenny, where he could join in the attack on that city.

Cromwell had appointed Colonel Hewson as governor and commander of Dublin in September 1649. Hewson found Dublin hedged in from the west by a series of royalist-held castles and small towns. As late as December there were no English garrisons in Kildare west of Naas.[69] On 26 February, as the first phase in his part of the winter offensive, Hewson led a force of 3,000 men and three siege guns into County Kildare. His goal was to take the strong castles held by his enemies at Kilmaog, in the Isle of Allen, and at Ballisonan. Upon the news of his approach, the royalist garrisons in Kilmaog, Maryborough (Portlaoise) and Athy destroyed their defences and fled to the west. Hewson continued his march to the double-moated fortress of Ballisonan, north-east of Carlow, without resistance. After his summons to the garrison to surrender was refused, he set up his siege artillery in a position to destroy the main tower of the defences. He also built a fort around his siege battery to protect it from the rear in the eventuality that Castlehaven might come to the relief of the place with his army from Kilkenny.[70]

Castlehaven failed to intervene. On 1 March the governor of Ballisonan chose to surrender on terms which allowed the garrison to march away with arms and colours. This easy triumph, along with the abandonment of Athy and Maryborough by the Catholics and their garrisoning by the English, opened the road from Naas to Carlow, allowing Hewson to continue his advance to join Cromwell.[71] Hewson next moved to Castledermot, where he hoped to find and fight Castlehaven's field force of 4,000 men. However, Castlehaven was unable to gather an army, allowing Hewson to capture and garrison Castledermot before returning to Dublin to replenish his supplies.[72]

After three days rest in Dublin, Hewson again led his army south, carrying fourteen days' supply of food in wagons and knapsacks. While on the march, Hewson received a letter from Ireton ordering him to capture Leighlinbridge, a town with a good bridge over the River Barrow. Ireton ordered this move to open overland communications between Dublin and Cromwell's forces in Munster.[73]

Hewson marched his force to Leighlinbridge without opposition from Castlehaven or Lord Dillon, the commander of the royalist forces in King's County (Offaly). This lack of response was astonishing. Dillon should have been able to attack Hewson's open flank as he marched south, thus hindering his advance. Lord Dillon's failure to resist Hewson prompted Clanricarde's secretary to write that while Dillon had been claiming £2,000 in monthly contribution for his forces from County Kildare, 'the truth is, they are men in the air and not visible'.[74] Hewson's advance was squeezing the royalist forces in Kilkenny in a vice between his and Cromwell's troops. Ormond, realising the danger of encirclement, had already withdrawn the Confederate Commissioners of Trust and his council from Kilkenny, leaving Castlehaven in command of the forces in the area.[75] Castlehaven had too few men to stop either wing of the English envelopment because Catholic garrisons would not leave their quarters to join him. His hope for timely support from Owen Roe O'Neill's main army in Cavan was slim, since that force had not yet chosen a successor to O'Neill and remained, as ever, short of money and munitions. Similarly, Castlehaven found Lord Dillon unable or unwilling to march south to help him resist the enemy's main army.[76]

Hewson arrived in Leighlinbridge on 18 March. That afternoon he summoned the garrison's commander, Captain Percy Brereton, to surrender or face the inevitable slaughter of a successful assault. Brereton capitulated the next day on terms which allowed the garrison to march away, giving the English an important bridge over the Barrow. He also surrendered 800 bushels of grain and 200 muskets in the town, providing Cromwell's offensive with welcome supplies. Leaving a strong garrison in Leighlinbridge, Hewson continued his march south to Gowran, a village and castle twelve miles east of Kilkenny.[77]

Castlehaven was unable to respond effectively to Hewson's moves owing to his shortage of provisions and his need to maintain strong garrisons in Clonmel and Kilkenny.[78] His only important success against the offensive was his capture of Hewson's garrison at Athy, but this minor triumph brought no relief to the desperate situation around Kilkenny since it came too late to divert Hewson. Castlehaven remained in the vicinity of Kilkenny with a force of cavalry for the next few weeks, but he could find no way to avert the hammer-blows about to strike the former Confederate capital.

While Hewson was dealing with Leighlinbridge, Cromwell and Reynolds captured Grennan Castle and Thomastown, to the south of Kilkenny, giving the garrisons easy terms.[79] Cromwell's capture of these places, along with Hewson's of Leighlinbridge, cut Kilkenny off from all relief and opened communications between the English positions in Leinster and Munster. Subsidiary operations led by Colonel Cook, from the garrison in Wexford, also restored Enniscorthy to English control and eliminated organised resistance in County Wexford.[80]

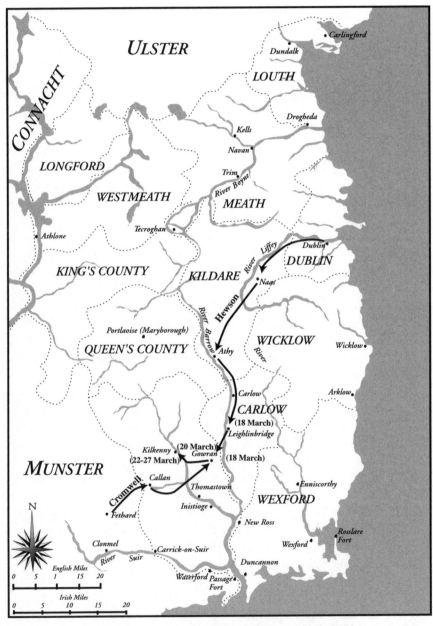

10. *Hewson's Winter Campaign, February–March 1650*

On 20 March Hewson's column met Cromwell's and Ireton's at Gowran. The governor of the castle, a Kentishman named Colonel Hammond, refused Cromwell's offer of generous terms of surrender, forcing Cromwell to deploy his artillery and prepare for an assault. On 21 March the guns opened fire, making a small breach in the wall. Seeing this, Hammond asked for a treaty, but Cromwell refused to deal with him. Instead Cromwell informed the soldiers in the garrison that he would give them 'quarter for their own lives', which they quickly accepted. The soldiers surrendered Colonel Hammond and their officers to Cromwell, who then gave orders for all but one of them to be shot, and for a priest captured in the castle to be hanged.[81]

THE BATTLE FOR KILKENNY, MARCH 1650

With Gowran in his hands, Cromwell had completed the isolation of Kilkenny. On 18 March he ordered Ireton to move the heavy artillery from Fethard to Gowran. On 22 March Cromwell led his army from Gowran, across the River Nore at Bennettsbridge, and north along the road known as the *Boher na Thoundish* to within a mile of Kilkenny Castle.

Castlehaven meanwhile had moved his army of 3,000 men to Ballyragget, a place that he claimed in his memoirs was seven miles north of Kilkenny, but which is really more like twelve miles distant. There he tried unsuccessfully to convince Lord Dillon to join him with the forces from Leinster.[82] Ormond by this time was well to the west, trying to rally support in Limerick. Outnumbered and poorly supplied, Castlehaven was able only to observe the English assaults on Kilkenny from a distance.

Kilkenny was one of the largest towns in Ireland. Kilkenny Castle, the home of the Marquis of Ormond, dominated the town, which in turn was divided into two parts (see Map 11). The High Town, next to the castle, was surrounded by a strong wall connected to the castle. The Irish Town, as it was called, was adjacent to the High Town on its north side. To the east, across the Nore, was a walled suburb as well, connected to the High Town by St John's Bridge.[83] This series of self-contained fortifications promised to be a difficult nut to crack if the garrison were to hold out resolutely.

The garrison and local population, however, had been the victims of the plague for the past several months. Fewer than 400 soldiers were still alive out of the 1,200 men whom Castlehaven had sent to garrison the town. Consequently, the mayor and city fathers were responsible for the defence of the Irish Town, while the soldiers held the High Town and the castle.[84] In spite of the immense odds against him, the governor, Sir Walter Butler, planned to 'maintain this city for his majesty, which, by the power of God, I am resolved to do', as he told Cromwell when the latter summoned him to surrender on 22 March.[85]

On the following morning the English tried to take the Irish Town by thrusting a cavalry regiment towards its gate. This attempt failed, as the townsmen stood firm. At the same time the attackers seized St Patrick's Church, just outside the south-western wall near a gate, and there established a battery of three cannon aimed towards a portion of the wall that was not flanked by other defences.

Seeing that the townsmen and garrison were going to resist vigorously, Cromwell planned a two-pronged assault. One infantry regiment, commanded by Colonel Hewson, would assault into the breach which the guns were going to establish near St Patrick's Church. Another regiment of 1,000 infantry, commanded by Colonel Ewer, was simultaneously to attack the Dean's Gate on the west side of the Irish Town, hoping to burn or batter it down.[86]

The English siege guns began to fire early on the morning of 25 March, and by noon a breach had been created by the 100 rounds fired at the wall near St Patrick's. Sir Walter Butler did not remain idle. As the English guns were firing he had his soldiers construct two retrenchments or counterworks opposite the inside of the breach. His troops palisaded these works and lined up behind them awaiting the English assault.[87]

When the signal to attack was given, Ewer's regiment charged the gate of the Irish Town, capturing it without significant resistance owing to the panicked flight of the townsmen-defenders. Once inside, the troops secured St Canice's Cathedral on the high ground overlooking Irish Town and advanced south towards the wall separating the High Town from the Irish Town. Ewer attempted to fight his way across the small stream that divided the two parts of the city near its juncture with the River Nore, in the north-east corner of the High Town. But the townsmen held their ground, inflicting forty or fifty casualties. Ewer also failed to take the gate in the centre of the High Town's north wall.

The assault did not proceed with equal success at the breach in the south wall of the High Town. There the attackers, led by Lieutenant-Colonel Axtell and Colonel Hewson, charged into the breach and were met by a withering fire from Butler's soldiers. Hewson claims that the signal to attack was given prematurely, before his men were ready, and that they were repulsed because the defenders had time to prepare to meet the onslaught. This might be true, but his claim that only four or five men were wounded does not agree with Cromwell's account or the predictable outcome of such an assault.[88] Cromwell reported in his letter to parliament that 'Our men upon the signal fell on upon the breach, which indeed was not performed with usual courage nor success.'[89] In any case, Butler's cleverly posted troops killed and wounded thirty to forty attackers, including Hewson, who was wounded slightly. This was the first significant repulse the royalists had inflicted upon an English assault during the entire winter offensive. Butler's skilful defence, however, only postponed the inevitable.

Butler's men still held the High Town and the castle on the evening of 25 March, but they were hemmed in by a very angry Cromwell, with no

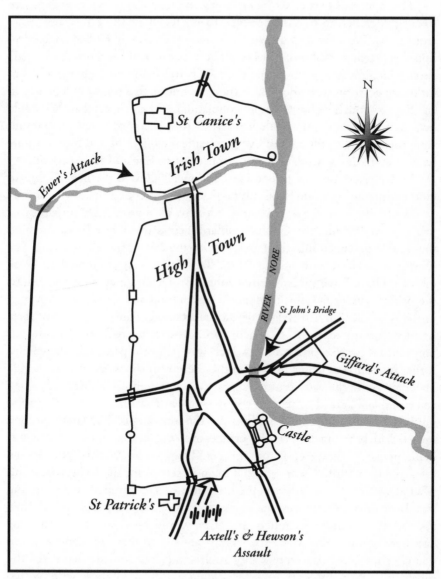

11. *Assault on Kilkenny, 25 March 1650*

hope of outside help reaching them. However, Cromwell renewed his offers to Butler to surrender on generous terms that would allow the townsmen to remain or to depart with their goods, and the garrison, with its priests, to march away.

This offer was part of Cromwell's new approach to convincing garrisons to surrender before it was necessary to go to all of the effort and losses required to take a town by a siege or an assault. Evidently he had concluded, from his defeat at Waterford in December, that fear of his reprisals to a garrison which refused terms before the assault was made no longer worked to make the garrison surrender. He turned, therefore, to a policy of leniency in an effort to convince the Catholic populations and garrisons that they could trust him to spare them and their priests if they accepted terms. The results were the same, but the method was dramatically different and more in tune with how the New Model Army had operated in England and Scotland.

Butler asked for time to consider. Cromwell allowed the negotiations to go on while he continued with his preparations for taking the city by force.

With the Irish Town in hand, Cromwell sent eight companies of infantry, commanded by Colonel Giffard, across the River Nore and into the weakly defended suburb of St John's, to the east of the High Town. The suburb was seized with minimal loss. This force next attempted to break into the High Town by crossing St John's Bridge and assaulting a gate near the bridge. Butler saw this manoeuvre developing and shifted enough men to the newly threatened wall to defeat the attack. Giffard's column lost forty or fifty men in the process. Then, as Cromwell related, '[we] made our preparations for a second battery, which was well near perfected: the enemy, seeing himself thus begirt', between the breach on the western side and the new battery on the east, 'sent for a treaty' on the night of 26 March.[90]

Cromwell agreed to receive commissioners from Butler and the mayor, but he refused to stop his operations. By the morning of 27 March a second breach had been made near the bridge over the Nore, and an assault was being prepared. However, before this could happen Sir Walter Butler agreed to surrender both the castle and the town in return for the favourable terms offered earlier. Cromwell accepted, feeling that continued battering and assaults against the defences would cost too many casualties and would damage the fortifications so much that they would be costly to repair. The agreement ending the siege of Kilkenny was signed that day. Cromwell had gained control of the second city of Ireland. He agreed to protect the inhabitants and their goods from his soldiers and to allow those who wanted to leave the town to do so. Butler and his men received a free pass to march away with arms, baggage and 150 horses, and were to be given an escort for the first six miles of their march away from Kilkenny.[91]

Cromwell had little time to reflect upon his success, since Clonmel remained well defended by Hugh O'Neill and his resolute garrison of

Ulstermen. Certainly the painful losses inflicted on the attackers by Butler's troops at the first breach in Kilkenny served as an indication to the Catholics of how a Cromwellian assault could be defeated. These defensive tactics were going to be repeated at Clonmel to great effect.

RESULTS OF THE WINTER OFFENSIVE

The winter offensive had lasted over fifty days. Cromwell had divided his army successfully into independent columns which allowed him to attack the inland counties of Munster on a broad front, while also protecting his forces from royalist counter-attacks from the west or north. His use of converging pincers around Kilkenny and Clonmel left these important towns isolated from reinforcements and supplies. His capture of the major crossing-points over the rivers Blackwater, Suir, Barrow and Nore left his communications secure and enabled him to move his artillery and infantry rapidly from west to east as needed. Conceptually, Cromwell's use of a double envelopment, with forces marching south from Dublin and north from the Munster ports, was brilliant and most successful. By early April 1650 only Clonmel held out in central Munster, and the Catholic and royalist forces had been pushed back against Connacht.

Cromwell's mastery of the logistical details of warfare had allowed him to refresh and reinforce his army in a brief period of winter quarters and then to conduct a remarkably successful campaign against the inland counties of Munster. By maintaining the initiative against his enemies, through the speed and geographical width of his manoeuvres, Cromwell kept Ormond and the royalists off balance. Thus he was able to capture their scattered garrisons piecemeal before Ormond, Castlehaven or Inchiquin could send help.

Ormond, Castlehaven and Clanricarde failed in their attempts to rally a overwhelming force against any of the English columns, largely as a result of their logistical difficulties and the refusal of regional commanders like Lord Dillon to obey orders to attend a rendezvous. English successes further divided the royalists politically, forcing Ormond to rely increasingly on the Catholic population of Ireland for his military power.

Consequently, during the campaign from 29 January to 30 March 1650 Cromwell's forces captured all of the major fortified towns of Munster except for Clonmel and Limerick, thereby denying the royalists the financial and logistical resources of one of the richest provinces in Ireland. The loss of Cahir, Cashel, Fethard, Callan and Kilkenny dramatically worsened the royalists' financial and logistical situation and destroyed any trust still held by Catholics in Ormond's leadership. Cromwell accomplished these military and political feats while suffering only moderate casualties. No military commander had ever done so much so rapidly in Ireland. His next objective was Clonmel.

6

The Collapse of the Royalist Coalition, March–May 1650

His Excellency's [Ormond's] army, through the aforementioned obstinacy and disobedience of the towns against receiving garrisons, was so far dispersed that there was no means of drawing them together; Neither if that were done, of keeping them in a body, for the country was destroyed and wasted, so that it could not supply him.

A Letter from Sir Lewis Dyve to the Lord Marquis of Newcastle,
10 July 1650[1]

The royalist situation looked bleak by March 1650, but it was not hopeless. Ormond and Clanricarde knew that Charles II was working hard to come to an agreement with the Scots which would bring the Scots again into the royalist war against the English Commonwealth.[2] A Scottish threat to the unpopular republican government in England would, they hoped, distract Cromwell and Ireton from completing their conquest of Ireland. For this strategy to succeed, the Irish royalists needed to inflict serious setbacks on English military progress in Ireland. A delay in the completion of the war in Ireland would increase the chances of a royalist uprising in England. The Commonwealth government's need to tax Englishmen more heavily to pay for the large armies it needed to deploy in Ireland and in the north of England would help precipitate such a revolt.

Clanricarde and Ormond hoped that they could wear down the English forces in Ireland through prolonged resistance by the remaining royalist strongholds.[3] Considerable military strength remained available to Ormond and his fellow-commanders, even after the heavy losses suffered in February and March. Clanricarde commanded a field army of 3,000 men in Connacht; Castlehaven had roughly 4,000 men in Munster; a total of at least 4,000 soldiers garrisoned Limerick and Waterford; and two regiments held Clonmel under the command of Hugh O'Neill. Inchiquin still commanded three weak regiments of cavalry in Kilmallock, and Colonel David Roche led another substantial force in County Kerry.[4] Manpower was not the royalists' most pressing problem. Financial and logistical shortages made it very difficult to pay, feed and arm the troops available.

Cromwell also faced serious problems which made it possible for the royalists to slow or even stop his advance. In early April he observed to William Lenthall, Speaker of the Parliament, that 'we have advanced our quarters towards the enemy a considerable way above Kilkenny', but 'our horse have not had one month's pay in five. We strain what we can that the foot may be paid, or else they would starve.' His need to garrison captured Irish towns further weakened his fighting strength, causing him to remind the Speaker that fresh troops were needed from England as soon as possible.[5] This was the situation which Ormond and the Irish tried to exploit in order to stop Cromwell's progress.

Even as the English forces were closing in on Kilkenny for an assault in late March, Ormond, Clanricarde and Castlehaven struggled to gather military forces to face Cromwell's columns in Munster and to take the offensive against parliament's army in Ulster.[6] These efforts depended for success ultimately on the willingness of the remaining Catholic-held areas of Ireland to pay their financial assessments to the Commissioners of Trust for the support of the troops and for the Catholic towns to provide bases for the remaining royalist units. Therefore Ormond worked to preserve his precarious political relations with the Catholic members of his coalition.

ORMOND'S POLITICAL PROBLEMS, MARCH 1650

The royalist alliance had been an uneasy one from the start. The defeats which Cromwell had inflicted upon its military forces since August steadily eroded Ormond's military and political positions. The relationship between the Protestant forces and the Catholic Old English in Ormond's coalition had been strained further in October when Owen Roe O'Neill agreed to join the cause with his Gaelic Irish forces, alienating many Protestant royalists in Ulster. The defection of so many of Inchiquin's garrisons to Cromwell and Lord Broghill in the late autumn only made matters worse for Ormond, Clanricarde and Castlehaven as they tried to rally forces and raise money to stop the English onslaught. Cromwell's winter offensive further strained relations within the royalist coalition as the Munster towns and castles fell like ripe fruit into his hands.

In December Ormond's discussions and agreement with the Catholic bishops at Clonmacnoise had papered over the divisions between the Protestants and the Catholics in the royalist cause, largely as a result of the conciliatory efforts of the Bishop of Clogher.[7] However, the deep distrust between the confessional factions continued to simmer. When Cromwell overran most of the inland counties of Munster in February and March, the political bonds of the royalist coalition snapped. In an effort to salvage what he could, Ormond met with the Catholic hierarchy in Limerick on 8 March 1650.

The bishops came prepared to shear Ormond of his military and political power and to expel Protestants from most positions of command. They demanded that Ormond accept the creation of a privy council which was to have veto power over his military decisions. Catholic bishops were to sit on this council as well. They further demanded that the size of the army be exactly stated and supernumerary forces disbanded to ease the logistical strain on the population. Strongholds garrisoned without the approval of the Catholic Commissioners of Trust were to be abandoned, and Catholic officers were to be given the same chances to command as Protestants.[8]

Ormond countered by pointing out that unless the people of Ireland trusted and obeyed him, there was little hope of success against the invaders. He demanded that the major towns, and especially the city of Limerick, accept garrisons of his choice and begin to pay their assessments for the support of the royalist army. Finally, he refused to countenance the dilution or undermining of his authority as Lord Lieutenant and commander of the king's forces in Ireland by the establishment of a privy council with veto authority over his military appointments and actions.[9]

Since both sides recognised their serious predicament, they worked out a compromise settlement. Ormond agreed to the demand that the size of the royalist forces be fixed and that free quarter no longer should be taken by the garrisons. He retained his power to select the officers of the army and his authority to make military decisions without having to submit them to the scrutiny of a privy council. For their part, the bishops promised to 'root out of men's hearts all jealousies and sinister opinions, conceived either against your Excellency or the present government. . . . And in conclusion, we leave to all impartial, judicious persons sad and serious considerations to think how incredible it is, that we should fail to oppose . . . a rebellious and malignant murderer of our late sovereign King Charles.'[10] Limerick and other towns agreed to accept Ormond's garrisons, but a substantial portion of those garrisons were to consist of Catholics and, if possible, Ulstermen. Such political manoeuvres were important. But the war could only be won by offensive military actions throughout Ireland which would prevent the English from massing their forces whenever and wherever they chose to attack.

THE ROYALIST COUNTER-OFFENSIVE IN THE NORTH, MARCH 1650

During the autumn of 1649 the successful progress of the parliamentary commanders in Ulster, Sir Charles Coote and Colonel Robert Venables, had driven organised royalist forces out of the coastal areas and most of the interior of the province. In the spring Coote and Venables hoped to push their offensive southwards into Connacht as well, but a shortage of ships prevented them from moving by sea the cannon and supplies needed to support a protracted campaign into the mountainous region of northern Connacht.[11] None the less, the threat of such operations forced the Connacht royalists to attempt to launch an offensive in March. This operation, to be commanded by Clanricarde, was to drive northwards from Sligo toward Derry to pre-empt Coote and Venables from launching an offensive in the other direction and to encourage O'Neill's Ulster army to attack the parliamentarian forces in Ulster.

Clanricarde, the royalist commander in Connacht, had failed to come to the assistance of Ormond during his summer offensive against Dublin in 1649. He also had failed to provide help to Ormond during Cromwell's autumn and winter campaigns in Leinster and Munster. Clanricarde had excused his failures to march his 3,000 soldiers to Ormond's aid by claiming, at various times, that shortages of money, the incidence of the plague in Galway and the need to defend the northern borders of Connacht from Sir Charles Coote prevented him from doing so.[12] These problems certainly made Clanricarde's tasks difficult. But he had consistently failed throughout the 1640s to aid Ormond materially, and he continued to find reasons to remain on the defensive in 1650. This situation, in a nutshell, showed how difficult it was for Ormond to co-ordinate royalist military activity.

As Cromwell was closing in on Kilkenny in March 1650 Ormond finally seemed to have convinced Clanricarde to launch an offensive against the English forces in south-western Ulster. However, even before he moved towards the royalist stronghold of Sligo, in northern Connacht, Clanricarde was getting cold feet, as was demonstrated when he observed to Ormond that if 'the forces of Munster and Leinster do not diligently attend Cromwell's motions, these parts in my absence, and especially my poor family here, will be in a very great danger'.[13] By 17 March Clanricarde was reporting that 'the want of provisions through the scarcity of carriages' had forced him to disperse his infantry into small garrisons in and around Sligo. The next day Clanricarde wrote again to tell Ormond that owing to the shortage of money, George Monro and his Scottish troops would not join the offensive against Sir Charles Coote. Clanricarde concluded, therefore, that he would have to retreat because he could not meet Monro's and 'his countrymen's greedy expectations'.[14] Clanricarde remained on the defensive, protecting the borders of Connacht but offering little help to Ormond in the crucial period from March to May.

Most of the Gaelic army of Owen Roe O'Neill remained equally inactive in winter quarters near Finea, County Longford. Since the death of O'Neill in November 1649 a major contingent of the Ulster army had served in Munster against Cromwell's onslaught. One thousand of these soldiers under the command of Lieutenant-General Richard Farrell played an important role in the successful defence of Waterford in November and remained in that city as the backbone of the garrison in the spring. Another contingent of two regiments under Colonel Hugh O'Neill, the nephew of Owen Roe O'Neill, was defending Clonmel in March.[15] The bulk of the Ulster army, however, remained in Finea, preparing to select a new commander to replace Owen Roe O'Neill. On 18 March the army's officers and the nobility and gentry of Ulster met at Belturbet to elect a new leader. The chief candidates included Lieutenant-General Farrell, Sir Phelim O'Neill, Randal MacDonnell, Earl of Antrim, Henry O'Neill, Owen's son, Hugh O'Neill, Owen's nephew, and Heber MacMahon, Bishop of Clogher.[16]

The most qualified candidates for military command were Richard Farrell, Hugh O'Neill and Henry O'Neill. However, Farrell was not popular with many Ulstermen, and Hugh O'Neill was away defending Clonmel. For reasons not entirely clear, the assembled Ulstermen voted unanimously for Heber MacMahon, Bishop of Clogher. This move may have been necessary to preserve unity. It certainly was not a wise choice, as the Bishop of Clogher was 'no more a soldier fit to be a general than one of Rome's cardinals' would have been.[17] In any case, Ormond could expect no more help in the short term from the Ulster army than he was already receiving, since it would take several months before Bishop MacMahon and Lieutenant-General Farrell could prepare their army for action in Ulster against Coote and Venables. As a result of these developments in Connacht and Longford, Ormond had to rely on the forces at hand in Munster to relieve Hugh O'Neill's garrison in Clonmel and Preston's in Waterford before hunger or a successful English assault forced them to surrender.

THE COLLAPSE OF THE PROTESTANT ROYALISTS, MARCH–MAY 1650

Ormond's most reliable military forces during his successful campaign in the summer of 1649 had been those commanded by Murrough O'Brien, Lord Inchiquin. During the summer of 1649 Inchiquin's Protestant forces from Munster had driven O'Neill's Ulstermen from their Leinster garrisons and had inflicted a serious defeat on Farrell's troops near Dundalk. Inchiquin's forces had also captured Drogheda, Dundalk and Trim in July. His infantry regiment, commanded by Colonel Giffard, had put up the stoutest resistance to Jones's attack at the disastrous battle of Baggotsrath/Rathmines in August. However, during the autumn campaign in Munster many of Inchiquin's garrisons had defected to Lord Broghill, giving Cromwell prime winter quarters in Cork, Youghal, Kinsale and Dungarvan. By March Inchiquin had fewer than 2,000 men still loyal to the royalist alliance. These troops were concentrated in and near Kilmallock, south-east of Limerick, where they had forced themselves on the local population for winter quarters.

When Ormond needed relief from Cromwell's winter offensive, Inchiquin responded with the limited forces at his disposal. In February he moved towards Cork with a cavalry regiment, forcing Broghill to screen the western flank of Cromwell's offensive. But his force of cavalry could not remain in the field for long owing to the scarcity of fodder for the horses at that time of year. In March Inchiquin again led three regiments of cavalry, totalling roughly 1,200 soldiers, towards Mallow. This time Lord Broghill and Henry Cromwell intercepted the royalist advance at a point close to the River Shannon in County Limerick with a larger force of cavalry, quickly routing Inchiquin's outnumbered men. Broghill's troops killed or captured several hundred royalists. Inchiquin barely escaped. Broghill gave orders for most of the captured royalist officers to be shot, further demoralising Inchiquin and his remaining officers.[18] As a result of this defeat, Inchiquin retreated with what was left of his regiments over the Shannon into Connacht. The Irish population around Kilmallock fled westwards with him, destroying their crops and driving their animals with them.[19]

Broghill's defeat of Inchiquin broke the last of the Protestant royalist regiments in Munster and convinced the Catholic prelates and the Old English lords that Protestant royalists were unreliable as soldiers or allies. Consequently, the Catholic leaders demanded that Ormond disband his remaining Protestant units so that they would no longer be quartered on the Catholic population.[20] Ormond agreed to do so, requiring in turn that the Protestant soldiers be paid enough of their arrears of pay to allow them to feed themselves on their journey into English-controlled territory.[21]

Cromwell was prepared to capitalise on the collapse of Ormond's coalition. He promised safe-conduct passes to Inchiquin and his family, and to the Protestant officers and soldiers whose units had been disbanded.[22] He offered to negotiate a peace treaty, excluding Inchiquin and Ormond, with those Protestants who desired to remain in Ireland. In response, the Protestants sent Colonel Robert Starling, Colonel John Daniel and Michael Boyle, the Protestant Dean of Cloyne, to meet with Cromwell at Cashel to discuss terms of surrender for all of Ormond's Protestant adherents.[23] Cromwell was prepared to be lenient, but he first tried to get Dean Boyle and the others to surrender unconditionally and to trust parliament to treat them fairly. The royalists knew better than to leave themselves so open to revenge and at the mercy of the English commanders in Ireland once Cromwell returned to England. They therefore held out for terms providing clear security for their lives and property. After two days of negotiations Cromwell accepted their conditions, signing terms with them on 26 April 1650.

Cromwell allowed the Protestant royalists to come to Cork, where they would be required to sign promises not to do 'anything to the prejudice of the Parliament or Commonwealth of England . . . during their continuance in our quarters'. They were then to be free to go anywhere in Protestant-controlled Ireland and to settle and work peacefully. Cromwell also allowed them, if they chose, to go overseas, except to England or Scotland. Officers were to be allowed to keep their horses and personal weapons until they were safely in English-held territory, and all of them were to be allowed to keep any money or property that they brought with them out of the Catholic-controlled areas of Ireland. Within six months they were to sell their arms and horses to the English quartermaster in Ireland for a fair price. Cromwell also agreed to let them recover their estates in Ireland, though only on payment of appropriate fines for their 'delinquency' towards parliament.[24] At the end of six months the Protestants could be required to leave Ireland, depending on the security needs of the Commonwealth.

The terms between Cromwell and Dean Boyle were to cover all of the Protestant royalists in Ireland. The remaining Scottish forces in Ulster, under the command of Lord Montgomery of the Ards, were included, as were the remainder of the Laggan troops under the Stewarts. The terms excluded Colonel Edward Wogan, the royalist commander of Duncannon, who had been captured in December and then escaped, and Inchiquin and Ormond. The latter two were offered safe-conduct passes from Ireland to any place other than Scotland and England, but they were not afforded the opportunity to recover their estates.[25] After Cromwell provided a further clarification of the terms to Dean Boyle, the remaining royalist forces surrendered and moved peacefully into English-held Ireland.[26]

The Ulster Protestants availed themselves of these terms, as did most Protestant royalists remaining in arms in Munster and Leinster. The royalist coalition was dead. Ormond remained titular commander of the Catholic forces in Ireland, but in fact there was little he could do to direct the affairs of the Catholic forces still in the field. Ormond seriously considered leaving Ireland at this point, even going so far as to have a frigate prepared in Galway to carry him and his family to France. He adopted this attitude not only because of the surrender of his fellow-Protestants, but also because of the refusal of the city government of Limerick to accept a garrison of Catholic troops from Connacht, and because of the rude treatment his personal servants were receiving in Limerick and other Catholic towns.[27] Clanricarde and a Catholic Assembly meeting in Loughrea, County Galway, convinced him to remain in Ireland for a little longer, in the hope that Catholic resistance could succeed in slowing Cromwell's advance, thus aiding the king's strategy in Britain by sapping English strength in Ireland.[28]

To further embarrass Ormond with the Catholics, Cromwell gave Dean Boyle passes for Inchiquin and Ormond to depart safely from Ireland. Ormond had foreseen such a move and had ordered Boyle not to ask for, nor accept, such an offer. Cromwell hoped by this move either to get Ormond to leave the country or to discredit him so badly in Catholic eyes that his authority would be diminished even further. Ormond made public his refusal of the offer, writing to Cromwell: 'By this trumpeter [I have] returned you your paper, and for your unsought courtesy do assure you, that when you shall desire a pass from me, and I think fit to grant it, I shall not make use of it to corrupt any that commands under you.'[29] The last line referred to Cromwell's attempt to convince Thomas Preston, the Catholic commander of Waterford, that Ormond had come to terms and, therefore, that further resistance at Waterford was hopeless. While these negotiations and ploys were going on, the war continued.

BROGHILL'S CAMPAIGN IN MUNSTER, MAY 1650

As Cromwell and Ireton closed in on Clonmel, capturing the remaining castles near that town and Waterford, the Catholic commander in western Munster, David Roche, gathered a force of 2,000 men in County Kerry to launch an attack to relieve Clonmel. When Roche started to march his army east, through Macroom and towards Cork, Cromwell sent Lord Broghill to intercept him with a force of 1,200 infantry and 800 cavalry. On 8 May Broghill arrived in Cork. The next morning he advanced towards Roche's force, then seven miles to the west. When Roche found out that a English force was advancing towards him, he withdrew his army to Macroom. Broghill, fearing that the Irish would escape, determined to pursue Roche with his cavalry alone, leaving his infantry to catch up as soon as they could.[30]

Broghill's tactic worked. On 10 May he caught up with Roche's troops near Macroom and immediately attacked. The speed of the English advance took Roche by surprise, before he could deploy or withdraw his predominantly infantry force. The results were catastrophic for the Irish. Broghill's cavalry slammed into the Irish as they tried to form a defensive front, riding down and sabering between five and six hundred Irish soldiers. The remainder of Roche's army retreated into the bogs and hills where the English cavalry could not follow. The English troopers took few prisoners, since Broghill ordered most to be killed.[31]

Broghill's decision to run down and attack an Irish force larger than his own demonstrated the tremendous faith the English leaders had in the tactical superiority of their soldiers and units over the Irish. The English soldiers were better trained and armed than their opponents at this stage in the war, and their officers generally were tactically more proficient than their Catholic counterparts. This differential in tactical skill was due to the tremendous losses inflicted on the cadre of trained royalist officers during the battles and sieges since Jones's great victory at Rathmines. The demoralising diet of defeat and retreat suffered by the Irish soldiers made things worse. When an Irish unit's cohesion was broken in a fight, panic and rout generally ensued, as at Macroom.

On 11 May Broghill sent Major John Nelson with a force of 200 infantry and 70 cavalry to capture Carrigadrohid Castle, several miles east of

Macroom. Broghill ordered Nelson to take the Catholic Bishop of Ross, who had been captured, with him and to use the bishop as a hostage to force the garrison to surrender. When Nelson arrived at Carrigadrohid, he told the garrison that if they did not capitulate, he would hang the Bishop of Ross. The garrison asked to see the bishop. When he was paraded in front of the defences, the bishop bravely told the garrison to ignore the English threat. They did so, and Nelson ordered his men to hang the bishop from a tree with his own reins, after they brutally tortured the cleric. Broghill rode up shortly after this barbarous act and offered the castle commander slightly more lenient terms.[32] The garrison commander accepted and was allowed to march away with sixteen muskets to protect his men from marauding bands of 'tories', the name now given to groups of disbanded soldiers roving throughout Ireland.

The atrocity at Carrigadrohid, committed on Broghill's order, was typical of Broghill's indiscriminate use of terror. He consistently ordered the shooting of prisoners as well. This contrasts sharply with Cromwell's employment of terror. When Cromwell used it at Drogheda, he believed 'that it will tend to prevent the effusion of blood for the future, which are the satisfactory grounds to such actions, which otherwise cannot but work remorse and regret'.[33] After losing control of his troops at Wexford, Cromwell no longer unleashed the terror of his soldiers. Instead he offered lenient terms of surrender to the defenders so as to shorten sieges. When a place refused to surrender before the assault, he executed justice only on the officers, as at Gowran. In contrast, Broghill consistently opted for the slaughter of the defeated enemy.

Following the actions near Macroom, Broghill returned to Cork to rest his troops briefly and to replenish his supplies from the tons of food and munitions shipped from England to Cork and to the other major Irish ports. In late March thirteen ships had arrived in Youghal carrying oats for the English horses.[34] English ships and smaller boats then carried the tons of fodder and food needed by the army up the major rivers to places like Cappoquin, Carrick-on-Suir, and New Ross, where magazines had been established. From these forward logistical bases the supplies were carted to the regiments operating inland during the winter and spring, when the grass would not support horses. Similar supply efforts took place in Ulster, where 30 tons of cheese, 27 tons of oatmeal groats, and 1,300 quarters of wheat arrived in April alone.[35] The sustained English logistical effort in the winter and spring of 1650 was remarkable for the seventeenth century, a period in which a leading expert has claimed that 'no logistic system of the time could sustain an army embarked on operations in enemy territory'.[36] There is no question that Cromwell and his generals could not have operated as they did in the winter offensive of 1650 without the steady stream of supplies. Such support allowed the English officers to maintain discipline and to prevent looting. As one officer wrote in a letter published in April 1650:

Our musters are strict, here is no free quarter allowed nor practised, either they [the soldiers] pay or give tickets, which being demanded by the poorest Irish, is not, dare not, be denied by any officer.[37]

Troop replacements also continued to arrive from England, even though the Scottish threat of military action was growing in the north of Britain. In March, April and early May seven regiments were shipped to Ireland to reinforce the 24,000 English soldiers already operating there.[38] These men and the supplies to sustain them were crucial to the English strategy of capturing and garrisoning all major towns and castles in Ireland while defeating all Catholic field forces.

CROMWELL AND THE ADVANCE TO CLONMEL, APRIL 1650

Cromwell accepted the surrender of Kilkenny on 28 March. His plans now turned to the problem of how to capture Clonmel and Waterford, while also keeping pressure on the Irish forces in western Leinster and western Munster. Cromwell returned to his headquarters in Knocktopher on the night after the surrender of Kilkenny, probably to avoid the plague that still raged in that city. He appointed Lieutenant-Colonel Daniel Axtell to serve as governor of Kilkenny, leaving him a small garrison of several hundred infantrymen. By 2 April Cromwell was back in Ormond's splendid Elizabethan manor-house in Carrick-on-Suir, from where he directed military operations and political negotiations for the next few weeks.

Colonel John Hewson led his regiments back to Dublin, ensuring along the march northwards that the castles he had captured earlier remained in English hands. Another column commanded by Colonel Reynolds, Theophilus Jones and Colonel Culme marched along the west side of the Barrow from Kilkenny to Carlow, laying siege to the Irish garrison in that town.[39] The capture of Carlow would push the English frontier west across the Barrow and improve communications with Dublin by removing a post from which the Irish could make sorties to attack English detachments moving on the east side of the river.

Castlehaven, with a force of 3,000 men, attempted to save Carlow, but Reynolds and Theophilus Jones led a large contingent of cavalry to the west of the town to block Castlehaven's force while Colonel Culme carried out the siege.[40] Castlehaven's only hope of disrupting this strategy would have been to attack Reynolds's and Jones's screening force. He failed to do so. As Castlehaven later wrote to exonerate himself, 'Understanding that Carlow Castle was besieged, I appointed a rendezvous intending to attempt the succour; but coming to the place [of rendezvous], I found not half my foot, the rest were marched into Munster, I know not by whose orders.'[41] Unable to raise sufficient infantry, Castlehaven withdrew his cavalry into County Clare. Unexpectedly, however, the Catholic garrison of Carlow

Castle hung on, forcing the English to besiege the place until the middle of July.

The attempt to capture Carlow was part of Cromwell's design to push the Irish back against the Shannon, on the border of Connacht, while his columns captured Irish posts in the counties of Tipperary, Limerick and Kilkenny.[42] To further this strategy, Adjutant-General Sadler led a column with a small artillery train to capture a number of castles to the west of Kilkenny. Sadler ruthlessly executed his mission. For example, when he summoned Polkery, a small castle near Clonmel, to surrender, the garrison refused. Sadler then 'battered it [with his two cannon], they refusing to come out, [he] stormed it, put[ting] thirty or forty of them to the sword, and the rest, remaining obstinate, were fired in the castle. He took Ballodoin, the enemy marching away leaving their arms behind them; he took also the Granny [Castle] and Dunkitt, two very considerable places [near] to Waterford upon the same terms.'[43]

At the same time another force commanded by Colonel Abbot captured the castle of Inistioge, hanging the garrison's two officers because they had formerly served under Colonel Michael Jones and had defected to the royalists.[44] Actions such as these soon cleared all of the major Irish outposts remaining in southern Munster except for Waterford, Duncannon and Clonmel. Cromwell was ready to move against these places, but first he had to deal with the order he received from London to return to England to consult with parliament about the growing Scottish threat.

The Westminster government had sent an order to Cromwell to return to London in January. Their message, which they dispatched on 8 January, was timed so that Cromwell could return to England during the quiet period of winter quarters. However, Cromwell had launched his winter offensive on 29 January, well before he received the summons to return. While he probably knew that a message had been sent from England to recall him, Cromwell did not receive the actual letter until 22 March, just as his army was closing in on Kilkenny.[45] By that time his return would have hindered operations, leaving matters hanging in Ireland. The arrival of this summons meant that he had little time left in Ireland before a further order for his return would be dispatched from London. This order, in duplicate copies, was signed by the Council of State on 27 March and dispatched via two couriers to ensure its safe arrival. This precaution reflected the Westminster government's growing concern about the activities of the Scots and Charles II.[46]

There was little time left for Cromwell to complete the conquest of Munster before his recall. With the negotiations with the Protestant royalists successfully completed, and after the capture of the small castles in Counties Kilkenny, Waterford and Tipperary, Cromwell was ready to concentrate his army for the capture of Clonmel.

The massacres of Protestants during the 1641 rebellion in Ulster were later represented in the most graphic form, as here. Such images inspired a spirit of retribution among Puritans to which Cromwell gave full expression.

James Butler, 12th Earl and 1st Marquis (later 1st Duke) of Ormond, as painted by Peter Lely (National Gallery of Ireland)

Archbishop Giovanni Battista Rinuccini, the papal nuncio whose uncompromising Counter-Reformation policies drove a wedge between Gaelic and Old English Catholics (National Gallery of Ireland)

Owen Roe O'Neill

Sir Phelim O'Neill

Richard Deane (National Maritime Museum, Greenwich)

King Charles I (National
Maritime Museum,
Greenwich)

*Roger Boyle, Lord Broghill
(later Earl of Orrery)*

Cromwellian roll of account of money delivered, received and paid for public use in Ireland
(National Library of Ireland)

Oliver Cromwell (National Maritime Museum, Greenwich)

The storming of Drogheda

George Monck (National
Maritime Museum, Greenwich)

THE SIEGE OF CLONMEL, APRIL–MAY 1650

Clonmel was a town of several thousand inhabitants on the north side of the River Suir, twelve miles west of Carrick. Hugh O'Neill had arrived to take command of the defences on 10 December. He brought 1,200 Catholic soldiers with him, most of whom were from Counties Cavan and Tyrone. O'Neill was a veteran of professional service in the Spanish army in Flanders and was well versed in the art of defending a besieged town. As nephew of Owen Roe O'Neill, he had great prestige among his soldiers and those who had favoured Rinuccini's position in 1648. A tactful and disciplined officer, he kept a firm grip on his soldiers, preventing them from getting out of hand. Consequently, his relations with the Mayor of Clonmel, John White, and the population were cordial, easing the normal problems of co-operation by the townsmen and the garrison during a siege.[47]

The defenders' biggest problems were a shortage of food and ammunition and the steady reduction of their numbers by the plague. In February and March Clonmel was reinforced by the garrisons ejected from Cashel and Kilkenny by Cromwell's advance. These reinforcements helped to maintain O'Neill's troop strength at around 2,000 men, in spite of the effects of plague. Because of the shortage of supplies, the town's fate would be sealed once it was besieged closely, unless Ormond could raise a relief force.

Clonmel was defended on its west, north, and eastern sides by a circuit of walls twenty to twenty-five feet high and six feet thick at the base. The walls were reinforced for most of their length by an escarpment of earth on the inside and a counter-escarpment on the outside, making them more difficult to breach with cannon fire. A deep ditch on the outside of the walls added further protection against mining.[48] Four gates protected by towers provided the only entrances into the place. Only minor works protected the south, since the swift and deep Suir provided good protection on that side (see Map 12). The low grounds to the west and east of the town were marshy, inundated by the rain-swollen river at that time of year. The only firm ground from which a battery of siege artillery could be placed to fire against the walls was to the north.

English forces began arriving before Clonmel in February. However, since the campaign against Kilkenny took priority until the end of March, they were too few to completely isolate Clonmel. After Kilkenny fell, Cromwell's diversion of the flying columns to the north and north-west to widen the belt of English-held territory prevented the English from completely surrounding Clonmel until late April. On 27 April Cromwell arrived to take charge of the siege of Clonmel.[49] He brought with him 8,000 infantry, 600 cavalry and twelve field guns.[50]

O'Neill did not await his fate passively. He launched numerous sorties against the English camp, inflicting heavy casualties on work parties. On one occasion the Irish sallied out through an unguarded section of the defences near the river and attacked an English force in an unfinished fort near the site at which the siege battery was being set up.[51] Catching the English by surprise, the Irish killed thirty or forty soldiers and escaped back into Clonmel through a gate opened nearby. The losses inflicted by sallies such as this possibly caused Cromwell to contemplate conducting the siege from further off. Such an option would have relied on the slow process of starvation rather than on the use of artillery and infantry to force O'Neill to surrender.

Cromwell, however, wanted to take Clonmel as quickly as possible so that he could return to England leaving most of Munster in English hands. He therefore chose not to rely on the slow process of starvation to reduce the garrison, but instead planned to blow a breach in the walls and take the town with a powerful assault by his infantry. The former course of action, while slower, would have worked because O'Neill was desperately short of gunpowder and food.[52]

Treachery was another ploy which Cromwell reportedly tried to use to take Clonmel. It seems that a Major Fennell, the commander of the two troops of royalist cavalry in Clonmel, offered to open one of the gates at midnight to admit 500 English soldiers, in exchange for £500. O'Neill, who inspected his guards several times a day, suspected treachery when he noticed that Fennell's cavalrymen were posted alone at the North Gate, a post normally defended by a mixed force of Irish foot and Fennell's troopers. O'Neill took immediate action, replacing the guard with Ulster infantry. He then allowed the English to enter the gate into an ambush. A short fight ensued as the Irish surprised the attackers. The English hastily retreated, and the defenders claimed to have killed 500 Englishmen.[53]

English sources are quiet about this costly débâcle, but it is a reasonable to accept that it took place because Cromwell and Broghill had used similar subterfuges elsewhere. Since most of the cavalry units operating in Munster were composed of Protestants from Ormond's or Inchiquin's forces, Fennell's cavalrymen would have been regarded with suspicion by O'Neill because most of their co-religionists had surrendered to the English. In any case, the treachery was thwarted. Cromwell found it necessary to batter a breach in the walls and launch a major assault if he wanted to seize Clonmel quickly.

Cromwell at first attempted to breach Clonmel's defences without bringing up the heavy cannon of his siege train. He hoped that he could avoid the time-consuming efforts needed to haul the guns, each weighing 6,000 pounds, overland to Clonmel with hundreds of oxen.[54] In early May his gunners bombarded Clonmel's wall on the north-west side with their twelve field guns, but the cannon-balls were too small to make a breach in the walls large enough to allow attacking troops to enter in a massed column. None the less, Cromwell ordered some of his infantry to attack small openings blown in the walls on several occasions.[55] O'Neill's pikemen and musketeers repulsed these attacks handily. Worse for the besiegers, following each day's bombardment by the light guns, the garrison repaired the damage, making it impossible for the English to open a large breach without heavy guns.[56] Cromwell was therefore obliged to send for the heavy cannon capable of firing balls weighing thirty-two to forty-two pounds.

On 27 May the following news in a letter written from the leaguer, or siege camp, before Clonmel on 14 May was published in London: 'Tis thus certified our army is hard at work before Clonmel [where] we have been battering three days at some towers that did annoy our men in their approaches; Our main battery will be ready within two days, by which time we intend to storm.'[57] By 16 May the heavy siege guns had arrived and the English gunners had placed them into a firing position on the north side of Clonmel, two hundred yards from the North Gate.[58] This location was chosen for several reasons. First, the North Gate led directly to Lough Street, the widest street in the town and the best place to deploy cavalry once the initial defences were breached. Second, the battery's location to the north of the town was at the base of Gallows Hill, a slight elevation above the walls and a place where the ground was firm enough to support the weight of the siege guns.[59]

Batteries of heavy guns could not be established to the west or east of Clonmel because the marshy terrain next to the river would not support the weight of the guns. This meant that the English could only attack from one direction, rather than from two, as they had been able to do at their successful attacks against Drogheda, Wexford and Kilkenny. As a result, O'Neill was able to concentrate the defensive efforts of the townspeople and his garrison against the site where the main attack was obviously going to come. The English delay in bringing up the battering pieces further allowed O'Neill to prepare for the assault that he knew would come at the breach which the cannon were steadily battering in the north wall.

On the morning of Thursday 16 May the heavy guns went into action. The forty-two-pound balls made an immediate impression on the walls, and the breach began to widen. By late afternoon the breach was wide and fairly level, and much of the rubble had fallen into the ditch in front of the wall. As the battering progressed, O'Neill 'set all men and maids to work, townsmen and soldiers . . . to draw dunghills, mortar, stones, and timber, and made a long lane a man's height and about eighty yards length, on both sides up from the breach, with a foot bank at the back of it; and caused [to be] place[d] engines on both sides of the same, and two guns at the end of it invisible opposite to the breach, and so ordered all things against a storm'.[60] These two competing actions continued into the evening. By the end of the day Cromwell concluded that the breach was ready for an assault to be launched the next day, 17 May.

Cromwell's plan for the assault was simple. The attack was to be led by the infantry regiments. Once through the breach, the infantry were to fight

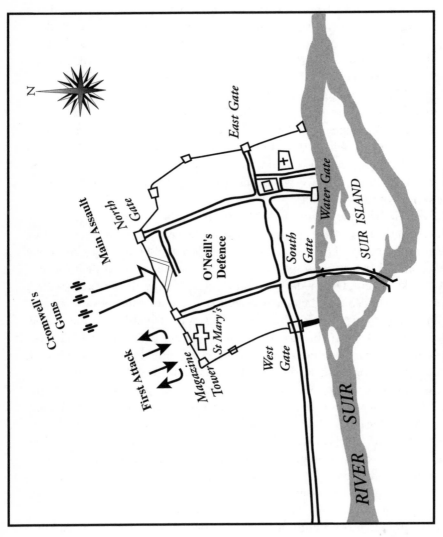

12. Siege of Clonmel, April–May 1650

their way east to capture the North Gate. Cromwell and the cavalry were to wait outside the North Gate, ready to charge into the town when the gate was opened by the infantry. Then the combined force of foot and horse was to fight its way through the town, killing the garrison. Unfortunately for the attackers, things did not work out this way.

O'Neill prepared his soldiers carefully for the expected assault. He lined the walls which he had built behind the breach with musketeers. He deployed his pikemen at the flanks of the breach and at the apex of the killing ground formed by the palisades inside the breach. The houses to the east of the breach also provided a good firing-point for some of his musketeers to shoot down into the killing zone.

The English attack commenced at 8 a.m. on Friday 17 May.[61] Cromwell's infantry entered the breach with little opposition and pushed their way into the V-shaped ambush. The front ranks soon realised that they were facing another major defensive work and that the defenders were preparing to cut their column off. They therefore began to shout 'Halt! Halt!' to the soldiers pushing into the breach behind them. However, these men thought that the leading ranks were shouting at retreating Irishmen inside, and they began to shout 'Advance! Advance!' so as to catch up with the action.

Once the ground between the breach and the improvised palisades was full of English infantrymen, O'Neill sprung his counter-attack. His pikemen bore down on the flanks of the attackers as his musketeers let loose a devastating volley into their faces from the houses and the palisades. Large logs suspended by some sort of device were flung at the flanks of the milling mass of English soldiers, and the gunners of the two cannon at the end of the lane fired their chain-shot at point-blank range into the packed crowd.[62] The slaughter of Englishmen was horrific. Perhaps as many as 1,000 were killed, and the remainder of Cromwell's finest infantry retreated from the breach.

Cromwell had been waiting near the North Gate for the successful storm troops to break through to the inside of the gate and let him and his cavalry into the town. When he heard the cannon fire inside the town, he began to suspect that things were not going well. Then he saw stragglers falling back from the breach to their initial positions. His first impulse was to go to the point of action and try to rally his soldiers for another effort. The bloodied and dispirited infantrymen would have none of it, refusing to throw their bodies into the fatal breach again. Instead they called for Cromwell to send the cavalry into the breach, especially since the horsemen were paid more than the foot-soldiers.[63]

Cromwell turned to his cavalry regiments for the next assault into the deadly breach. The regimental commanders volunteered immediately to lead the attack, and their example and pleas to their men succeeded in rallying sufficient numbers for another try. Remarkably, Cromwell made no attempt to revise his scheme of manoeuvre. Since he had at least 10,000 soldiers stationed near Clonmel, he could have tried to attack the defences with ladders at several places along the north wall in addition to the breach near the North Gate. Such a tactic would have forced O'Neill to split his heavily outnumbered forces to defend several points. Cromwell also could have taken a few more days to pound another breach in the wall further to the west of the main breach, forcing the defenders to divide their efforts against two major breaches. However, he either felt there was too little time to attempt such additional efforts, or he thought the defenders were nearly at the end of their strength and resources.

It was several hours before the next assault could be readied. At around 3 p.m. Colonels Sankey and Culme led a massed column of dismounted cavalry back into the breach. The technique of leading an assault with dis- mounted cavalry had been used before in England, where it was felt that the more heavily armoured cavalrymen had a better chance of surviving an assault than would the infantry, who lacked the body armour provided for the horse regiments.[64] The cavalrymen quickly drove the defenders from the original breach and entered the body-strewn area between the wall and O'Neill's palisades. The Irish defenders reacted violently to the renewed assault, attacking the cavalrymen with every conceivable weapon from cannon to pitchforks. Again the slaughter was horrific. Colonel Culme and many officers were killed at an early stage of the assault, but the troopers refused to withdraw. Hand-to-hand fighting continued for as long as three hours. The attackers retreated only after most of their officers and up to 2,000 English soldiers were killed or wounded.[65]

Cromwell reluctantly ordered the retreat to be sounded after the long afternoon struggle. He tried to keep a force in the breach through the night to prevent the garrison from repairing the damage, but his soldiers refused to stay in that body-strewn battlefield. 'Neither the threats of the General nor the bloody swords of inferior officers was sufficient enough to keep them from turning tail to the assault.'[66] Cromwell's prospects looked bleak indeed. He had lost nearly ten per cent of the entire English army in Ireland in one day. He could not afford to risk another assault. As a result, he had to resort to a long siege to starve O'Neill into submission. His return to England would either have to be delayed, or he would have to return to London after his army had suffered the worst military defeat ever inflicted on the New Model Army (the highest loss, other than Clonmel, was suffered at Naseby, where 400 New Model soldiers died).[67] The political repercussions of returning to England after such a defeat would have been immense.

O'Neill, however, could no longer sustain the fight for Clonmel. His ammunition was exhausted. He had several hundred wounded soldiers, and there remained almost no food for garrison or townsmen. Consequently, O'Neill decided to lead his soldiers out of the town that night and to arrange for Mayor White to approach the English for favourable terms of surrender. After dark on 17 May O'Neill slipped his column of soldiers and camp-followers across the Suir to the south of town. The English evidently had not tightly blockaded the south side, since they never intended to attack across the river. It was thus easy for the Irish troops to get away unnoticed. Some time around midnight, after he was sure that O'Neill had a good start, White sent a message to Cromwell asking for terms.

Anxious to get the siege of Clonmel behind him, Cromwell readily offered lenient terms to the townsmen in the following articles:

> 1st. That the said town and garrison of Clonmel, with arms, ammunition and other furniture of war that are now therein shall be surrendered and delivered up into the hands of his Excellency the Lord Lieutenant by eight of the clock this morning.

> 2nd. That in consideration thereof the inhabitants of the said town shall be protected as to their lives and estates, from all plunder and violence of the soldiery, and shall have the same right, liberty, and protection as other subjects under the authority of the Parliament of England have, or ought to have and enjoy within the dominion of Ireland.[68]

After Cromwell and White had signed the articles of surrender, Cromwell asked White to tell him how O'Neill had reacted to the surrender. White replied that he did not know, since O'Neill had departed the night before with his troops. Cromwell was furious, having thought that he had captured over 1,000 of the finest Irish troops still in the field against him. However, he kept his word with White, allowing the townspeople to remain in Clonmel in possession of their property.[69]

The English launched an immediate pursuit of O'Neill's column, which had moved south-east towards Waterford. English cavalrymen cut down at least 200 of O'Neill's camp-followers and wounded soldiers who could not keep up with the main body. However, since the English infantry regiments were still licking their wounds north of Clonmel, most of the Irish soldiers got away through the rough terrain south of the Suir where the cavalrymen were reluctant to ride.[70] When O'Neill reached Waterford, Major-General Thomas Preston would not allow him or his starving troops to enter. O'Neill was forced to disperse his men and order them to find their way back to Ulster in small groups. This final indignity to the brave defenders of Clonmel was due to the fact that Preston already had too many mouths to feed in Waterford and, possibly, because the Old English Preston had always harboured a great deal of antipathy to Owen Roe O'Neill and the Ulster Gaelic Irish.

Cromwell quickly secured the gates of Clonmel and established a garrison there under the command of Colonel Sankey. While there may have been some looting, the accounts generally agree that the English faithfully observed the terms of the surrender. However, some Catholic priests were murdered in the area, and the town was forced to begin paying assessments to support its occupiers.

Cromwell and the English newspapers were remarkably quiet about the bloody losses suffered by the English during the assault on Clonmel. This is not surprising. While the English eventually succeeded in taking the town, the siege was the costliest operation they had carried out in Ireland. O'Neill had been forced to evacuate the place because of shortages of food and ammunition, rather than by a successful English assault. This strong rebuff had to have hurt the morale of the English soldiers and officers involved in the battle. Cromwell had little time to dwell on the disaster, since he was on a ship sailing from Youghal on 27 May and he arrived in London by 1 June.[71] He, like many of his soldiers, regarded the costly victory as God's will. As such, it was not something to be analysed and dwelt upon; it was, rather, a sign that atonement through prayer and greater effort needed to be made to seek God's blessings.

The capture of Clonmel was an English victory in spite of the enormous casualties the English army suffered. Waterford was hopelessly isolated, and Ormond's military impotence was demonstrated again. Cromwell was able to demonstrate his clemency towards defeated Catholics at Clonmel, as he had done at Kilkenny, proving to the inhabitants of other Irish towns that his promise to respect lives and property would be honoured. The future reduction of Ireland to obedience required the Old English burghers to come to terms with the English. If the Old English submitted, the Gaelic Irish would be isolated and incapable of sustaining large military units. In this way the war would be shortened.

Ormond, for his part, was not happy with the outcome, no matter how costly it was to the English. He had lost another of his major garrisons, and his communications to Waterford and Duncannon were now completely at the mercy of the English. His inability to raise a relief force was symptomatic of the decline of his military and political power. He and Inchiquin became increasingly marginalised figures in the war after May 1650. With the surrender of most Protestant royalists to Cromwell and the fall of Clonmel, the war in Ireland had become purely and simply a religious war. The Catholic military prospects were next to hopeless. However, the uncompromising Puritanism of the men who ruled the English Commonwealth prevented the war from ending in the summer of 1650. Their unwillingness to give to Catholics the same tolerance that Cromwell demanded for the 'tender consciences' of English Protestants and Jews forced the Old English to continue to resist alongside the Gaelic Irish. So the war continued, even as Oliver Cromwell departed for England and the beginning of his conquest of Scotland.

7

Ireton's Summer Campaign, 1650

The Enemy here is much divided and more weakened, yet the obstinacy of the priest, [and the] desperation and guiltiness of some prime gentlemen and lords still keep up a poor shifting war. The taking of Tecroghan and Carlow will clear Leinster: the reducement of Charlemont, Ulster: the crossing of the Shannon gains Connacht, where are but two garrisons considerable, and then the Tories and lurching Ulsters are the only enemies to settlement.

Report by Colonel John Reynolds, 28 May 1650[1]

The capture of Clonmel was Cromwell's last military endeavour in Ireland. His costly success there ensured that the Catholic forces in Connacht would be unable to supply or reinforce their garrisons in Waterford and Duncannon. Cromwell spent his last few days in Ireland wrapping up the political arrangements he had made for the surrender of the Protestant royalists. On 27 May he boarded a ship at Youghal, and two days later he disembarked at Bristol. By 1 June he was received by the government and population of London with a great show of respect and appreciation for what he had accomplished in Ireland. After providing parliament with a full report of his tour of duty in Ireland on 11 June, Cromwell prepared for his forthcoming campaign to conquer Scotland.[2]

English operations in Ireland remained in the hands of a group of talented professional soldiers. Cromwell's son-in-law, Henry Ireton, assumed command of all English forces in Ireland and was soon appointed Lord Deputy to the Lord Lieutenant of Ireland. Sir Charles Coote and Robert Venables continued to command the forces in Ulster, and John Hewson those in Dublin. Lord Broghill and Henry Cromwell were the leading commanders in Munster, ably seconded by Colonel John Reynolds. Thus a remarkably able and tight-knit group of New Model Army veteran officers, joined by the ruthless and efficient Broghill and Coote, remained in charge of the campaign to conquer Ireland. None the less, Cromwell's departure removed a source of relentless energy, and the result would be a decrease in the intensity of operations of the main army under the Lord Deputy Ireton.

CROMWELL'S MILITARY ACHIEVEMENTS IN IRELAND

Cromwell had failed to conquer Ireland completely before his recall to England to prepare for the war against Scotland. The fragmented nature of the Irish and royalist causes in Ireland, which had facilitated Jones's and Cromwell's victories in 1649–50, made it difficult to bring the war to an end. There was no single political or military centre of gravity against which the English could concentrate their resources. The capture of castles and fortified towns did not end the war. New Irish military bands rose up in the countryside as if springing from the soil to attack scattered English outposts. The few remaining cities and towns in Irish hands were well fortified and would be difficult to attack.

Most Catholics in Ireland recognised that their military situation was desperate. In normal circumstances, men who found themselves in such a situation would probably have submitted to an enemy who had gained the upper hand. But English hostility to Catholicism made a political settlement between the English and the Irish Catholics almost impossible in 1650. By English law, all Catholics who had fought against parliament in Ireland stood to lose their land and their right to practise their religion openly, thus depriving them of both their livelihood and their faith. Consequently, religious prejudice created a strategic problem which, more than any other military or geographical challenge, lengthened the Irish war far past the point at which it needed to be fought to ensure English victory.

Cromwell's greatest failure was his inability to accept the need to allow Catholics to practise their faith in the same manner in which he allowed Quakers, Jews and Baptists to practise theirs. He expressed his view of religious freedom for Catholics when he answered the request of the governor of New Ross for toleration in October 1649:

> For that which you mention concerning liberty of conscience, I meddle not with any man's conscience. But if by liberty of conscience you mean a liberty to exercise the mass, I judge it best to use plain dealing, and to let you know, where the Parliament of England have power, that will not be allowed of.[3]

This view is radically different from his views about toleration for Protestants. For example, following the New Model Army's victory at Naseby, he had written to the Speaker of the House of Commons reminding him that the soldier 'who ventures his life for the liberty of his country, I wish he trust God for the liberty of his conscience, and you for the liberty he fights for'.[4]

Cromwell, none the less, accomplished a great deal militarily and politically during his nine months in Ireland. He had successfully organised an expeditionary force that was large enough and sufficiently equipped for extended operations in a foreign country. He had arranged for the steady flow of supplies, money and replacements needed to sustain the fighting strength of the army and to support hundreds of garrisons throughout the conquered land. His attention to the logistical and financial details of the expedition mark him as one of the great military commanders in European history.[5]

Cromwell used all human resources available to hasten the campaign in Ireland. He readily accepted the services of Michael Jones, Sir Charles Coote and Lord Broghill. These men were not kindred spirits with Cromwell. Broghill was a royalist Protestant *en route* to France to serve Charles II when Cromwell met him in London in 1649 and convinced him to accept a general officer's commission in the expeditionary force. Cromwell ensured that all available resources and troops were hastened to Dublin to reinforce Jones's garrison in the spring of 1649, even though there was rumour that Jones had not favoured the trial and execution of the king. Cromwell never displayed the least hint of jealousy of Jones, even though Jones had won the most important Protestant victories in Ireland in 1647 (Dungan's Hill) and in 1649 (Rathmines). A great commander can generally surround himself with competent subordinates. Cromwell's ability to do so in Ireland allowed the English to divide their forces into several regional armies capable of hunting down and destroying the royalist and Irish forces in three provinces simultaneously.

During his service in Ireland Cromwell displayed the ability to envision how to manoeuvre several forces simultaneously to achieve decisive results. His detachment of Robert Venables and Theophilus Jones with 5,000 soldiers into Ulster in September 1649 quickened the defeat of royalist forces there while Cromwell marched the main army to Munster in the south. He increasingly divided his forces in the autumn campaign, compelling the royalists to face multiple thrusts and therefore to remain on the defensive. He sent John Reynolds and Michael Jones north towards Kilkenny in November, and then swung his entire force south to exploit the quick capture of Carrick-on-Suir and the road to Waterford. While he failed to complete the conquest of Munster in the autumn, he was able to refit and rest his army in winter quarters that were provided to the English by the defection of most of the Protestant royalists of Munster.

His understanding of the political fissures that lay within the royalist coalition allowed him to play a clever game of deception designed to lure the Munster Protestants back to the English parliament's cause. He used Broghill and his connections with the Munster Protestants to suborn the loyalty of the garrisons of Cork, Bandon and Youghal in November 1649.

This political coup came just in time to save his army from defeat by Ormond's allies, Colonels Winter and Disease.

The winter campaign of February and March 1650 was one of Cromwell's finest manoeuvres. He surprised the royalist leaders with his early resumption of operations. This was possible because of the English ability to reinforce and supply the parliamentary army in Ireland with replacements, fodder and food. The three prongs of the English advance isolated the major inland towns of Munster from each other and from Connacht, making it very difficult for Ormond and Castlehaven to decide which town to reinforce first. The English divisions soon became pincers that closed around Kilkenny, forcing the evacuation of the royalists' government from their capital and leaving the town at the mercy of the converging English columns. Similar operations were carried out against Clonmel, leading to its capture and the total isolation of Waterford and Duncannon from the main royalist forces in Connacht.

The tactical operations carried out by the forces under Cromwell were not uniformly brilliant, although most were effective. The assault on Drogheda in September was well planned and vigorously executed. Two separate breaches in the southern walls of the well-defended town forced the defenders to face converging assaults by three battle-hardened regiments. Cromwell's placement of his artillery and his organisation of his troops was competent. His personal courage in leading the second assault into the breach was crucial to the final outcome. In spite of the active and skilful defence, the town fell quickly, allowing Cromwell's army to move south to Leinster.

In March 1650 Cromwell's tactics at Kilkenny were similarly competent. He assaulted the city from three directions and established a second breach well removed from the first break in the defences, compelling the garrison to surrender before the final assault. However, Cromwell's assault on Clonmel was his greatest tactical failure. He lost nearly ten per cent of the entire English army in Ireland because he underestimated the strength, skill and resolve of the defenders. He tried to breach the defences at two places, but he gave up on one of them and concentrated his total effort on the other site. This allowed the Irish commander, Hugh O'Neill, to concentrate most of his force of Ulster veterans at that point and to slaughter the assaulting English infantry. None the less, Clonmel fell because the English had isolated it from all hope of supply with their previous manoeuvres, causing the garrison to run out of food and ammunition.

The campaigns in southern Leinster and Munster demonstrated Cromwell's grasp of the essentials of logistical operations. He chose courses of action that allowed him to use naval forces to support and sustain his army as it marched through and captured towns like Wicklow, Arklow, Ferns and Enniscorthy. The combined operation against Wexford by the navy and the army was very effective. The army seized Rosslare Fort quickly, allowing the fleet to enter Wexford harbour unmolested by royalist artillery. Thus the fleet was able to land supplies and the artillery siege train for the army's operations against Wexford. Cromwell put pressure on several points in the defences, making it necessary for the defenders to spread their troops. The treachery of a royalist commander precluded the need for a breach and formal assault. However, the aggressive and unbridled behaviour of the troops during the capture of the town was responsible for one of the darkest blots on the reputation of Cromwell, who had temporarily lost control of the men under his command.

Cromwell's skilful use of the terror instilled by English brutality at Drogheda brought him some results at Dundalk, Trim and New Ross in September and October 1649, and a lot more success at Fethard, Cashel, Cahir and Kilkenny in the winter campaign in 1650. But terror was of limited utility against Irish Catholic garrisons at Waterford, Clonmel and Limerick. In fact it may have prolonged their resistance. Worse, his use of terror at Drogheda and Wexford made it unlikely that Irish Catholics would ever be reconciled to the English, helping to lead to England's ultimate loss of Ireland, her greatest strategic failure in modern history.

When the threat of terror began to encourage prolonged resistance, Cromwell changed his approach for dealing with Catholic garrisons that were willing to surrender.[6] Cromwell's remarkable adaptation of his policy allowed Irish soldiers to depart with their weapons and the towns' populations to remain safely in possession of their homes.[7] Cromwell also protected the townsmen and the country-people from the depredations of his soldiers by executing soldiers who disobeyed his orders and proclamations against stealing from farmers and townsmen. This last policy helped his officers to maintain the discipline of their soldiers while encouraging the local population to co-operate. In a century marked by the ravages of the Thirty Years' War, this forward thinking and intelligent policy was made possible by the English financial and logistical support that Cromwell ensured flowed steadily to Ireland.

Cromwell exhibited a great understanding of how to motivate soldiers to fight and die for a cause. He constantly exposed himself to danger and personally took an interest in the material well-being of his men. He travelled to all of his garrisons in Munster during the harsh winter weather in December and January, ensuring that his soldiers knew that he and the other commanders shared their hardships. On campaign, he lived with the troops and shared their short rations and exposure to the weather. His correspondence is full of letters written on behalf of his officers and concern for the widows and orphans of those killed in action. His character was above reproach to his fellow-Protestants.

Cromwell's sensibility, however, was typical of his age, reflecting as it did the strongly held religious enthusiasms and prejudices common among seventeenth-century Europeans, as recently exemplified during the Thirty Years' War. To his uncompromising attitude may be attributed his failure to treat the defeated garrisons of Drogheda and Wexford with the same fairness that he had generally exhibited in his victories in England and Scotland.[8] The plain fact is that he allowed his troops to slaughter Protestant and Catholic soldiers and townsmen who were ready to surrender. The classic explanation is that he allowed these atrocities because he believed these garrisons were morally complicit in the massacres of Protestants by Catholics in 1641–2.[9]

The noted English historian C. V. Wedgwood characterised Cromwell's extraordinarily complex personality well when she wrote that his 'career illustrates the irreconcilable contradictions between ethics and politics, between the right and the expedient. . . . He was consumed by an intense, narrow, burning patriotism, so closely interwoven with his religion that he could not distinguish one from the other.'[10] Cromwell's time in Ireland proved that he was a great military commander, but not a great man. He failed to transcend the narrow bounds of his Puritan hostility towards Catholicism. In these failures, he was typical of so many Christians of both faiths in the Irish war. His departure from Ireland marked neither the end of the English conquest nor the end of the atrocities committed by all parties involved. Hard-fought and bitter campaigns lay ahead of the English in Ireland in the summer of 1650.

ALIGNMENTS AND STRATEGIES, MAY 1650

Henry Ireton took command of all parliamentarian forces in Ireland on 27 May. He faced a badly scattered enemy torn by military defeat and political disintegration. He was soon to be joined by parliamentary Commissioners for Ireland who would help him rule the country even as the English forces continued the conquest. The men who made up this commission — Edmund Ludlow, John Jones, Miles Corbet, John Weaver and Ireton himself — were committed Puritans who believed that only a totally defeated and subjugated Catholic Ireland could be acceptable and safe for England. However, these were not to be results easily or swiftly achieved.

Facing Ireton and his dispersed subordinates was an array of Catholic military forces that numerically at least equalled the English forces. Inchiquin continued to raise troops in the west of Leinster. Ormond commanded a force reckoned at 2,000 men near Limerick. Castlehaven continued active service in western Munster with several thousand men. Clanricarde commanded at least 3,000 men in Connacht, while Bishop Heber MacMahon of Clogher commanded the Catholic army of Ulster, numbering as many as 6,000 veteran troops. The Catholics also controlled a number of strongly garrisoned towns and castles. A contemporary observer noted:

For they have Waterford, Galway, and Limerick, three of the strongest and most considerable towns of the kingdom still untaken, any of which, if they be well garrisoned (as questionless now they are) will be near a summer's work to reduce; The forts of Duncannon and Sligo, the castles of Carlow, Athlone, Charlemont and Nenagh are not easy purchases; the Province of Connacht is still preserved entire by my Lord of Clanricarde, who will be able to bring 4,000 men of his own into the field, now that Galway and his country is somewhat cleared from the infection of the plague.[11]

Ormond remained titular head of a royalist–Catholic coalition. The defection of most Protestant royalists made it predominantly a Catholic alliance. However, there remained strong divisive forces at work within the Catholic cause. The Ulster Gaelic Irish still distrusted, and were distrusted by, Old English Catholics such as Clanricarde, Lord Taaffe and Lord Dillon. Bishop MacMahon kept the Ulster army in the north, rather than moving it south to work with Castlehaven against the English forces in western Leinster. Clanricarde co-operated to a certain degree with Castlehaven, but he remained very reluctant to risk his forces outside the borders of Connacht for extended periods of time.

In Munster, General Thomas Preston's refusal to admit Hugh O'Neill and his Ulster troops into Waterford after their daring escape from Clonmel in May was just one example of the Old English Catholics' antipathy towards the Gaelic Irish Catholics.[12] This divisiveness among Catholics was also evident when Bishop MacMahon's requests for reinforcements and supplies were ignored.[13]

At a conference in Loughrea in May the Irish leaders agreed that their best strategy was to continue to attack those areas under English control in order to destroy the crops and herds from which the English drew a large part of their supplies.[14] They believed that such raids would prevent the English from sustaining their offensives against Connacht and the places still held by Catholic forces in Ulster, Leinster and Munster. They also hoped that the diversion of English resources in Britain to face the Scots would prevent the English from fully conquering Ireland and revive Irish chances of expelling the English. There was only a remote chance that this strategy would succeed, depending as it did on Scottish success and English inactivity in Ireland. However, it was the best strategy available to the Irish at that time.

IRISH OFFENSIVE IN LEINSTER, JUNE 1650

Before Clonmel fell, Ormond and Clanricarde had hoped to reinforce Castlehaven and march to the relief of their garrisons there and in Waterford.[15] With the fall of Clonmel, their attention turned north, to western Leinster, where the English forces under Colonels Hewson and Reynolds were besieging the formidable castle of Tecroghan.[16]

Tecroghan was a castle situated about seven miles west of Trim, on an island in a forested and boggy area. It was near the main road from Dublin to Athlone, posing a threat to English garrisons in the Pale. A garrison of about 1,500 men, commanded by Sir Robert Talbot and inspired by the presence of Lady Fitzgerald, wife of Sir Luke Fitzgerald, defended the castle and the sixteen cannon stored there.[17] The English strategy for the summer campaign of 1650 was to capture the remaining Irish strongholds in Munster and Leinster, in preparation for a final campaign that would then be launched against the province of Ulster. The capture of Tecroghan was an important part of this strategy.

In late May, shortly after the English arrived before Tecroghan, tories raided up to the walls of Dublin, stealing a number of cattle and burning crops. Hewson, the governor of Dublin, was forced by this raid to march his regiment back to Dublin to hunt down the tory partisans.[18] This move weakened the force besieging Tecroghan, offering Clanricarde and Castlehaven an opportunity to unite and attempt its relief. By 18 June Clanricarde and Castlehaven had led a force of several thousand men to Tyrrellspass, to the west of Tecroghan.[19] There they halted and assessed the situation. An English force of about 1,400 infantry and 1,200 cavalry had surrounded the castle and had erected palisades and entrenchments to protect themselves from sallies from within the castle and attacks from relieving forces. The only way that a relief force could carry supplies of gunpowder and food into the castle was to march through the bogs so as to avoid meeting the superior English cavalry in open terrain. An Irish council of war determined that the effort should be made and that the infantry and 300 of the cavalry, dismounted, would make the trip. Each soldier was to carry his weapons and bundles of food and gunpowder. Clanricarde agreed that the attempt should be made because of the valuable cannon held in the castle. However, he refused to accompany the column because he felt too weak to make the trek through the bog.[20]

On 19 June the Irish column moved through the bog to within four miles of the castle, where they ran into a force of 2,600 English troops deployed in a line for battle. The Irish deployed, and their left wing, commanded by Richard Burke, attacked the English right wing. The English gave way under the weight of the assault about half an hour before dark, retreating across the Toghan stream. At the same time the English left wing attacked the Irish right wing, commanded by Sir Thomas Dillon. The English attack, made by cavalry and infantry against the Irish infantry, drove Dillon's men into the woods and turned the flank of the Irish army. Castlehaven, who had accompanied the column, was unable to rally the Irish centre, which quickly retreated under the weight of the English onslaught. Castlehaven later claimed that the Protestant commander of Ormond's lifeguard, which was present at the battle, treacherously refused to bring his men to the assistance of the faltering Irish infantry. This claim is unsubstantiated in other sources.[21] In any case, most of the Irish army retreated.

Several hundred of the Irish troops on the left side of the Irish line were able to make their way into the castle with some food and gunpowder. On the way in they destroyed part of the English siege works and captured an English cannon. This success ensured that the garrison could not be quickly destroyed, making it likely that the English commander, John Reynolds, would grant lenient terms if the Irish decided to surrender. For several days afterwards the reinforced garrison sallied out against the English, killing a number of them. Their efforts were not assisted further by the relief force under Clanricarde and Castlehaven, primarily because Ireton reinforced Reynolds with a further 400 infantrymen and 400 cavalrymen, giving Reynolds overwhelming superiority in the open ground with a force of 1,600 horse.[22]

By 23 June all the Irish leaders near Tecroghan except Castlehaven concluded that further efforts to relieve the place were hopeless. Clanricarde decided to return to Connacht and to release his officers to their quarters since he was out of money and supplies. Castlehaven marched his troops south to Munster.[23] As usual, Clanricarde placed the blame for failure on others, telling Ormond that he was departing on 24 June, 'and when I shall have time to inform your Excellency how barbarously I have been used ever since my coming into Leinster that your Excellency must trust [I] have little reason to engage or endanger my party any further for them [the Leinster Catholics]'.[24]

Sir Robert Talbot and Lady Fitzgerald surrendered Tecroghan on 25 June. The terms were lenient, allowing the garrison of 1,700 men to carry away some of the artillery stored in the castle.[25] However, on a pretext that tories were raiding in the area and had received help from the garrison, Reynolds reneged on the portion of the treaty allowing the cannon to be taken out.[26] The fall of Tecroghan was not in itself a major defeat. The garrison marched away with their weapons and continued to serve in the Irish armies. But the animosities which the campaign produced between Castlehaven and Clanricarde, and between Connacht Catholics and Leinster Catholics, further weakened Irish resistance to the English advance. Reynolds and Hewson could now approach Athlone without fear of attack from a major fortress in their rear. Western Leinster up to the Shannon was under firmer English control. The Shannon crossings at Athlone were to be the next target of the English troops in Leinster.

IRISH OFFENSIVE IN ULSTER, JUNE 1650

While Castlehaven and Clanricarde attempted unsuccessfully to drive the English away from Tecroghan, the Catholic army of Ulster launched a major offensive into the English quarters in northern and eastern Ulster. The army of Ulster was the most successful Irish or royalist military force raised in Ireland during the 1640s. By 1646 Owen Roe O'Neill had shaped the ill-disciplined Ulster recruits into a well-organised and well-trained fighting force. With this army of nine regiments he defeated Robert Monro's Scottish army at Benburb. Following that victory, O'Neill's army played a pivotal role in Rinuccini's coup against the Old English in the Confederate Supreme Council. In 1647, when Thomas Preston and Lord Taaffe lost, respectively, the Catholic Confederate armies of Leinster and Munster at the battles of Dungan's Hill and Knockanuss, O'Neill had preserved his army by avoiding battle with Michael Jones's parliamentarian army. Consequently, by 1649 the Ulster troops were the best Catholic soldiers remaining in a body in Ireland.

After the fall of Drogheda in September 1649 O'Neill finally had decided to join Ormond's royalist coalition. However, his illness in October and death in November kept most of his army from playing an active part against the English advance in Leinster and Munster. A few Ulster regiments, commanded by Richard Farrell and Hugh O'Neill, did contribute a great deal in the successful defence of Waterford in November and the hard-fought siege of Clonmel in April and May 1650. These Ulster troops were the only Irish forces which dealt Cromwell's forces heavy blows during his nine months in Ireland.

On 18 March 1650 Heber MacMahon, Bishop of Clogher, was elected by the gentry and clergy of Ulster to command O'Neill's army of Ulster. For the next several months that army remained in winter quarters, unable to campaign until the grass needed to feed its horses and cattle began to grow. In early June Bishop MacMahon decided to march his army into the English-held areas of northern and eastern Ulster to destroy crops and, if possible, to catch and crush the forces of Sir Charles Coote and Colonel Robert Venables separately. This strategy was promising, since Venables had been forced to march his troops to Toome, on the border of Ulster and Leinster, to recover that place from an Irish force that had taken it by surprise.[27] MacMahon also hoped to rally the Scottish settlers in eastern Ulster to the anti-English cause.[28]

By the end of May Bishop MacMahon had assembled his army of 4,000 foot and 600 horse at his base near Loughgall, County Armagh, for his offensive in Ulster.[29] Sir Charles Coote meanwhile had dispersed his forces to defend major towns like Derry and Enniskillen from marauding tory raiders; he thus faced the Irish offensive with only 800 infantry and 600 cavalry in his field force. MacMahon first advanced to and captured Dungiven, County Londonderry. His troops massacred the garrison of sixty Protestants, sparing only the commander, Colonel Michael Beresford, whom they sent to Charlemont for future use as a hostage. The Irish army

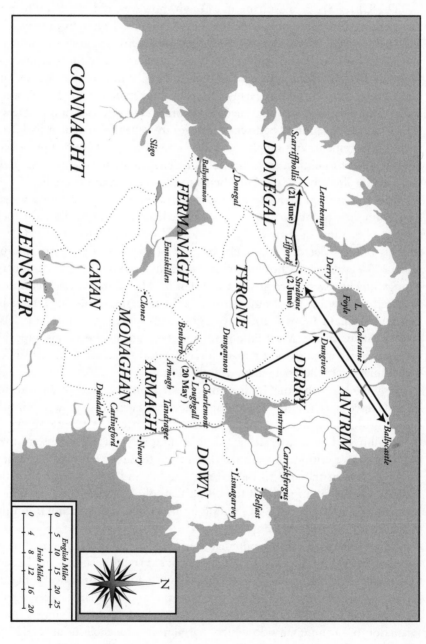

13. The Army of Ulster's Offensive, May–June 1650

continued its march north-east into Antrim, where it captured Ballycastle without opposition.[30] So far the campaign seemed to be going according to plan, catching the forces of Coote and Venables off guard and divided.

The Ulster Scots of Antrim and Down, however, did not flock to join the invading Catholic army, as Bishop MacMahon had thought they would. This meant that the Irish army was deep in enemy territory without an adequate supply base and without the siege artillery needed to capture one from the British. Hoping to crush Coote before reinforcements could join him, MacMahon turned his army westward and marched towards Coote's badly outnumbered force stationed at Lifford, fifteen miles south of Derry. Coote, in the meantime, had sent messages to Venables to return to Ulster with reinforcements and supplies as soon as possible. As O'Neill approached, Coote gathered companies of the local defence units to augment his field force, while also sending reinforcements to the garrison of Enniskillen.[31]

The Irish troops arrived near Coote's encampment on 2 June, 'where they continued for about four hours; but at length began to draw off their ground with most of their forces over a pass' over the River Foyle. Coote and his officers decided to attack the rear of the retreating Irish column with 200 cavalrymen, hoping to start a rout among the Irish infantry. Things quickly went wrong for the English. The Ulster cavalry counter-attacked, throwing the English horse into disarray. Only an attack by Colonel Richard Coote's infantry regiment stopped the advancing Irish cavalry. Surprisingly, MacMahon did not take advantage of his superior numbers by attacking Coote's main force. Instead the Irish army continued to withdraw over the Foyle in an orderly fashion.[32]

It is unclear why the Irish units retreated in the face of an inferior English force near Lifford — although they had been short of ammunition earlier in the campaign and perhaps were still short.[33] As Coote observed, the English 'had been in great hazard of being totally cut off'. Coote realised the dangerous position he was in and retreated towards Derry, giving orders to the settlers in the area to move their families and farm animals into the fortified towns, out of reach of the Ulster Catholics.[34] MacMahon continued his march by stages to the west, ending up in a camp at Scarriffhollis, on the River Swilly, near Letterkenny.

By 18 June Sir Charles Coote had been reinforced by infantry regiments commanded by Venables and Colonel Fenwick. Having received intelligence that the Irish Ulster army had encamped on a hillside near Scarriffhollis, Coote marched his forces west from Derry and Strabane, arriving on 21 June near the Irish camp. There he found the Irish troops drawn up in formation on a mountainside which was almost impossible to attack. Most of MacMahon's officers, including Owen Roe O'Neill's son Henry, urged the bishop to stay where he was and wait for the English supplies to run out, rather than to attack an enemy army whose cavalry outnumbered their own.[35] MacMahon ignored their advice, perhaps believing that his superiority in infantry would win a battle fought on rough terrain.[36] After berating his officers for being cowardly, the bishop deployed his army to lower ground, as Coote reported later:

> Where upon sight of our party (they being then encamped upon the side of a mountain, inaccessible either for horse or foot) they drew forth into a piece of ground, which though extremely bad, yet it pleased God to put into our hearts to advance towards them.[37]

The Irish army had been reduced to roughly 4,000 infantry by the need to garrison places they had captured during their march in eastern Ulster and by the natural attrition of a campaign. MacMahon drew his numerically superior infantry into a large mass formation with an advance guard in front, facing the English. Coote, on the other hand, arrayed his troops in smaller formations, 'handsomely disposed to succour one another' as the fight progressed.[38]

The English opened the battle with the attack of a forlorn hope (advance guard) of 150 soldiers led by Colonel Fenwick. The Irish responded with the attack of their own forlorn hope led by a captain. Colonel Fenwick and the Irish captain were soon killed, and the Irish started to give ground. The English reinforced their attack and began to win the 'push of pike'. The battle was fierce, with musketeers using their muskets as clubs after firing their first round. The massed Irish infantry could not manoeuvre, as the English units slammed into them from several directions at once. But they fought on rather than flee, as is shown by the fact that 2,000 Irishmen were killed on the battlefield. At the decisive moment in the battle Coote ordered a regiment of infantry to attack the Irish flank. This move threw the Irish into disarray. Once the English infantry had broken the cohesion of the defenders, a rout commenced. English cavalry pursued the fleeing Irish soldiers for ten or eleven miles, killing hundreds of them.[39] As the Irish retreated, Protestant settlers in the area joined in the chase, avenging the massacres of 1641–2. Coote himself proved to be the most vindictive of the victors.[40]

Coote destroyed Owen Roe O'Neill's Ulster army at the battle of Scarriffhollis. By the time the battle and pursuit were over 3,000 Irish soldiers had been killed, along with hundreds of their officers. The English casualties were fewer than 100, showing the importance of maintaining the cohesion of the infantry in such a battle and the disastrous results when an army was broken and pursued. Most of the weapons and baggage of the Irish army were captured. Owen Roe O'Neill's son Henry was captured and beheaded on orders of 'the unchristian and tigrish doom of the thrice-cruel butcher and human blood-sucker, Sir Charles Coote'.[41] Many other high-ranking officers were similarly executed after the battle, although Sir Phelim O'Neill, the first Irish commander in 1641–2, managed to escape.

The Bishop of Clogher escaped to the south, where English troopers captured him several days later after a bitter fight near Enniskillen.[42] He was taken to Derry and hanged on Coote's order, even though he had surrendered with a promise of quarter. At least nine Irish colonels and generals died in the fighting, along with four lieutenant-colonels and three majors. The loss of these officers, and the twenty captains killed as well, made it impossible for anyone to rebuild the Gaelic Catholic army of Ulster. Although sufficient manpower remained available in Ulster from which to recruit a new army, the loss of trained leaders and weapons made it impossible to put together an effective fighting force.[43] Irish garrisons in Dungiven, Ballycastle and Lifford departed before English forces arrived to attack them. This was the greatest military disaster suffered by the Irish since their defeat by Mountjoy in 1601.

The Irish defeat at Tecroghan and disaster at Scarriffhollis radically altered the strategic situation in Ireland. There was no longer a well-trained force opposing the English advance in southern Ulster and western Leinster. Sir Charles Coote could march from Ulster into Connacht and threaten Clanricarde's garrisons at both Sligo and Athlone (see Map 15). At the same time Hewson and Reynolds could lead a force towards Athlone, striking Connacht from the east. Lord Deputy Ireton was free to intensify the sieges of Waterford and Duncannon, and Sir Hardress Waller was able to bring the siege of Carlow to a successful conclusion. Once these operations were complete, Ireton could lead the main English army against Limerick. Connacht would then be under attack from three directions by converging English pincers.

THE CAMPAIGN IN THE SOUTH: THE SECOND SIEGE OF WATERFORD, JULY–AUGUST 1650

The royalist and Catholic causes remained in disarray in the face of the growing English threat. The defeats in the north further divided Ormond from the Catholic bishops, making it nearly impossible to concert resistance. Ormond continued to command an army centred on the area around Loughrea and Limerick and to serve as the titular head of the Irish forces. Inchiquin commanded a small force in Kerry, in western Munster. Ormond's and Inchiquin's forces, along with Hugh O'Neill's survivors from Clonmel, were the only troops available to attempt any relief of Waterford and to defend Limerick. The people of Limerick had steadily refused to accept Ormond's garrison or to help support his troops in the area. The defeat of Scarriffhollis seemed for a time to convince them to do so, but they soon reneged on an agreement they had made with Ormond to accept his orders in early July.[44] This situation was extremely dangerous, because if there was not a strong garrison in Limerick, it would be easy for an English cavalry force to swoop down on the city by surprise and capture it and its vital bridge across the Shannon. Clanricarde feared such a move, recognising that it would open south-eastern Connacht to attack just as his army was moving north to secure Sligo and to try to rally the survivors of the army of Ulster.[45]

After more negotiations the Limerick city fathers accepted Ormond's suggestion that Hugh O'Neill and his Ulster soldiers should serve as their garrison. Clanricarde had proposed this solution because he knew that O'Neill's inspired defence of Clonmel had heartened the Limerick citizens. O'Neill's ability to deal tactfully with the civilian element of Clonmel was just the sort of skill needed to deal with the testy population of Limerick. In fact O'Neill was so popular with the citizens of Galway and Limerick that both places wanted him as their governor. Clanricarde convinced Ormond to place O'Neill in the most threatened town first, and appointed Colonel Maurice Lynch to command Galway in his absence.[46]

Bad news continued to come in to Ormond in July. Word arrived from England that Charles II had signed an agreement with the Scots which denounced the 1649 treaty between Ormond and the Catholic Confederates of Ireland. The royalist uprising in Scotland led by Montrose had been crushed and Montrose brutally executed in Edinburgh, after the king disavowed him as well. Efforts to raise £10,000 in loans to sustain a field force failed, as merchants in Limerick and Galway refused to advance money to the cause.[47] In the words of Ormond's biographer, 'This obstinacy and disobedience of Limerick made it impossible for the Marquis of Ormond either to gather or keep the body of an army together.'[48] English reinforcements continued to arrive in Ireland, and parliament appointed Edmund Ludlow, a distinguished officer of the New Model Army, to serve as the Lieutenant-General of Horse in Ireland under the command of Ireton.[49]

Closer to Ormond, Inchiquin's force in Kerry was scattered on 13 July by a force of English cavalry led by Colonel Robert Phayre, and the council of Waterford reported that the city could not hold out much longer.[50] Waterford had been cut off from easy access from the west since January. The fall of Kilkenny, Clonmel and the towns of central Munster to the English had further hindered communications with the city. After the English victories in Leinster and Ulster, it was only a matter of time before Waterford would be under closer siege. To make matters worse, the plague was killing 400 soldiers and citizens in Waterford every week in July. As the mayor reported to Ormond, 'Our men and means are now come to an end together.'[51] There was nothing Ormond or anyone else could do for Waterford in the face of the active operations carried out by Lord Broghill and Henry Ireton in western Munster.

In the midst of this discouraging situation, Inchiquin proposed to Ormond that a rendezvous be held of all available forces in western Munster, including O'Neill's Limerick garrison, and that the united army march to the relief of Waterford. This proposal came to naught owing to the lack of money to pay the army and the unwillingness of Ormond to pull O'Neill's garrison out of Limerick. A similar effort by Ormond to gather the remaining forces in western Leinster failed as well, as most Catholics turned their back on the Protestant Lord Lieutenant and refused to obey his orders.[52]

Waterford was left to its own resources. By late July, with the defeat of the royalists' attempts to move forces into western Munster, Ireton was free to launch the final campaign against Waterford and Duncannon. He left Sir Hardress Waller with a large force at the siege of Carlow. Broghill was reinforced with a cavalry unit commanded by Colonel Henry Ingoldsby to help Broghill prevent any Irish attempts to relieve Waterford from the west. Ireton also established a large body of cavalry at Carrick-on-Suir to serve as a mobile reserve against any incursions into central Munster by Castlehaven. He then marched a large troop of infantry to Waterford to reinforce the siege and interdict all communications in and out of the place.[53] As Ireton marched additional infantry regiments to Waterford to finish the siege, the English navy blockaded the port and brought supplies to the besiegers. Well-supplied English soldiers dug entrenchments ever closer to the defences and set up the siege batteries.[54]

With his forces in place, Ireton summoned Thomas Preston, the royalist governor of Waterford, to surrender. Preston refused. Ireton then moved two batteries of heavy artillery into easy range of the walls at locations where the defences did not appear too formidable. As the guns were being set up and trenches dug closer to the walls, news reached Ireton that the English forces besieging Carlow had assaulted and captured the castle over-looking the town. The garrison had sought and received generous terms which allowed it to march away to Athlone and the townsmen to remain undisturbed in Carlow.[55] The fall of the last Irish strong point on the River Barrow freed additional forces for the expected assault against Waterford, allowing Ireton to order the infantry from the Carlow siege to join the troops in front of Waterford and Duncannon.[56]

Before these reinforcements arrived Preston agreed to surrender Waterford. He had little choice. As a result of starvation and disease, he had fewer than 700 soldiers and townsmen left who were fit to man the extensive walls of the city. He reported to Ormond that even before Ireton had arrived the town's supply of gunpowder had dwindled to less than 500 pounds. Waterford's mayor and aldermen wanted to surrender on terms before the English launched a final assault that could end in the slaughter of garrison and townsmen alike. Preston therefore decided to surrender on the best terms he could get.[57]

Ireton granted generous terms to Preston and the townspeople of Waterford on 10 August 1650. The garrison could depart to Athlone with their weapons, luggage, horses and colours. The town's citizens were allowed to depart or stay. If they chose to stay, they would not be molested, apart from being obliged to pay their taxes. If the English decided later that the citizens should leave the city, they promised to give them three months in which to settle their affairs before departure. This last provision was different to those in the terms given to the citizens of Clonmel and Kilkenny, who were allowed to remain indefinitely in their homes. This additional clause in the standard terms was the beginning of a shift in English policy towards one which favoured the eventual expulsion of Catholics from Munster, Leinster and Ulster. Preston also agreed to surrender all artillery, ammunition and ships in Waterford.[58] General Thomas Preston was too ill to leave the city with his troops, but his son James led the remaining 700 defenders on their march to the north. Without an assault, but after a long and costly siege, the English had finally captured the great port of Waterford.

Duncannon did not hold out much longer. Although Duncannon was nearly impregnable, owing to its modern fortifications, its commander saw nothing to be gained by further resistance once Waterford had fallen. On 12 August articles of surrender were signed. The English allowed the garrison to depart to either Athlone or Galway with arms, baggage and personal belongings. The crews of two small Irish ships in the harbour were also allowed to sail to the Scilly Isles, Jersey or Guernsey, but with only a few of their cannon. When the English entered the fortress, they found it still well stocked with food and ammunition.[59] Its surrender without a more prolonged siege was a good gauge of the progressive demoralisation of the Irish. These English victories eliminated the last major Irish strongholds in Leinster and Munster except for Athlone and Limerick, and English forces were already operating on the outskirts of those places.

The defeats suffered by the Irish in Ulster, Leinster and Munster in the summer of 1650 destroyed the last vestiges of loyalty by the Catholic prelates to Ormond. Deserted by most of his countrymen of both religions, Ormond prepared to depart from Ireland. The Catholic clergy and Old English lords now scrambled to reorganise their command structure and to find some way to save themselves from the Puritan onslaught into Connacht.

ORMOND DEPOSED, AUGUST 1650

As the military blows fell on his cause throughout the year, Ormond had to deal with the growing distrust felt in him by the Catholic clergy. Their concerns were valid. Ormond had failed to prevent his commanders from surrendering places such as Cahir and Tecroghan before they had expended all supplies. His inability to march to the relief of the garrisons of Kilkenny, Clonmel and Waterford had been especially damaging to his position with the clergy.[60] The fall of Carlow seems to have been the catalyst for decisive action by the Catholic prelates against the royalist Lord Lieutenant. On 24 July the Archbishop of Tuam wrote to Ormond notifying him that the archbishops and bishops were going to meet at Jamestown, County Leitrim, on 6 August 'to do what in us lies for the amendment of all errors, and the recovery of this afflicted people'.[61] Ormond was invited to send a representative, but not to attend.

The prelates meet at Jamestown from 6 to 10 August. They determined that it was best for Ireland and the Catholic Church for Ormond to leave. However, they were worried that he would do so before he appointed a deputy Lord Lieutenant, acceptable to them, who could continue the theory of the king's authority in the Irish cause. Consequently, the four archbishops sent Lord Dromore and Dr Charles Kelly to negotiate with Ormond before the publication of their decision in an effort to ease the blow and to persuade Ormond to appoint Clanricarde to serve as Lord Deputy.[62]

The immediate effect of the clergy's message to Ormond was to divide the anti-English cause further. Ormond initially refused to comply with the request that he appoint a successor, feeling that he did not have the king's authority to do so. He related to the Commissioners of Trust the gist of the prelates' demands and wrote to Clanricarde with the latest news. The bishops did not wait long for a reply. On 12 August they published their initial decisions and on 13 August wrote to Ormond again, ordering him to 'speedily repair out of the country and join His Majesty'.[63]

While the Catholic prelates and Ormond were exchanging letters, Sir Charles Coote and Colonel Venables continued to pound away at the defences of Charlemont, the last Irish stronghold in Ulster. Charlemont had been held by the Irish since the autumn of 1641. It was one of the most modern fortifications in Ireland and proved to be impervious to capture by assault. Consequently, Coote and Venables were forced to bring up siege artillery, including mortars, and to work from late July until early August to batter a breach in the fortifications.[64]

Once a breach had been made, Coote ordered his troops to cut approach trenches up to the walls. On 8 August the English launched a major assault. Phelim O'Neill, the Irish commander, rallied his entire garrison and the civilian inhabitants to mount a vigorous defence at the breach. They killed between 500 and 800 English soldiers while driving the rest of the attackers out of the breach and back to their lines. After this effort the garrison was exhausted. Many defenders were wounded, and ammunition was in short supply. Consequently, O'Neill requested and was granted terms of surrender on 14 August.[65] He and his garrison were allowed to march away with weapons and baggage, a remarkably lenient set of terms from Coote. This leniency can best be explained by Coote's unwillingness to loss hundreds of men in another assault.

News of the loss of Charlemont further demoralised Ormond. While there was no immediate threat of an invasion from western Ulster into northern Connacht, it was only a matter of time before Coote could move west to threaten Sligo and then south to strike Athlone.[66] The bishops saw the fall of Charlemont as another sign of Ormond's failure as a commander. They continued to push for his departure. Clanricarde reacted negatively to the bishops' hopes that he would succeed Ormond. He even wrote to them and to Ormond announcing that he was planning to leave Ireland together with Ormond; at the same time he tried to persuade Ormond to remain.[67]

Ormond and the clerical representatives met at Loughrea from 26 August to 3 September in an attempt to find some way out of the impasse. Ormond refused to surrender his command or to depart; the prelates, for their part, refused to allow Catholics to serve under him any longer. This stand-off forced the bishops to resort to their only weapon: excommunication. On 15 September they issued a proclamation against the continuance of the king's power through Ormond. Any Catholic who served Ormond was to be excommunicated. By this time the king's brother, James, Duke of York, had sent a frigate to meet Ormond and his family at Galway and transport them to France. The king made it easier for Ormond to depart by sending him authority to do so and to appoint Clanricarde to serve as the Lord Deputy of Ireland.[68]

By the end of August Ireton was moving his forces from Waterford towards Limerick and Athlone. In this crisis situation, attempts were made by Clanricarde and some bishops friendly to Ormond to get the troops to ignore the excommunication.[69] These efforts may have had some impact, because no one was in fact excommunicated; it is probable that Ormond's evident lack of authority made any such drastic action unnecessary by this stage. Clanricarde and Castlehaven did all they could to reinforce Lord Dillon in Athlone and Hugh O'Neill in Limerick. None of the clergy could object to these moves since they were all threatened if the English captured either of these bridge sites across the Shannon. Nevertheless, Ormond's tenure of office as Lord Lieutenant was now clearly at an end.

James Butler, Marquis of Ormond, left Ireland on 11 December aboard the *Elizabeth of Jersey*, a twenty-four-gun frigate sent by the Duke of York. In the weeks before his departure several more attempts were made to compose the differences between the prelates and Ormond, all to no avail. On 6 December Ormond appointed the Earl of Clanricarde as Lord Deputy. Long before that date Clanricarde had assumed most of the responsibilities of military command.

ORMOND'S PLACE IN HISTORY

Ormond had been the most important royalist figure in Ireland since 1641. His loyalty to the House of Stuart and the Church of Ireland never wavered. He loyally jeopardised his position in Ireland to serve the strategy of Charles I when he sent a number of Protestant infantry regiments to England to serve with the king in 1644. He successfully defended Dublin from the Catholic armies of Owen Roe O'Neill and Thomas Preston in 1646. In 1647 he chose to go into exile in France rather than to serve parliament. And he returned from his safe exile in France in 1648 to create the royalist co-alition which nearly took possession of the whole of Ireland for Charles II by July 1649.

Ormond, as a Butler, was a Protestant Old English nobleman. He was related to many of the Old English Catholic lords of Munster and Leinster, and he shared the king's tolerance towards Roman Catholics as long as they acknowledged the king's authority in church and state. Through his family relationships and his remarkable diplomatic skills, Ormond had built up a major faction within the Catholic Confederation. These 'Ormondists' often dominated the Confederate Supreme Council. It was this faction which had signed the Cessation of 1643 that declared a truce between the Confederates and the royalists so that they could each fight their other enemies. In 1645 Ormond succeeded in concluding a peace with the Confederate Supreme Council without totally compromising the king on the religious issue. Such political accomplishments preserved the Protestant and royalist causes in Ireland and demonstrated Ormond's strongest attributes as a political operator and negotiator.

Ormond served as the commander of the Protestant and royalist armies in Ireland from November 1641 until July 1647. He won only one major battle, at Ross in 1643, but he was victorious in many skirmishes against Catholic forces. He was not a great military commander. He lacked the ability to conceive of how to bring the enemy's main force to battle. He was a master of tactical and strategic defence and relied on Fabian tactics and strategies to wear his opponents down. This made some sense in the larger picture of the war between the royalists and the parliamentarians in Ireland and Britain. The royalist cause could only have succeeded by achieving a victory in England. Ireland was a secondary theatre of operations for Charles I. Ormond's role was to prevent either a Catholic or a parliamentarian victory in Ireland. This meant that to risk a major battle against an enemy who had superior manpower resources was extremely dangerous. It also meant that, from the royalist point of view, no decisive positive results could be achieved in Ireland.

When the king was defeated in England in 1645, Ormond tried to form a royalist coalition with the Catholics and Scots in Ireland. The Ormond Peace of 1645 was the main instrument used to form that alliance. He failed because he refused to give the Catholics full toleration in Ireland and permanent control of the churches in their possession. The arrival of the papal nuncio, Archbishop Rinuccini, put the final quietus to his attempts to cut a deal. He was forced to turn to parliament and to hand Dublin over to Colonel Michael Jones in July 1647. By this act, Ormond saved the Protestant cause in Ireland.

After he created a new royalist coalition, in January 1649, he had an opportunity to drive the parliamentarians out of Ireland before they could consolidate their power in England. The refusal of Owen Roe O'Neill to join with him against the Westminster government was ultimately a decisive factor in his failure to do so. The time and energy which the Confederates and royalists spent fighting O'Neill's forces in 1648 and 1649 would have been better spent in driving Michael Jones out of Dublin and Sir Charles Coote out of Derry. In the 1649 campaign Ormond again displayed his weaknesses as a military commander. He failed to direct his forces against the decisive point. He tried to capture every other parliamentarian garrison in Ireland before concentrating overwhelming strength against Dublin. His delay in doing so allowed the English to reinforce Jones's garrison with sufficient forces to sally out at Baggotsrath and set in motion the disaster of Rathmines.

After Rathmines Ormond never recovered the tactical or strategic initiative. He failed to find a way to make Cromwell pay a high cost for capturing the major garrisons of Leinster. In the winter of 1650 he was again caught off balance by Cromwell's manoeuvres and watched helplessly as the English systematically overwhelmed his garrisons in Munster. The only major check that he helped to deliver against Cromwell was at the successful defence of Waterford in November 1649. Cromwell's costly success at Clonmel was due to the resistance of Hugh O'Neill's Ulstermen, rather than to Ormond's efforts to relieve or supply the town. The fall of Carlow and Waterford was the last straw for the Catholics, who had watched as most Protestant royalists deserted the royalist cause and accepted Cromwell's lenient surrender terms.

Although Ormond failed militarily, he was the most politically consistent figure in the Irish wars. Owen Roe O'Neill, Inchiquin and most Old English leaders made deals with the parliamentarians at some point. Ormond never wavered in his loyalty to the king and to what he thought best for the Stuart kingdom of Ireland. He was *politique* in his religious views, although a committed member of the Church of Ireland. Had he possessed greater military abilities, things may have been appreciably different. When the monarchy was restored in 1660, Ormond returned to Ireland as the first Duke of Ormond and Lord Lieutenant of Ireland. As such, he was the most powerful man in Ireland for another two decades.

A PAUSE IN OPERATIONS, SEPTEMBER–NOVEMBER 1650

As the Catholics removed Ormond, the war continued. The English had cleared all major Irish forces from Munster, Ulster and Leinster, except for those in the Catholic fortress of Limerick. Connacht remained the only province not conquered. It was going to be difficult for the English to break into Connacht because of its geographical isolation from the rest of Ireland.

A major readjustment of forces and supplies was clearly required before the conquest of the province could be attempted. The English Lord Deputy, Henry Ireton, underestimated the logistical and tactical problems this created and he wasted precious time in September before finally settling on a plan for the final thrust against Catholic Ireland. Consequently, English operations in September, October and November 1650 were poorly co-ordinated and failed to capture the crucial bridgeheads into the western province. The onset of winter forced an end to active campaigning in 1650.

8

The Advance on Limerick, 1650–51

It is further certified that the enemy lurk much in the woods and so unanimous are the inhabitants there that though there were a law made to make it immediate death to relieve the enemy, yet would they undergo the danger, and give them money though they want it themselves, (being imbued with the spirit of monarchical belief, though often slashed for their ignorance) so that they [the English] find there is a necessity in many parts of Ireland to burn up the country, without which there can never be an end of wars in that nation.

Mercurius Anglicus, 24 Sept.–1 Oct. 1650[1]

Ireton's capture of Waterford and Duncannon in mid–August 1650 allowed the English to concentrate their forces and resources on the conquest of Connacht. Connacht was the last of the four provinces of Ireland still free of English forces or rule and had by now become the base of operations for the remaining Irish military units. A campaign to seize the gateways into the province at Limerick and Athlone was entirely feasible and was the obvious way to crush the remaining organised Irish military resistance. Cromwell or Michael Jones would have pursued aggressively such an opportunity to end the war before the onset of another Irish winter. A quick attack by the English against Limerick in August would have allowed them to capitalise on the political disputes within the royalist coalition between Ormond and the Catholic prelates. It also would have exploited the psychological momentum generated by their string of major victories in July and August.

The selection of Henry Ireton as Cromwell's successor as commander of all English forces in Ireland was due primarily to his close relationship with his father-in-law Oliver Cromwell. Ireton had served bravely as a regimental and brigade commander during the English Civil Wars. He had commanded the left wing of cavalry at the battle of Naseby in 1645, where he was severely wounded and captured while leading a counter-attack against Prince Rupert's cavalry.[2] He had served competently as Commissary-General of the army in the Civil Wars and in the expedition to Ireland in 1649. While he never displayed tactical brilliance in these military roles, he was at least tactically competent. A more important reason for Ireton's selection as Lord Deputy was Cromwell's complete trust in him politically. They shared similar Independent religious and political views and had worked closely together during the New Model Army's coup against king and parliament in 1648–9.[3] The other logical choices for command in Ireland, Lord Broghill and Sir Charles Coote, lacked Ireton's family and political connections and his identification with the regicides.

By mid-August 1650 English forces had moved into positions from which they could launch a concentric attack against Connacht (see Map 15). Ireton had sent cavalry units to Limerick to prevent interference by Irish detachments from that city in his operations against Waterford. Sir Charles Coote, after his capture of Charlemont on 14 August, had marched his army south from Ulster to Athlone, where he planned to seize the bridge over the Shannon.[4] Athlone's capture would open the direct road from Dublin to Galway, the last major city other than Limerick still held by the Irish. With his capture of Waterford on 6 August, Ireton was free to reinforce his troops around Limerick with the infantry and siege guns used at Waterford and Duncannon. The Irish commander of Limerick's garrison, Hugh O'Neill, was not at that time prepared to resist a long siege. The capture of Limerick should have been the immediate objective of Ireton's campaign. Its capture would have opened the route from the Munster ports to Galway and would have eliminated the last Irish fortress in Munster. Its symbolic importance was nearly as great as its tactical value.

Ireton decided, however, not to pursue the capture of Limerick as his immediate objective. Refusing to discuss campaign plans with his key subordinates, he kept his own council and decided to divide his army.[5] He sent one column, commanded by Sir Hardress Waller, to Limerick to reinforce the siege, while he himself led a substantial force north through Counties Carlow and Wicklow and then on to Athlone. Consequently, substantial military resources and the personal efforts of the English commander-in-chief were diverted away from Limerick for the next two months. Ireton reportedly made this decision to divide his army and march to Athlone because the English needed to capture supplies from the Irish entrenched in the glens and bogs of County Wicklow. He also hoped to crush the tory guerrillas who were raiding from there into the English-held areas up to the outskirts of Dublin.[6] This long detour to Connacht eventually consumed as many resources as Ireton's column captured, and the defeat of the Wicklow tories eventually had to be left to Hewson and the Dublin garrison.

Meanwhile Ireton and Sir Charles Coote hoped that Athlone might fall quickly without a costly assault. They had been tricked into believing that Lord Dillon, the Irish commander of Athlone, was planning to surrender Athlone and its bridge over the Shannon in exchange for money and an assurance of personal safety.[7] Ireton reasoned that if Athlone were captured quickly, his army could move across the river and down the west side of the Shannon to Limerick, cutting that city off from supplies and reinforcements from Connacht. However, while Lord Dillon was indeed negotiating with Coote at Athlone in August, he was doing so with Ormond's approval and had no intention of surrendering the Athlone bridge to the English. This planned deception helped to draw Ireton away from the course of action which promised the best chance of ending the war quickly. His march north certainly gave Limerick's garrison the chance to prepare for a long siege.[8]

IRETON'S MARCH TO ATHLONE AND LIMERICK, AUGUST– OCTOBER 1650

On 16 August 1650 Ireton and his column of infantry and cavalry departed from Waterford *en route* to Leighlinbridge, and thence into County Wicklow (see Map 14). One of the officers with him later described their progress: 'On the 21st, we encamped at Ravilla, three miles westerly from Hacketstown, on the border of Wicklow, from whence my Lord [Ireton] in person with about 600 foot and 200 horse entered the mountains to be better advertised of those notoriously wicked Tories and of their haunts.'[9] As this punitive column marched north through the mountains smaller detachments raided into the glens and bogs, capturing cattle, sheep and horses, while killing any armed Irishmen they could find. In this manner the Lord Deputy began a 'savage war of peace'.[10]

The main column marched steadily northwards to Naas, about twenty miles south-west of Dublin, where it received a fresh supply of bread from Dublin bakeries. While marching through Wicklow, the English captured thousands of cattle and sheep, but the soldiers and their horses were worn down physically, making it necessary for Ireton to stop and rest his troops at Naas and then at Tecroghan before moving on to Athlone. Owing to their fatigue, they were able to capture or kill only a few tories. Finally, on 16 September, after four weeks of hunting for tories and livestock, Ireton's weary soldiers joined Sir Charles Coote's regiments in front of Athlone.[11]

Coote greeted Ireton with the news that Lord Dillon had burnt the part of Athlone on the east side of the Shannon and had withdrawn his troops to the western side of the river. Ireton's and Coote's army 'kept before it about 14 days, but could not pass the bridge for a drawbridge was on it, and the castle stood with the other part of town on the other side [of] the Shannon, over[watching] the bridge'.[12] Lacking boats or bridging equipment, the English could not force their way across the Shannon in sufficient strength

14. *Ireton's Campaign, August–September 1650*

to seize the castle and town on the western side. While Ireton could have sent lightly armed units across the Shannon without a bridge, he could not have supplied them for long nor have supported them with the heavy artillery needed to reduce Irish fortifications.

After waiting for two weeks for Dillon to betray the bridge and castle of Athlone, Ireton decided to leave Coote and his troops at Athlone while he marched his regiments south along the eastern side of the Shannon to join Sir Hardress Waller at Limerick. As he did so, Ireton captured a number of small castles in King's County and posted small garrisons at the fording sites over the Shannon to prevent Irish forces from crossing the river and raiding English-held territory.

On 6 October Ireton's column reached Limerick and linked up with Waller's troops on the east side of the Shannon. During their march through Wicklow to Athlone, and then on to Limerick, Ireton's soldiers had every opportunity to witness the devastation that nine years of war had inflicted on Ireland. As one soldier wrote, they often marched '30 miles together and hardly [saw] a house, or any living creature . . . only ruins and desolations in a plain pleasant land'.[13] Ireland had come to resemble some of the most desolated regions of Germany in the Thirty Years' War.

Ireton's circuitous and distracted march to Limerick produced few beneficial results to the English. While they captured a few animals and killed some tories, the will to resist of the Irish guerrillas in Wicklow remained unbroken. Large bands of tories continued to operate in Wicklow and Wexford, destroying valuable crops and raiding to the outskirts of the major towns.[14] When Ireton finally got to Athlone, the gate into Connacht had been firmly shut. Coote's delay in attacking the Athlone bridge had given Clanricarde time to send reinforcements to Lord Dillon and had enabled James Preston to arrive at Athlone with the Irish garrison from Waterford. These forces checked any attempt by Coote to raid to the west of the Shannon.

Ireton's absence from Limerick in August and September 1650 gave Hugh O'Neill, the Irish commander in Limerick, time to prepare his garrison and the townsmen for a prolonged siege. Although Sir Hardess Waller had arrived with his English regiments before the town on 9 September, he had lacked the manpower and artillery needed to cut the city off from supplies and to breach its defences.

It was incredible that Ireton did not march immediately from Waterford to Limerick with his entire army in August. Limerick was not much more than one hundred miles west of Waterford. A siege of Limerick could have been supported by the English naval squadron already anchored in the River Shannon near the city.[15] Ireton could have conducted amphibious operations to land a large force on the western side of the Shannon to cut communications into Limerick from Ennis and Loughrea. Since most of the harvest had not yet been gathered in August, a swift move to Limerick would have increased the defenders' logistical problems by preventing them from bringing grain supplies into the town in large quantities. By October the English had lost these opportunities.

Ireton could ill afford to lose any advantage he could gain in his struggle to capture Limerick. Limerick was one of the most strongly fortified towns in Ireland. The main part of the city was located on King's Island in the Shannon, with only a single bridge connecting it to the mainland on the eastern side of the river. A large and well-fortified suburb lay on the eastern side of the river, providing a strong defensive system to protect the bridge to the main part of town. The fortifications were in good repair, and the walls had been reinforced in most places with earthen ramparts. These ramparts made it very difficult to blow a breach in the walls. Major-General Hugh O'Neill's garrison of 2,000 men were veterans of the siege of Clonmel, where they had given the English army its bloodiest defeat since 1645. Ireton was not likely to order an assault against defences held by these experienced Irish soldiers, even if he had been able to move a large enough artillery train into place to blow a breach.

Hoping that he could take the city without a fight, Ireton summoned the mayor and aldermen to surrender on easy terms on 6 October.[16] They rejected his terms. Lacking sufficient infantrymen or artillery to cut off and assault the city, Ireton now faced a difficult decision. Should he remain in front of Limerick in the wet autumn weather, with winter approaching, hoping that the Irish would change their minds and surrender? Or should he withdraw to winter quarters and organise the forces, supplies and artillery that were needed to take such a well-defended city? For the first time since his appointment as commander in Ireland, Ireton called a council of his senior officers to help him select a course of action. This council recommended to Ireton that he abandon the siege until the return of more favourable weather. Ireton agreed with their recommendation.[17]

On 19 October most of the English units encamped outside Limerick withdrew, much to the surprise of the Irish.[18] A number of small garrisons in castles on the eastern side of the Shannon remained to prevent Irish raiding parties from moving easily into the English-held areas of Munster or Leinster. The remainder of the English regiments marched to winter quarters. Limerick remained in Irish hands. The respite Ireton had given to the Irish by means of his roundabout campaign through Leinster had allowed them to reorganise their military structure and prepare for the defence of Connacht.

CLANRICARDE'S COUNTER-OFFENSIVE, SEPTEMBER–OCTOBER 1650

In August 1650 the Catholic prelates' excommunication of anyone who obeyed Ormond's orders left the Catholic forces without a supreme military or political commander. The bishops were agreed that Ormond had to go, but no other leader was acceptable to serve as commander-in-chief to all parties in the Catholic coalition. The Catholics had a number of possible candidates, but few acceptable choices. Professional soldiers like Major-General Thomas Preston or Lord Taaffe had been defeated too many times by the English to engender any faith by the rank and file in their leadership capacities. Although the Earl of Castlehaven had a great deal of experience in command, he was English rather than Irish, and memories of his uninspired and cautious command of the expedition to Ulster in 1644 hardly aroused enthusiasm for his appointment.

Randal MacDonnell, the Marquis of Antrim, was another possibility. Antrim was the leading Catholic nobleman of north-eastern Ulster. He had organised the Gaelic Irish expedition led by Alasdair MacColkitto MacDonnell to Scotland in 1644. MacDonnell and his Irish regiments had provided invaluable help to the Earl of Montrose in his remarkably successful royalist campaign against the Edinburgh government. Antrim, however, had deserted the Catholic cause in May 1650, shortly after the officers of the Catholic army of Ulster refused to select him as their new commander to replace Owen Roe O'Neill.[19] Antrim fled to Dublin in June, throwing himself on the mercy of the parliamentarians, who were more than glad to have him serve as an example of how Irish nobles would be allowed to surrender peaceably.

None of the Catholic bishops aspired to command, especially after the disastrous results of the Bishop of Clogher's leadership of the army of Ulster and his execution after the Irish defeat at Scarriffhollis in June. The only Catholic and Irish nobleman in Ireland who had the social and political stature necessary to replace Ormond was Ulick Burke, fifth Earl and first Marquis of Clanricarde.

Clanricarde was an Old English Catholic and a devoted royalist. He had retained close ties with both Ormond and the Catholic royalists in the Confederation of Kilkenny throughout the 1640s. During the political crisis in the Catholic coalition in the summer of 1650 Clanricarde had worked diligently to prevent the prelates from deposing Ormond and excommunicating those soldiers who continued to obey Ormond.[20] He had served as the royalist political and military commander in Connacht from the beginning of the Irish rebellion of 1641. While his military accomplishments were not brilliant, he had maintained a modicum of internal peace in his province throughout the decade. In addition, he was well connected by family ties and education with the English nobility.[21] Finally, he was Ormond's first choice for selection as Lord Deputy of Ireland.[22]

Clanricarde had shown more vigour in his military actions during the summer of 1650 than he had in any comparable time in the past decade. The approach of the English armies to the borders of his province of Connacht accounted for this increased energy. Although he was not appointed Lord Deputy until December, he was the *de facto* Irish commander from at least September. By October Clanricarde had organised an army of 3,000 men to relieve the pressure being exerted on Lord Dillon's garrison in Athlone.[23] When Ireton marched south from Athlone to Limerick in early October, Clanricarde's army was in a position to launch a counter-attack over the Shannon to destroy the supply areas then supporting the English forces in King's County and to cut English communications between Athlone and Limerick.[24]

The Irish offensive caught the English off guard when Clanricarde's army crossed the Shannon at several fords south of Athlone, probably near Shannonbridge, in early October. The Irish surprised and captured the English garrison in Ferbane Castle and pushed Colonel Axtell's regiment south, across the River Brosna. After a brief skirmish at a ford over the Brosna, Axtell withdrew towards Birr, allowing the Irish to seize the three small English posts at Cary Castle, Streamstown Castle and Cloghan.[25] Fearing that he might be cut off in Birr, Axtell retreated to Roscrea, leaving a strong garrison in Birr to defend some important siege artillery stored there.

While Axtell retreated, James Preston joined Clanricarde with reinforcements, bringing Irish numbers to 'upwards of four thousand foot and five hundred horse'. By mid-October English reinforcements were on their way to Axtell as well. Ireton sent Colonel Abbot with a regiment of dragoons and Colonel Shelborne with one of infantry to Axtell from Kilkenny, while the governor of Wexford, Colonel Cook, advanced with additional infantry and cavalry. These forces linked up with Axtell's troops at Roscrea on 21 October. Axtell then began to move this army towards Birr and Clanricarde's army.

When Clanricarde learned that the English were approaching, he decided to withdraw his troops to Meelick Island, in the River Shannon, about eight miles north-west of Birr. There he placed his soldiers in excellent defensive positions overlooking the fords from the east which the English would have to cross if they wanted to attack the Irish entrenchments.[26] Clanricarde probably believed that in such positions his soldiers could defeat an attack by Axtell's column which they also outnumbered.

Things did not go as Clanricarde planned. An English participant later reported that:

> Upon five and twentieth of October, half an hour before night, our forces made an attempt upon the enemy, and after a small dispute beat them from the first and second guard on the pass; But at the third the dispute was so hot that they came to butt-end of musket, and God being pleased to give our forces an entrance into the island, the whole body of the enemy was presently routed.[27]

Evidently the English attack completely surprised the Irish. Once the rout began, the Irish lost perhaps as many as 1,000 men who drowned in the

Shannon while trying to cross the river in the dark. English losses were light. The English captured Clanricarde's personal wagons and tents, along with the entire baggage train of his army.[28] The loss of weapons, tents and horses was perhaps as serious a loss as the manpower for the Irish.

The disaster at Meelick ended the most promising Irish offensive operation in months. The castles which they had captured on the east side of the Shannon quickly surrendered, and the tactical superiority of the English troops and commanders was again demonstrated to anyone thinking of joining the Irish army. Clanricarde wrote to Ormond on 2 November, telling him that 'I found my forces in great disorder having lost their baggage and much of their arms and so disheartened that they could not be drawn to any service, until they were refreshed.'[29]

THE CATHOLIC COALITION UNDER NEW LEADERSHIP, NOVEMBER–DECEMBER 1650

After the defeat at Meelick all that remained for Ormond to do was to appoint Clanricarde as his successor and depart as soon as possible. Ormond had the king's permission to do so, and Clanricarde was ready, reluctantly, to accept the office of Lord Deputy. He even agreed to try to unite and lead the various factions in the Catholic coalition, including, as he wrote to Ormond, 'those obdurate senseless people' in Galway, with whom he had experienced stormy relations in the past ten years.[30]

However, before he appointed Clanricarde as Lord Deputy, Ormond launched one last blast against the Catholic prelates in an effort to salvage some of the king's authority in Ireland. On 23 October he wrote to the Commissioners of Trust, demanding that they negotiate with the prelates to get them to agree to rescind the edict of excommunication for those who upheld Ormond's and the king's authority.[31] He also convened the Confederate General Assembly at Loughrea on 15 November and demanded that the delegates reaffirm their obedience to the king before he appointed anyone to govern Ireland.[32] Ormond's letters were ill-received by the bishops, but there were enough Ormond sympathisers in the General Assembly to temper their response. A committee was formed to discuss Ormond's account of things and to answer his demands. The General Assembly, dominated by laymen anxious to preserve some unity and to get on with the war, responded to Ormond in a moderate fashion, reaffirming royal authority in Ireland:

> We the Lords spiritual and temporal, and Gentry met in this assembly, conceiving that there is no better foundation and ground of our union, then the holding to, and obeying his Majesties authority . . . nor is there any power in the Lords spiritual or temporal, Gentry or people, clergy or laity of this kingdom that can alter or change or take away his Majesties authority.[33]

In return, Ormond agreed to 'leave that authority with us in some person faithful to his Majesty, and acceptable to this nation'.[34] The General Assembly's reply included a final paragraph, however, which pointedly recalled how the royalist coalition had lost so much ground against the English while led by Ormond.

Ormond accepted this reply and on 6 December appointed the Earl of Clanricarde as Lord Deputy. He shortly thereafter left Ireland in a frigate sent by the Duke of York to transport him to France. He was followed into exile by Lord Inchiquin and the remaining Protestant royalist commanders in Ireland.[35]

Ormond had failed to preserve the Stuart cause in Ireland or to prevent the English parliamentarians from conquering three of the four Irish provinces. None the less, while he had not accomplished what he set out to do when he returned to Ireland in 1648, he had contributed to Charles II's attempts to defeat the regicides in London. Ormond had united most of the factions of royalists, Catholics and anti-parliamentarians in a great coalition which came very close to bringing all of Ireland under royalist control. This achievement made Cromwell's conquest much more difficult than it would have been had the Irish, Scots, royalists and Old English remained fragmented and at war with one another in 1649.

The Catholic coalition tied down increasing numbers of English troops in 1650, forcing the English republic to provide a continuous flow of men, money and resources to Ireland. This meant that English resources were stretched thin when Scotland prepared for war against the English Commonwealth in the spring and summer of 1650. Consequently, Cromwell was not able to lead as large an army as he would have liked into Scotland in July. England's need to continue to pour resources into Ireland, even after the capture of all of the ports of Leinster and Munster, prolonged the war in Scotland and increased the odds in favour of a royalist victory there. This was a significant contribution to the overall royalist strategy in Britain. Had the numerically superior Scots defeated Cromwell, the royalist strategic situation would have been dramatically improved. Cromwell's unexpected victory over the Scottish army at Dunbar with his badly outnumbered army on 3 September 1650 was due mostly to the Scottish commander's mistake in giving the English an opportunity to fight the kind of pitched battle in which English tactical dominance could be exploited. Had the Scottish commander, David Leslie, continued to pursue a Fabian strategy, he might have broken the English republic financially by prolonging the Scottish war.[36] The opportunity to do so owed much to the stiff resistance offered by Ormond's royalist coalition in 1649–50.

Ormond, however, lacked the tactical and leadership skills needed to stop the English onslaught in Ireland. As S. R. Gardiner correctly concluded, 'If nobility of character combined with almost infinite patience could have availed him, Ormond might have saved Ireland from impending ruin. As it was, not only were the conditions of action persistently adverse to him, but his inbred royalism made it impossible for him to inspire confidence in his Celtic countrymen, who were sufficiently keen-sighted to perceive that they must exist without Charles, or that they could not exist at all.'[37]

Clanricarde and the Catholic coalition now faced overwhelming odds in their attempt to prevent the completion of the English conquest of Ireland. They lacked the financial resources for purchasing the weapons and munitions needed to equip the still abundant Irish manpower. Equally as bad, they lacked the experienced officers needed to train and lead their soldiers in the kind of pitched battles which had to be won if they were to drive the English out. They lacked the artillery necessary to breach the defences of the walled towns and castles held by English garrisons. Finally, they did not have the unity necessary to exploit fully the resources that were available to them.

However, the Irish were still not conquered. Lacking any way to negotiate an acceptable peace with the anti-Catholic Puritans, the Irish fought on in the only way they could. Conventionally organised Catholic units continued to defend Connacht, while bands of tory guerrillas struck English garrisons in the other three provinces.

By the summer of 1650 it was impossible for Englishmen to travel outside the cities and towns of Ireland without a sizeable military escort.[38] English tax-collectors and purchasing agents were prevented from gathering money or supplies from the Irish countryside because of the military activity of guerrilla bands which were becoming numerous and strong enough to raid up to the walls of English garrisons. The English had not anticipated this situation, believing instead that once their armies had defeated the Irish royalists and captured their towns, the Irish would have no choice but to surrender. This did not happen, in large part because the English offered no way for a Catholic population to surrender honourably.

This situation placed an unbelievable strain on English resources, forcing Ireton and the London government to change their estimates of how much manpower and money would need to be sent from England in order to win the Irish war.

THE ENGLISH LOGISTICAL EFFORT, 1650–51

Ireton sent the English forces into winter quarters in November 1650. Sir Charles Coote and Colonel Venables quartered their regiments in the coastal towns of Ulster, with strong garrisons on the northern and eastern borders of Connacht. The English billeted large units in Dublin, Kilkenny, Wexford, Waterford and Cork. At least another 120 smaller garrisons of up to 100 soldiers each guarded castles throughout Leinster and Munster to prevent tories from finding refuge.[39]

The campaigns of 1650 had worn down the English army in Ireland in a number of ways. The return to winter quarters was needed to reconstitute the physical power and fighting spirit of the English soldiers. The *Calendars of State Papers* for 1650 and 1651 are full of requests from Ireton and Coote to the Council of State and parliament for replacements, supplies and money. The constant refrain was that the soldiers were exhausted, often hungry, and inadequately clothed. The guerrilla operations conducted by the tories had exhausted the food resources of many Irish counties, exacerbating the English logistical problems. As the English commissioners in Dublin observed, 'The stock of cattle in the country is almost spent so that about four parts in five of the best and most fertile lands in Ireland lie waste and uninhabitable.'[40]

English commanders and commissary officers bought as many foodstuffs as possible in Ireland. But the army, which had grown to 25,000 men by May 1650, and to 35,000 men by July 1651, was too large to be supplied fully in a country impoverished by ten years of warfare. The London government had little choice but to provide a steady supply of food, money, replacements and equipment if it intended its armies to maintain the offensive in Ireland.

Complicating English logistical difficulties was the simultaneous need to support the army of over 16,000 soldiers engaged in the Scottish campaign, beginning in July 1650.[41] Although this English army was victorious in the battle of Dunbar in September, the Scots had raised fresh regiments and forced a stalemate on Cromwell's army along the line of the Firth of Forth throughout the winter and spring of 1650–51. At the same time the Commonwealth's navy expanded from forty-four to seventy-two major combatant vessels, with major squadrons deployed to Lisbon, in the Irish Sea, the English Channel and the North Sea. These military deployments throughout Britain and Ireland and on the high seas cost immense amounts of money to support. By November 1650 the English parliament found it necessary to raise the land tax, known as the Assessment, to £120,000 per month to provide the largest part of the £2.5 million needed per year to pay and supply its military forces.[42]

The Irish war was the largest drain on English resources in 1650. At least 12,000 soldiers were required to man the hundreds of English garrisons scattered throughout Ireland. The field armies operating against Connacht and Limerick required another 12,000 to 18,000 men. Disease, desertion and combat losses constantly reduced these numbers, forcing the English to send a steady stream of replacements to Ireland from England. Between August 1649 and March 1650 the English sent 7,000 replacements to Ireland to reinforce Cromwell's regiments.[43] By August 1650 the need for additional replacements had become pressing.

The Westminster government responded to the requests from its field commanders by raising additional regiments to send over and by recruiting individual replacements to refill the regiments already in Ireland. Companies and regiments of replacements marched from throughout England to ports of embarkation such as Chester, Bristol and Milford Haven. The government armed and equipped these soldiers before they were transported to Ireland.[44] The officers and many of the men sent in 1650 were veterans of the English Civil Wars. Their arrival in Ireland provided an immediate boost to the fighting power and spirits of Ireton's army. At least 6,940 English soldiers travelled in this manner to Ireland between March and December 1650.[45]

In spite of these replacements, the combat losses due to the assault on Clonmel in May 1650 and the steady attrition caused in the English ranks by disease throughout 1650 continued to erode English combat strength. This trend was intensified by the need to install so many garrisons throughout the Irish countryside in an effort to defeat the tory menace. By October 1650 the English manpower situation was serious. A shortage of infantrymen was one of the reasons why Ireton's council of war recommended that the army withdraw from its position before Limerick and go into winter quarters.

The Council of State in London responded to the continued need for replacements by redoubling its recruiting efforts. However, the concurrent requirement to supply a steady stream of replacements to Cromwell's army in Scotland made it impossible any longer to find sufficient numbers of veterans of the Civil Wars willing to enlist for overseas service. Consequently, in April 1651 parliament passed legislation to allow the Council of State to raise 10,000 men by impressment to be sent to Ireland to fill the regiments deployed there. The Council of State quickly ordered the county militia committees to select these draftees from the militia.[46] These recruits were impressed into service and marched to embarkation ports with an armed escort. By May the Council of State was able to issue orders to its agents in the ports to transport these men to Ireland, and by June they had arrived there.[47] These soldiers did not fare as well as did those soldiers who arrived as part of organised military units. They were not properly armed or clothed before leaving England, and they were not assigned to units until they reached Ireland. They seem to have died at a much higher rate from disease than the soldiers recruited and shipped over in organised units.[48]

In addition to these individual replacements, the Westminster government raised a number of complete companies and regiments, totalling 7,200 men, for service in Ireland during the period from January to October 1651. These soldiers were commanded for the most part by veteran officers. They were armed and equipped in England and shipped to the front as units.[49] These troops were much better cared for than the impressed men who travelled to Ireland under armed escort.

The English government sent at least 43,000 soldiers to Ireland between June 1649 and December 1651. These men joined the parliamentary forces already stationed there, totalling about 9,000 men in Dublin and Derry alone. At least another 2,000 Protestants defected from the royalist coalition to the parliamentary cause in November 1649. By December 1651 over 55,000 soldiers had served in the English armies in Ireland. However, by the summer of 1652 no more than 35,000 English soldiers remained alive in Ireland.[50] There is no evidence that any regiments were shipped back to Britain, nor do the contemporary accounts mention desertion as a problem.

Roughly 37 per cent of the English forces raised for the Irish campaigns since March 1649 had died by July 1652. Most losses were the results of disease. Plague was probably the biggest killer, especially in the spring and summer of 1650, when the disease ravaged most of Ireland's towns and cities, killing English and Irish alike. In Dublin, a major garrison, as many as 1,300 people died per week as a result of the plague during the summer of 1650.[51] The disease killed the lieutenant-colonel, major and many soldiers in Colonel Hewson's Dublin garrison in August and September 1650 alone, badly weakening the defences of that city.[52] The plague probably killed as many Irish soldiers as English, helping in that way with the conquest.

The assault on Clonmel was the only battle in which significant numbers of English soldiers were killed (2,000 died in that assault). Another 2,000 English troops died at the siege of Limerick in 1651, again mainly from disease. England's ability to conquer Ireland was due first and foremost to her ability not only to replace these losses, but steadily to increase the size of her forces in Ireland so that the entire country could be occupied.

Clothing the troops in Ireland was another persistent logistical problem. Only a small percentage of the clothing needs of the English forces could be met by Irish production. Consequently, most of the clothes worn by the English soldiers had to come from England. During the winter of 1649–50 the English government sent more than 17,000 complete sets of clothing to Cromwell's soldiers in Ireland.[53] This supply of shoes, shirts, breeches and cloaks was essential for the soldiers during Cromwell's winter campaign. By the summer of 1650 the need for clothing had increased with the size of the army. While English soldiers often used the clothes of their deceased comrades to replace worn clothing, this source was not sufficient. Therefore the English state had to provide a steady stream of clothing to Ireland.

During 1650 the flow of supplies, including clothing, diminished, probably owing to the strain of supplying men, money and materials for Cromwell's invasion of Scotland. Only 6,000 pairs of shoes, 5,000 sets of clothes, 1,200 pairs of boots and 16,200 stockings were shipped to Ireland from March to December. With the increase in tax revenues in early 1651, the English government was able to increase significantly the amounts of material, food and munitions sent to Ireland. From January to October 1651 the government bought and shipped 23,000 complete sets of clothing, 28,000 shirts, 16,000 pairs of stockings, 10,000 hats and 8,000 yards of cloak cloth to Ireland.[54] Additional clothing was purchased in Ireland by the soldiers with some of the £196,000 in cash shipped over to pay the troops from March 1650 to October 1651.[55]

Feeding the armies in Scotland and Ireland was equally difficult and important for the English Commonwealth. The ravaged Irish countryside, increasingly pillaged by Irish irregulars and English punitive expeditions, could not feed the forces. During the winter of 1649–50 the English government sent millions of pounds of wheat, rye, oats, salmon and cheese to Ireland.[56] Between March and December 1650 no less than 149 tons of oatmeal and 10,400 bushels of wheat were shipped to the forces in Ireland to supplement the food which the reasonably well-paid soldiers could purchase.[57] However, with the growing devastation of Ireland, English shipments of food supplies had to be increased. Between January and October 1651 the government shipped at least 57,000 bushels of wheat, 54 tons of oatmeal, 1,000 tons of cheese and 1,340 barrels of wheat flour to its troops in Ireland.[58]

These food shipments were considered part of the soldiers' pay, and deductions were made from the amounts owed to the troops. The troops also received 1,030 kettles in which they could prepare their food while on campaign, and over 2,000 tents to shelter them from the elements.

The English government also harnessed the market economy in England to provide food for its forces in Ireland. Dozens of merchants requested and received export licences to ship grain and food duty-free to Ireland to sell to the soldiers and the populations of English-held towns.[59] The ingredients for beer and ale made up the largest proportion of such food exports in the period 1650–52. For example, the Council of State issued export licences for the export of at least 84,160 bushels of malt and 43,360 bushels of barley between November 1651 and October 1652. Brewers in Dublin, Derry, Waterford and the other major towns used these grains to brew beer which was then sold to the soldiers in retail shops and to the government in bulk for the use of the field armies. The Council of State also issued licences for the export of significant amounts of other food such as peas, beans, beer and salmon.[60]

The need for firearms and ammunition placed additional strain on English resources. The English sent 12,000 matchlock and snaphance muskets, 4,500 pikes and 200 pairs of pistols to Ireland in 1650–51. These weapons, along with 10,000 bandoleers, were in addition to the arms carried by all of the soldiers sent over, except for the 10,000 pressed men, who were armed in Ireland. Eighteen tons of lead bullets, eleven tons of iron, and thousands of barrels of gunpowder provided the army in Ireland with the means to carry on the war.[61]

England's ability to raise and ship such large amounts of food, clothing and munitions to Ireland prevented its large army from disintegrating, as

English overseas expeditions had routinely done in the 1620s. The royalists in a politically divided and war-ravaged Ireland could not compete successfully in the long run against a nation that could marshal such manpower and material resources. In the face of England's immense resources, the Irish struggled to raise even the paltry sum of £20,000 to buy munitions in Europe in the autumn of 1650. By that time the Catholic forces had lost all of their sources of organised logistical support, except for that which was provided by the towns and population of Connacht. Their only hope was to raise money from foreign sources. ▄

France, the wealthiest Catholic monarchy that might have helped the Irish, was badly distracted by the Fronde, by a major war against Spain, and by its need to support the exiled English royal family. The French also feared that if the Catholics in Ireland succeeded without royalist help, the position of Spain and the papacy in Ireland would be improved at the expense of the French position.[62] So France remained aloof, other than to harbour fleeing royalists such as Ormond. Spain, the other most likely benefactor of the Catholic cause in Ireland, was equally preoccupied with wars throughout Europe and the Mediterranean region. In fact Spain was seeking the goodwill of the English Commonwealth, respecting both its naval and military power. The main Spanish concern seemed to be to maintain access to the manpower resources of Ireland while denying the same access to her mortal enemy, France.[63]

By 1650 the growth of English naval power made it risky for any European power openly to support the enemies of the English Commonwealth. Portugal found this out when she allowed Prince Rupert to seek sanctuary in Lisbon harbour with his royalist fleet in the autumn of 1649. Shortly thereafter the English General at Sea, Robert Blake, arrived with a squadron of English warships and blockaded Lisbon for the next three months. The papacy, the last logical resort for the Irish, was near bankruptcy owing to her military exertions in Italy. More important, the papacy was unwilling to support the heretical monarch Charles II. The Catholic Assembly's decision in December 1650 to maintain Stuart authority in Ireland made it unlikely that much help would be forthcoming to the Confederates from Rome.

In a desperate effort to secure foreign help, some of the Irish Catholic gentry and prelates sought the help of the Duke of Lorraine. The duke was a professional soldier who had made large amounts of money as a mercenary commander and contractor during the Thirty Years' War. He was unemployed in 1650 and had lost his province of Lorraine to the French monarchy in 1634. Such a man had little to lose by considering the Irish offer. The Irish leaders who approached the duke offered him the position of 'Royal Protector of Ireland' and the use of some 'cautionary towns' to secure the large loans which they hoped he would make to them. They hoped that Lorraine would provide the money, munitions and cadre of trained soldiers needed to transform the still abundant Irish manpower into the kind of army that could defeat the English in pitched battles.[64]

Ormond and Clanricarde opposed such an approach to a foreign prince because of its potential threat to Stuart authority in Ireland in the long term. However, given the desperate Irish military condition, these negotiations progressed to the point where the Duke of Lorraine advanced £6,000 in cash and weapons to the Irish. However, the continued deterioration of the Irish military situation and Clanricarde's reluctance to accept the duke's authority deterred the Duke of Lorraine from undertaking an Irish adventure.

THE SAVAGE WAR OF PEACE, 1650–51

The fighting between major units abated during the winter of 1650–51 as both armies went into quarters.[65] The English forces regrouped, and Ireton carefully prepared 'all things that were necessary for the army, that they might be ready to march into the field early the next spring, making provisions of tents, arms, clothes, and bread for the soldiers; sending cannon and ammunition of all sorts towards Limerick by vessels provided to that end'.[66] Clanricarde lacked the money, food and arms to equip his forces for a major offensive, but he could rest his men and keep his regiments in existence for the coming struggle. Strategically, Clanricarde could only hope that the war in Scotland would prevent the English from supplying and reinforcing their forces in Ireland sufficiently for an offensive into Connacht. He concentrated his main efforts on defending Limerick and the major towns of Connacht, prompting an English correspondent to observe from Ireland 'that as they design that place for their garrison, we shall endeavour to make it their prison until as such time God makes way for us to go over amongst them.'[67]

Irish forces did not remain completely idle during the winter. Tory bands raided English garrisons and ravaged the farms and villages in English-held territory. They carried out these raids to support themselves and to deny resources to the English, and the results could be bloody. In the words of a contemporary news report,

> They come out of the wood, being persuaded to it by acuteness of the winter, and expecting prey, have been made a prey themselves: and have been surprised by our forces. . . . They have done great harm when they came in, killing the country people with the sword, and consuming their houses with fire, but being taken by our forces, they have answered for their cruelty with the forfeit of their lives.[68]

Often the raiders surprised their prey and then escaped, as when in December 'some of their men killed and robbed some of Kilmallock merchants, between Cork and Mallow, whereupon a party of 300 foot and 200 and odd horse of ours went out . . . but through the extremity of weather . . . could not overtake the enemy, but have driven them up to

Kerry mountains'.[69] Tory raiding parties often numbered several thousand men, especially in the counties of Wicklow and Cavan, where there were bogs and mountains in which they could hide. These formations lacked the discipline and equipment needed to stand up to considerably smaller English units. They could not prevent English punitive expeditions from applying scorched-earth tactics to their subsistence areas.[70]

When tories were able to surprise smaller English units, they inflicted considerable damage. In November the Irish guerrilla leaders Scurlock and Sir John Dungan surprised and defeated a column of several hundred English soldiers with a force of 500 tories, killing forty Englishmen. The guerrilla bands also frequently succeeded in capturing small isolated English garrisons, usually of fewer than twenty soldiers, before reinforcements could be sent to them. These attacks steadily eroded English strength and caused great alarm in Dublin, where Hewson ordered the removal of Catholics from that city and other English-held garrison towns, fearing that they might help the tories from within.[71]

In response to these tory raids, the English organised a number of campaigns during the winter to destroy tory strongholds and supply areas. Some of these punitive raids were local, as when 'Colonel Axtell hath again marched into the enemy's quarters 17 miles from Kilkenny, and there was a strong castle kept by 140 men with provisions for their supply this winter. Colonel Axtell summoned the castle, the governor refused to yield, he then battered some five hours and fell to storming, and then the Irish submitted to mercy.'[72] Farther north, the English maintained pressure on the isolated Irish strongholds, as when, in January 1651, 'a party of ours went into the King's County to a place called Balenoy and took it, putting those [Irish] which were there (six score and eighteen persons) to the sword'.[73] The Irish responded, 'plundering up and down' near Dublin, 'killing the country people, and firing and burning of houses, corn, and other provisions'.[74]

Some English expeditions were major efforts, as when the English launched a two-pronged campaign into the counties of Longford, Cavan and Westmeath. These counties had been controlled by the Irish since 1641. Owen Roe O'Neill had used this region as a major supply base on a number of occasions, owing to their remoteness from major English garrisons and their proximity to the Ulster recruiting grounds of his army. As late as 1651 much of this area remained hostile territory to the English.

In February 1651 Colonel Hewson led a force of 2,300 men from Dublin to Tecroghan, south-west of Trim. From there he drove west towards Mullingar, where several thousand tories were harassing an English garrison. As Hewson moved west, Commissary-General John Reynolds led another English column north from Kilkenny and into southern Westmeath, driving before him a large number of tories. These English columns captured castles at Kilbride, Erlestown and Donaghmore before meeting near Ballymore in Westmeath. As they moved, the English established garrisons in strategically important castles and seized significant quantities of food in the places abandoned by the Irish.[75] While Reynolds strengthened the defences of Ballymore, Hewson drove the Irish out of Ballinalack, 'a considerable pass [over the Inny River] out of Westmeath unto Longford'.[76]

From Ballinalack, Hewson reported, 'the Commissary-General and I agreed to march to Finea, where we heard was great store of forces to entertain us'. When they neared Finea, on about 12 March, they saw a large Irish force marching south from Cavan towards them. Although the two forces exchanged musket fire, the English could not attack the Irish because a small castle stood between the two armies. While Reynolds watched the tory band with his troops, Hewson planted his artillery and began to batter the castle. On his third shot, the Irish garrison 'did quit the castle, and run away unto the bog'. The English army then advanced to Finea, as the Irish force retreated 'much faster back from us'. Sending Sir Theophilus Jones with 400 cavalrymen and a regiment of infantry to pursue the Irish, Hewson stormed Finea's defences. The Irish garrison repulsed his assault, forcing Hewson to summon the garrison and to offer lenient terms.[77]

Meanwhile Jones had caught up with the rear of the retreating tories, killing upwards of 400 of them. When he returned to Finea with this news, the Irish commander there saw that his situation was hopeless and accepted Hewson's terms. The garrison was allowed to depart, after surrendering all weapons and supplies. The capture of Finea and the castles in Westmeath gave the English a much stronger position in the area, while the loss of supplies and winter quarters badly crippled the Irish forces.[78]

This punitive expedition, and others like it, did not stop the guerrilla campaigns. The capture of famous tory leaders like Scurlock did not end the war either, as many others came forward to take their place. The Irish could not stand up to the English in pitched battles; the English could not hunt the Irish out of every bog and mountain range in Ireland. None the less, the English continued to apply the torch to areas harbouring tories, and the tories continued to raid English-held areas. The tories' raids could not defeat their enemies, since the English received most of their supplies from England. Additionally, such guerrilla actions added little or nothing to the military situation of the Catholics, while inflicting untold misery on the local inhabitants caught in the middle. The often indiscriminate nature of these attacks prompted Clanricarde to condemn the tory partisans, especially since the tory campaigns diverted men, weapons and food away from the main Catholic efforts to defend Connacht from the anticipated English offensives in the spring.[79]

During the long winter of raid and counter-raid the English reinforced their regiments and stockpiled the supplies and equipment needed to launch a major offensive into Connacht from three directions. Clanricarde's forces received little help from outside. Given the paucity of their resources, it is remarkable that the Catholic regiments survived at all as organised units. All attempts to get help from France, Spain and the papacy had failed. The scheme to bring the Duke of Lorraine in as the Catholic 'Protector' had foundered as well. The only hope for Clanricarde and the Irish now was that Charles II would somehow defeat Cromwell in Scotland, thus compelling the Westminster government to withdraw its support from its army in Ireland.

Had the English offered the Catholics some way to surrender honourably, without loss of religion or life, the war might have ended at this point. But the English Puritans refused to do so, leaving the Catholics no choice but to fight on until total exhaustion. The English, however, did begin to consider a way to end the tory threat that did not require the extermination of every Irish soldier. The method would be simple, though not cheap. The English could allow the French and Spanish to hire Irish mercenaries to serve in their respective armies in the ongoing Franco-Spanish war. This policy would remove from Ireland thousands of men who had known nothing but war for the past ten years and who had little prospect of finding a place in post-war society. It could not be initiated, however, until the Irish were finally convinced that they had no military hope in Ireland, and to do that would require the occupation of Limerick and Connacht.

By April 1651 the only thing preventing Ireton from launching his offensive against Limerick, Athlone and Sligo was the need to wait for the spring grass to grow so that his cavalry and artillery horses could be fed.[80] By May, as the English columns began to close in on Connacht, time had run out for Clanricarde's forces.

9

The Conquest of Connacht and the Collapse of the Catholic Cause, 1651–3

All Irish are generally dejected, even the prelates themselves, despairing of either ability of defence or of gaining conditions.

Clanricarde to Ormond, 26 Nov. 1650[1]

lthough the savage guerrilla war in Ireland continued, the strategic situation changed little from November 1650 to May 1651. The English maintained their hold on all of the major towns and castles of Ulster, Leinster and Munster, with the notable exception of Limerick. The Catholic–royalist coalition controlled all of the province of Connacht, County Clare and the city of Limerick. No political solution was possible as long as the English refused to end their war of annihilation against Catholicism and to allow Catholics to exercise their religion in Ireland. English aims made the Irish fight with grim determination to defend Catholic religious liberties.

By May 1651 nearly 35,000 English soldiers were under arms in Ireland, backed by a powerful artillery train and unchallenged naval power.[2] Sir Charles Coote and Colonel Robert Venables held Ulster in a firm grip and had prepared a field army of over 4,000 men for offensive operations once the spring grass could support their horses. Colonels John Hewson and Edward Cook commanded the garrisons in Dublin and Wexford and maintained steady pressure on the tory bands in the Wicklow hills between those two places.[3] Roger Boyle, Lord Broghill, commanded the English forces in Cork and western Munster, where he and Colonel Henry Cromwell waged a war of attrition against the Irish forces in Kerry. And Lord Deputy Henry Ireton operated out of Kilkenny against any major Irish raids launched from across the Shannon, while he also prepared for the spring offensive against Limerick.[4]

Roughly 30,000 Irish Catholic soldiers remained in the field against the invaders. However, over half of these soldiers were scattered throughout Ireland, serving in isolated tory bands and strongholds.[5] The heart of Irish resistance to the English was in County Clare, the province of Connacht, and especially in the towns of Galway, Limerick, Sligo, Athlone and Loughrea. The Earl of Clanricarde had assumed Ormond's duties as political and military commander of all of the king's forces in Ireland, although his effective control did not reach far outside Connacht. Geography favoured the defenders of Connacht and Clare. The River Shannon provided a strong natural barrier against the English advance, since the river was fordable at few places, and all of the likely passage points over the river were in Irish hands (see Map 15). Clanricarde, however, displayed a misplaced sense of security in the face of English preparations for an assault on Connacht when he wrote that the 'enemy is drawing strongly together about Killegat; but I cannot imagine what design they can have worth their labour and spoil of horse, the Shannon I presume very *jure* against any attempt they can make.'[6]

CLANRICARDE'S STRATEGIC SITUATION, 1651

Clanricarde and the members of the Catholic–royalist coalition faced a difficult, but not hopeless, military and political situation in 1651. Lacking adequately trained and armed soldiers, Irish units could not defeat large English formations in the kind of pitched battles that they needed to win if they were to turn the tide of the war against the invaders. Without an acceptable political solution to their predicament, the Irish could only hope for a royalist victory over Cromwell's army in Scotland. This was not impossible, at least theoretically. Charles II had gathered a well-equipped royalist army of 15,000 infantry and 5,000 cavalry near Perth and was waiting for the right opportunity either to defeat Cromwell in Scotland, or to evade his army and march into England, where Charles and his advisers hoped to ignite another English civil war.[7] However, English military strength in Scotland and England increased significantly over the winter as Cromwell anticipated Charles's options. By June over 21,000 English soldiers were with Cromwell in Scotland, and the English were bringing a large number of regiments in England up to full strength to face a possible Scottish–royalist invasion.[8]

During the winter of 1650–51 Clanricarde and many of the prelates and Catholic lay leaders made every effort to heal the wounds within their coalition that had been caused by the ousting of Ormond. The Catholic Assembly, meeting in Loughrea in December 1650, proclaimed its allegiance to Charles II and to Clanricarde as his Lord Deputy.[9] The bishops called upon all Catholics to serve together with Catholic royalists such as Clanricarde against the common foe. But these efforts barely papered over the deep fissures between Clanricarde and his Old English supporters and the Gaelic Irish. The efforts of conciliation made by the Catholic Assembly failed to absolve Clanricarde for his efforts against the Gaelic Irish during the early years of the rebellion. Internal distrust and bitter memories of past betrayal remained perilously close to the surface, as a contemporary source described:

> The realists and the royalists by woeful experience were severally ascertained of Clanricarde's double dealing and thwarting of proceedings since these commotions [began in 1641] . . . and consequently, not well pleased with such whom he reputed his antagonists; notwithstanding [this, he] winked at the matter until he had the king's sword and managing of the kingdom in his power, as the *non plus ultra* to be aimed at. True it is they could never assure themselves in his fidelity in the execution of his charge, nor he of their loyalty and reality towards him.[10]

A number of Irish leaders still hoped that foreign military aid would arrive to turn the tide of war. Consequently, Clanricarde agreed to continue negotiations with Charles, Duke of Lorraine, for military and financial assistance from that mercenary in exchange for recognition of his title as Protector of Catholic Ireland.[11] The Stuart court in exile in France approved of this approach to the duke as well, probably recognising that he would pose no effective threat to Stuart sovereignty in Ireland, even if he bolstered Irish resistance. Representatives of the duke and the Catholic Assembly conducted negotiations in Ireland from February to April 1651, while Lord Taaffe met in Brussels with the duke's representatives at the same time.[12] Little real help for the Irish came of these negotiations, in part because the English victories in Scotland and Ireland showed the duke the hopelessness of the royalist military situations in Ireland and Britain. None the less, some Irish leaders believed that the Duke would deliver. 'Let none doubt the said duke be able to do it,' observed the royalist Colonel Richard Plunket, 'for he is a wise prince, very rich, wants no good council nor commanders, hath a good army, and the best horsemen in the world.'[13]

By May 1651 the Duke of Lorraine had cooled towards the idea of accepting the office of Protector, partly because Spain refused to let him embark his troops from the Netherlands, and probably also because he recognised the futility of a military effort in Ireland with the limited forces at his disposal.[14] Taaffe, negotiating in Brussels for Clanricarde, became desperate for an agreement as the news from Ireland worsened. Consequently, on 22 July he signed a compact granting the duke far greater sovereignty over Ireland than either Clanricarde or Charles II would ever consider accepting.[15] However, military events in Ireland and actions of the English navy in June made it impossible for the duke to embark troops for or to sail to Ireland safely.[16] By October Clanricarde's repudiation of the July agreement ended the Lorraine episode in the Irish war.

Irish royalists also hoped to receive help from the continental Catholic powers, but it was obvious to informed observers that by May 1651 the Spanish and French were both courting 'or in league with the rebels [i.e. the republican government in London]'.[17] This was not surprising, given the tremendous growth in English naval power, Cromwell's victories over the Scots at Dunbar (September 1650) and Edinburgh (December 1650), and Admiral Blake's defeat of the last royalist naval squadron in the Mediterranean.[18] The French and Spanish remained interested in Ireland only for its value as a recruiting ground for Irish Catholic soldiers to serve in their armies on the continent. The English government was more than willing to meet this demand for manpower by shipping defeated Irish regiments from Ireland to Spain or France.[19]

Clanricarde had heard nothing from Charles II in six months and was definitely feeling the burdens of his office.[20] His time and efforts were taken up fully with the need to organise his forces in Connacht to face the expected English offensive. In pursuit of this objective, he commanded a coalition of Irish Catholics who, 'whatever lip-service Irish priests and patriots might render to the idea of Royalty . . . had made up their minds to fight their own battles without reference to a king who in Presbyterian hands was a hindrance rather than a strength'.[21]

The Catholic coalition's military forces were deployed to defend Connacht and Clare against attacks from all directions. In the west several thousand soldiers led by Major-General Thomas Preston, the veteran professional soldier who had commanded Waterford during its long siege, garrisoned the city of Galway. In the south Hugh O'Neill commanded another 3,000 soldiers in the garrison of Limerick. O'Neill was probably the best Catholic commander in Ireland. He had performed brilliantly in the siege of Clonmel, inflicting on Oliver Cromwell the costliest military setback in that great general's career; he had also thwarted Ireton's first attempt to capture Limerick in October 1650. Lord Muskerry mustered a force of 3,000 men in western Kerry, while in the east Lord Dillon commanded a garrison of 500 men in Athlone, the critical crossing-point of the River Shannon on the road between Dublin and Galway. In the centre the Earl of Castlehaven led a mobile force of roughly 3,000 soldiers in Clare, from where they could quickly march to support Galway, Athlone or Limerick, depending on which was threatened. Clanricarde commanded another reserve in central Connacht. The initiative lay with the English, but the Irish forces were as ready as they could be to defend civil and religious liberty for Catholics.[22]

THE ENGLISH STRATEGY, 1651

Oliver Cromwell's departure from Ireland in May 1650 had left a vacuum in the English political and military structure which had only partially been filled by the appointment of Henry Ireton as Lord Deputy. Ireton was, at best, an able soldier. He lacked the time and energy needed to command both the field forces and to serve as chief executive of a conquered nation. Perhaps as serious, he lacked the political skills needed by a chief governor of Ireland to placate the various political factions that made up the Protestant coalition in Ireland.

Ireton displayed remarkable political naïveté, as when he failed to give Lord Broghill a suitable military promotion during the reorganisation of the English forces for the spring offensive of 1651. Broghill had expected to be made Lieutenant-General for his services in the 1649–50 campaigns. He therefore felt neglected and threatened politically when Ireton appointed Edmund Ludlow to that post. In an angry letter Broghill told Ireton that he would obey only the orders of Oliver Cromwell. This challenge was deflected when Ireton made Broghill Lieutenant-General of the Ordnance, a rank accompanied by a considerable salary.[23]

The English Council of State recognised the need for a civil government in Ireland. In June 1650 it appointed two commissioners, Edmund Ludlow and John Jones, to serve in Ireland as the political executive of the English occupation. The Commission for Ireland was later enlarged to four members (with the addition of John Weaver and Miles Corbet) and vested with the task of re-establishing a judicial system and civil administration in Ireland and with the supervision of tax collection.[24] The four commissioners, who were men of stature within the regicide cause in England and close adherents of Cromwell, finally arrived in Ireland in January 1651.[25]

Since it was evident by the autumn of 1650 that the conquest of Ireland would be successful, the English Commissioners for Ireland organised a government structure for the more effective establishment of political order. Initially six 'precincts' were established in the areas firmly under parliamentarian control. As the English forces extended their effective control, additional precincts were added, until by 1652 there were twelve.[26] In each of these precincts the sub-commissioners worked closely with the local military commanders to stamp out resistance to English rule and to begin the collection of taxes. Before the Dublin government could hope to raise much money in the way of taxes, it was essential that they re-establish a system of civil justice, protected, of course, by the local military garrisons. The power and role of Ludlow and the other commissioners increased significantly with the death of Ireton in November 1651. From then until 1653 there was no Lord Deputy in Ireland, and the commissioners assumed all of the powers of that office.

The 'commissioners spent a considerable time in debating and resolving in what manner justice should be administered for the present [in 1651] in each precinct, till the state of affairs could be reduced into a more exact order'.[27] They appointed sub-commissioners for Dublin, Waterford, Cork, Clonmel, Kilkenny and Ulster to collect the excise, customs, and assessment taxes. These administrators served alongside the military governors such as Hewson in Dublin and Axtell in Kilkenny. The commissioners appointed two special inspectors (Colonels Herbert and Markham) to travel from place to place in order to ensure that the sub-commissioners were executing their duties properly.[28]

Eventually, by 1653, the English were able to return the government of Ireland to more tradition civilian control. At that point the judicial system of pre-war Ireland was again in operation, manned in large part by the same New English planters who had held the judicial offices in 1641. Charles Fleetwood, another son-in-law of Oliver Cromwell, had assumed the duties of Lord Deputy of Ireland, and a traditional council had replaced the commissioners in Dublin. By 1655 a Lord Chancellor again oversaw the administration of justice through the 'traditional "four courts" — chancery, upper bench (in place of king's bench), common pleas, and exchequer — and the pre-war system was virtually restored'.[29] However, all that was in the future in the spring of 1651.

With the political commission established in Dublin to handle the civil administration, Ireton was free to plan his offensive. In early May, as re-inforcements and supplies flowed into his garrisons, Ireton summoned his leading officers to Clonmel to plan the attack against Connacht. Ireton's council of officers determined that the city of Limerick was the key to the Irish defence of Connacht. Until that city on the east side of the Shannon fell, English forces operating to the west of the Shannon would be vulnerable to attack or harassment from their rear. However, they concluded that a direct attack against Limerick would fail and that the capture of Limerick 'could not be expected till we had blocked them up in both sides [of the Shannon]'.[30] A plan was therefore developed that called for three simultaneous attacks against the remaining Catholic strongholds, making it necessary for the Irish to divide their forces and confusing them as to the main English attack.

Sir Charles Coote was to lead the northern prong of the offensive from Ulster into Connacht, along the coast near Ballyshannon and Sligo. Coote's army of 5,000 men was to bypass the River Shannon to the west and to sidestep around the Irish garrison in Sligo. He was then to march south-wards to Athlone, the key Irish position in the centre of the Shannon line. Commissary-General Reynolds was to ford the Shannon north of Limerick with a mounted force of 1,500 men and to march across country towards Athlone to reinforce Coote's column.[31]

Venables was to maintain the pressure on the tories in Ulster and north-ern Leinster with a force of 4,300 men, of whom 1,300 were to serve as a mobile striking force.[32] Hewson was to campaign against the tories in King's County and make a feint toward Athlone from the east side of the Shannon. Ireton was to muster the main force of 8,000 infantry and cavalry at Cashel and march in the direction of the Shannon north of Limerick. As Ireton's column moved towards Limerick, Lord Broghill and Henry Cromwell were to lead a company of 2,500 men west of Mallow in order to provide flank protection against any threat from Muskerry's Irish forces in western Kerry. Finally, the English navy was to sail a major flotilla up the Shannon to Limerick, 'with our artillery, ammunition, provisions, and all things necessary for the siege of Limerick'.[33]

THE ENGLISH OFFENSIVE, JUNE 1651

Ireton's council of officers at Clonmel broke up in mid-May and set the campaign against Clare and Connacht in motion. By early June Sir Charles Coote's column had marched past the Irish garrison of Sligo, through County Mayo, and was moving south-east towards Athlone and Portumna.[34] This move took the Irish by surprise, as they had expected Coote to march from Enniskillen southwards into Connacht across the Curlew Mountains and had fortified the passes on that route against him.[35] Clanricarde reacted promptly, calling for a rendezvous of all available forces which could be used to march north against Coote, who he thought would try either to take Sligo or perhaps march into Mayo.[36]

Clanricarde's move northwards with an army of 3,000 men to protect Sligo and Mayo played into the English plan. Coote had no intention of besieging Sligo, a course of action which might have taken weeks and diverted him from the main campaign against Athlone, Limerick and Galway. His immediate objective was Athlone. Although Clanricarde thought he held a good position from which to stop Coote, 'Coote, wheeling about, got 15 miles in this side of him ere he had knowledge of it, which amazed him much'.[37] Clanricarde could only pursue Coote's column southwards.

At about the same time as Coote was manoeuvring into Connacht and around Clanricarde's army, Ireton marched his army from Cashel through Nenagh to the Shannon opposite Killaloe. There he was faced across the river by Castlehaven's troops in fortifications which blocked the passage to the western side of the river.[38] Ireton's move towards Killaloe prevented Clanricarde from concentrating all of his forces in the north to fight Coote or to reinforce the garrison at Athlone.

Ireton's column remained hung up opposite Castlehaven's positions at Killaloe only for a short time. After a reconnaissance of the Shannon from Killaloe south to Castleconnell, Ireton determined that the river could be crossed by small boats south of O'Briensbridge, almost half way between Killaloe and Limerick. Once a force could be transported across the river, the English could build a bridge which would allow large units to be supplied on the Clare side of the Shannon.[39] The approaches to this crossing-point traversed the bogs on the east side of the river, and it was therefore necessary for Ireton's soldiers to build a corduroy road with logs and earth so

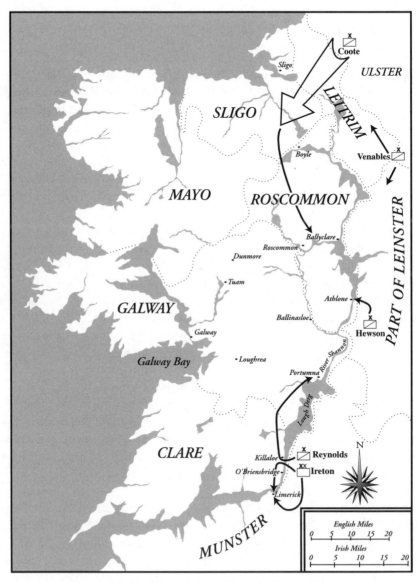

15. *English Assault on Connacht, June 1651*

that troops and cannon could be marched to the river's edge in readiness for the crossing.

Remarkably, an English regiment commanded by Colonel Reeves built the road without attracting the attention of Castlehaven's scouts. On 1 June, when the road was completed, one cavalry and three infantry regiments with four cannon marched 'silently to the place where boats were ordered to lie'. Three files of infantry and some cavalrymen crossed in the first three boats just before dawn on 2 June. They reached the western bank un-opposed, with the horsemen leading their swimming horses from the boats. Once ashore, this small force surprised a nearby Irish garrison in a small castle and then protected the crossing of additional English troops from an Irish force that was approaching from the west. Cannon fire from the English artillery on the eastern bank of the river helped the advance guard to break the assault of an Irish regiment that attacked the bridgehead.[40]

As the English consolidated their position on the western bank, the Irish decided to withdraw, 'to provide against our [the English] falling upon them'.[41] Ireton's crossing near O'Briensbridge and Coote's movements towards Portumna forced Castlehaven to withdraw his troops from Killaloe. Consequently, the Irish troops protecting the remaining crossing-sites over the Shannon either surrendered or abandoned their posts.

The Catholic commander of Athlone, James Dillon, found his garrison caught between Coote's advancing column and Hewson's troops on the east side of the Shannon. Either because he felt his situation was hopeless, or because of treachery, Dillon decided to surrender Athlone on 18 June with-out facing a long siege or an English assault.[42] The *Aphorismical Discovery* commented: 'By this surrender, all human hope of the Irish is now at a stand, for all the enemies of Ireland may now come together without control into the province of Connacht.'[43] The loss of Athlone opened a major breach in the Shannon defences of Connacht, giving Coote direct communications with Dublin for reinforcements and supplies. Coote captured thirty barrels of gunpowder, eight cannon and three months' provisions in Athlone. He quickly continued his march toward Galway.[44]

Castlehaven still commanded a force of at least 2,000 men which could either have reinforced Clanricarde against Coote or hindered Ireton's advance towards Limerick. Ireton understood these dangers and moved quickly against Castlehaven to prevent him from reinforcing Clanricarde. Castlehaven hesitated in deciding what to do next. This hesitation gave Ireton the chance to attack his force with two converging columns, causing the rapid disintegration of the poorly commanded Irish. 'Whereupon' (in the words of a contemporary report) 'both commander and other [troops] with mighty disorder and speed ran away.'[45]

Ireton and Coote had broken Clanricarde's hold on the Shannon from Athlone to Limerick. As the *Aphorismical Discovery* noted, 'The said

Shannon, the Irish bulwark and loyal spouse of the nation, was now become a prostitute, rendering free passage unto all comers, and denied any favour unto its former possessors.'[46] Ireton now was able to march his main force, unopposed, south along the west bank of the Shannon to Limerick, where he was met by an English fleet carrying his heavy guns and tons of supplies and siege equipment. Simultaneously he unleashed Commissary-General Reynolds with a column of 1,500 soldiers to drive north to reinforce Coote.[47]

As Reynolds marched to join him Coote moved against the Catholic garrison at Portumna, the seat of the Earl of Clanricarde. Clanricarde, meanwhile, had marched his army south to Loughrea, where he learned that he was too late to save Athlone or to prevent Ireton from crossing the Shannon. Even then, however, he still could have attacked Coote before Reynolds joined him, possibly saving Portumna and inflicting a defeat on the English. At this opportunity, Clanricarde displayed the same timidity that had prevented him from taking the initiative against enemy forces for the past ten years. As he paused at Loughrea some of his Connacht units retired to their homes, leaving Clanricarde with a force made up largely of Leinster and Ulster Irish commanded by Lieutenant-General Richard Farrell. Farrell urged an immediate attack against Coote, but Clanricarde ordered a withdrawal to the west. This decision left the English columns free to unite near Portumna. 'Standing upon the defensive part, [Clanricarde] did never measure his strength or resistance to the assailer, nor ever offered to prevent or divert his motion till past recovery.'[48] Clanricarde never demonstrated his military incompetence more clearly than in these actions.

Receiving no help, Portumna's commander surrendered, leaving Coote free to march towards Loughrea and Galway.[49] Castlehaven's force had disintegrated and Clanricarde's had retreated toward Galway, leaving towns like Loughrea, Gort, Tuam and Roscommon vulnerable to English attack and with no hope of relief. Clanricarde soon 'left the army, and with a sad heart fled to some place,' while 'Castlehaven himself is so confounded (through the Lord's justice) [that he is] flying to and fro with his shattered horse, intending it is thought to break through Athlone into Leinster to turn tory.'[50]

With Coote's capture of Portumna and Clanricarde's retreat to Galway, Ireton was free to continue his march south to Limerick. On 3 June he arrived opposite Limerick, cutting that city off from all communications with Clare. Ireton's main force faced Limerick from the north-west side of the Shannon, near the Thomond Bridge to King's Island, on which the main part of the city was situated. On 14 June, after establishing a battery of twenty-eight siege guns aimed at the castle on the north end of the Thomond Bridge, Ireton summoned Hugh O'Neill to surrender.[51] O'Neill refused. The final siege of Limerick had begun.

Ireton's move against Limerick provoked a vigorous response by the Irish forces in western Kerry. In mid-June Lord Muskerry marched towards

Mallow with nearly 3,000 soldiers, hoping to take that town and castle.[52] If he succeeded at Mallow, from there he could attack the English garrisons on the eastern side of the Shannon that had cut Limerick off from supplies and reinforcements from Munster. Muskerry also hoped to unite his force with the large tory bands operating in western Leinster and Munster.[53] Such an operation, if successful, could badly upset Ireton's siege of Limerick.

Lord Broghill had expected such a move. To defeat it, he had divided his forces to cover the approaches from western Kerry towards Mallow and Limerick. Hearing of Muskerry's advance, Broghill marched to Mallow with about 1,000 soldiers on 21 June. Upon his approach, Muskerry withdrew westwards towards the mountains. Broghill pursued with about 400 cavalrymen, catching up with the Irish at an encampment about midnight on 22 June. Surprised, the Irish 'drew away in haste and disorder' into the hills. Broghill continued the pursuit, closing to within four miles of Muskerry on the 23rd. But Muskerry was able to elude Broghill's pursuit and retreat across the rain-filled Blackwater river to Drishane on the 25th. The English abandoned the pursuit at that point, returning to Mallow for supplies.[54] Muskerry's retreat in the face of a numerically inferior enemy demonstrated the tactical superiority of the English and its continuing negative impact on Irish military operations.

With Clanricarde's force in retreat, and now commanded by Lieutenant-General Richard Farrell, and with Castlehaven's and Muskerry's forces dispersed, most of the soldiers of the Irish army joined the ever-swelling ranks of the tory bands. The English took most of the towns of Connacht rapidly and without resistance. Sligo and Galway held out in that province, and Limerick remained the only significant place held by the Irish in the rest of Ireland. The Irish war was reduced to the sieges of Galway and Limerick, and the anti-tory war throughout the kingdom.

THE ANTI-TORY CAMPAIGN, 1651–2

'By breaking to pieces of their army, the country is everywhere very full of Tories': thus wrote an observer in Waterford in June 1651.[55] The defeat and disintegration of the larger Irish formations gave the English an additional major military problem. Until they defeated the tory resistance, the English could not end the war and reduce the enormous cost of maintaining an army of 35,000 soldiers in an island ravaged by a decade of almost continuous warfare. The English decided to use a scorched-earth strategy to defeat the bands of guerrillas whom they could not easily hunt down and destroy. The first steps of this strategy had been taken in the autumn of 1650 with Ireton's march through Wicklow. That punitive expedition had failed to end the tory presence in Wicklow. The bitter war waged against the tories in the winter of 1650–51 proved equally futile in ending the partisans' attacks on English supply columns and garrisons, although it devastated large swaths of Irish countryside. So, in April 1651, the Commissioners for Ireland decided to launch a still more ruthless campaign against the tory threat.

The war against the tories came increasingly under the direction of the Commissioners for Ireland. They had to deal with the problems of reconstituting civil order in a conquered society that had known only war for ten years. The establishment of hundreds of garrisons throughout the towns and countryside had not ended the menace that thousands of armed soldiers, who had been scattered by the defeats of the royalist armies, posed to the English.[56] These soldiers took cover in the bogs, woods and hills throughout the country. From these refuges they attacked English supply columns, tax-collectors and small military units. Therefore, in order to deny the tories intelligence and supplies from sympathisers living close to English garrisons, the commissioners

> ordered and declared, that all and every person and persons whose parents, husbands, sons, or brothers are in actual rebellion . . . or live in any woods, bogs, or other places, . . . do within fifteen days . . . remove themselves, their children and families out of the said garrisons and places adjacent within two miles distance of every respective garrison.[57]

The commissioners also ordered garrison commanders to demolish any huts, cottages and cabins that might be used to shelter tories or their relatives within two miles of the garrisons. In this way the English hoped to drive the Irish still in arms into the remoter parts of the country where they could do the least harm to the English and to those many Irish who had made their peace with the conquerors. These measures did not defeat the guerrillas, but they did impede tory access to supplies and information. It is also clear from the evidence that many ordinary people had come to accept the English occupation. English rule was not demonstrably harsher than that of the displaced Catholic gentry, and the English provided markets for Irish farm produce, while the tories could only seize food and goods without payment. Further, tory brutality to those who collaborated could backfire, as the country-people grew tired of depredations from both sides and opted to support the stronger English forces.

With their enemies theoretically driven away from the major towns, the commissioners hoped that they had forced the tories into areas that could be identified as hostile territory. This would allow the occupied areas to recover without threat of guerrilla raids. The commissioners issued proclamations protecting those people who had come to terms with the English occupation and providing for the encouragement of tillage of abandoned land and the restocking of the flocks and herds which made up much of the agricultural wealth of Ireland. They included in these measures tax incentives for farmers who raised hay for the use of the English army as well.[58]

After ordering the expulsion of all people related to suspected tories, the commissioners found that there was no appreciable decline in attacks on

English columns or officials. Consequently, they decided to quarantine the tory-infested areas of occupied Ireland, and to declare those areas 'free-fire zones' in which English forces could destroy any person or habitation without cause, other than the fact that a person or building was in a designated hostile area:

> And whereas the places . . . hereafter named, are known to be harbours for the enemy, and for other bloody and mischievous persons, who do there assemble and meet together . . . thence to commit daily murders, rapines, thefts, and all kinds of spoil and villainy, upon such as desire to live peaceably under the protection of the English Army . . . it is ordered, that from the tenth of April 1651, until the tenth of April 1652 . . . all such as shall continue to inhabit the same, after the said tenth of April next, shall be, and are hereby declared to be places and persons excepted and excluded from the protection of the Parliament and Commonwealth of England.[59]

The commissioners' proclamation listed parts of the counties of Tipperary, Waterford, Wicklow, Carlow, Queen's County, King's County, Kilkenny, Cork, Limerick and Wexford as excluded from English protection. They ordered all persons willing to live at peace with the English to abandon their homes in the proscribed areas. Anyone remaining after 10 April 1652 could be 'taken, slain, and destroyed as enemies, and their cattle and other goods there found, shall be taken or spoiled, as the goods of enemies'.[60] The commissioners allowed people willing to leave the free-fire zones to settle on any waste or untenanted lands within the protection of the English parliament, as long as these abandoned lands were not already allocated to support the English garrisons or to recompense men who had advanced money for the conquest of Ireland in the 1640s.[61] It is unclear how many people responded to this order.

English commanders also found that many of their soldiers had become acquainted with Irish women during the winter. Numerous marriages had resulted,[62] and this particularly disturbed Lord Deputy Henry Ireton. Ireton did not believe that many of these Catholic women had really seen the light of Protestantism and converted sincerely to that faith, although that was a prerequisite before they were allowed to marry English soldiers. Ireton therefore issued an order which threatened to reduce to the enlisted ranks any officer marrying a Catholic woman unless the sincere conversion of the woman could be confirmed by reputable Protestant ministers. Similarly, he ordered that any cavalryman who did so was to be reduced to a foot-soldier, and foot-soldiers who did so were to be reduced to pioneers, the lowest military caste.[63] There is no evidence of whether or not this policy was enforced with any vigour. Certainly the proportion of Irish females to males was excessive, owing to the losses which the war had inflicted on the male population. The presence of so many well-paid and well-fed Englishmen was too good an opportunity for some Irish women to ignore. No army in history has been able to separate the sexes in such situations, and it is doubtful that Puritan rigour did any better.

As the campaigns against Limerick and Connacht continued during the summer, the English deployed troops to reinforce the social and economic policies aimed at breaking the Irish insurrection. In July Colonel John Hewson led a punitive expedition from Dublin into the outlawed areas of County Wicklow, where his mission was to cut the unripened grain, thereby denying it to the local population. On another similar foray to the west, he destroyed the fortifications at Tecroghan, west of Trim, and other castles not needed by the English, preventing the tories from using them as bases. English commanders in Munster and Ulster conducted similar campaigns in an effort to drive the guerrillas away from the Irish population.[64] The English waged these brutal campaigns against women and children as well as against armed men for an entire year, but they failed to end the tory threat. Only the eventual English deportation of Irish soldiers overseas to serve in the armies of Spain and France would relieve Ireland of a population of young men who had known little but soldiering as a trade for the past decade. But the English had to conquer Ireland fully before they could implement such a policy. The punitive strikes did, however, prevent the tories in Ulster, Leinster and Munster from interfering effectively in the English campaigns against Limerick and Connacht.

THE SIEGE OF LIMERICK, JUNE–OCTOBER 1651

The initial phase of the English offensive against Connacht had gone remarkably well. The advance by three converging columns had prompted Clanricarde to divide and dissipate his reserves. Coote had outmanoeuvred Clanricarde and opened the front door to Connacht by capturing Athlone. A strong force of English cavalry thenceforth was maintained at Athlone to prevent Irish soldiers from escaping into Leinster and to protect the rear of Coote's siege of Galway and Ireton's of Limerick. Lieutenant-General Richard Farrell had assumed command of Clanricarde's dispirited army and had quickly retreated through Tuam to western Galway, pursued by English cavalry. Ireton followed up his defeat of Castlehaven by marching his army south to Limerick . By July Galway, Sligo and Limerick remained the only major towns still in Catholic hands.[65]

While Coote faced Galway, Ireton deployed the main strength of the English field army in a close siege of Limerick. Ireton had prepared meticulously for his second attempt to take Limerick. To improve his communications, he ordered the construction of 'a strong (not a floating) bridge' over the Shannon near O'Briensbridge, providing a solid crossing for his field artillery and supply trains. In addition, his engineers built a floating bridge much closer to Limerick, enabling the English to move troops quickly to either side of the Shannon, depending on the military situation.[66] Ireton organised the logistical details of the campaign equally well. English naval forces convoyed a flotilla of supply ships up the Shannon estuary, to where 'our ships near Limerick very comfortably furnish [the army] with biscuit, cheese, and what else they had'. Ireton's regiments had been filled with replacements before he moved, and he reported to London from Limerick in June that no more soldiers should be sent, 'we having men enough (with the remainder of the pressed men expected) to fill up all our regiments to 1,200 apiece, or very near (if not more)'. At least 9,145 soldiers had arrived in Ireland since March 1651, allowing Ireton to deploy 8,000 men against Limerick while his subordinates conducted active campaigns against Galway and the tories throughout Ireland with thousands more.[67]

The English began their attempt to take Limerick in late June with an attack on a small Irish-held castle on a fishing-weir upriver from the city. The English took this post quickly, after the first few rounds of artillery fire made direct hits on the castle, killing three members of the garrison. The surviving Irish soldiers fled from the castle in small boats, called cots, but the English artillery and musketeers on both sides of the river prevented them from escaping to Limerick. As a result, the Irish surrendered to English troops on both sides of the river, having been promised quarter. However, Colonel Tothill, an English regimental commander on the Clare side of the river, ordered his men to slaughter the captured Irish in cold blood, claiming that he had not given them quarter and that his soldiers had not been authorised to do so.[68]

This atrocity did not go unpunished. Ireton relieved Tothill of his command and had him tried by a court martial for his violation of the rules of war. The court of officers found Tothill guilty, cashiering him and his ensign, and ordered him home to England. Ireton also offered to make recompense to the families of the murdered Irish soldiers. Ireton's actions in this case were clearly designed to maintain discipline in his army and to offer hope of quarter to the garrison of Limerick if it surrendered on terms. To his credit, Ireton thought the punishment of the court 'fell short of the justice of God, requiring therein to the acquitting of the army from the guilt of so foul a sin'.[69]

Shortly afterwards Ireton ordered an attack against the fortified bridge leading from the Thomond side of the Shannon to King's Island, the main part of Limerick. The English, 'having battered and opened the nearer side of the castle on the bridge, and filled up . . . the open arch under their drawbridge before the castle, stormed it, and God gave it into our hands'.[70] The Irish defenders responded by breaking down two more spans of the bridge between the outer and inner castles, preventing the English from gaining access to the city by means of the Thomond Bridge.

On 23 June the English tried an audacious manoeuvre which might have led to the immediate capture of Limerick.[71] According to Ireton's report, 'We attempted (by great boats drawn from the ships below over land, towards the upper end of their island, and by other lesser boats, and a great float brought over from Castle Connell) to storm and possess the island . . . which if we had possessed we might suddenly have been masters of the town.'[72] This assault against King's Island, if successful, would have allowed English troops to enter the main part of Limerick over the low walls on the east side of town.

The initial amphibious assault was to have been carried out by 500 infantrymen commanded by Major Walker from Ireton's own regiment, using eleven boats and the great float.[73] However, ninety men in the first four boats separated from the remainder of the flotilla in the morning fog and landed on the island by themselves. Before the other boats arrived Walker and his men impulsively assaulted the Irish fortifications and succeeded in driving the Irish guards from the wall. Hugh O'Neill quickly rallied his garrison to face this threat, sending a regiment of at least 500 men to attack the English advance guard. The English were scattered by their early success and were unable to stand up to the determined Irish counter-attack. The entire English force was driven 'unto the river again, where pressing into the fifth boat that was but then landing, and half sunk before with shot from the enemy, they sunk her, and so all the officers and soldiers that went in those five boats . . . were all drowned or killed before the rest of the boats which were coming and the float could get over to second or relieve them'.[74] The remainder of the assault force did not attempt to land on the well-defended shore.

English attempts to take Limerick by storm had failed. Ireton now reverted to a close siege to starve the city into submission: 'We have strong forts and sconces raised on this [east] side, and unless they come down presently to low conditions, [we] can spare time and force to starve them out.'[75] The besiegers built defensive works on the north-west side of the Shannon as well, cutting off the approaches from Clare and Connacht. They constructed two additional large forts within musket range of the south-eastern walls of Limerick to prevent any aid or food from reaching the city from Munster.[76] Ireton manned these larger fortifications with 800 soldiers each, while maintaining a mobile reserve that could respond to threats from Irish forces on either side of the river. Broghill, Reynolds and Hewson continued to operate to the north and south of the city, repulsing any Irish forces that attempted to obstruct the siege. The fortifications surrounding Limerick kept the garrison confined within and prevented any relief of the place from without. Once these defensive works were completed, Ireton was able to send some of his infantry to reinforce Coote in his positions in front of Galway.

In July Muskerry again decided to attempt to relieve Limerick with an army of 3,000 soldiers, hoping to catch Lord Broghill unprepared in the process. By then Broghill had repositioned his units between the Catholic forces in Kerry and the ring of forts on the east side of Limerick to prevent the Irish from breaking the siege of Limerick. He had also conducted a number of raids into Irish territory to deter the assembling of an Irish force. As he was returning with a column from such a raid, he got word that a force of Muskerry's Irish cavalry was advancing toward his rear-guard. Hoping to fight a pitched battle, Broghill turned and deployed his units in open ground and advanced toward Muskerry's men. The Irish brought forward their infantry and attacked as the English moved forward. The fighting was fierce, as reflected by Broghill's account:

> We fired into each other's faces, and mingled. I had the happiness to kill the officer which led the division I charged, and after a round dispute, though we were so very much outnumbered and winged, that they charged us in flank and rear, and their pikes too galled us exceedingly, yet after a second charge on one of their rallying divisions, we gave them a total rout, and carried all that wing of horse and foot before us.[77]

The English pursued the Irish for three miles. Broghill ordered the killing of all prisoners except for men of 'good quality'. The Irish lost most of their weapons and many of their remaining veteran officers, along with hundreds of men killed. The English claim to have lost only 26 dead and 130 wounded; these low figures in comparison with Irish casualties are entirely believable in such a battle where defeated and fleeing infantry become vulnerable to pursuing cavalry.[78] This English victory ended the Irish threat to Ireton's siege from the south-west for some time.

As a result of victories such as Broghill's, Limerick was isolated from all Irish centres of resistance by early July. At this point in the siege Hugh O'Neill, the military governor of Limerick, offered to discuss possible surrender terms with Ireton.[79] O'Neill hoped to delay another English assault, giving Clanricarde, Castlehaven and Muskerry more time to break the siege. These negotiations went on for a number of days, but were abandoned when O'Neill refused to accept terms that did not allow the practice of Catholicism by the inhabitants. In the meantime it became clear that Clanricarde and Castlehaven were 'now slighted and suspected as much as Ormond and Inchiquin' had been in the previous summer.[80] The Limerick garrison could no longer expect any relief from outside.

Hugh O'Neill was a talented and inspiring military commander. He and his garrison of 2,000 Ulstermen were determined to make the English pay as dearly for Limerick as they had for Clonmel in May 1650. They even hoped that by holding out until winter they could force Ireton to raise the siege and send his troops into winter quarters, as he had done the previous

October. Therefore, in order to stretch out the limited supply of food in Limerick, O'Neill ordered the expulsion of many women, children and old men from the city. O'Neill's soldiers sent these obvious non-combatants towards the English lines, but Ireton refused to allow them to pass. Instead Ireton ordered his soldiers to send them back, as had been done by the besiegers at Colchester in England in 1648. None the less, O'Neill continued to eject members of the civilian population. Ireton, in desperation to prevent O'Neill from reducing the number of mouths to feed in Limerick, ordered his soldiers to execute four of the refugees now caught between the lines. But, through 'mistakes of orders, all the others (about 40) were put to the sword'.[81] This brutal move, as cruel as O'Neill's order to expel these people had been in the first place, eventually stopped the flow, but not before the English killed a number of innocent civilians.[82]

The major manoeuvres of the English summer offensive were completed by July 1651. Ireton's army of 8,000 men ringed Limerick on both sides of the Shannon. These well-supplied soldiers had constructed a ring of strong forts sited to cut the city off from all relief. Further away, Coote with nearly 5,000 soldiers had settled down to conduct a loose siege of Galway, preventing Clanricarde or Lieutenant-General Farrell from marching to Limerick's relief from the north. The English navy escorted a steady flow of supply ships to Galway Bay and the Shannon estuary to support these operations logistically. By the end of July most of the towns of central Connacht had surrendered and English forces were containing the tory bands in western Leinster, eastern Connacht and Munster.[83]

Hugh O'Neill, however, refused to give up easily. Whenever he saw an opportunity to surprise an isolated English unit, he attacked. Such sallies were always defeated, albeit with losses on both sides, mainly because of the superiority of the English cavalry.[84] But O'Neill's resistance kept Irish hopes alive in the summer of 1651. Consequently, Ireton's need to secure the newly conquered areas of Connacht and to maintain the sieges of Limerick and Galway obliged him to transfer forces to Connacht from the English garrisons in the more secure areas of Ireland. These transfers helped him to maintain his army's and Coote's strength, in spite of the loss of at least 2,000 English soldiers at Limerick alone as a result of disease and combat.[85] Because of these troop deployments, Irish tories were able to step up their raids against the English garrisons throughout the rest of Ireland. While these raids were costly to both the English and Irish, the Irish were unable to exploit this opportunity because a combat-effective Irish army no longer existed outside Galway.

O'Neill's garrison in Limerick could not hold out for ever. The food supplies dwindled as disease and battle casualties reduced the effective combat strength of the Irish regiments. The English suffered similar or greater losses, but these could be replaced, and the English soldiers remained well-fed.

Ireton was prepared to stay all winter if necessary, and O'Neill had no hope of relief. By September O'Neill faced increasing hostility from a faction of people within the city who wanted to end the siege by surrendering. These people felt it was essential to reach terms before the English found a way to breach the defences and sacked the city in accordance with the practice of war exhibited by the English at Drogheda. A majority of the city councillors agreed with this faction, along with Colonel Fennell, the officer who had tried to betray Clonmel to Cromwell the year before.[86]

Throughout September O'Neill had overruled this faction with the help of the Catholic clergy, who threatened to excommunicate anyone who surrendered. However, by late October the sentiment in favour of surrender increased, especially after Ireton established a battery of twenty-eight heavy siege guns 'against a part of the wall, which though it was of the same height and thickness with the rest of it, and also well flanked, yet it proved not to be lined with earth within as all other parts were, nor had any counterscarp without'.[87] Once these guns were in place and had began to demolish the wall, the pessimists decided to act before the English infantry assaulted the breach. On 23 October Fennell seized the gate on the south-eastern end of St John's Street and turned several cannon inward against O'Neill's loyal soldiers.[88] O'Neill had reached the end of his strength, and the excommunication threatened by the clergy no longer prevented the hungry and frightened citizens from surrendering. O'Neill asked for terms.

On 27 October O'Neill surrendered the city on terms far less lenient than had been offered by Ireton in June and July. The inhabitants received quarter for their lives and the right to keep their personal property. They were allowed to remain in Limerick, with the provision that they could be ejected from their homes with three months' warning. The soldiers of the garrison were allowed to march away to Galway with their baggage, but without weapons and ammunition. Twenty-two of the leaders and clergy in Limerick were excepted from the provisions granting quarter for life. These men, including Hugh O'Neill, several aldermen, the mayor and two bishops, were to be dealt with as the English saw fit.[89] Ireton's soldiers occupied the city on 28 October.

The siege had been costly. Over 2,000 English soldiers had died, along with at least twice that number of Irish soldiers and citizens. The majority of these casualties were due to disease. Only 1,300 Irish soldiers marched out. Not a single horse remained alive, testifying to the effects of the siege on the city's food supply. The English took possession of over 3,000 weapons in the city. Most importantly, the English had captured the last major Irish stronghold in Munster, without having to face the rigours of a winter siege.

The English took an awful revenge on the Irish leaders of the defence of Limerick. Major-General Purcell, the Bishop of Emly and Alderman

Thomas Strick were hanged after a brief trial and their heads placed on the city wall. Colonel Fennell was executed as a soldier of fortune, in spite of his services in opening the city to the English. Hugh O'Neill was tried by court martial for the crimes of resisting too well at Clonmel and Limerick. The court of officers was bullied by Ireton into finding O'Neill guilty and passing the sentence of death on him twice. But then Ireton, 'observing some of the officers to be unsatisfied with this judgment, referred it again to the consideration of the court, who by their third vote consented to save his life'.[90] O'Neill was spared, while seven of the twenty-two excepted persons were executed.

Ireton did not long outlive his victims. As Lieutenant-General Edmund Ludlow observed, Ireton 'had so totally neglected himself during the siege of Limerick, not putting off his clothes all the time, except to change his linen, that the malignant humors which he had contracted, wanting room to perspire, became confined to his body, and rendered him more liable to be infested by the contagion'.[91] He refused to take a rest before riding to Galway to see how Coote's siege there was progressing. After a number of exhausting rides from one garrison to another, and back to Galway, Ireton became mortally ill. Exhausted and weakened by his work, and having driven himself harder than he drove his soldiers, Ireton died on 26 November. Edmund Ludlow was appointed to serve temporarily in his place as parliamentary commissioner and commander-in-chief by the Commissioners for Ireland in early December. The prisoner of war Hugh O'Neill accompanied Ireton's corpse to London, where Ireton received a state funeral and was buried in Westminster Abbey.

THE FALL OF GALWAY AND THE END OF TORY RESISTANCE, NOVEMBER 1651–FEBRUARY 1653

After the surrender of Limerick, Galway remained the only major Irish-held town in Ireland. Major-General Thomas Preston commanded a garrison of 2,000 troops in the town, while Lieutenant-General Richard Farrell led an army of as many as 3,000 soldiers to the north of Galway, in Counties Mayo and Galway. The Marquis of Clanricarde remained titular head of the Catholic forces, but he exercised little if any effective authority. Thousands of Irish soldiers remained in arms throughout Ireland, commanded by regional leaders. These men were incapable of forming armies that could stay in the field as an organised force for any length of time or defeat any substantial body of English soldiers.

The English had overcome nearly all of Ireland, although their control of the countryside generally reached only a few miles outside of the hundreds of castles and towns they garrisoned. To end the war, the English needed to capture Galway and find a way to deal with the scattered but numerous Irish soldiers remaining in arms. Ireton held a council of his chief officers shortly after the capture of Limerick, hoping to craft a strategy that would end the war quickly. At this council he and Ludlow tried to persuade the leading officers that the army should be shifted to Galway to tighten the siege, believing that Galway 'would probably be soon brought to reason'. The majority of his commanders disagreed with this strategy, feeling that their soldiers had already suffered too much from the weather and the toils of a five months' siege in front of Limerick. They also believed that Galway would not be taken without a protracted siege.[92] In November Ireton reluctantly gave in to their advice, ordering most of the army into winter quarters.

The English units found winter quarters in County Clare and central Connacht. However, Ireton did ride to Galway with some reinforcements for Coote's army. While there, he sent a summons to Major-General Preston to surrender the town. Preston refused, and the siege continued while the English consolidated their grip on Connacht.[93]

Galway was not an easy town to encircle. The town lay on the eastern side of the River Corrib, and was protected on the south by Galway Bay, and on its northern approaches by Lough Corrib. Sir Charles Coote had established his forces only on the eastern side of the river, unable to surround the city because he had too few troops to do that and to defend his rear from Richard Farrell's Irish army to the north. Coote had been steadily reinforced from Athlone and Limerick during the summer. His supply situation was well in hand since the Commonwealth's navy had established a strong presence and blockade in Galway Bay. But Coote had not been able to prevent the Irish from sending supplies and reinforcements into the town. Owing to the difficulties of terrain, weather and shortage of troops, it looked as if Galway would be able to hold out until the English forces came out of winter quarters in the spring. Coote, therefore, put most of his soldiers into villages and castles in the immediate vicinity of Galway.

Irish morale had fallen to new depths with the loss of Limerick and the news that the last royalist army in Britain had been smashed on 3 September at Worcester by Oliver Cromwell and 40,000 English soldiers. In spite of this situation, Clanricarde tried one more time to rally the demoralised Irish by summoning a Catholic Assembly to meet in Jamestown, County Leitrim, in early November.[94] Little came of this meeting, and on 11 November Clanricarde dismissed the few delegates who had been able to attend. In January 1652 he tried to gather an army in front of Galway to use against Coote. However, this attempt to rendezvous the Irish forces was an abysmal failure. The Ulster contingents refused to attend, and, 'as for Munster and Leinster armies, there is no possibility of their going thither, all passages taken by the enemy.'[95] The Catholic bishops supported Clanricarde against the recalcitrant Ulstermen by excommunicating the officers and men who had refused to attend the rendezvous. This seemed to have as little affect on the Ulster troops as had a similar threat at Limerick in October.

After these futile attempts to resist the English, Clanricarde and most Irish leaders recognised the inevitable. At a council of Irish commanders in Galway in March, that included Clanricarde, Muskerry, Castlehaven, the Earl of Westmeath and Sir Lucas Dillon, it was decided that Clanricarde should open negotiations with the English to try to end the war. Accordingly, Clanricarde wrote to Ludlow:

> Many of the nobility, clergy, and other persons of quality, subjects of this kingdom, with the corporation of Galway, having considered the ruinous effects which this long war hath produced, have solicited me to desire you a conference for the establishment of the repose of this nation.[96]

Having little to offer in return for lenient terms, Clanricarde could only threaten that the Irish would sell their lives dearly and 'render your former conquests of little advantage'. Ludlow, who had spent a number of weeks directing operations against the tories in Leinster, returned a clear reply: 'That the settlement of this nation doth of right belong to the Parliament of England, to whom we are obliged to leave it; being assured that they will not capitulate with those who ought to submit to them . . .'.[97] Ludlow, the acting chief governor of Ireland since Ireton's death, refused to deal with the Irish council in Connacht. Instead he demanded that each Irish force in Ireland surrender individually. By refusing to deal with Clanricarde and his council, Ludlow made it clear that the Commonwealth did not recognise the existence of an Irish or a royalist government in Ireland.

The English demanded unconditional surrender from people they viewed as rebels. They had good reason to believe that they could end the war on these terms, especially after 7 March 1652, when Colonel John Fitzpatrick became the first regional tory commander to surrender his forces in Leinster on English terms. Fitzpatrick was spared and allowed to keep his estate, pending the decision of parliament about the ultimate land settlement. His action was followed shortly afterwards by Colonel Edmund O'Dwyer's surrender of the Irish brigade in Tipperary and Waterford (23 March) and Captain Edmund Daly's surrender of Roscommon (3 April). From then on, the floodgates were open, and most remaining Irish commanders surrendered over the next three months.[98]

Major-General Preston followed the trend by surrendering Galway to Sir Charles Coote on 12 May 1652. The lenient terms granted by Coote exceeded his authority by agreeing to let the citizens retain their property and homes permanently. Parliament's commissioners in Dublin quickly reneged on these terms, granting instead terms similar to those given to Waterford and Limerick.[99] There was little the Irish could do about this betrayal without resuming the hopeless armed struggle.

Most of the terms of surrender granted by the English in 1652 allowed the commanders of the Irish units surrendering to recruit their soldiers for service in the army of any state that was not at war with the Commonwealth of England. Thus Preston and O'Dwyer were allowed to recruit up to 5,000 men each and to transport them overseas. Lord Muskerry accepted similar terms for his army in Munster on 22 June 1652.[100] By allowing the Irish commanders to take regiments of Irish fighting men overseas, the English solved the major problem preventing the consolidation of their control over Ireland. They got rid of over 34,000 Irishmen who had known only war as an occupation since 1641. The departure of these veterans from Ireland ended the most dangerous tory threats to English rule. As the historian Gardiner succinctly commented, 'In this way the peace of despair was secured for at least a generation.'[101]

By August the English parliament was busy passing the legislation that would put into motion the 'Cromwellian' settlement of Ireland. This is a subject beyond the scope of the present account of Ireland's conquest by Puritan England; it has recently been analysed and described ably by Karl Bottigheimer's book *English Money and Irish Land*. On 28 June 1652 Clanricarde and his closest advisers accepted English passes to stay in or to depart from Ireland in safety. Clanricarde himself remained in Ireland for some time, and he also received permission to recruit soldiers for foreign service. The final surrender of some of the small Irish garrisons and tory units stretched into 1653. The misery of the Irish people continued, after more than a decade of war in which Sir William Petty estimated that over 600,000 out of a population of 1,500,000 had disappeared.[102] Worse, the divisions among the peoples of Ireland which had played such a large role in the defeat of the Irish and Catholic causes continue to this day. With the fall of Galway and the surrender of the Irish armies, the Cromwellian conquest of Ireland was complete.

10

Ireland: Aftermath and Settlement

This country is like to be a sad place this ensuing year for want of bread, many of the inhabitants perishing daily from want, and the common food of them in many places being horseflesh, grass and green ears of corn, so as there cannot be any considerable supply of bread, or other provisions for your forces.

Commissioners for Ireland to Council of State, 22 July 1652[1]

The collapse of large-scale organised resistance to the English army in Ireland in 1652 did not end the social disruption caused by the war. Over the next four years the defeated Catholic forces had to be disarmed and demobilised. During this process over 34,000 Irish soldiers were shipped overseas to serve as mercenaries in the armies of the major Catholic powers. The large English army in Ireland also had to be paid off and returned to civilian life, a task that required immense amounts of money from a government already badly strapped for cash. Ultimately the arrears in pay owed to the soldiers would be settled with expropriated Irish land, bringing about the largest land transfer in Irish history. The terms of this Cromwellian land settlement had to be finalised and a massive expropriation and transplantation of Catholic landowners put into effect. Amidst these traumatic events, the people of Ireland suffered the effects of disease, hunger and military occupation.

As a result of the war and these post-war crises, the social and economic patterns of life in Ireland were transformed and the population decline that had begun in the 1640s continued to take its toll. How extensive an impact did the wars and the period of Cromwellian rule have on the people of Ireland? How drastic was the population decline? How much land did Catholic proprietors lose, and how did the land settlement affect their tenants? Which groups of people suffered and gained most from the war, the Cromwellian regime, and the restoration of Charles II in 1660?

POPULATION LOSS AND CASUALTIES

There is no way to determine exactly the casualties and population losses caused by the war and the collapse of the Irish economy from 1641 to 1654. However, some evidence does exist that has enabled historians to estimate the magnitude of the disaster. The total population of Ireland in 1641 was probably between 1.5 and 2 million people. William Petty, the man responsible in the 1650s for surveying and valuing the lands of Ireland that were used to pay the debts the English government had incurred in the conquest, estimated that the population fell from 1,466,000 people in 1641 to 850,000 in 1652.[2] According to Petty's estimate, 616,000 people disappeared from Ireland. This is as good an estimate as we will probably ever have. Petty's detailed breakdown of these losses provides evidence concerning the magnitude of the Irish disaster.

According to Petty, a total of 112,000 British Protestants died between 1641 and 1652. Of these, he estimated that 37,000 were killed in the first year of the Irish insurrection. He estimated that 167,000 Catholic Irish were killed by the sword and by famine during the war. He thought that a minimum of 275,000, and perhaps as many as 400,000, died from the effects of the plague of 1649–52. Finally, he believed that between 1649 and 1652 a total of 40,000 Catholic soldiers and civilians were transported to the continent to serve in the armies of France and Spain. The sum of these categories is a minimum of 594,000 persons. This would mean that roughly 40 per cent of the pre-war population disappeared. The difference between this total of 594,000 and Petty's total of a population decrease of 616,000 is attributable to plague deaths, for which Petty gave a range.[3]

While these estimates must be regarded as tentative since they rely on Petty's limited means of counting population, they are by no means far-fetched. For comparison's sake, it should be remembered that of the 43,000 English soldiers shipped to Ireland from 1649 to 1652, solid evidence indicates that at least 8,000 had died by July 1652. Most of these deaths were due to disease. This was 18 per cent of the total force sent over to Ireland in three years. These soldiers had been reasonably well-fed and well-clothed. Their morale was relatively high, and they had tents to sleep in while on campaign. If 18 per cent of such a well-supplied force could be killed by battle and disease, it is not unreasonable to accept Petty's estimate that as much as 40 per cent of the population of Ireland died as a result of all causes during eleven years of war, famine and plague.

Much of the Irish population was starving by 1650. The English policy of free-fire zones, coupled with the raids carried out by both sides to deny food and shelter to their enemy, left much of the Irish population homeless and hopeless. Such a population was a perfect target for infectious disease. The bubonic plague that hit Ireland in 1649 found a weakened population. The plague raged for at least three years. It has been estimated that it killed

20,000 people in Galway alone in 1649–50. Another 5,000 Catholics died in Limerick during the siege of July–October 1651, and reports from Dublin placed the weekly plague deaths at 1,300 at the height of its visitation. The plague, on top of the economic disruption and misery of eight years of war, 'caused total collapse in the Irish economy, and it was not until the late 1650s that any sign of improvement can be detected'.[4] In such a situation, Petty's estimate that at least 275,000 people were plague victims is not unreasonable.

The exact number of deaths due directly to battle is impossible to determine, but it was significant. They royalists lost roughly 2,500 men at Drogheda, 3,000 at Rathmines, 2,000 at Wexford, and over 3,000 at Scarriffhollis in the year from August 1649 to July 1650. During the 1640s Catholic Confederate armies lost as many as 3,000 men at Dungan's Hill, 3,000 at Knockanuss, and several thousand more each at the battles of Liscarroll, Clones, New Ross and Bandonbridge. A large number of Catholic soldiers were also killed by the English when they captured dozens of castles during Cromwell's and Ireton's campaigns.

The war's impact on the agricultural system of Ireland was even more devastating, as crops were destroyed year after year by the armies moving about the land. During the period from 1641 to 1649 military operations and the accompanying destruction of crops and cottages were mostly confined to the contested areas between Catholic-controlled Ireland and the Protestant enclaves on the eastern coasts of Leinster, Ulster and Munster. The Cromwellian campaigns of 1649–52, however, spread death and destruction throughout Ireland. The results were catastrophic for the Irish population.[5] Petty's estimate that 167,000 Catholics were killed by the sword and by famine is not unreasonable in light of these battle losses and the desolation caused by military operations.

Casualties suffered by the English troops and British settlers were significant as well. Petty estimated that 37,000 Protestants died during the initial rising of 1641–2. Petty's estimate is well below the figure of 154,000 put forth by the English Protestant propagandist Sir John Temple in 1646.[6] These claims concerning the number of Protestants that the Catholic insurgents killed in the first year of the struggle have been hotly contested.[7] While there is no doubt that Temple's estimate was far too high, Petty's should not be so quickly dismissed.

The historian S. R. Gardiner provided one of the most reasonable discussions of this question in his *History of England* (1863–81). He concluded that not more than 4,000 or 5,000 Protestants were slain at the outbreak of the insurrection in 1641. But he also concluded that between 20,000 and 25,000 were 'slain and allowed to die of starvation in the first two or three years' of the war.[8] These estimates are in line with the estimates of historians today, who believe that as much as 20 per cent of the Protestant population (of between 125,000 and 200,000 people) died during the struggle.[9] In any case, it is clear that substantial numbers of Protestants died in the war.

Once the war was over, at least 34,000 Irish soldiers were transported to the continent to serve as mercenaries. They were accompanied by an estimated 6,000 women and children. Thousands more Irish soldiers had been shipped overseas during the 1640s to serve in royalist armies in Scotland and England, as well as to serve in the Spanish and French armies. These earlier overseas levies have been estimated to have totalled as many as 20,000 men or more, but there is no way to fix the exact number.[10]

Although there is debate about the exact numbers of deaths and the size of the population of Ireland in the 1640s, there is no doubt that the country suffered a demographic disaster at least equal in magnitude to that suffered by Germany during the Thirty Years' War. The memory of these deaths has haunted Anglo-Irish relations ever since. The land settlement that grew out of the war also transformed Ireland and remains one of the defining memories of modern Irish consciousness into this century. On the part of Irish Catholics, confiscation, transplantation and the slaughter of Drogheda stand as symbols of English oppression and Irish suffering. To Irish Protestants, the rebellion of 1641, with its attendant horrors, remains a potent element in their fear of Catholic rule. These are powerful and depressing legacies of the long Irish war of 1641–52.

THE CROMWELLIAN SETTLEMENT

What came to be called the 'Cromwellian' settlement of Ireland had its roots in the practice of English governments during the previous century of confiscating the land of Irish 'rebels' and of redistributing that land to those who paid for or took part in the defeat of the rebellion. In these confiscations, only the landowners, and not their tenants, were dispossessed. For example, the Munster Fitzgeralds and their chief vassals forfeited 574,645 acres in the 1580s as the penalty for their part in the Desmond rebellions. Over 200,000 of these acres were eventually planted with English Protestant landowners, but the Irish tenants and labourers remained to work the land.[11] The hope was that the newly planted landowners would bring Protestantism and order to Ireland, providing a firm base for royal power.

It was no surprise, therefore, when the English government in 1642 proposed that the anticipated costs of suppressing the Catholic insurgency in Ireland should be paid for by £1 million advanced by investors (or 'Adventurers') who would be repaid with confiscated Irish land. This proposal was readily accepted by a parliament that lacked the money needed to pay for the English and Scottish armies then to be sent to Ireland. Parliament passed and Charles I signed 'An Act for the Speedy and Effectual Reducing of the Rebels in His Majesty's Kingdom of Ireland' in March 1642. This act promised the Adventurers 2.5 million acres to repay their investment of £1 million. As a result of this act, 1,281 Adventurers advanced £306,718 to the Westminster government for the costs of the conquest. Most of this money was never used to support forces in Ireland. In spite of attempts to coax more money out of investors, the Adventurers' scheme of 1642 failed to provide the millions of pounds needed to pay for the conquest of Ireland.[12] One of the most important results of the 1642 act, however, was that many of the original contributors were prominent parliamentarians, making it likely that the confiscation of Irish land would be a prominent part of English policy in a conquered Ireland.[13]

After the surrender of Limerick the parliamentary Commissioners for Ireland and the Rump Parliament in Westminster turned to deal with the Irish settlement. By July 1652 the English army in Ireland had grown to 34,128 soldiers. These men were owed at least £1.5 million in back pay, and their estimated annual pay and costs of £523,000 greatly exceeded the £197,000 annual revenue of Ireland in 1652.[14] It was soon proposed to pay the soldiers' arrears with Irish land, saving the Commonwealth immense amounts of money. Such a proposal was not new, considering that the soldiers' arrears in England in 1649 had been also paid through the sale of the crown lands. What was new in Ireland was the idea that these soldiers would settle on the land they were paid with, thereby providing the Protestant interest with a permanent bulwark against the Irish Catholic population.

The Rump Parliament passed the act implementing the confiscation of Irish land to pay the Adventurers and the soldiers in Ireland on 12 August 1652. During the next two years the 'Cromwellian' settlement emerged as the English government and its Irish commissioners dealt with the often contradictory needs of paying off the Adventurers and soldiers, demobilising the English army, and destroying the economic and political power of the leading Catholic landowners in Ireland.[15]

The 1652 act laid out the basic scheme for who would be penalised, and in what manner, for the rebellion. If the act had been adhered to strictly, as many as 100,000 Catholics could have been condemned to death for their parts in the long war. However, financial exigencies and the need to restore order and economic activity in Ireland soon limited the application of the full power of the act to Catholic landowners and to not more than several hundred Catholic military leaders. A High Court was established to try those men responsible for the atrocities allegedly committed in the first years of the war. This court sat for two years and ordered the execution of fifty-four men. Remarkably, it seems that there were a number of acquittals in this process.[16] Beyond this, and the banishment of leaders such as Ormond, Clanricarde and Inchiquin, the reign of terror was brief.

The Act of Settlement of 1652 required additional clarification and modification before it could be implemented. A struggle soon developed between the Adventurers and the officers of the army in Ireland over who would get first access to the best Irish lands. The former wanted to be paid first with lands still populated by the Irish tenants and labourers who were essential to the profitable cultivation of the land. The soldiers wanted to receive their land at the same time as the Adventurers so that they did not receive the poorer lands. Additionally, many of the army officers believed that the entire Catholic population should be removed from the land, opening the country for a massive migration of tenants and labourers from England. After a great deal of debate parliament decided that the Catholic landowners who were guilty of rebellion under the provisions of the Act of Settlement should forfeit their lands and transplant themselves to lands in Connacht and Clare, where the local Catholic landowners were to make way for them. These men would be permitted to take their tenants and labourers with them.

As the specifics of the land transfer and transplantation to Connacht were debated and modified, a committee was established in Loughrea with which Catholic landowners were to register and to receive their allotted Connacht lands. Initially this process, including the actual transplantation, was to be completed by 1 May 1654. Reality soon set in, however, as it became obvious that no one even knew how much arable land there was in Connacht, let alone in Ireland, available for transfer. Furthermore, the issue of exactly who should be transplanted was only slowly resolved. Army officers such as Fleetwood and Axtell called for the strictest interpretation of the act, while the 'Old Protestant' landowners such as Lord Broghill recognised that such a policy would leave them and the newly planted Adventurers and soldiers with no tenants and labourers to work the land.

It took several years to resolve this debate in favour of the Old Protestants. In the meantime most of the soldiers sold the debentures they had received in settlement of their arrears of pay to their officers and to the Old Protestants in the vicinity. Consequently, by the time the land settlement was implemented, only 7,500 of the 34,000 soldiers eligible to buy confiscated land did so. The soldiers and the Adventurers shared the initial spoils, with the first pick of lands going to the politically well-connected Adventurers. Ultimately only 500 of the initial investors remained on the land after 1660, along with about 7,000 soldiers.[17]

Approximately 3,000 Catholic landowners forfeited their land and transplanted themselves to Connacht. The share of Irish land owned by Catholics was reduced from roughly 59 per cent in 1641 to 22 per cent in 1660.[18] In spite of the vague promises made by Charles II in the 1650s that the settlement would be reversed when he regained his throne, the Restoration left this Cromwellian settlement intact.

The majority of the land confiscated from Catholics and sold by the government fell into the hands of the Old Protestants, men whose families had come to Ireland before 1641. These men had formed an alliance with Henry Cromwell, the Lord Deputy of Ireland, by 1657 and eventually defeated the extreme anti-Catholic transplantation policies of the army officers and Puritan zealots in Ireland. They did so out of self-interest, but common sense was on their side as well. Since few Protestant tenants or labourers were willing to move to Ireland from England, Catholic tenants and labourers were essential if the lands were to be farmed and taxes paid to support the government and an army of occupation of 14,000 men.[19]

The English confiscated something like 11 million out of 20 million acres in Ireland, and transplanted 3,000 Catholic landowners and over 40,000 of their servants and families to Connacht. However, the wealthiest Catholic landowners for the most part escaped the penalty of confiscation. The Marquis of Ormond received the protection of Henry Cromwell, who allowed Ormond's wife to retain most of his extensive holdings. The Earls of Antrim and Clanricarde similarly escaped forfeiture of most of their land. The former made a deal with the Cromwellian officers in the 1650s, and both of these great landowners received special favours from Charles II in the 1660s.[20] Ormond was rewarded for his consistent loyalty to the king with the greatest Irish plum. Having been created a duke by the newly restored king, he was reappointed Lord Lieutenant of Ireland and served in that capacity, with intermissions, until the 1680s. From this position he was able to protect his extensive network of Catholic Butler relatives.

Protestant royalists such as Broghill escaped most of the penalties for their loyalty to Charles II and Ormond because they had shifted their loyalty to Cromwell early in the autumn of 1649. Those Protestants who had remained loyal to Ormond until the royalist coalition disintegrated in the summer of 1650 were allowed to save their estates by paying a composition fine. However, the Dublin government of Henry Cromwell evidently decided not to collect this money.

THE ULTIMATE LOSERS AND WINNERS

The common people of Ireland were the ultimate losers, especially the Catholic majority. Hundreds of thousands of men, women and children were killed by war, famine and disease. The Catholic merchants of the major towns were driven from their homes and forced to emigrate to the continent to continue their commercial activity. Three thousand Catholic landowners, most of whom had relatively small holdings, and many of their servants were forced to transplant to Connacht and to build a new life on smaller and less fertile estates. Those who refused faced execution or transportation to England's Caribbean colonies. While the majority of Irish Catholics were not transplanted to Connacht, those remaining on the land in the other three provinces exchanged their Catholic landlords for Protestants.[21]

The Old Protestants were the big winners in the 1650s. They increased their economic stake in the kingdom by preserving their estates and by buying confiscated land from the soldiers and Adventurers who had received that land as payment for money owed to them by the English

16. *Petty's Map of Great Britain and Ireland*

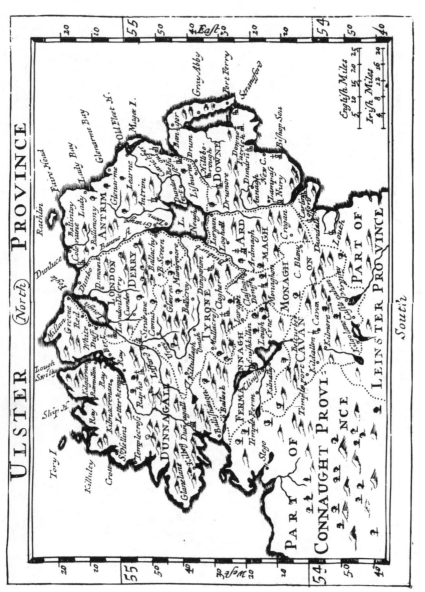

17. Petty's Map of Ulster

18. *Petty's Map of Leinster*

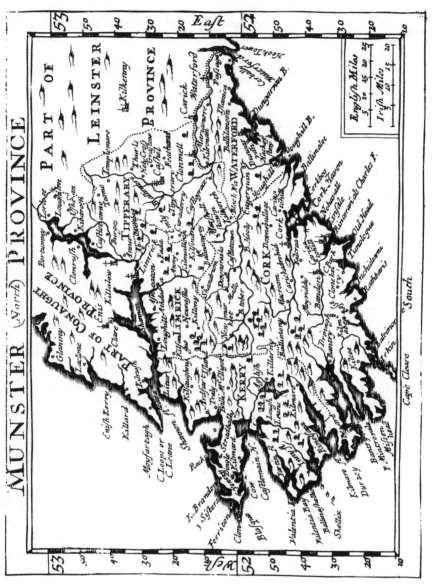

19. Petty's Map of Munster

20. *Petty's Map of Connacht*

Commonwealth. The Old Protestants gained politically, first by becoming closely aligned with Oliver Cromwell and his son Henry, and then by destroying the political power of the Old English Catholics.[22] These gains were consolidated in the Irish parliaments after 1660 in which Catholics no longer sat.

Tens of thousands of Irishmen felt that they had no place under the new dispensation that had been imposed upon Ireland. Well over 40,000 of these men and their families departed from their homeland for ever and served as mercenaries in Spanish, French and papal armies. Thousands more continued a spasmodic and disconnected opposition to the new regime. These recalcitrant rebel activists, or 'tories', brought misery to friend and foe alike, while never effectively shaking the English grip on the kingdom. Again, the chief victims were the Irish people.

Finally, any chance of conciliating Catholic and Protestant in a tripartite British state was destroyed. Ulster Protestants harboured grim memories of the massacres of 1641 which through successive generations embittered their relations with their Catholic neighbours. Similarly, Catholic memories of Drogheda and the transplantation to Connacht permanently stained Anglo-Irish relations. In the best of times these memories remained latent. In times of stress they fed old fears and fuelled new rebellions against oppression and religious intolerance.

THE EFFECTS OF THE WAR ON BRITAIN

Cromwell's successful campaign in Ireland from August 1649 to May 1650 was extraordinarily important to the fledgling English Commonwealth. The defeat of most of the major royalist field armies in Ireland eased the threat of a royalist counter-attack directed against the republic from Ireland. Charles II lost his chance to lead his most loyal supporters against the regicides in England when the royalist coalition in Ireland was defeated. This forced Charles to turn to the Scots as his last hope of military assistance to reclaim his patrimony. However, since Cromwell's success secured the parliamentarian state from interference from royalist forces operating from Ireland, it was able to turn the full fury of its naval and military might against the Scots. The Anglo-Scottish war of 1650–52 was disastrous for the Scots.[23] They, like the Irish, lost their independence in a united Commonwealth of Great Britain.

COULD THE CATHOLICS OR ROYALISTS HAVE WON?

The defeat of the Catholic cause in Ireland was not inevitable. By consistently proclaiming their loyalty to the Stuart monarchy, the Catholics maintained the possibility that if the king defeated the Puritans in Britain, he might have rewarded them for their loyalty by granting religious toleration in Ireland. Given the large number of Catholics closely associated with

Charles I in the English Civil Wars, such hopes were not far-fetched. The Catholics in Ireland succeeded to a remarkable extent in creating an autonomous Catholic Ireland. The Catholic Confederation provided much of Ireland with a government recognised, at least *de facto*, by Charles I and his Lord Lieutenant of Ireland, the Marquis of Ormond. The Confederates maintained diplomatic relations with the continental Catholic powers and routinely negotiated with the king and Ormond. They made several binding agreements with Ormond that recognised their control of much of the kingdom.[24]

The significant military power of the Catholic and royalist coalitions in Ireland has not been given its full due, probably because of the eventual outcome of the Cromwellian conquest. The forces raised by the Confederates outnumbered those fielded by their enemies for much of the period from 1643 to 1650.[25] Only determined military and logistical efforts by the English state over a period of eleven years were able to overcome the royalist and Catholic military forces in Ireland. Ireland was a very difficult military challenge and danger to the English state in the 1640s.

Ultimately, effective military and political leadership made the difference and won the day for the parliamentarians. In the 1640s Inchiquin, Robert Monro, Sir Charles Coote and George Monck led the parliamentarian and anti-Catholic forces in Ulster and Munster. They prevented the Catholic Confederates from completely overrunning those provinces while the English were distracted by their civil wars. When Inchiquin changed sides for the last time in 1648, he gave the Confederates a remarkable military advantage. But his previous efforts against the Catholics, crowned in his victory over Lord Taaffe at Knockanuss in 1647, had badly weakened their forces in Munster.

The parliamentarian commander who did the most to preserve the English bridgehead in Ireland was Michael Jones. His campaigns against the Confederates in Leinster, culminating with his victory over Preston's army of Leinster at Dungan's Hill in 1647, might have led to the final defeat of the Catholics had the Second Civil War not broken out in Britain. While heavily outnumbered in 1649, Jones skilfully defended Dublin against the armies of the royalist coalition. When given the chance to attack the royalist forces piecemeal at Baggotsrath/Rathmines in August, he achieved decisive results.

Jones's efforts set the scene for Cromwell to achieve rapid success in Ireland. Cromwell and his subordinates exploited their opportunity in a way that such opportunities are seldom exploited. They first of all focused on the destruction of royalist military strength near Dublin, at Drogheda. Then they divided their army into two offensive forces to overrun eastern Ulster and southern Leinster in the autumn of 1649. After a pause to refurbish their units in December 1649 and January 1650 the Cromwellians resumed their offensive. The winter campaign of 1650 attacked the main royalist forces and strongholds in Munster. Using four columns that converged on the Confederate capital in Kilkenny, Cromwell paralysed the royalist high command and picked off most of their major garrisons one by one. Even the costly operations against Clonmel did not stop Cromwell's rapid exploitation of English material superiority. By May Cromwell could safely return to England, secure in the knowledge that only Limerick and Waterford held out in Munster, and that the royalist field armies were heavily depleted.

Cromwell's successors did not perform in a manner equal to his tactical and operational virtuosity, but they got the job done. Ireton captured Waterford and Duncannon in 1650 without suffering a major loss such as that experienced by Cromwell at Clonmel. In 1651 he and his able subordinates broke into Connacht, again using three converging columns to confuse and divide the Catholic defenders. Ireton isolated and captured Limerick, and Galway fell without an assault. As a result, all major Catholic and royalist leaders in Ireland surrendered by the summer of 1652.

The royalists and Catholic forces in Ireland also had some remarkably talented leaders. The Marquis of Ormond performed political miracles throughout the period from 1643 to 1650. He played the Catholic Confederates off against the Scots and parliamentarians in the years 1643–6. He united most royalists, Catholics and Scots in a royalist coalition in 1649 that came very close to driving all parliamentarians out of Ireland. Catholic military leaders such as Thomas Preston, Owen Roe O'Neill and Theobald, Lord Taaffe, raised provincial armies from scratch. They and the Catholic clergy of Ireland created the Catholic Confederation and the provincial committees that gave much of Catholic Ireland independence in the 1640s. However, their military efforts were always hampered by shortages of money and military equipment. When they lost a skirmish or a battle, they could replace the manpower but not the weapons and trained leaders that were lost. This steadily undercut their efforts to stand up to the veteran parliamentarian regiments from 1649 on.

Dissensions within the Catholic Confederation and the Ormond royalist coalition constantly hampered their efforts to expel the parliamentarians from Ireland. In 1644 O'Neill, Castlehaven and Preston worked poorly together in the Confederate offensive in Ulster. Their disunity and unwillingness to risk a battle against Robert Monro's Scottish army ended this first chance to drive the Protestants out of Ulster. In 1646 animosities within the Catholic Confederation between the 'nuncioists', led by Rinuccini and Owen Roe O'Neill, and the 'Ormondists' prevented them from exploiting the greatest Catholic military victory in the decade. O'Neill's victory over the Scots at Benburb might have led to the expulsion of the Scottish garrisons from Ulster and then to a Catholic campaign against Dublin. Finally, the Catholic civil war of 1648–9 dissipated Catholic military power in a struggle between the forces of the Catholic Confederation and O'Neill's army of Ulster. O'Neill's failure to join Ormond's royalist coalition in 1649 until after the disasters at Baggotsrath/Rathmines and Drogheda greatly eased the Cromwellian conquest.

The English Commonwealth, after executing the king and asserting its control in England, wasted little time in launching a massive invasion of Ireland. This invasion, led by Oliver Cromwell, thoroughly defeated the royalist and Catholic forces in Ireland. This conquest, however, took three years and cost the English immense amounts of treasure and large numbers of men to complete. Cromwell himself played a pivotal role in this effort. He commanded the English forces in Ireland during the first year of the conquest, and he defeated the Scottish and royalist forces in Britain in 1650–51, sealing the fate of Ireland as well.

Cromwell's conduct during the conquest will always be darkened by the blood shed by his soldiers at Drogheda on his orders, and by his out-of-control soldiers at Wexford. However, there was unbelievable brutality by all participants during the long war, reflecting the religious bitterness and prejudices on both sides.

Notes

Abbreviations

Abbott	*The Writings and Speeches of Oliver Cromwell*, ed. W. C. Abbott, 3 vols, Oxford: Clarendon Press, 1989
Aphorismical Discovery	*An Aphorismical Discoverie of Treasonable Faction* (Trinity College Library, Dublin, MS F. 3. 28) in Sir John T. Gilbert, ed., *A Contemporary History of Affairs in Ireland, from* A.D. *1641 to 1652*, 3 vols, Dublin: Irish Archaeological and Celtic Society, 1879–80
BL	British Library, London
Bodl.	Bodleian Library, Oxford
CJ	*Journals of the House of Commons* [England]
CSPD	*Calendar of State Papers, Domestic*
CSPI	*Calendar of State Papers, Ireland*
Carte MSS	Carte Manuscripts, Bodleian Library, Oxford
Gardiner, *C & P*	Samuel R. Gardiner, *History of the Commonwealth and Protectorate, 1649–1656* [1894–1901], repr., 4 vols, New York: AMS, 1965
NHI, iii	T. W. Moody, F. X. Martin and F. J. Byrne, eds, *A New History of Ireland*, iii: *Early Modern Ireland, 1534–1691*, Oxford: Clarendon Press, 1976
PRO	Public Record Office, London
TT	Thomason Tracts, British Library, London

Introduction (pp 1–5)

1. Denis Murphy, *Cromwell in Ireland: A History of Cromwell's Irish Campaign*, new ed., Dublin: M. H. Gill, 1897, v.
2. Ibid., vi.
3. *An Aphorismical Discovery of Treasonable Faction* in Sir John T. Gilbert, ed., *A Contemporary History of Affairs in Ireland, from* A.D. *1641 to 1652*, 3 vols, Dublin: Irish Archaeological and Celtic Society, 1879–80. It has its utility, but like all contemporary sources it must be used with care.
4. S. R. Gardiner, *History of the Great Civil War, 1642–1649*, London: Longmans, 1893; S. R. Gardiner, *History of the Commonwealth and Protectorate, 1649–1656*, new ed., 4 vols, London: Longmans, 1903.
5. T. W. Moody, F. X. Martin and F. J. Byrne, eds, *A New History of Ireland*, iii: *Early Modern Ireland, 1534–1691*, Oxford: Clarendon Press, 1976.

6. Thomas Bartlett and Keith Jeffery, eds, *A Military History of Ireland*, Cambridge: Cambridge University Press, 1996.
7. See Jane Ohlmeyer, ed., *Ireland from Independence to Occupation, 1641–1660*, Cambridge: Cambridge University Press, 1995, for a good example.
8. Jason McElligott, *Cromwell: Our Chief of Enemies*, Dundalk: Dundalgan Press, 1994, 14–15; Toby Barnard, 'Irish Images of Oliver Cromwell' in R. C. Richardson, ed., *Images of Oliver Cromwell*, Manchester: Manchester University Press, 1993, 180–84; S. R. Gardiner, *Cromwell's Place in History*, repr., Freeport, NY: Books for Libraries, 1969.

Chapter 1: The War of the Three Kingdoms, 1641–8 (pp 6–39)

1. TT, E121 (44), *A True Copy of Two Letters brought by Mr Peters, this October 11. From my Lord Forbes from Ireland*, London: Henry Overton, 12 Oct. 1642.
2. Hugh Kearney, *Strafford in Ireland, 1633–41: A Study in Absolutism*, Cambridge: Cambridge University Press, 1959, 209–15.
3. Charles Carlton, *Going to the Wars: The Experience of the British Civil Wars, 1638–1651*, London: Routledge, 1992, 213–14, places the total deaths in Ireland at 618,000 out of 1.5 million people. R. F. Foster, *Modern Ireland, 1600–1972*, London: Penguin, 1988, 130, estimates the population to have been about 2 million in 1640 and 1.7 million in 1672. Raymond Gillespie, 'The Irish Economy at War, 1641–1652' in Ohlmeyer, ed., *Ireland from Independence to Occupation, 1641–1660*, 160–80, concludes that the population losses and the economic devastation were worse in the 1640s war than in the Williamite conquest of the 1690s.
4. R. A. Stradling, *The Spanish Monarchy and Irish Mercenaries: The Wild Geese in Spain, 1618–1668*, Dublin: Irish Academic Press, 1994, 163–8, calculates that from 1641 through 1652, 22,531 Irish soldiers arrived in Spanish ports as part of organised military units. Most of these men left Ireland after 1649.
5. Conrad Russell, 'The British Problem and the English Civil War', *History*, lxxii (Oct. 1987), 395–415; Conrad Russell, *The Fall of the British Monarchies, 1637–1641*, Oxford: Clarendon Press, 1991; Conrad Russell, *The Causes of the English Civil War*, Oxford: Clarendon Press, 1990.
6. Brian Mac Cuarta, ed., *Ulster 1641: Aspects of the Rising*, Belfast: Institute of Irish Studies, 1993, 1–6.
7. Ibid., 1–2; Foster, *Modern Ireland*, 36–9; James Tuchet, Earl of Castlehaven, *The Earl of Castlehaven's Review: or his Memoirs of his Engagement and Carriage in the Irish Wars*, London: Charles Brome, 1684, 22–3, where Castlehaven labels the Old Irish as 'meer Irish'.
8. TT, E52 (17), *Mercurius Hibernicus: or, A Discourse of the Late Insurrection in Ireland . . . the True Causes of It*, Bristol, 1644, 8–9.
9. J. C. Beckett, *Confrontations: Studies in Irish History*, London: Faber & Faber, 1972, 53–5; Conrad Russell, 'The British Background to the Irish Rebellion of 1641', *Historical Research*, lxi (June 1988), 180–81; S. R. Gardiner, *History of England, 1603–1643* [1863–81], new ed., 10 vols, London: Longmans, Green & Co., 1883–4, x, 49–50; TT, E52 (17), *Mercurius Hibernicus*, 8.
10. TT, E149 (34), *An Exact Relation of all such Occurrences . . . in the North of Ireland, since the Beginning of this Horrid, Bloody, and Unparalleled Rebellion*, by Lieutenant-Colonel Audley Mervyn, London, 4 June 1642.
11. Kearney, *Strafford in Ireland*, 20–23, 56–63; Foster, *Modern Ireland*, 3–5.

12. TT, E37 (31), *The Motives and Reasons occasioning the Catholic Subjects to Take Up Arms*, Feb. 1643; TT, E91 (9), *Orders . . . of the Popish General Assembly . . . of Kilkenny*, London, 28 Feb. 1648.

13. TT, E91 (9), *Orders . . . of the Popish General Assembly . . . of Kilkenny*, 5.

14. Thomas Carte, *The Life of James, First Duke of Ormond*, 2nd ed., 6 vols, Oxford: Oxford University Press, 1851. Vols v and vi contain complete copies of original letters to and from Ormond. The originals are in the Carte MSS in the Bodleian Library, Oxford. See v, 254–5, letter from William Cole, Enniskillen, to the Lords Justices in Dublin, 11 Oct. 1641, in which Cole warns them that Sir Philem O'Neill and Lord Maguire have been busy recruiting troops for some unspecified action.

15. TT, E134 (26), *A Proclamation of the Lords Justices for the Apprehension of the Chief Rebels*, Feb. 1642, 1–4.

16. Nicholas Canny, 'What Really Happened in 1641?' in Ohlmeyer, ed., *Ireland from Independence to Occupation*, 32–6; Gardiner, *History of England*, x, 64–9, where Gardiner notes that no large or universal massacre took place in 1641. He placed the total number of settlers killed in the initial rising at between 4,000 and 5,000.

17. TT, E149 (34), *An Exact Relation of all such Occurrences . . . in the North of Ireland*, 3–5. This early news-sheet provides a good example of how the term British had come to mean the settler communities in Ulster.

18. Jane Ohlmeyer, 'The Wars of Religion, 1603–1660' in Bartlett and Jeffery, eds, *Military History of Ireland*, 163; Mac Cuarta, *Ulster 1641*, 4–5, where Mac Cuarta notes that 'it is possible that about one-fifth of the Protestant population' of County Armagh were killed in 1641–2.

19. Ethan Howard Shagan, 'Constructing Discord: Ideology, Propaganda, and English Responses to the Irish Rebellion of 1641', *Journal of British Studies*, xxxvi (Jan. 1997), 4–34; Ohlmeyer, 'Wars of Religion, 1603–1660', 163; see also John Kenyon and Jane Ohlmeyer, eds, *The British and Irish Civil Wars: A Military History of Scotland, Ireland, and England, 1638–1660* (Oxford: Oxford University Press, 1998), 73–7, for Ohlmeyer's discussion of the massacres.

20. Castlehaven, *Memoirs*, 29.

21. TT, E131 (35), *A Perfect Relation of the Beginning and the Continuation of the Irish Rebellion, from May last to this present 12th of January 164[2]*, London, 12 Jan. 1642, 5–15; TT, E110 (9), *A Remonstrance of the Beginnings and Proceedings of the Rebellion in the County of Cavan . . . Whereunto is added the Acts, and Twenty-Nine Conclusions of that Great and General Congregation of Archbishops, Bishops, and Others of the Romanish Clergy in Ireland, met in the City of Kilkenny [May 10–13, 1642]*, London, 11 Aug. 1642; Keith J. Lindley, 'The Impact of the 1641 Rebellion upon England and Wales, 1641–45', *Irish Historical Studies*, xviii (1972), 143–75. Shagan, 'Constructing Discord', 9–17, points out that the propaganda was set in an English tradition of anti-Catholic sensibility which connected Irish Catholicism with an international Catholic Counter-Reformation in which Charles I was involved. This tradition had a lot to do with John Pym's and Oliver Cromwell's attitudes and action against all Catholicism in Ireland and Britain.

22. Nicholas Canny, *From Reformation to Restoration: Ireland 1534–1660*, Dublin: Helicon, 1987, 210.

23. Kevin J. McKenny, 'The Landed Interest, Political Ideology and Military Campaigns of the Northwest Ulster Settlers and their Lagan Army, 1641–1685' (Ph.D. thesis, State University of New York, Stony Brook, 1994), 71–3.

24. TT, E149 (34), *An Exact Relation of all such Occurrences . . . in the North of Ireland*, 4 June 1642.

25. Hugh Hazlett, 'A History of the Military Forces Operating in Ireland, 1641–1649' (Ph.D. thesis, Queen's University, Belfast, 1938), 330.

26. E. D. Hogan, ed., *The History of the War of Ireland from 1641 to 1653, by a British Officer of the Regiment of Sir John Clotworthy*, Dublin: McGlashan & Gill, 1873, 12–13.

27. Carte, *Ormond*, v, 256, letter from Endymion Porter to Ormond, 29 Oct. 1641; Gardiner, *History of England*, x, 54.

28. Richard Bagwell, *Ireland under the Stuarts and the Interregnum*, 3 vols, London: Holland Press, 1909–16, ii, 14.

29. Ibid., 15; Hugh Hazlett, 'The Recruitment and Organisation of the Scottish Army in Ulster, 1642–9' in H. A. Cronne, T. W. Moody and D. B. Quinn, eds, *Essays in British and Irish History in honour of James Eadie Todd*, London: Frederick Muller, 1949, 108–9, 123; David Stevenson, *Scottish Covenanters and Irish Confederates: Scottish–Irish Relations in the Mid-Seventeenth Century*, Belfast: Ulster Historical Foundation, 1981, 72–98.

30. TT, E149 (12), *A True Relation of the Proceedings of the Scottish Army now in Ireland*, London, 13 May 1642, 1–4; Hogan, ed., *History of the War of Ireland*, 25–7.

31. McKenny, 'Lagan Army', 80–81; Hogan, ed., *History of the War of Ireland*, 25–7; Hazlett, 'Scottish Army in Ulster', 123; TT, E108 (47), *A True Relation of the Taking of Mountjoy in the County of Tyrone by Colonel Clotworthy*, London, 4 Aug. 1642, 5–7; TT, E149 (33), *A True Relation of the Proceedings of the Scots and English Forces in the North of Ireland*, 8 June 1642, 1–6.

32. TT, E149 (12), *A True Relation of . . . the Scottish Army*, 2–3. The prisoners taken near Lochbricklane were hanged, while sixty prisoners were shot at Newry.

33. McKenny, 'Lagan Army', 77–81.

34. J. C. Beckett, *The Cavalier Duke: A Life of James Butler, 1st Duke of Ormond*, Belfast: Pretani Press, 1990, 13–23.

35. Carte, *Ormond*, ii, 2–4.

36. TT, E137 (31), *Good and Bad News from Ireland*, 14 Mar. 1642, 1.

37. Canny, *Reformation to Restoration*, 213–14.

38. Castlehaven, *Memoirs*, 34–5.

39. Canny, 'What Really Happened in 1641?', 40–41.

40. Castlehaven, *Memoirs*, 41.

41. Ibid., 4–5; Stevenson, *Scottish Covenanters and Irish Confederates*, 72, 98; Hazlett, 'Recruitment and Organisation of the Scottish Army in Ulster', 125; Ian Ryder, *An English Army for Ireland*, London: Partizan Press, 1987, 14–17.

42. TT, E132 (36), *The Latest Intelligence from Ireland*, letter from Richard Johnson, 1 Feb. 1642, 3; Castlehaven, *Memoirs*, 42.

43. TT, E132 (36), *The Latest Intelligence from Ireland*, 5–7.

44. TT, E146 (14), *A True Report of the Late Good Success in Ireland*, London, 2 May 1642, 4–6; TT, E145 (16), *Captain Yarner's Relation of the Battle fought at Kilrush upon the 15th day of April*, London, 4 May 1642, 1–3.

45. TT, E149 (12), *A True Relation of the . . . Scottish Army now in Ireland*, 13 May 1642, 2–6, for Monro's account; TT, E149 (33), *A True Relation of the Proceedings of the Scots and English Forces in the North of Ireland*, 8 June 1642, 1–7, for the British account of the same campaign; TT, E149 (24), *The English and Scottish Protestants' Happy Triumph over the Rebels in Ireland*, London, 4 June 1642.

46. Stevenson, *Scottish Covenanters and Irish Confederates*, 120.

47. Jane Ohlmeyer, 'Ireland Independent: Confederate Foreign Policy and International Relations during the Mid-Seventeenth Century' in Ohlmeyer, ed., *Ireland from Independence to Occupation*, 89–111.

48. TT, E149 (13), *A New Remonstrance of Ireland*, London, 2 June 1642, 2–3.

49. TT, E116 (24), *Exceeding Happy News from Ireland*, 9 Sept. 1642, 3–5; TT, E125 (5), *Special Passages*, 11–18 Sept. 1642, 87.

50. TT, E108 (15), *Bad News from Ireland, in a Letter dated from Dublin, 20 July 1642*, London, 28 July 1642, 2–3.

51. TT, E52 (17), *Mercurius Hibernicus*, 15–16; TT, E118 (45), *Special Passages*, 20–27 Sept. 1642, 1–2; TT, E108 (15), *Bad News from Ireland*, 3.

52. TT, E137 (31), *Good and Bad News from Ireland*, London, 14 Mar. 1642, 2; Jane Ohlmeyer, 'The Dunkirk of Ireland: Wexford Privateers during the 1640s', *Journal of the Wexford Historical Society*, x (1988–9), 23–49; Jane Ohlmeyer, 'Irish Privateers during the Civil War, 1642–50', *Mariner's Mirror*, lxxvi (May 1990), 119–33.

53. TT, E125 (15), *A Journal of the Most Memorable Passages in Ireland*, London, 19 Oct. 1642, 1–3.

54. Nicholas Perry, 'The Infantry of the Confederate Army of Leinster', *Irish Sword*, lxi (winter 1983), 233–5.

55. Ohlmeyer, 'Ireland Independent: Confederate Foreign Policy', 99–103.

56. Jerrold Casway, *Owen Roe O'Neill and the Struggle for Catholic Ireland*, Philadelphia: University of Pennsylvania Press, 1984, 54, 63; Stevenson, *Scottish Covenanters and Irish Confederates*, 120–22.

57. Ohlmeyer, 'Ireland Independent: Confederate Foreign Policy', 90–96.

58. Casway, *O'Neill*, 63.

59. Ibid., 64–6; Pádraig Lenihan, '"Celtic" Warfare in the 1640s' in John Young, ed., *Celtic Dimensions of the British Civil Wars*, Edinburgh: John Donald, 1997, 126–8.

60. Casway, *O'Neill*, 75–8.

61. Carte MS 6, fos 38, 62, George Monck to Ormond, 4 July 1643, reporting in each case an inability to stay in the field due to lack of supplies.

62. Ibid., fo. 26, Sir Richard Grenviles to Ormond, 6 July 1643, reporting Preston's strength; TT, E89 (31) *Newest Intelligence . . . from Ireland*, 1 Feb. 1643, 1–2; Carte *Ormond*, v, 436–8, Ormond to Mr Secretary Nicholas, 13 Apr. 1643, reporting that Preston continued to advance in April, in spite of his setback at New Ross; Castlehaven, *Memoirs*, 63–4, for a Confederate's account of the battle.

63. Hazlett, 'Scottish Army in Ulster, 1642–9', 120–23.

64. McKenny, 'Lagan Army', 94.

65. Casway, *O'Neill*, 79–82; Patrick J. Corish, 'The Rising of 1641 and the Catholic Confederacy, 1641–5' in *NHI*, iii, 308; McKenny, 'Lagan Army', 95–7; Hogan, ed., *History of the War of Ireland*, 29–31.

66. Corish, 'Rising of 1641', 304–5; TT, E90 (16), *Continuation of Certain Passages*, 16–23 Feb. 1643, 1.

67. Carte, *Ormond*, v, 444–5, Charles I to Lords Justices, 23 Apr. 1643; ibid., 445–6, Charles I to Ormond, 23 Apr. 1643; Carte MS 6, fo. 13, Charles I to Ormond, 2 July 1643, ordering him to finalise the cessation and to send regiments to England; TT, E52 (17), *Mercurius Hibernicus*, 18–23.

68. TT, E69 (22), *A Proclamation concerning a Cessation*', Dublin, Sept. 1643; TT, E35 (4), *Ireland's Lamentation for the Late Destructive Cessation, or, A Trap to Catch Protestants*, by Childey Coote, London, Mar. 1644.

69. Carte MS 6, fos 118–19, Monro to Ormond, 25 July 1643.
70. Ibid.; Casway, *O'Neill*, 92–3.
71. Carte MS 6, fo. 119, Monro to Ormond, 25 July 1643.
72. McKenny, 'Lagan Army', 117–18, 130–33.
73. Casway, *O'Neill*, 98.
74. McKenny, 'Lagan Army', 119.
75. Donal F. Cregan, 'The Confederation of Kilkenny: Its Personnel and History' (Ph.D. thesis, National University of Ireland, 1947), 147–8.
76. Carte MS 8, fo. 243, Ormond to Supreme Council, Jan. 1644. Ormond sent a further 1,300 men in late January: see ibid., fos 517, 555; *CSPI, 1633–47*, 369, 420, 431–4; Hazlett, 'History of the Military Forces Operating in Ireland', 336. Castlehaven, *Memoirs*, 79, places the number of Protestant soldiers sent to England at 10,000, but there is no evidence that more than 6,300 were sent.
77. Hazlett, 'Scottish Army in Ulster, 1642–9', 126–7; McKenny, 'Lagan Army', 71–3.
78. John Lowe, 'The Earl of Antrim and Irish Aid to Montrose in 1644', *Irish Sword*, iv (1959–60), 191–8; Jane Ohlmeyer, *Civil War and Restoration in the Three Stuart Kingdoms: The Career of Randal MacDonnell, Marquis of Antrim, 1609–1683*, Cambridge: Cambridge University Press, 1993, 159–70.
79. Hazlett, 'Scottish Army in Ulster, 1642–9', 126–7.
80. Ibid., 102–13; Castlehaven, *Memoirs*, 82–3.
81. Casway, *O'Neill*, 113.
82. Ulick, Marquis of Clanricarde, *Memoirs and Letters of Ulick, Marquis of Clanricarde*, London: J. Hughes, 1757, 397–8, a paper by Clanricarde listing the advantages that a cessation would provide to the king's cause.
83. Casway, *O'Neill*, 93–6.
84. Carte MS 11, fos 491–2, Inchiquin to Charles I, 17 July 1644, telling the king that there can be no peace with the rebel Irish; ibid., fos 520–22, Inchiquin to Sir John Paulett, 23 July 1644; ibid., fos 533–4, Inchiquin to Lieutenant-Colonel St Leger, 21 July 1644 telling him that they must defend themselves against the Catholics; ibid., fo. 538, Inchiquin to Col. William Jephson, governor of Portsmouth, 20 July 1644, asking him to ask parliament to accept Inchiquin and his forces.
85. Stevenson, *Scottish Covenanters and Irish Confederates*, 193–6; Casway, *O'Neill*, 102–4.
86. Castlehaven, *Memoirs*, 82–95; Casway, *O'Neill*, 105; Carte MS 12, fo. 101, Edward Mitchell to Ormond, 13 Aug. 1644; Hogan, ed., *History of the War of Ireland*, 37–41; McKenny, 'Lagan Army', 137–41.
87. Hogan, ed., *History of the War of Ireland*, 38; Castlehaven, *Memoirs*, 92–3.
88. Hogan, ed., *History of the War of Ireland*, 39; Casway, *O'Neill*, 108.
89. Casway, *O'Neill*, 108–9.
90. Ibid., 110–11.
91. McKenny, 'Lagan Army', 137–8; Hogan, ed., *History of the War of Ireland*, 40.
92. Castlehaven, *Memoirs*, 95.
93. Hogan, ed., *History of the War of Ireland*, 42; Casway, *O'Neill*, 120–21.
94. Carte MS 14, fo. 293, Edward Conway to Ormond, 25 Mar. 1645.
95. Ibid., fos 351, 385, Edward Mitchell to Ormond, 4 Apr. 1645; Hazlett, 'Scottish Army in Ulster, 1642–9', 127.
96. Carte MS 15, fo. 240, Lord Dillon to Ormond, 10 July 1645, telling Ormond of the fall of Sligo on 9 July; ibid., fo. 268, Edward Mitchell to Ormond, 19 July 1645, telling Ormond of the operations of the Stewarts in Connacht.

97. Gillespie, 'Irish Economy at War', 170–75.
98. Carte MS 13, fo. 3, Edward Mitchell to Ormond, 2 Dec. 1644.
99. Carte MS 14, fo. 121, Mitchell to Ormond, 24 Feb. 1645.
100. Ibid., fo. 317, for Duncannon; Gardiner, *Civil War*, iii, 31, for Castlehaven; Castlehaven, *Memoirs*, 107–12.
101. Casway, *O'Neill*, 121; Hogan, ed., *History of the War of Ireland*, 42–3; Carte MS 14, fos 351, 385, Edward Mitchell to Ormond, 4 Apr. 1645.
102. Patrick J. Corish, 'Ormond, Rinuccini, and the Confederates, 1645–49' in *NHI*, iii, 317.
103. Carte MS 17, fo. 367, Owen Roe O'Neill to Ormond, 10 May 1646.
104. TT, E342 (6), *Kingdom's Weekly Account*, 23–30 June 1646, 147–9, for Monro's account of the campaign; Carte MS 17, fo. 482, Monro to Ormond, 10 June 1646, telling Ormond about the campaign.
105. Hogan, ed., *History of the War of Ireland*, 49–51; Hazlett, 'Scottish Army in Ulster, 1642–9', 127–8.
106. Hazlett, 'Scottish Army in Ulster, 1642–9', 128; McKenny, 'Lagan Army', 154–5.
107. Gardiner, *Civil War*, i, 334; Cregan, 'Confederation of Kilkenny', 147.
108. Carte, *Ormond*, vi, 258, Charles I to Ormond, 27 Feb. 1645.
109. Carte MS 14, fos 502–4, Ormond to Charles I, 8 May 1645.
110. Carte, *Ormond*, vi, 279, Ormond to Charles I, 16 Apr. 1645.
111. Cregan, 'Confederation of Kilkenny', 168–72.
112. TT, E316 (29), *The Irish Cabinet, or His Majesty's Secret Papers for Establishing the Papal Clergy in Ireland*, 20 Jan. 1646, 3–5.
113. Cregan, 'Confederation of Kilkenny', 185.
114. Corish, 'Ormond, Rinuccini, and the Confederates', 317.
115. Ibid., 318; TT, E316 (29), *The Irish Cabinet . . .*, 20 Jan. 1646, 5–13, for terms of the Glamorgan treaty.
116. Gardiner, *History of England*, i, 408–41; Foster, *Modern Ireland*, 45–52.
117. Carte MS 15, fos 330–36, Lord Digby to Ormond, 2 Aug. 1645, telling him of the poor state of royalist affairs after Naseby; ibid., Digby to Lord Muskerry and the Supreme Council in Kilkenny, 1 Aug. 1645, promising them that the king would be very accommodating about religious concessions; C. V. Wedgwood, *The King's War, 1641–1647*, New York: Book of the Month Club, 1991, 455. The king's defeat at Naseby was 'total'.
118. Carte MS 16, fo. 405, Ormond to Charles I, 9 Jan. 1646; ibid., fo. 9, Digby to Ormond, from Oxford, 26 Mar. 1646.
119. Ibid., fo. 53, Supreme Council to Ormond, 3 Apr. 1646, telling him that it was not feasible to ship 10,000 soldiers to Britain.
120. Ibid., fo. 525, Commissioners to Ormond, 16 Feb. 1646; Carte MS 17, fos 95–7, Ormond to the Derby House Committee in London, 8 Apr. 1646, telling the parliamentarians that he could only hold Dublin for a short period of time without some logistical help, and asking for safe-conduct passes for himself, Clanricarde, Digby and other Protestant royalist leaders in Ireland; ibid., fo. 146, Protestant Commissioners, in Carrickfergus, to Ormond, 15 Apr. 1646, asking him to surrender Dublin to them; ibid., fo. 271, Commissioners to Ormond, granting safe conduct for Ormond's representatives to come to Carrickfergus to negotiate.
121. Carte MS 16, fos 590–610, drafts of treaty and exchange of letters between Ormond and the Supreme Council, Mar. 1646; Corish, 'Ormond, Rinuccini, and the Confederates', 320.

122. Carte MS 17, fo. 484, Charles I, in Newcastle (where he was held in captivity by the Scots), to Ormond, 11 June 1646.
123. Carte MS 18, fo. 261, Preston to Ormond, 13 Aug. 1646; ibid., fo. 412, Preston to Ormond, 1 Sept. 1646; ibid., fo. 519, Preston to Ormond, 19 Sept. 1646, explaining to Ormond that he and his officers can no longer obey Ormond's orders.
124. Ibid., fo. 658, Sept. 1646, a copy of a notice from Ormond's headquarters to his garrisons in Newry, Drogheda, Trim, Carlingford, Dundalk, Greencastle, Castlejordan and Slane updating them about O'Neill's advance; Casway, *O'Neill*, 168–72, for Casway's analysis of the failed campaign in the autumn of 1646, in which lack of unity due to the 'racial' divisions within the Confederate camp figure prominently; Cregan, 'Confederation of Kilkenny', 233–4.
125. Carte MS 19, fo. 206, William Cadogan to Ormond, 17 Oct. 1646, from Preston's camp, telling Ormond that Preston had no intention whatever of joining O'Neill; Castlehaven, *Memoirs*, 124–8.
126. Carte MS 20, fo. 416, Lords Clandeboye, Montgomery and Conway to Ormond, 10 May 1647; Carte MS 21, fos 18, 36, 48, 59, an exchange of letters between the British lords and Ormond, 7–12 May 1647, in which he called for a rendezvous and they refused to come.
127. Carte MS 21, fo. 87, George Monro to Ormond, 14 May 1647; Hazlett, 'Scottish Army in Ulster, 1642–9', 129–31.
128. Casway, *O'Neill*, 174, 184.
129. Carte MS 23, fo. 604, Ormond to Charles I, 27 Sept. 1646, telling the king that Ormond was negotiating with parliament.
130. Ibid., fo. 313.
131. Carte MS 20, fo. 117, Charles Rambert to Ormond, 12 Jan. 1647; ibid., fo. 133, Nicholas Plunket (on behalf of the Supreme Council) to Ormond, 15 Jan. 1647; ibid., fo. 140, Preston to Ormond, 25 Jan. 1647, proclaiming the continued goodwill and good faith of the Confederates.
132. Ibid., fos 291–2, Ormond to Charles I, Feb. 1647; ibid., fos 260–61, Ormond to Derby House Committee, 6 Feb. 1647, agreeing to turn his garrisons over; ibid., fo. 341, parliament to Ormond, 22 Feb. 1647, accepting the terms; *CSPI, 1647–60*, 742, for the financial terms; Carte MS 21, fo. 397, order of the Derby House Committee to pay Ormond £5,438, 27 Aug. 1647.
133. McKenny, 'Lagan Army', 162–4.
134. Carte MS 20, fo. 367, Derby House Committee to Ormond, 27 Feb. 1647.
135. Carte MS 21, fo. 250, Ormond to Michael Jones, 21 June 1647, setting 28 July as his date of departure; ibid., fo. 268, the final agreement, signed by Jones and the other parliamentary commissioners, 28 June 1647.
136. Casway, *O'Neill*, 183–4.
137. Ibid., 184–7.
138. Ibid., 190.
139. Carte MS 20, fo. 431, Derby House Committee to Major Robert Astley, Mar. 1647, ordering him to go to Dublin with letters of credit; Carte MS 21, fo. 215, 15 June 1647, resolution of parliament to send 5,000 sets of arms, 200 barrels of powder, 30 tons of match, and 200 pikes to Dublin.
140. Carte MS 21, fo. 215, parliamentary resolution, 15 June 1647.
141. Archibald W. M. Kerr, *An Ironside of Ireland: The Remarkable Career of Lieutenant-General Michael Jones*, London: Heath Cranton, 1923.

142. Carte MS 20, fos 371–2, 'A Diary and Relation of Passages in and about Dublin from the first of August 1647 unto the tenth'.

143. Ibid., fos 371–2. The muster book of Preston's army was captured; it listed his army's strength at 7,300 infantry and 1,047 cavalrymen at the most recent muster.

144. Ibid.

145. Ian Gentles, *The New Model Army in England, Ireland, and Scotland, 1645–1653*, Oxford: Blackwell, 1992, 190–234, for the clearest account of the complicated political struggles in England, 1646–8.

146. Carte MS 118, fos 33a–34b; TT, E412 (4), *The Late Successful Proceedings of the Army commanded by Colonel Michael Jones*, London, Oct. 1647, 4–5.

147. Carte MS 118, fo. 34b; TT, E416 (22), *News from Dublin . . . relating how Colonel Jones . . . fell upon the Rebels*, Nov. 1647, 3–6.

148. Corish, 'Ormond, Rinuccini, and the Confederates', 324.

149. TT, E417 (14), *A Mighty Victory in Ireland*, 29 Nov. 1647, for the quote; TT, E418 (6), *A True Relation of a Great Victory obtained by the Forces under the command of the Lord of Inchiquin*, 30 Nov. 1647, 2–5.

150. Henry Cary, ed., *Memorials of the Great Civil Wars in England from 1641 to 1652*, 2 vols, London: Henry Colburn, 1842, i, 360–67, Inchiquin to the Speaker of the House of Commons, 18 Nov. 1647, for Inchiquin's detailed account of the battle. (The letters in Cary's compilation are from the Tanner MSS in the Bodleian Library); Bagwell, *Ireland under the Stuarts*, ii, 158.

151. TT, E431 (10), *Kingdom's Weekly Intelligencer*, 29 Feb.–7 Mar. 1647, 858–9, Inchiquin to parliament, Feb. 1648.

152. TT, E434 (21), ibid., 28 Mar.–4 Apr. 1648, 893–6.

153. TT, E452 (10), *Declaration of the Protestant Army . . . in Munster*, Cork, Apr. 1648.

154. Patrick J. Corish, 'Rinuccini's Censure of 27 May 1648', *Irish Theological Quarterly*, xviii (Oct. 1951), 326–8.

155. Ibid., 330–31.

156. Ibid., 323.

157. Hazlett, 'Scottish Army in Ulster, 1642–9', 129; McKenny, 'Lagan Army', 173–4.

158. TT, E536 (5), *Kingdom's Weekly Intelligencer*, 19–26 Dec. 1648; TT, E537 (26), *The Moderate*, 2–9 Jan. 1649.

Chapter 2: The Catholic Civil War of 1648–9 and the Royalist Confederacy (pp 40–63)

1. Corish, 'Ormond, Rinuccini, and the Confederates', 328; Patrick J. Corish, 'Bishop Nicholas French and the Second Ormond Peace, 1648–9', *Irish Historical Studies*, vi (1948), 84–5.

2. TT, E452 (10), *Declaration of the Protestant Army . . . in Munster*, Cork, Apr. 1648.

3. Carte MS 22, fo. 5, Inchiquin to Ormond, 19 Jan. 1648, telling Ormond that the moderates under Muskerry had won most of the seats on the Supreme Council; Corish, 'Ormond, Rinuccini, and the Confederates', 325.

4. TT, E435 (33), *Papers presented to Parliament against the Lord Inchiquin . . . and the Lord Inchiquin's Declaration*, 3–4; TT, E435 (34), *The Testimony of Several Eminent Commanders, Late of the Army commanded by the Lord Inchiquin*, 15 Apr. 1648, 1–4, provides a similar account.

5. Patrick J. Corish, 'The Crisis in Ireland in 1648: The Nuncio and the Supreme Council: Conclusions', *Irish Theological Quarterly*, xxii (July 1955), 232–3.
6. Carte MS 22, fo. 67, Barry to Ormond, 15 Apr. 1648.
7. Ibid., fo. 99, 'Terms of the Agreement between Inchiquin and Lord Mountgarret and the rest of the Supreme Council', 20 May 1648.
8. Corish, 'Rinuccini's Censure of 27 May 1648', 322–3, 327–8, 335–7.
9. Corish, 'Ormond, Rinuccini, and the Confederates', 330–31.
10. Carte MS 22, fos 58–9, memorandum by Ormond, 'All that I conceive necessary to be done by way of preparation for the business of Ireland', 5 Apr. 1648.
11. Ibid.
12. Gardiner, *Civil War*, iv, 87–101; Martyn Bennett, *The Civil Wars in Britain and Ireland, 1638–1651*, Oxford: Blackwell, 1997, 284–305; Kenyon and Ohlmeyer, eds, *British and Irish Civil Wars*, ch. 3.
13. Carte MS 22, fos 67–67b, Jack Barry to Ormond, 15 Apr. 1648.
14. Carte, *Ormond*, vi, 549–53, Inchiquin to Ormond, 29 May 1648, acknowledging receipt of the royal commissions.
15. Ibid., 550.
16. Gardiner, *Civil War*, iv, 119–20.
17. Carte, *Ormond*, vi, 551, Inchiquin to Ormond, 28 May 1648.
18. Gardiner, *Civil War*, iv, 121–71.
19. Carte, *Ormond*, vi, 549, Inchiquin to Ormond, 15 Apr. 1648.
20. Carte MS 22, fo. 167, Supreme Council proclamation, 13 Aug. 1648.
21. Murphy, *Cromwell in Ireland*, 13.
22. Carte MS 22, fos 245–6, Ormond to Prince of Wales, 28 Sept. 1648; ibid., fo. 257, Ormond to Lord Jermyn, 30 Sept. 1648.
23. Ibid., fo. 245, Ormond to Prince of Wales, 28 Sept. 1648.
24. Ibid.
25. Ibid., fos 264–8b, 298, Ormond to Mr Blake, Chairman of the General Assembly, 4 Oct. 1648.
26. J. C. Beckett, 'The Confederation of Kilkenny Reviewed' in his *Confrontations in Irish History*, 57–8, 62.
27. TT, E536 (14), *Full Satisfaction concerning the Affairs of Ireland*, letter from Cork, 30 Nov. 1648, London, Dec. 1648.
28. Carte MS 22, fo. 301, Clanricarde to Ormond, 4 Oct. 1648.
29. TT, E468 (3), *The Proceedings of the Army under . . . Colonel Michael Jones*, Dublin, 2 Oct. 1648.
30. Ibid., 2–3.
31. Ibid., 4–6.
32. TT, E536 (5), *Kingdom's Weekly Intelligencer*, 19–26 Dec. 1648, 1198.
33. TT, E537 (3), *Moderate Intelligencer*, 28 Dec. 1648–4 Jan. 1649, 1813.
34. Carte MS 22, fos 555–6, Ormond to Prince of Wales, 2 Nov. 1648; TT, E473 (25), *The Declaration of the Lord Lieutenant of Ireland, for Settling the Protestant Religion, Maintaining His Majesty's Just Rights . . .*, Cork, 27 Nov. 1648.
35. Carte MS 22, fo. 601, Inchiquin's speech to his 'Fellow Soldiers', 2 Nov. 1648.
36. Ibid., fo. 641, Inchiquin to Ormond, 16 Nov. 1648.
37. Carte MS 23, fo. 60, Ormond to the Supreme Council, 19 Dec. 1648.
38. TT, E475 (8), *His Majesty's Declaration and Message to the Marquis of Ormond*, London, Dec. 1648, 1, in which Charles ordered Ormond to cease his negotiations and told Ormond that he had given parliament the power to

settle with the Irish. Even though it was clear that this proclamation was either a forgery or a document forced on the king, its publication made Ormond's task more difficult.

39. Carte MS 23, fo. 141, Ormond to Inchiquin, 29 Dec. 1648, telling Inchiquin that the Supreme Council had accepted the Peace; ibid., fo. 166, Ormond to Blake, 1 Jan. 1649, arranging to extend the truce; ibid., fo. 265, resolution of the General Assembly to accept the Peace, 16 Jan. 1649.

40. TT, E555 (21), *Articles of Peace made and concluded with the Irish Rebels, and Papists, by James, Earl of Ormond . . . and a Representation of the Scotch Presbytery at Belfast in Ireland*, London, 16 May 1649, 3–4. (The articles were signed on 17 Jan. 1649.)

41. Murphy, *Cromwell in Ireland*, 6; Carte MS 23, fos 590–92, for discussion of the Waterford customs.

42. Murphy, *Cromwell in Ireland*, 20–21. The money came in slowly, and Ormond had to borrow against its security to get the cash to pay the soldiers. But he raised enough money to pay the army under Inchiquin and Castlehaven through the month of May, according to Carte MS 24, fo. 762, Ormond to Castlehaven, 22 May 1649.

43. For the British settlers' rationale see TT, E556 (15), *The Declaration of the British in the North of Ireland*, London, 9 Apr. 1649, 1: 'We declare against the public enemies of our God, such as are now the prevalent party in England, who have overturned authority.' For the Catholic Confederates' view see TT, E545 (12), *Ormond's Proclamation concerning the Peace . . . with a Speech delivered by Sir Richard Blake, Speaker of the Assembly at Kilkenny*, 17 Jan. 1649. For the Ulster Scots' view see TT, E555 (21), *A Necessary Representation . . . by the Presbytery at Belfast*, 15 Feb. 1649, 41–5.

44. Carte MS 23, fo. 303, Ormond to Lord Digby, 22 Jan. 1649.

45. TT, E545 (12), *The Marquis of Ormond's Proclamation . . . together with a List of their Several Numbers of Foot and Horse*, London, 27 Feb. 1649, 16. These numbers specifically excluded O'Neill's army, estimated to number 5,000 infantrymen.

46. Carte MS 23, fo. 528, Clanricarde to Ormond, 20 Feb. 1649.

47. Ibid., fos 69–70, Ormond to the Lord President of Munster, telling him that O'Neill has little ammunition; ibid., fo. 595, Lord Dillon to Ormond, telling him that O'Neill has marched into Longford with 4,000 foot and 200 horse.

48. Ibid., fo. 532, Ormond to Francis Nugent, 28 Feb. 1649.

49. Carte MS 24, fos 794–7, Ormond to Edward Nicholas, 29 May 1649. Ormond noted that O'Neill had lost all but one of his Leinster garrisons and was restricted to Ulster.

50. TT, E616 (7), *A Letter from Sir Lewis Dyve to the Lord Marquis of Newcastle of the Whole Account of the King's Affairs in Ireland*, The Hague, 17 Nov. 1650, 35.

51. Gardiner, *Civil War*, iv, 135; Bernard Capp, *Cromwell's Navy*, Oxford: Oxford University Press, 1989, 19–24; J. R. Powell, *The English Navy in the Civil Wars*, London: Archon Books, 1962, chs 10–12.

52. Carte MS 23, fo. 27, Robert Long to Ormond, 12 Dec. 1648; ibid., fo. 353, Inchiquin to Ormond, 26 Jan. 1649; ibid., fo. 348, Rupert to Ormond, 27 Jan. 1649; ibid., fo. 349, Mr Brookbank, Ormond's agent in Kinsale, to Ormond, 28 Jan. 1649, telling him that Rupert had arrived and that he had a total of sixteen warships; ibid., fo. 365, Ormond to Inchiquin, 30 Jan. 1649.

53. Ibid., fo. 436, Rupert to Ormond, 7 Feb. 1649; Carte MS 24, fo. 228, Ormond to Charles II, 23 Mar. 1649, telling the king about how he hoped to use Rupert's ships to cut Dublin off from supplies from England.

54. Carte MS 24, fo. 448, Rupert to Ormond, 9 Feb. 1649; Ohlmeyer, 'Irish Privateers during the Civil War', 119–34; Ohlmeyer, 'The Dunkirk of Ireland: Wexford Privateers during the 1640s', 23–49.

55. Ohlmeyer, 'Irish Privateers during the Civil War', 131.

56. Carte MS 23, fo. 576, Mayor of Waterford to Ormond, 27 Feb. 1649; Carte MS 24, fo. 6, Commissioners of Trust to Ormond, 2 Mar. 1649, suggesting that loans of £60,000 be raised on the security of the tenth share of prizes.

57. TT, E542 (6), *A Great and Bloody Fight at Sea*, reported from Bristol, 9 Feb. 1649, 3–5.

58. Bodl., Rawlinson MS A223, fo. 97 (this number includes 33 hired warships and 45 state-owned warships); Bulstrode Whitelocke, *Memorials of the English Affairs*, London: Nathaniel Ponder, 1682, 371. See TT, E542 (11), *The Moderate*, 6–13 Feb. 1649, 299, for a report about the royalist and Irish naval forces consisting of 18 ships under Rupert and 40 other major vessels in the Wexford privateer force.

59. *CJ*, vi, 138.

60. Carte MS 24, fos 461–2, Rupert to Ormond, Apr. 1649; ibid., fos 795–7, Ormond to Sir Edward Nicholas, 29 May 1649, telling him that Rupert had failed to respond to Ormond's request to blockade Dublin.

61. TT, E531 (11★), *A Perfect Diurnal of Some Passages in Parliament*, 25 June–2 July 1649, 2610.

62. Carte MS 24, fo. 716, Charles II to Ormond, 16 May 1649.

63. Ibid., 765–6, William Legg, Ormond's agent in Kinsale, to Ormond, 22 May 1649.

64. Whitelocke, *Memorials*, 361.

65. McKenny, 'Lagan Army', 185.

66. TT, E555 (21), *Articles of Peace made and concluded with the Irish Rebels, and Papists, by James, Earl of Ormond, . . . and a Representation of the Scotch Presbytery at Belfast in Ireland*, London, 16 May 1649, 43.

67. Whitelocke, *Memorials*, 381.

68. TT, E562 (1), *General O'Neill's Letter to Colonel Monck . . . together with Colonel Monck's Answer*, letters dated Apr. 1649, London, 28 June 1649, 1–5; TT, E562 (15), *The Propositions of Owen Roe O'Neill sent to Colonel Monck, and a Cessation for Three Months concluded between Them*, Apr. 1649, Cork, 1649, 1–7.

69. TT, E545 (2), *Moderate Intelligencer*, 15–22 Feb. 1649, 2.

70. TT, E544 (13), *The Declaration of . . . Ormond . . . concerning the Death of His Sacred Majesty*, Cork, 20 Feb. 1649, 4.

71. McKenny, 'Lagan Army', 185–99.

72. TT, E573 (4), *A True Relation of the Twenty Weeks' Siege of London-Derry, by the Scotch, Irish, and Dis-affected English*, Londonderry, 19 June 1649, 1.

73. McKenny, 'Lagan Army', 199–200, 204–5; TT, E573 (4), *The Twenty Weeks' Siege of London-Derry*, 2–3.

74. TT, E573 (4), *The Twenty Weeks' Siege of London-Derry*, 3–4.

75. Ibid., 4; TT, E562 (12), *A Bloody Fight in Ireland and a Great Victory Obtained by Sir Charles Coote*, 29 June 1649, London, 2 July 1649, 2.

76. TT, E573 (4), *The Twenty Weeks' Siege of London-Derry*, 4–5.

77. TT, E530 (3) *Perfect Summary of an Exact Diary of Passages of Parliament*, 4–11 May 1649, 140.

78. TT, E556 (15), *The Declaration of the British in the North of Ireland*, 9 Apr. 1649, London, 25 May, 1649, 1.

79. Ibid., 2–4; Whitelocke, *Memorials*, 400, reports that 500 of Monck's 700 soldiers deserted.

80. Carte MS 24, fo. 36, O'Neill to Ormond, 4 Mar. 1649, telling Ormond that he planned to discuss the 'promising terms' which Ormond sent him with his council of colonels; Casway, *O'Neill*, 230–34.

81. Foster, *Modern Ireland*, 100.

82. Carte MS 23, fo. 586, Ormond to Clanricarde, 28 Feb. 1649.

83. Carte MS 24, fo. 69, Ormond to Inchiquin, 6 Mar. 1649.

84. Ibid., fo. 125, Clanricarde to Ormond , 13 Mar. 1649; ibid., fo. 124, Ormond to Clanricarde, 14 Mar. 1649.

85. Castlehaven, *Memoirs*, 135–6.

86. TT, E555 (21), *A Necessary Representation of the Present Evils . . . by the Presbytery at Belfast'*, 41–5, listing the reasons why the kirk and the Ulster Scots had joined Ormond; TT, E556 (15), *The Declaration of the British in the North of Ireland*.

87. TT, E562 (1), *General Owen O'Neill's Letter to Colonel Monck . . . together with Colonel Monck's Answer*, 1; Jerrold Casway, 'George Monck and the Controversial Catholic Truce of 1649', *Studia Hibernica*, xvi (1976), 55–9.

88. Carte MS 24, fos 69–70, Ormond to Clanricarde, 6 Mar. 1649.

89. TT, E562 (15), *The Propositions of Owen Roe O'Neill sent to Col. Monck*, Cork, Apr. 1649, 2–3.

90. Carte MS 24, fo. 50, Ormond to Mayor of Athlone, 5 Mar. 1649; ibid., fo. 330, Inchiquin to Ormond, 30 Mar. 1649.

91. Bagwell, *Ireland under the Stuarts*, ii, 182.

92. Whitelocke, *Memorials*, 401; Casway, 'George Monck and the Controversial Catholic Truce of 1649', 68–9; Casway, *O'Neill*, 250.

93. Casway, 'George Monck and the Controversial Catholic Truce of 1649', 68; Whitelocke, *Memorials*, 400.

94. TT, E562 (12), *A Bloody Fight in Ireland and a Great Victory Obtained by Sir Charles Coote*, 1–3.

95. TT, E531 (16) *A Perfect Diurnal of Some Passages in Parliament*, 2–9 July 1649.

96. TT, E573 (4), *The Twenty Weeks' Siege of London-Derry*, 8–10.

97. Ibid., 10.

98. Ibid., 11–12; McKenny, 'Lagan Army', 208.

99. TT, E573 (4), *The Twenty Weeks' Siege of London-Derry*, 13–14; Kerr, *An Ironside of Ireland*, 101–2.

100. TT, E616 (7), *A Letter from Sir Lewis Dyve to the Lord Marquis of Newcastle*, 13–16; Casway, *O'Neill*, 247–51.

101. The preparations of Cromwell's expeditionary force and the problems and delays which hindered it will be fully discussed in the next chapter. See Gentles, *New Model Army*, ch. 10 for the preparations, and ch. 11 for the Cromwellian conquest.

102. TT, E542 (11), *The Moderate*, 6–13 Feb. 1649, 306.

103. Carte MS 24, fos 493–4, Bradshaw, President of the Council of State, to Monck, 23 Apr. 1649, telling Monck about the size of the force being raised and telling him to hang on.

104. Ibid., fos 103–4, Ormond to Jones, 9 Mar. 1649; see also TT, E548 (28), *The Marquis of Ormond's Proclaiming of Charles II . . . with his Summons to Colonel Jones . . . and the Answer of Colonel Jones*, London, 29 Mar. 1649, 2–5; TT, E 555 (21), *Articles of Peace, made and concluded with the Irish Rebels*, 34–9, Ormond to Jones, 9 Mar. 1649, and Jones to Ormond, 14 Mar. 1649; TT,

E529 (28), *A True Copy of Two Letters, the first sent from the Earl of Ormond to the Honourable Colonel Michael Jones . . .*, Dublin, 17 May 1649, 4–16, Ormond to Jones, 27 Mar. 1649, and Jones to Ormond, 31 Mar. 1649.

105. Carte MS 24, fo. 129, Jones to Ormond, 14 Mar. 1649.

106. Ibid., fo. 392, Ormond to Clanricarde, 8 Apr. 1649; ibid., fo. 405, Ormond to Charles II, 10 Apr. 1649.

107. Ibid., fo. 717, Inchiquin to Ormond, 16 May 1649; ibid., fo. 730, Castlehaven to Ormond, 18 May 1649.

108. Ibid., fo. 527, Clanricarde to Ormond, 27 Apr. 1649, complaining of abuses committed by Inchiquin's soldiers against Catholic landowners; ibid., fo. 736, Castlehaven to Ormond, 18 May 1649, telling him that the soldiers were paid to 13 May.

109. Ibid., fo. 755, Castlehaven to Ormond, 21 May 1649; ibid., fo. 764, Castlehaven to John Lane, 22 May 1649, asking for money to be sent to pay the Munster cavalry who had just arrived; ibid., fos 795–7, Ormond to Sir Edward Nicholas, secretary to Charles II, 29 May 1649, for troop strength estimate.

110. Carte MS 25, Ormond to Charles II, 1 June 1649. Murphy, *Cromwell in Ireland*, 23, puts Ormond's total strength in his field forces at 14,500 foot and 3,000 horse, but he cites no evidence.

111. *CJ*, vi, 138–9.

112. Ibid., 157 for the troops, and 176 for Cromwell's appointment; *CSPD, 1649–50*, 28, 41, 61, 66–7, for the immediate dispatch of reinforcements and supplies.

113. Carte MS 25, fos 19–20, Ormond to Charles II, 28 June 1649, from near Dublin.

114. Ibid., fo. 21.

115. Murphy, *Cromwell in Ireland*, 24–5.

116. TT, E566 (7), *A Modest Narrative of Intelligence*, 21–28 July 1649, 132–4; TT, E531 (11), *Moderate Messenger*, 25 June–2 July 1649, 59–60.

117. *CSPD, 1649–50*, 572–3.

118. TT, E562 (11), *The Present Condition of Dublin*, Dublin, 22 June 1649.

119. TT, E562 (17), *Two Great Fights in Ireland, near the City of Dublin*, 2 July 1649, 1–3, a letter from David Cotton in Dublin, 24 June 1649.

120. TT, E563 (6), *A Bloody Fight at Dublin*, 1–3, in a letter, Dublin, 4 July 1649.

121. Ibid.; TT, E531 (16), *A Perfect Diurnal of Some Passages in Parliament*, 2–9 July 1649, 2629.

122. Carte MS 25, fos 56–7, Ormond to Charles II, 18 July 1649.

123. TT, E566 (7), *Modest Narrative*, 21–28 July 1649, for the desertions from Dublin; TT, E566 (2), *A Great and Bloody Fight at Dublin*, 26 July 1649, 1–3, for the estimate that the Confederate coalition had 20,000 men in the field. This estimate probably included the troops under Monro in Ulster.

124. TT, E568 (17), *Moderate Intelligencer*, 2–9 Aug. 1649, 2191.

125. Carte MS 25, fos 56–8, Ormond to Charles II, 18 July 1649.

Chapter 3: Cromwell's Preparations, Arrival and Campaign from Dublin to Drogheda, August–September 1649 (pp 64–88)

1. H. J. Habakkuk, 'Public Finance and the Sale of Confiscated Property during the Interregnum', *Economic History Review*, xv (1962), 70–88; Ian Gentles, 'The Arrears of Pay of the Parliamentary Army at the End of the First Civil War', *Bulletin of the Institute of Historical Research*, xlviii (1975), 52–73.

2. *CJ*, vi, 138–9.
3. Gentles, *New Model Army*, 258–65.
4. Abbott, ii, 40–50; Gardiner, *C & P*, i, 24–8.
5. *CJ*, vi, 239.
6. Gentles, *New Model Army*, 141–50, and ch. 6, 'The Political Wars, 1646–8'.
7. Ibid., 157: *CSPD, 1649–50*, 28, 41.
8. *CSPD, 1649–50*, 572–3; PRO, SP 25/118, 'A Particular of the Charges of Raising and Paying the Eight Regiments of Foot and the Six Regiments of Horse . . . for Ireland' [1650], fos 19–24 (hereafter cited as PRO, SP 25/118).
9. Whitelocke, *Memorials*, 383–4.
10. Gentles, *New Model Army*; Gardiner, *C & P*, i, 40.
11. Whitelocke, *Memorials*, 371.
12. PRO, E351/2288–9, the declared accounts of the Navy Treasurer, 1 Jan. 1648–31 Dec. 1650. For the size of the army in 1649 see Sir William Clarke, *Manuscripts, 1640–1664*, ed. G. E. Aylmer, Hassocks: Harvester Microform Edition, 1979, MS 2/11, 'Letters and Other Papers dealing with the Army . . . 1640–1660'. The total strength of the army in the summer of 1649 was, excluding Coote's and Jones's troops, 38,842. The monthly cost was estimated to be £97,952 for a 28-day 'mensem', yielding a total annual cost of £1,273,376.
13. PRO, E134/357, the declared accounts of the treasurers for the sale of dean and chapter lands, 1649–57.
14. Bernard Capp, 'George Wharton, "Bellum Hybernicale", and the Cause of Irish Freedom', *English Historical Review*, cxii (1997), 671–77; Norah Carlin, 'The Levellers and the Conquest of Ireland in 1649', *Historical Journal*, xxx (1987), 269–88; Chris Durston, '"Let Ireland Be Quiet": Opposition in England to the Cromwellian Conquest of Ireland', *History Workshop Journal*, xxi (1986), 105–12.
15. Gardiner, *C & P*, i, 31–48; Gentles, *New Model Army*, 318–29.
16. Gentles, *New Model Army*, 329.
17. Gardiner, *C & P*, i, 48–54.
18. Ibid., 50; TT, E530 (3), *Perfect Summary of an Exact Diary of Some Passages of Parliament*, 4–11 May 1649, 150–51, for the most extensive first-hand account; Abbott, ii, 67.
19. Abbott, ii, 67–8.
20. Ibid., 69–70; Gardiner, *C & P*, i, 53–4; Gentles, *New Model Army*, 331–45.
21. Abbott, ii, 91–2; TT, E531 (21), *A Perfect Diurnal of Some Passages in Parliament*, 9–16 July 1649, 5; Whitelocke, *Memorials*, 398, states that Cromwell left London on 10 July; Gardiner, *C & P*, i, 96, erroneously states that he left London on 12 July; Gentles, *New Model Army*, 353, gives the date as 9 July. Gardiner's and my source are the *Perfect Diurnal*, which is corroborated by Whitelocke.
22. *CSPD, 1649–50*, 583.
23. C. H. Firth and R. S. Rait, eds, *Acts and Ordinances of the Interregnum, 1642–1660*, 3 vols, London: HMSO, 1911, ii, 160, 168, 200.
24. PRO, SP 28 contains numerous examples of the audits of the pay accounts of individual soldiers and units.
25. PRO, E351/603, the declared account of John Dethicke, treasurer for the sale of crown lands; H. J. Habakkuk, 'The Parliamentary Army and the Crown Lands', *Welsh History Review*, iii (1960), 403–60, for an account of how the soldiers disposed of their debentures.

26. Gerald Aylmer, *The State's Servants: The Civil Service of the English Republic, 1649–1660*, London: Routledge & Kegan Paul, 1973, 320.
27. James S. Wheeler, 'Logistics and Supply in Cromwell's Conquest of Ireland' in Mark C. Fissel, ed., *War and Government in Britain, 1598–1650*, Manchester: Manchester University Press, 1991, 38–56.
28. Austin Woolrych, 'Cromwell as a Soldier' in John Morrill, ed., *Oliver Cromwell and the English Revolution*, London: Longman, 1990, 93–118.
29. Gardiner, *C & P*, i, 97.
30. Ibid., 94.
31. Murphy, *Cromwell in Ireland*, 26–8.
32. Ibid., 95; Abbott, ii, 84; Gentles, *New Model Army*, 356. Gentles uses Gardiner and Abbott exclusively as his sources for his conclusion that Cromwell was headed to Munster. Gardiner admits the ambiguity of the sources concerning Cromwell's destination. Abbott relies heavily on Gardiner and admits no ambiguity.
33. Abbott, ii, 88.
34. TT, E566 (19), *A Great and Bloody Fight at Dublin*, London, 1 Aug. 1649, 2; TT, E532 (2), *A Perfect Diurnal*, 23–30 July 1649, 2672.
35. TT, E569 (1), *Lieutenant-General Jones's Letter to the Council of State of a Great Victory'*, Dublin, 6 Aug. 1649, London, 11 Aug. 1649, 3–5; Abbott, ii, 101–3, Cromwell to Richard Mayor, 13 Aug. 1649; *CSPD, 1649–50*, 275.
36. TT, E571 (15), *Perfect Weekly Account*, 15–22 Aug. 1649, 574.
37. Abbott, ii, 104.
38. Whitelocke, *Memorials*, 407–8.
39. Carte MS 25, fo. 25, Ormond to Digby, 19 July 1649; Carte, *Ormond*, iii, 461.
40. TT, E569 (1), *Lieutenant-General Jones's Letter to the Council of State of a Great Victory*, 4, listing the prisoners and weapons taken by Jones at Rathmines on 2 August.
41. TT, E566 (2), *A Great and Bloody Fight at Dublin*, 26 July 1649; Cary, ed., *Memorials*, ii, 159–60, Michael Jones to Speaker of Parliament, 6 Aug. 1649.
42. TT, E532 (13), *Every Day's Journal in Parliament*, 28 July–3 Aug. 1649, 1212; TT, E571 (16), *Ormond's Letter to His Majesty King Charles II*, 24 July 1649.
43. TT, E568 (14), *Perfect Weekly Account*, 1–8 Aug. 1649, 567; TT, E568 (22), *A Modest Narrative*, 1 Aug. 1649, 147.
44. TT, E568 (14), *Perfect Weekly Account*, 1–8 Aug. 1649; Whitelocke, *Memorials*, 402; Murphy, *Cromwell in Ireland*, 26.
45. Carte MS 25, fo. 39, resolution of the council held at Rathmines, 27 July 1649; Castlehaven, *Memoirs*, 143–4.
46. Carte, *Ormond*, iii, 465–6; Murphy, *Cromwell in Ireland*, 27–9.
47. TT, E568 (16), *A Great Victory Obtained by the Marquis of Ormond, 9 August 1649*, 3.
48. Ibid., 2; Gardiner, *C & P*, i, 100.
49. TT, E569 (1), *Lieutenant-General Jones's Letter to the Council of State of a Great Victory*, 3.
50. Carte, *Ormond*, iii, 465–7.
51. Ibid., 467. Carte's biography of Ormond provides one of the few detailed accounts of the events leading up to the fight at Baggotsrath and of the battle of Rathmines. Carte based his account on Ormond's letter to Charles II, written several days after the battle. My account of these events adds details and corroboration to Carte's account from the newsbooks and Jones's detailed accounts to the Council of State and to parliament.

52. Ibid., 467–8; Murphy, *Cromwell in Ireland*, 30.

53. Cary, ed., *Memorials*, ii, 159–60, Jones to the Speaker, 6 Aug. 1649.

54. Ibid., 160.

55. Ibid., 161; TT, E569 (1), *Lieutenant-General Jones's Letter to the Council of State*, 3.

56. Carte, *Ormond*, iii, 468; Murphy, *Cromwell in Ireland*, 30.

57. TT, E569 (1), *Lieutenant-General Jones's Letter to the Council of State*, 4.

58. Carte, *Ormond*, iii, 469–70; Gardiner, *C & P*, i, 102. Carte gives an account far more generous to Dillon than does Gardiner.

59. Carte, *Ormond*, iii, 469.

60. Carte MS 25, fo. 132, Ormond to Clanricarde, 3 Aug. 1649.

61. TT, E569 (1), *Lieutenant-General Jones's Letter to the Council of State*, 3–5; Cary, ed., *Memorials*, ii, 160–61, Jones to the Speaker, 6 Aug. 1649; Abbott, ii, 101–3. Cromwell received news of Jones's victory on 8 August. Jones put the number of royalist dead at 4,000 and the captured at 2,715. Ormond put the dead at 600, but admits that the captured numbered in the thousands; Carte MS 25, fo. 128, Jones to Ormond, 3 Aug. 1649, when Jones told Ormond that since the rout he had so many prisoners that all of their names could not be taken; he further told Ormond that he had 1,500 common men and about 300 officers as prisoners.

62. TT, E569 (1), *Lieutenant-General Jones's Letter to the Council of State*, 4.

63. Ibid., 6–7.

64. TT, E571 (9), *Another Great and Bloody Fight in Ireland*, London, 21 Aug. 1649.

65. Carte MS 25, fo. 235, Ormond to Clanricarde, 12 Aug. 1649; ibid., fo. 237, Ormond to Lord Montgomery, 12 Aug. 1649.

66. Ibid., fo. 120, Clanricarde to Ormond, 1 Aug. 1649; ibid., fo. 270, Clanricarde to Ormond, 17 Aug. 1649; ibid., fo. 362, Clanricarde to Ormond, 27 Aug. 1649.

67. Ibid., fos 212–13, Lord Montgomery to Ormond, 10 Aug. 1649; Gardiner, *C & P*, i, 107–8, for a discussion of O'Neill's arrangements with Coote.

68. Carte MS 25, fo. 366, Ormond to O'Neill, 27 Aug. 1649; ibid., fo. 369, Ormond to Colonel O'Neill (Owen's nephew), 27 Aug. 1649; ibid., fo. 377, Owen Roe O'Neill to Ormond, 28 Aug. 1649, asking for a settlement, but delaying final arrangements.

69. TT, E532 (17), *A True Day's Journal of Perfect Passages in Parliament*, 7–14 Aug. 1649, 30–32; Carte MS 25, Ormond to George Monro, 19 Aug. 1649.

70. Carte MS 25, fo. 173, Thomas Armstrong to Ormond, 7 Aug. 1649; ibid., fo. 195, Ormond to Charles II, 8 Aug. 1649; Ormond to Clanricarde, 12 Aug. 1649; ibid., fos 251–2, Ormond's letters to Clanricarde and Lord Montgomery, 13 Aug. 1649, telling them that Jones had withdrawn from before Drogheda; Ormond to the Commissioners of Trust at Trim, 13 Aug. 1649; TT, E571 (9), *Another Great and Bloody Fight in Ireland*.

71. Gardiner, *C & P*, i, 110–12.

72. Abbott, ii, 107–9; Gardiner, *C & P*, i, 109.

73. PRO, SP 25/118, fos 1–18, listing the regiments and the amounts they were paid in July and August; ibid., fos 19–27 listing supplies sent over in June and July to sustain Jones's garrison.

74. Abbott, ii, 110–11.

75. Ibid., 111–12, a proclamation issued at Dublin, 24 Aug. 1649.

76. TT, E533 (12), *Perfect Occurrences*, 21–28 Sept. 1649, 1275.

77. Abbott, ii, 116–17; Gardiner, *C & P*, i, 112–14.
78. Abbott, ii, 124–7, Cromwell to Lenthall, 17 Sept. 1649.
79. Murphy, *Cromwell in Ireland*, 91–2. Murphy's account of the technical details of the attack on Drogheda is superior to Gardiner's.
80. Abbott, ii, 125–7; TT, E533 (15), *Perfect Occurrences*, 28 Sept.–4 Oct. 1649, 1275; J. G. Simms, 'Cromwell at Drogheda', *Irish Sword*, xi (1974), 386–93; James Burke, 'The New Model Army and the Problems of Siege Warfare', *Irish Historical Studies*, xxvii (1990), 10–12; Tom Reilly, *Cromwell at Drogheda*, Drogheda: Broin Print, 1993; Gardiner, *C & P*, i, 115 n. 2.
81. Abbott, ii, 125, where Cromwell specifically mentions that the assault troops would initially be without cavalry support while the royalist cavalry could counter-attack from within the town.
82. Carte MS 25, fo. 509, Cromwell to Sir Arthur Aston, 10 Sept. 1649; Abbott, ii, 118.
83. Abbott, ii, 126, Cromwell to Lenthall, 17 Sept. 1649.
84. TT, E533 (15), *Perfect Occurrences*, 28 Sept.–4 Oct. 1649, 1275–76, letter from Colonel Hewson in Dublin, 22 Sept. 1649.
85. Whitelocke, *Memorials*, 412, 'More Letters of the Particulars of the Taking of Drogheda', 1 Oct. 1649. Cromwell does not mention his role in the assault in his letters to parliament or the Council of State. Hewson makes no mention of Cromwell's presence at the eastern breach, leading me to be convinced that Cromwell was at the southern breach with Castle's and Ewer's troops.
86. Abbott, ii, 120, 124, Cromwell to Lenthall, 17 Sept. 1649; Murphy, *Cromwell in Ireland*, 97–8, 97 n. 3; Gardiner, *C & P*, i, 118.
87. Gardiner, *C & P*, 117–20; TT, E553 (17), *Perfect Diurnal*, 1–8 Oct. 1649, 2811–20.
88. TT, E533 (15), *Perfect Occurrences*, 28 Sept.–4 Oct. 1649, 1276, for Hewson's account.
89. Carte MS 25, fos 596–9, Ormond to Charles II, 27 Sept. 1649, giving Ormond's assessment of the strategic situation.
90. For refusals to provide the prescribed allocations of money to Ormond's field army see ibid., fo. 360, Lord Taaffe to Ormond, 26 Aug. 1649 (Limerick); ibid., fo. 362, Clanricarde to Ormond, 27 Aug. 1649 (Galway).
91. Ibid., fo. 533, Ormond to Rupert, 18 Sept. 1649.
92. Ibid., fo. 526, Colonel David Galbraith to Ormond, 12 Sept. 1649.
93. Abbott, ii, 127, Cromwell to Lenthall, 17 Sept. 1649.
94. Gardiner, *C & P*, i, 118.
95. PRO, SP 25/118, fos 103, 105–6, details of the medical support Cromwell provided for his army; Abbott, ii, 124.

Chapter 4: Cromwell's Southern Campaign, September–November 1649 (pp 89–115)

1. Carte MS 25, fos 596–9, Ormond to Charles II, 27 Sept. 1649.
2. Ibid., fo. 533, Ormond to Rupert, 18 Sept. 1649.
3. Ibid., fo. 360, Lord Taaffe to Ormond, 26 Aug. 1649, telling Ormond that Limerick would only send £100 for the cause; ibid., fo. 362, Clanricarde to Ormond, 27 Aug. 1649, telling Ormond that Galway refused to contribute.
4. Ibid., fo. 579, O'Neill to Ormond, 24 Sept. 1649, telling Ormond that he has begun to march south, but that no treaty has yet been signed; ibid., fo. 586, O'Neill to Ormond, 25 Sept. 1649, still with no treaty signed.

5. Ibid., fo. 679, Clanricarde to Ormond, 4 Oct. 1649.
6. Ibid., fo. 362, Clanricarde to Ormond, 27 Aug. 1649; ibid., fo. 120, Clanricarde to Ormond, 1 Aug. 1649; ibid., fo. 270, Clanricarde to Ormond, 17 Aug. 1649, and fo. 679, Clanricarde to Ormond, 4 Oct. 1649, for representative letters of Clanricarde explaining his inability to support the main effort; ibid., fos 579, 586, for letters from O'Neill to Ormond, 24 and 25 Sept. 1649, discussing the incomplete negotiation.
7. Ibid., fos 596–9, Ormond to Charles II, 27 Sept. 1649.
8. Abbott, ii, 125, Cromwell to John Bradshaw, President of the Council of State, 16 Sept. 1649.
9. PRO, SP 25/118, fos 79–87, listing the supplies carried by the artillery train. There were 56 great guns and 600 barrels of powder shipped to Ireland in August, and 10 tons of shot sent in October.
10. Abbott, ii, 104 n. 199. The original fleet in August was too small, even with over 130 ships, to carry all of the invasion force, causing Cromwell to leave three regiments in Milford Haven for later shipment. The collection of shipping for the August operation diverted many merchant ships from other tasks. Once the army was in Ireland, many of these ships were needed to carry the steady flow of supplies to Dublin and Derry. See Wheeler, 'Logistics and Supply in Cromwell's Conquest of Ireland'.
11. TT, E533 (15), *Perfect Occurrences*, 28 Sept.–4 Oct. 1649, 1282, contains a discussion of these two operational options. The direct route to Kilkenny was deemed dangerous because of the many places in the mountains where ambushes could be set. The analysis concludes that Wexford 'may [be] first set upon because it is the great receptacle for pirates'. See also Ohlmeyer, 'The Dunkirk of Ireland: Wexford Privateers during the 1640s', 23–39; Ohlmeyer, 'Irish Privateers during the Civil War', 119–32.
12. Murphy, *Cromwell in Ireland*, 139–40, esp. 140 n. 2.
13. TT, E533 (18), *Perfect . . . Scout*, 2–12 Oct. 1649, 265, for the abandonment of the garrisons in Leinster; TT, E575 (35), *The Taking of Wexford . . . A Letter*, London, 26 Oct. 1649, 5, for an estimate of Ormond's field army; TT, E533 (20), *Several Proceedings in Parliament*, 19–26 Oct. 1649, 26, for Hugh Peter's account, 3 Oct. 1649, of the reinforcement of Wexford and New Ross.
14. TT, E575 (39), *A Brief and Particular Relation of the Several Marches and Proceedings of the Army in Ireland*, 29 Oct. 1649, 2; Abbott, ii, 131–5; ibid., 140–43, Cromwell to Lenthall, 14 Oct. 1649; Murphy, *Cromwell in Ireland*, 140–44.
15. TT, E575 (39), *A Brief . . . Relation of the Several Marches*, 3–6; TT, E576 (6), *Full and Particular Relation of the Army*, 31 Oct. 1649, 50–51.
16. Abbott, ii, 127–8, Cromwell to Lenthall, 17 Sept. 1649.
17. Gentles, *New Model Army*, 544 n. 163. If each of these 450 garrisons consisted of 50 men on the average, 22,500 men would have been absorbed. This does not take into account the large garrisons in Dublin, Drogheda, Wexford, and the other large towns captured in Munster.
18. PRO, SP 63/281, 'An Account of English Money Issued to the Army in Ireland, 1649–1656', fos 9–12, lists 28 infantry, 2 dragoon and 13 cavalry regiments in Ireland in the 1650s; Karl S. Bottigheimer, *English Money and Irish Land*, Oxford: Clarendon Press, 1971, 117, states that there were 35,000 English troops eligible to be paid off in Irish land in 1656.
19. *CSPD, 1649–50*, 182, 183, 207, 220, 247, and *CSPD, 1650*, 63, 515, for details of the recruiting process, to include the bonds of £1 per man posted

by the recruiters; PRO, SP 25/118, fos 137–8, for a description of a warrant to pay Colonel Pride to raise, equip, pay and ship 2,000 men to Ireland in 1649–50.

20. PRO, SP 25/118, fos 139–48 for replacements sent by February 1650; *CSPD, 1649–50*, 591, for the warrants to Colonels Pride, Waller, Whalley, Fleetwood, Harrison and Desborow to raise 4,000 men for immediate shipment to Ireland.

21. PRO, SP 25/118, fos 19–27, 55–77, for food and supplies sent to Ireland; *CSPD, 1649–50*, 585–600, lists the warrants for the thousands of tons of supplies, munitions and arms sent over from England to Ireland by February 1650.

22. Wheeler, 'Logistics and Supply in Cromwell's Conquest of Ireland', 48, for a list of the food sent to Ireland in the first eight months of the campaign.

23. TT, E576 (6), *Full and Particular Relations of the Army*, London, 31 Oct. 1649, 51 (Enniscorthy), 52 (Wexford).

24. Carte MS 21, fos 507–8, for an account of Jones's campaign of October 1647.

25. Gardiner, *C & P*, i, 126–8.

26. Abbott, ii, 140–42, Cromwell to Lenthall, 14 Oct. 1649, from Wexford.

27. TT, E576 (6), *A Very Full and Particular Relation of the Army*, 31 Oct. 1649, 51; Abbott, ii, 135, for Jones's seizure of the fort.

28. TT, E576 (6), *Full and Particular Relation of the Army*, 52; Carte MS 25, fo. 716, for Ormond's reinforcements, conclusions and actions.

29. Castlehaven, *Memoirs*, 145–6; Murphy, *Cromwell in Ireland*, 144–6.

30. Abbott, ii, 143, Cromwell to Lenthall, 14 Oct. 1649.

31. Ibid., 135–9.

32. Murphy, *Cromwell in Ireland*, 149; Gardiner, *C & P*, i, 129.

33. Carte MS 25, fo. 718, Cromwell to Commander-in-Chief in Wexford, 11 Oct. 1649.

34. Cary, ed., *Memorials*, ii, 181–4; Murphy, *Cromwell in Ireland*, 152–4.

35. TT, E576 (6), *Full and Particular Relation of the Army*, 52–3; Abbott, ii, 138–9.

36. There are conflicting accounts about the amount of resistance offered by the garrison after they abandoned the walls and about the number of civilians killed in the assault. See Murphy, *Cromwell in Ireland*, 155–72, for an extended discussion of the fighting. He accepts accounts published in 1758 as reliable primary sources for the murder of 300 women. D. M. R. Esson, *The Curse of Cromwell: A History of the Ironside Conquest of Ireland, 1649–53*, Totowa, N.J.: Rowman & Littlefield, 1971, 120–22, is the weakest of modern accounts of the siege and assault. Esson discusses the events only briefly, and he gets the date of Jones's seizure of Rosslare wrong. See Gardiner, *C & P*, 130–33, for a rationalisation of the atrocities that occurred.

37. Abbott, ii, 140–43, Cromwell to Lenthall, 14 Oct. 1649.

38. Gardener, *C & P*, i, 130–33; Abbott, ii, 142, Cromwell to Lenthall, 14 Oct. 1649.

39. Abbott, ii, 142, Cromwell to Lenthall, 14 Oct. 1649; TT, E576 (6), *Full and Particular Relation of the Army*, 56; TT, E575 (36), *A Letter from the Attorney of Ireland concerning the Taking of the Town of Wexford*, 26 Oct. 1649, 2–3, lists 51 pieces of ordnance, 40 good vessels in the harbour, powder and ammunition, tallow, hides, salt, and other commodities as captured, and adds that 1,700 Catholics were slain; TT, E579 (10), *Hugh Peters' Letter from Ireland*, 22 Oct. 1649, 4, estimates the spoils as 80 ships and 100 boats, and Irish losses as 2,000 slain.

40. Corish, 'Cromwellian Conquest' in *NHI*, iii, 340.

41. Carte MS 25, fo. 774, Rupert to Ormond, 18 Oct. 1649, from Kinsale, reporting that he had not received the £4,000 needed to outfit his fleet.

42. TT, E533 (17), *Several Proceedings*, 30 Nov.–7 Dec. 1649, 121, for the three ships left behind without guns; Whitelocke, *Memorials*, 413; Cary, ed., *Memorials*, ii, 187, Richard Deane to Lenthall, from Cork, 17 Oct. 1649.

43. Carte MS 21, fos 371–3, 'A Diary . . .' of Jones's campaign in August 1647 provides a good example of this earlier pattern; Ohlmeyer, 'Wars of Religion, 1603–1660', 168–70.

44. Murphy, *Cromwell in Ireland*, 171–2; J. C. Beckett does not mention Wexford or New Ross in his biography of Ormond.

45. Carte MS 26, fo. 25, Barry to Ormond, 15 Oct. 1649.

46. Whitelocke, *Memorials*, 406, 408 for Ireton's destination and for discussion of his ten days at sea off the Munster coast.

47. Murphy, *Cromwell in Ireland*, 198.

48. TT, E533 (25), *Several Proceedings*, 16–23 Nov. 1649, 70, Cromwell to Lenthall, 25 Oct. 1649, describing the surrender of New Ross and the defection of 500 Protestant troops from the royalist garrison.

49. TT, E581 (4), *A Brief Relation of Some Affairs . . . Civil and Military*, 13–20 Nov. 1649, 89, report from Cork, 5 Nov. 1649.

50. TT, E579 (13), *A Letter from the Lord Lieutenant General*, London, 26 Oct. 1649, 6, Cromwell to Taaffe, 17 Oct. 1649; see also Abbott, ii, 145.

51. TT, E581 (4), *A Brief Relation of Some Affairs*, 90.

52. TT, E579 (13), *A Letter from the Lord Lieutenant General*. This selection includes all of Cromwell's letters to Taaffe and a copy of the terms. Taaffe's responses are not published in Abbott.

53. TT, E579 (13), *A Letter from the Lord Lieutenant General*, 7, Cromwell to Taaffe, 19 Oct. 1649; see also Abbott, ii, 146.

54. TT, E581 (4), *Several Passages*, 13–20 Nov. 1649, 93; Gardiner, *C & P*, i, 135.

55. Carte MS 25, fo. 592, Castlehaven to Sir Edmund Butler, 27 Sept. 1649, telling Butler that Wexford was unprepared for defence.

56. Carte MS 25, fos 366, 369, 377, 386, 579, 586, 650, 702, for the correspondence between Ormond and O'Neill; TT, E579 (10), *Colonel Hewson's Letter from Dublin*, 29 Oct. 1649, announcing that O'Neill and Ormond had come to terms.

57. TT, E581 (3), *A Perfect Relation of . . . the Army in Ireland*, 29 Nov. 1649, 16, a letter from New Ross, 26 Oct. 1649; Abbott, ii, 150–56, for a good account of the defection of the garrisons of Cork, Youghal, Bandon and Kinsale.

58. Cary, *Memorials*, ii, 185–6, Richard Deane to Lenthall, 8 Nov. 1649; Abbott, ii, 151.

59. Abbott, ii, 158–9, Cromwell's 'Answer to the Several Desires of the Inhabitants of Cork, sent by their Commissioners and received 12 November 1649'; Murphy, *Cromwell in Ireland*, 203–6.

60. TT, E584 (11), *Brief Relation*, 27 Nov.–4 Dec. 1649, 125–6; TT, E581 (4), ibid., 13–20 Nov. 1649, 86–8, Blake to [Cromwell?], 5 Nov. 1649, from Cork harbour, describing the defection of Youghal's garrison to the English cause; TT, E583 (1), ibid., 20–27 Nov. 1649, 112; TT, E584 (14), ibid., 4–11 Dec. 1649, 129–30, Blake to Cromwell, Nov. 1649, explaining that the defectors asked for no terms, instead putting 'themselves upon your goodness'; ibid., 131–5, Cromwell to Blake, 14 Nov. 1649.

61. Murphy, *Cromwell in Ireland*, 212–13.

62. Gentles, *New Model Army*, 364.
63. Abbott, ii, 130, Cromwell to Lenthall, 27 Sept. 1649; TT, E608 (15), *A History or Brief Chronicle of the Chief Matters of the Irish Wars*, London, 26 July 1650, 3.
64. Bagwell, *Ireland under the Stuarts*, ii, 197.
65. TT, E579 (8), *Brief Relation*, 6–13 Nov. 1649, 73–4; TT, E608 (15), *A History or Brief Chronicle . . . of the Irish Wars*, 4.
66. Carte MS 26, fo. 11, Ormond to George Monro, 23 Oct. 1649; McKenny, 'Lagan Army', 219.
67. TT, E579 (8), *Brief Relation*, 6–13 Nov. 1649, 74–5; Carte MS 26, fos 286–8, Ormond to Charles II, Nov. 1649; TT, E608 (15), *A History or Brief Chronicle of . . . the Irish Wars*, 4.
68. Carte MS 26, fos 286–8, Ormond to Charles II, 30 Nov. 1649.
69. Ibid.; TT, E608 (15), *A History or Brief Chronicle of . . . the Irish Wars*, 5; McKenny, 'Lagan Army', 219.
70. TT, E587 (1), *Two Letters from William Basil . . . of a Great Victory Obtained by the Parliament's Forces*, London, 24 Dec. 1649, 3; McKenny, 'Lagan Army', 221–2.
71. TT, E587 (1), *Two Letters from William Basil*, 5.
72. Carte MS 26, fo. 351, Lord Montgomery of the Ards to Ormond, 10 Dec. 1649.
73. TT, E608 (15), *A History or Brief Chronicle . . . of the Irish Wars*, 6.
74. Bagwell, *Ireland under the Stuarts*, ii, 227; McKenny, 'Lagan Army', 224–5.
75. Casway, *O'Neill*, 259; Gardiner, *C & P*, ii, 139.
76. Carte MS 26, fo. 7, Castlehaven to Ormond, 21 Oct. 1649.
77. J. G. Simms, 'Cromwell's Siege of Waterford, 1649' in his *War and Politics in Ireland, 1649–1730*, ed. D. W. Hayton and Gerard O'Brien, London: Hambledon Press, 1986, 13–15.
78. Carte MS 26, fo. 23, Ormond to Castlehaven, 24 Oct. 1649, telling Castlehaven that Ormond's lifeguard was *en route* to Duncannon; ibid., fo. 54, for the replacement of Roche with Wogan.
79. TT, E581 (4), *Brief Relation*, 13–20 Nov. 1649, 93.
80. Carte MS 26, fo. 106, Castlehaven to Ormond, 6 Nov. 1649, reporting that the English gave up the siege on the previous night, having lost two cannon.
81. Ibid., fo. 526, Charles II to Ormond, 23 Jan. 1650, telling Ormond that the king had made a preliminary agreement with the Scots; Gardiner, *C & P*, i, 203–4, for Charles's double-dealing with the Scots and the Irish and for the final agreement with the Scots.
82. Carte MS 26, fos 286–8, Ormond to Charles II, 30 Nov. 1649.
83. Ibid., fo. 225, Ormond to his commanders, 17 Oct. 1649.
84. Ibid., fo. 70, draft copy of Ormond's appraisal of royalists' strategic options, Oct. 1649.
85. Ibid., fo. 132, Castlehaven to Ormond, 8 Nov. 1649, in which Castlehaven mentions that his sister's footman had told him about the movement of this English force; TT, E583 (1), *Brief Relation*, 20–27 Nov. 1649, 112.
86. TT, E583 (1), *Brief Relation*, 20–27 Nov. 1649, 112.
87. TT, E533 (26) *Several Proceedings*, 23–30 Nov. 1649, 98–9, Colonel Hewson's account from Dublin, 19 Nov. 1649; TT, E584 (2), *Several Letters of a Great Fight in Ireland*, London, 28 Nov. 1649, 1–4; E584 (11), *Brief Relation*, 27 Nov.–4 Dec. 1649, 125; Abbott, ii, 162–5, Cromwell to Lenthall, from Ross, 14 Nov. 1649; Murphy, *Cromwell in Ireland*, 176–8.
88. Abbott, ii, 164.

89. TT, E533 (26), *Several Proceedings*, 23–30 Nov. 1649, 98; TT, E583 (1), *Brief Relation*, 27 Nov.–4 Dec. 1649, 112; Murphy, *Cromwell in Ireland*, 178; Esson, *Curse of Cromwell*, 125. Esson gives a slightly different account in which he says the English column was accompanied by two field guns which played an important part in driving the Irish off. Neither the newsbooks' nor Cromwell's accounts mention the presence of cannon. Esson provides no citation of evidence.

90. Carte MS 26, fo. 96, Clanricarde to Ormond, 4 Nov. 1649, telling Ormond not to trust Inchiquin's men in battle.

91. TT, E533 (26), *Several Proceedings*, 23–30 Nov. 1649, 88, listing Ormond's strength as 8,000 foot and 3,000 horse, compared with Cromwell's of 4,000 foot and 2,000 horse; TT, E533 (27), *Several Proceedings*, 30 Nov.–7 Dec. 1649, 119, where Ormond's strength is estimated to be 5,000–8,000 foot, superior in numbers to Cromwell's forces at New Ross; Carte MS 26, fo. 37, Confederate Supreme Council to Ormond, 27 Oct. 1649, telling him that the garrison of Meath refused to join the army as ordered.

92. TT, E584 (16), *A Letter from . . . the Lord Lieutenant of Ireland*, London, 12 Dec. 1649.

93. *A Perfect Diurnall of Some Passages and Proceedings of, and in relation to the Armies in England, Ireland, and Scotland*, 10–17 Dec. 1649, 10 (hereafter cited as *Diurnall of the Armies*). This publication was licensed by Lord General Fairfax and provides a useful account of the operations of and the happenings in the armies. It is in the Thomason Tracts, but the edition used in this book is from a collection of the publication on microfilm.

94. TT, E616 (7), *A Letter from Sir Lewis Dyve to the Lord Marquis of Newcastle*, The Hague, 17 Nov. 1650, 31.

95. Abbott, ii, 172.

96. TT, E584 (16), *A Letter from . . . the Lord Lieutenant*, 5–6.

97. TT, E585 (5), *Brief Relation*, 11–18 Dec. 1649, 158–9.

98. TT, E584 (16), *A Letter from . . . the Lord Lieutenant*, 5–6; Murphy, *Cromwell in Ireland*, 222–3. Murphy gives the Irish losses as 500 dead. Cromwell, in his letter said there were about forty bodies under the walls and another 400 buried in the fields nearby.

99. Carte MS 26, fo. 256, Ormond to Lyvett, 23 Nov. 1649, telling him about the reinforcements; ibid., fo. 263, Lyvett to Ormond, 23 Nov. 1649, telling him about the delaying tactic.

100. Ibid., fo. 265, Lyvett to Cromwell, 23 Nov. 1649; Abbott, ii, 170–71, Cromwell to Lyvett, 24 Nov. 1649.

101. Abbott, ii, 173, Cromwell to Lenthall, 25 Nov. 1649, for the quotes; TT, E585 (5), *Brief Relation*, 11–18 Dec. 1649, 159; TT, E584 (16), *A Letter from Cromwell to Lenthall*, London, 12 Dec. 1649, 6.

102. Abbott, ii, 174; Simms, 'Cromwell's Siege of Waterford', 16–17.

103. TT, E583 (1), *Brief Relation*, 20–27 Nov. 1649, 113–16, for the terms of the treaty between O'Neill and Ormond.

104. TT, E533 (27) *Several Proceedings*, 30 Nov.–7 Dec. 1649, 120–21, for a list of the winter quarters of Cromwell's forces in the south.

Chapter 5: Cromwell's Winter Campaign: Waterford to Kilkenny, December 1649–March 1650 (pp 116–139)

1. Carte MS 26, fo. 326, Ormond to Clanricarde, 5 Dec. 1649.
2. Gentles, *New Model Army*, 370.
3. Abbott, ii, 176–9, Cromwell to Lenthall, 19 Dec. 1649; Carte MS 26, fo. 300, Ormond to Charles II, 30 Nov. 1649. Ormond estimated the royalist strength to be 18,000 foot, although he could muster only 5,000 foot and 1,300 horse.
4. Abbott, ii, 176, Cromwell to Lenthall, 19 Dec. 1649.
5. Ibid., 177; Gardiner, *C & P*, ii, 142.
6. Abbott, ii, 177, Cromwell to Lenthall, 19 Dec. 1649; Kerr, *Ironside of Ireland*, 123–6.
7. Kerr, *Ironside of Ireland*, 123–6, where Kerr notes the poison story and discounts it; Murphy, *Cromwell in Ireland*, 236–7, 236 n. 1, where Murphy repeats the story as if it were true.
8. *Diurnall of the Armies*, 31 Dec. 1649–7 Jan. 1650, 38–9.
9. *CSPI, 1649–50*, 349, 351, 391, 399, 592–600; *CSPI, 1650*, 572–80.
10. *Diurnall of the Armies*, 31 Dec. 1649–7 Jan. 1650, 30, 34, 39; ibid., 14–21 Jan. 1650, 24, letter dated 6 Jan. 1650.
11. Abbott, ii, 179, Cromwell to Lenthall, 19 Dec. 1649.
12. The detailed account mentioned in *CSPI, 1649–50*, 516, is found in PRO, SP 25/118. The money referred to in *CSPD, 1649–50*, 465, included the £20,000 sent to Venables on 1 Jan. 1650 for the forces in Ulster.
13. PRO, SP 63/281, 'Account of Money transmitted out of England upon the Army in Ireland . . . 1649–1656' [1656–7], fos 2–6.
14. PRO, SP 25/118, fos 101–3, 105–6.
15. TT, E534 (20), *Several Proceedings*, 14–21 Mar. 1650, 347, Colonel Hewson to William Lenthall, 3 Mar. 1650, noting that several large detachments of recuperated soldiers had marched from Dublin to Cromwell's forces in Munster.
16. *Diurnall of the Armies*, 14–21 Jan. 1650, 48, for accounts of men arrested for fraud connected with recruiting and with the counterfeiting of pay warrants and debentures used to pay soldiers' arrears.
17. *Diurnall of the Armies*, 4–11 Feb. 1650, 78–9; Whitelocke, *Memorials*, 424.
18. TT, E534 (7) *Several Proceedings*, 25–31 Jan. 1649, 250–51.
19. PRO, SP 25/118, fos 38–77, 111, 116.
20. Ibid., and fos 79–87.
21. Whitelocke, *Memorials*, 424; Murphy, *Cromwell in Ireland*, 240–43.
22. Abbott, ii, 175, proclamation issued on 8 Dec. 1649.
23. Carte MS 26, fo. 300, Ormond to Charles II, 30 Nov. 1649.
24. Ibid., fo. 320, Mayor of Limerick to Ormond, 4 Dec. 1649; ibid., fo. 347, Clanricarde to Ormond, 19 Dec. 1649; ibid., fo. 349, Mayor Lyvett to Ormond, 10 Dec. 1649.
25. Ibid., fo. 292, Ormond to Charles II, 30 Nov. 1649.
26. Ibid., fo. 772, Clanricarde to Ormond, 19 Feb. 1650.
27. Ibid., fo. 318, proclamation of the Catholic clergy, 4 Dec. 1649.
28. Murphy, *Cromwell in Ireland*, 246–8; Carte, *Ormond*, iii, 517–20.
29. Murphy, *Cromwell in Ireland*, appendix ix, 411–23, for a copy of the final proclamation of the clergy, 14 Dec. 1649; Carte MS 26, fos 318–19, for the proclamation of 4 Dec. 1649.

30. Abbott, ii, 196–205, 'A Declaration of the Lord Lieutenant of Ireland for the Undeceiving of Deluded and Seduced People', 21 Mar. 1650.

31. Gardiner, *C & P*, i, 147–9. Gardiner believed Cromwell to have been sincere, although incorrectly informed, concerning Irish history. While not excusing Cromwell directly, he posited that Cromwell's 'exaggerations of Irish crimes were common to all who thought or spoke on the subject. He had the mind of England as well as its sword at his disposal.'

32. Ibid., 197–9.

33. Carte MS 26, fo. 602, Ormond to Charles II, 2 Feb. 1650.

34. See Abbott, ii, 191, where Abbott mentions that three letters were sent by Cromwell to parliament, dated 1, 5 and 16 Jan. 1650, and that 'there seems to be no trace save in various notices of them'; TT, E534 (4), *Several Proceedings*, 25–31 Jan. 1650, 243, contains the letter. *CSPD, 1649–50*, 496, confirms that a letter from Cromwell was read in parliament on 29 January, and that the book that Cromwell mentioned in the letter of 16 January was received. The editor of the *Several Proceedings* in 1649–50 was Henry Scobell, the clerk to parliament and the man responsible for compiling the journals of the House of Commons, 'of which *Several Proceedings* was merely a diluted digest' (Joseph Frank, *The Beginnings of the English Newspaper, 1620–1660*, Cambridge, Mass.: Harvard University Press, 1961, 201).

35. Whitelocke, *Memorials*, 421; *Diurnall of the Armies*, 14–21 Jan. 1650, 44; ibid., 18 Jan.–4 Feb. 1650, 68, letter from Cork, 5 Jan. 1650.

36. *Diurnall of the Armies*, 31 Dec. 1649–7 Jan. 1650, 39–40, letter from Cork, 20 Dec.; ibid., 14–21 Jan. 1650, 42.

37. Carte MS 26, fo. 288, Ormond to Charles II, 30 Nov. 1649.

38. Ibid., fo. 495, Charles II to Ormond, 12 Jan. 1650, telling Ormond of the Scottish negotiations; similar letters are in fos 512, 526, 552.

39. TT, E534 (27), *Several Proceedings*, 4–11 Apr. 1650, 404, letter from Robert Saunders, now governor of Youghal.

40. PRO, SP 25/118, fos 88–91 (at least £128,000 worth of provender and stables' supplies were sent from England to Ireland from 1649 to 1656); Abbott, ii, 175, for Cromwell's proclamation of 8 December telling his cavalry to content themselves with the peas, oats, hay and other local forage available; TT, 534 (27), *Several Proceedings*, 4–11 Apr. 1650, 404, a letter reporting that 13 ships laden with oats for horses had just arrived; TT, E534 (31), ibid., 18–25 Apr. 1650, 434, a letter from Cork noting that 'indeed the horse in many places have wanted pay, but by supply of oats from England, have made good shift with straw'.

41. TT, E594 (5), *Irish Mercury*, 25 Jan.–25 Feb. 1650, 2–3.

42. Abbott, ii, 212–13, Cromwell to Lenthall, 15 Feb. 1650; Cary, ed., *Memorials*, ii, 210–11, Cromwell to Lenthall, 15 Feb. 1650; *Diurnall of the Armies*, 25 Feb.–4 Mar. 1650, 99–100.

43. Whitelocke, *Memorials*, 429.

44. Murphy, *Cromwell in Ireland*, 253.

45. Whitelocke, *Memorials*, 429.

46. Abbott, ii, 213, Cromwell to Lenthall, 15 Feb. 1650; Murphy, *Cromwell in Ireland*, 254.

47. Murphy, *Cromwell in Ireland*, 254–6; Abbott, ii, 213–14, Cromwell to Lenthall, 15 Feb. 1650.

48. Abbott, ii, 213–14, Cromwell to Lenthall, 15 Feb. 1650; Murphy, *Cromwell in Ireland*, 256–7, for the terms.

49. Carte MS 26, fo. 602, Ormond to Charles II, 2 Feb. 1650; ibid., fo. 654, Ormond to Clanricarde, 11 Feb. 1650, speculating that Cromwell's targets were Clonmel and Kilkenny; ibid., fo. 717, Clanricarde to Ormond, 9 Feb. 1650, telling him that the people of Roscommon refused to raise money and supplies for a force to be marched to Ormond's support.

50. Ibid., fo. 747, Hugh O'Neill to Ormond, 23 Feb. 1650.

51. *Diurnall of the Armies*, 10–18 Mar. 1650, 126; ibid., 18–25 Mar. 1650, 131, for reports of the plague in Galway, Limerick and Kilkenny.

52. Gillespie, 'Irish Economy at War, 1641–1652', 177–8.

53. TT, E534 (29), *Several Proceedings*, 11–18 Apr. 1650, 411, Hewson to Lenthall, 4 Apr. 1650, claiming that his troops were not affected by the plague in Gowran even though the local population was dying all around them.

54. Abbott, ii, 212, Cromwell to Lenthall, 15 Feb. 1650.

55. Ibid., 214.

56. *Diurnall of the Armies*, 10–18 Mar. 1650, 113–14, letter from Mallow, 28 Feb. 1650.

57. Abbott, ii, 214, Cromwell to Lenthall, 15 Feb. 1650.

58. Ibid., 211, Cromwell to Colonel Phayre, in Cork, 9 Feb. 1650.

59. TT, E595 (10), *A Particular Relation of . . . Ireland*, Dublin, 11 Mar. 1650, 4; Castlehaven, *Memoirs*, 151–5.

60. Abbott, ii, 214, Cromwell to Lenthall, 15 Feb. 1650.

61. Murphy, *Cromwell in Ireland*, 269–70.

62. Carte MS 26, fo. 740, Cromwell to Mathews, 24 Feb. 1650. He offered to allow Mathews to march away with baggage, arms and colours, free from injury or violence.

63. Murphy, *Cromwell in Ireland*, 270; Abbott, ii, 216–18.

64. Abbott, ii, 216–17; Carte MS 26, fo. 741, Cromwell's terms to Mathews, 24 Feb. 1650.

65. Carte MS 27, fo. 18, Ormond to Mathews, 3 Mar. 1650.

66. Ibid., fo. 90, 'Reasons alleged by Captain George Mathews for his surrender of the Castle of Cahir', Mar. 1650.

67. Abbott, ii, 216, 217–18, Cromwell to Council of State, 5 Mar. 1650.

68. Ibid., 218; Murphy, *Cromwell in Ireland*, 272.

69. TT, E534 (20), *Several Proceedings*, 14–21 Mar. 1650, 346, Hewson to Lenthall, 4 Mar. 1650; ibid., 347–8, Hewson to Lenthall, 3 Mar. 1650.

70. Ibid., 347–8; E595 (10), *A Particular Relation of . . . Ireland*, 1–4; TT, E534 (19), *Several Letters from Ireland*, 18 Mar. 1650, 1–3, Hewson to Lenthall, 3 Mar. 1650; Dan Bryan, 'Ballyshannon Fort, Co. Kildare, 1642–1650', *Irish Sword*, iv (1959–60), 93–8.

71. TT, E534 (19), *Several Letters from Ireland*, 6, letter from William Basil, Attorney-General of Ireland, 2 Mar. 1650.

72. TT, E534 (20), *Several Proceedings*, 4–11 Apr. 1650, 351, Hewson to Lenthall, 3 Mar. 1650, telling Lenthall that he was departing that night from Ballisonan to Castledermot, where he hoped to fight Castlehaven; TT, E534 (29), *Several Proceedings*, 11–18 Apr. 1650, 410, Hewson to Lenthall, 4 Apr. 1650, discussing his need to withdraw to Dublin for supplies..

73. TT, E534 (29), *Several Proceedings*, 11–18 Apr. 1650, 410, Hewson to Lenthall, 4 Apr. 1650.

74. Carte MS 27, fo. 39, 27 Feb. 1650, Clanricarde's secretary's notes.

75. Castlehaven, *Memoirs*, 151.

76. Ibid., 153.

77. TT, E534 (29), *Several Proceedings*, 11–18 Apr. 1650, 412, Hewson to Lenthall, 4 Apr. 1650.
78. Castlehaven, *Memoirs*, 152–3.
79. Abbott, ii, 222, Cromwell to Ireton, 18 Mar. 1650.
80. Whitelocke, *Memorials*, 424–5.
81. TT, E534 (29), *Several Proceedings*, 11–18 Apr. 1650, 411, Hewson to Lenthall, 4 Apr. 1650.
82. Castlehaven, *Memoirs*, 153–6.
83. Murphy, *Cromwell in Ireland*, 296–305.
84. Ibid., 295.
85. Ibid., 297; Abbott, ii, 224.
86. Abbott, ii, 225–7, for Abbott's account; ibid., 233–5, for Cromwell's account in his letter to Lenthall, 2 Apr. 1650; TT, E534 (29), *Several Proceedings*, 4–11 Apr. 1650, 410–13, for Hewson's account in a letter to Lenthall, 5 Apr. 1650; Murphy, *Cromwell in Ireland*, 296–310, offers a slightly different account. My account relies on Cromwell's and Hewson's accounts for details of the assaults, and on Murphy for a discussion of Kilkenny and the entire siege.
87. Abbott, ii, 233, Cromwell to Lenthall, 2 Apr. 1650.
88. TT, E534 (29), *Several Proceedings*, 4–11 Apr. 1650, 412.
89. Abbott, ii, 233, for Cromwell's account, 2 Apr. 1650; TT, E534 (29), *Several Proceedings*, 4–11 Apr. 1650, 412, for Hewson's account, 5 Apr. 1650.
90. Abbott, ii, 233, Cromwell to Lenthall, 2 Apr. 1650.
91. Ibid., 229, agreement between Cromwell and Sir Walter Butler, 27 Mar. 1650.

Chapter 6: The Collapse of the Royalist Coalition, March–May 1650 (pp 140–158)

1. TT, E616 (7), *A Letter from Sir Lewis Dyve to the Lord Marquis of Newcastle*, 17 Nov. 1650, 45.
2. Carte MS 26, fo. 495, Charles II to Ormond, 12 Jan. 1650.
3. Ibid., fo. 146, Clanricarde to Ormond, 8 Nov. 1649; Carte MS 27, fo. 437, Clanricarde to Ormond, 3 May 1650.
4. Carte MS 26, fo. 551, Ormond's list of the winter garrisons, 26 Jan. 1650. The garrisons of many places taken by Cromwell were allowed to march away to another Irish post.
5. Abbott, ii, 234, Cromwell to Lenthall, 2 Apr. 1650.
6. Carte MS 27, fo. 7, Clanricarde to Bishop MacMahon, 2 Mar. 1650, calling for a rendezvous with the Ulster Catholic forces; ibid., fo. 131, Clanricarde to Ormond, 17 Mar. 1650, telling Ormond that he was going to move against Sir Charles Coote near Sligo.
7. See above, ch. 5.
8. Carte MS 27, fos 96–101, correspondence between the Limerick clergy and Ormond, 8 Mar. 1650; Gardiner, *C & P*, i, 153.
9. Carte MS 27, fo. 104, Ormond to the Catholic prelates, 21 Mar. 1650; Murphy, *Cromwell in Ireland*, 273–4.
10. Murphy, *Cromwell in Ireland*, 276.
11. *Diurnall of the Armies*, 6–13 May 1650, 254, letters from Derry, 18 Apr. 1650.
12. For examples see Carte MS 25, fo. 270, Clanricarde to Ormond, 17 Aug. 1649; ibid., fo. 679, Clanricarde to Ormond, 4 Oct. 1649; ibid., MS 26, fo. 415, Clanricarde to Ormond, 30 Dec. 1649; fo. 619, Clanricarde to Ormond,

5 Feb. 1650; fo. 772, Clanricarde to Ormond, 19 Feb. 1650; MS 27, fo. 131, Clanricarde to Ormond, 17 Mar. 1650.

13. Carte MS 27, fo. 37, Clanricarde to Ormond, 5 Mar. 1650.
14. Ibid., fo. 136, Clanricarde to Ormond, 18 Mar. 1650.
15. Simms, 'Cromwell's Siege of Waterford', 15–16.
16. Murphy, *Cromwell in Ireland*, 351, places the election on 8 March; Ohlmeyer, *Antrim*, 236, places it on 18 March, as does Gardiner, *C & P*, i, 153.
17. Murphy, *Cromwell in Ireland*, 353 n. 1.
18. Abbott, ii, 239; TT, E534 (24), *Several Proceedings*, 28 Mar.–4 Apr. 1650, 390, letter from Dublin, 22 Mar. 1650; Carte MS 27, fo. 166, Inchiquin to Ormond, 22 Mar. 1650.
19. Murphy, *Cromwell in Ireland*, 321.
20. Carte MS 27, fo. 207, Inchiquin to Ormond, 27 Mar. 1650; ibid., fos 213–15, Ormond to Inchiquin, 27 Mar. 1650, ordering him to disband his forces.
21. Ibid., fo. 219, order of the Catholic Council at Loughrea, 31 Mar. 1650, ordering Ormond's commands to be carried out and the Protestant troops to be given one month's pay and sent to Galway.
22. Ibid., fo. 259, Cromwell's letter allowing safe passage, 8 Apr. 1650; ibid., fo., 316, Cromwell's letter allowing the Protestant officers to keep their horses and weapons, 26 Apr. 1650.
23. Gardiner, *C & P*, i, 151–2.
24. Abbott, ii, 241–3, terms of agreement, 26 Apr. 1650.
25. Ibid., 243.
26. Ibid., 246–7, explanatory articles by the Lord Lieutenant of Ireland, 5 May 1650.
27. Carte, *Ormond*, iii, 553.
28. Ibid.; Carte MS 27, fo. 437, Clanricarde to Ormond, 3 May 1650.
29. Quoted in Abbott, ii, 249.
30. TT, E602 (13), *Brief Relation*, 21–28 May 1650, 590–91, Broghill's letter from Cork, 13 May 1650.
31. TT, E777 (6), *Several Proceedings*, 23–30 May 1650, 502–3, published a letter from Cork which the editor said had been written on 16 April; this date is incorrect. TT, E777 (9), *Several Proceedings*, 30 May–6 June 1650, 514–15, published a letter from Cork dated 28 May 1650 which gives the date for the fight at Macroom by Broghill as 10 May, not 10 April 1650; TT, E602 (13), *Brief Relation*, 21–28 May 1650, 581–2, corroborates the 10 May date and the executions; ibid., 589–91, Broghill's account confirms the date; Gardiner, *C & P*, i, 151, incorrectly dates the fight at Macroom as 10 April 1650.
32. TT, E602 (13), *Brief Relation*, 21–28 May 1650, 590–91, Broghill's account.
33. Abbott, ii, 127, Cromwell to Lenthall, 17 Sept. 1650.
34. TT, E534 (27), *Several Proceedings*, 4–11 Apr. 1650. 404, Robert Saunders, governor of Youghal, to Lenthall, 26 Mar. 1650.
35. *CSPD, 1650*, 570–90. Hundreds of warrants were issued by the Council of State for the supply of the English forces in Ireland from April to September 1650.
36. Martin van Creveld, *Supplying War: Logistics from Wallenstein to Patton*, Cambridge: Cambridge University Press, 1977, 7.
37. TT, E534 (21), *Several Proceedings*, 18–25 Apr. 1650, 434.
38. *CSPD, 1650*, 570–90, for the list of regiments sent to Ireland; *Diurnall of the Armies*, 1–8 Apr. 1650, 182, for the estimate of the number of English soldiers in Ireland at that time.

39. *Diurnall of the Armies*, 15–22 Apr. 1650, 191; Abbott, ii, 230.

40. *Diurnall of the Armies*, 15–22 Apr. 1650, 195–201.

41. Castlehaven, *Memoirs*, 156–7.

42. Abbott, ii, 234–5, Cromwell to Lenthall, 2 Apr. 1650.

43. TT, E534 (29), *Several Proceedings*, 11–18 Apr. 1650, 418.

44. Ibid.; Carte MS 27, fo. 140, Cromwell to Ireton, 18 Mar. 1650.

45. Abbott, ii, 235, Cromwell to Lenthall, 2 Apr. 1650.

46. Ibid., 237.

47. Carte MS 27, fo. 369, James White to Ormond, 27 Apr. 1650; Gardiner, *C & P*, i, 155–6.

48. Patrick F. Dineen, 'The Siege of Clonmel' in P. O'Connell and W. C. Carmody, eds, *Tercentenary of the Siege of Clonmel, 1650–1950*, Clonmel: Nationalist Newspaper Co., 1950, 6–15.

49. Carte MS 27, fo. 402, Colonel John Lyvett in Waterford to Ormond, 30 Apr. 1650, telling him that Clonmel had been besieged by Cromwell for the past three days. There are few English accounts of the siege of Clonmel. No account written by Cromwell survives, if he ever wrote one.

50. Burke, 'The New Model Army and the Problems of Siege Warfare', 16.

51. Hogan, ed., *History of the War of Ireland*, 106.

52. Dineen, 'Siege of Clonmel', 12.

53. Ibid.; Abbott, ii, 245–6; Murphy, *Cromwell in Ireland*, 330–31.

54. W. G. Ross, *Military Engineering during the Great Civil War, 1642–9*, London: Ken Trotman, 1984, 35, 'A Table of Ordnance used in England'.

55. Abbott, ii, 250.

56. *Diurnall of the Armies*, 20–27 May 1650, 278; Burke, 'The New Model Army and the Problems of Siege Warfare', 16–17; Murphy, *Cromwell in Ireland*, 333–4.

57. *Diurnall of the Armies*, 20–27 May 1650, 278.

58. TT, E602 (13), *Brief Relation*, 21–28 May 1650, 580–81, a report from Youghal, 17 May 1650, stating 'that the batteries are now ready before Clonmel, and my Lord's intending a sudden action there before his coming toward you'; Murphy, *Cromwell in Ireland*, 333–4, incorrectly locates the site of the final breach to the 'west wall, about twenty yards south of the tower called the magazine, where a portion of the wall is still standing'. This location may have been the site of one of Cromwell's earlier attempts to blow a breach with his light field guns.

59. William Burke, *History of Clonmel*, Kilkenny: Roberts Books, 1983, 74–5.

60. Hogan, ed., *History of the War of Ireland*, 107.

61. Accounts vary about the timing and the number of assaults made on 17 May. The best first-hand account is Hogan, ed., *History of the War of Ireland*, 106–9; good secondary accounts are found in Murphy, *Cromwell in Ireland*, 334–7, Abbott, ii, 250–53, and Burke, *History of Clonmel*, 76–8. There is a great deal of disagreement as to when Cromwell launched his final assault against the main breach in Clonmel's north wall. A number of normally reliable secondary sources, such as Gardiner, incorrectly place the assault on 9 May. Murphy's *Cromwell in Ireland* gives no date for the assault in the text, although the footnote for the attack observes that one account places the assault on 9 May. Abbott, ii, 250, places the opening of the breach on 16 May and the final assault on 17 May, as does Burke, 'The New Model Army and the Problems of Siege Warfare', 17. Gentles, *New Model Army*, 374, places the assault on 16 May. The correct date for the final assault was 17 May, and the surrender took place on 18 May 1650.

The erroneous date of 9 May for the final assault came from a letter which was incorrectly dated when it was published. It is clear from the context of the newsbooks that the letter was misdated. The initial letter, published in *Several Proceedings*, 23–30 May 1650, was dated 10 May, but it was published in the newsbook between letters dated 17 May and 19 May. The report in the *Diurnall of the Armies*, 20–27 May 1650, 280, prints a notice from Holyhead, dated 20 May, which reports that 'this morning arrived the post-barque here. The news at present from Ireland is that Clonmel is taken.' A time-lag of two days to Holyhead is reasonable.

Ormond's correspondence contains evidence that the final assault and fall of Clonmel took place on 17–18 May. There is no mention of it in letters to and from Ormond before 21 May. In fact on 18 May Inchiquin speculated in a letter to Ormond that Cromwell would like Clonmel to fall quickly (Carte MS 27, fo. 523). On Tuesday 21 May the Mayor of Limerick wrote to Ormond telling him that 'The enemy, having taken Clonmel last Saturday [18 May], are now (we are told) coming to besiege this place' (ibid., fos 528–30). On 22 May Clanricarde lamented 'the so sudden fall of Clonmel', the first reference made by him to the fall of the place. The terms of the surrender are clearly dated 18 May 1650 in Abbott, ii, 252.

62. Hogan, ed., *History of the War of Ireland*, 108.
63. Ibid.; Abbott, ii, 251; Gentles, *New Model Army*, 374.
64. C. H. Firth, *Cromwell's Army*, repr., intro. John Adair, London: Greenhill Books, 1992, 73–4.
65. Gardiner, *C & P*, i, 156, puts the total number killed at 2,500. This estimate is perhaps too high. Gentles, *New Model Army*, 543 n. 137, thinks that a contemporary estimate of 1,500 dead is more realistic.
66. Burke, *History of Clonmel*, 77, quoting *Aphorismical Discovery*.
67. Burke, 'The New Model Army and the Problems of Siege Warfare', 19 n. 136, provides a chart listing the losses suffered by the New Model Army from its creation in 1645 to 1660.
68. Abbott, i, 252, 'Articles', signed by Cromwell on 18 May 1650.
69. Ibid.; Murphy, *Cromwell in Ireland*, 338–9.
70. Cary, ed., *Memorials*, ii, 218, letter from S. Dillingham to Mr Sandcroft, May 1650.
71. Whitelocke, *Memorials*, 440.

Chapter 7: Ireton's Summer Campaign, 1650 (pp 159–180)

1. *Diurnall of the Armies*, 10–17 June 1650, 302, an analysis of the current situation in Ireland by Colonel John Reynolds, 28 May 1650.
2. *Diurnall of the Armies*, 27 May–3 June 1650, 278–9: Whitelocke, *Memorials*, 440, 442; *Diurnall of the Armies*, 3–10 June 1650, 284; TT, E777 (11), *Several Proceedings*, 6–13 June 1650, 531.
3. Abbott, ii, 146, Cromwell to Governor of New Ross, 19 Oct. 1649.
4. Ibid., i, 360, Cromwell to Lenthall, 14 June 1645.
5. Wheeler, 'Logistics and Supply in Cromwell's Conquest of Ireland', 38–56.
6. McElligott, *Cromwell: Our Chief of Enemies*, 12.
7. Abbott, ii, 208–59, for terms given to Fethard, Cahir, Cashel, Kilkenny and Clonmel.
8. Gentles, *New Model Army*, 361–3; Patrick J. Corish, 'The Cromwellian Conquest, 1649–53' in *NHI*, iii, 341.

9. Gardiner, *C & P*, i, 118–25.

10. C. V. Wedgwood, *The Life of Cromwell*, New York: Collier Books, 1966 ed., 13–14.

11. TT, E616 (7), *A Letter from Sir Lewis Dyve*, 17 Nov. 1650, 50–51.

12. *Diurnall of the Armies*, 3–10 June 1650, 295.

13. Gilbert, ed., *Contemporary History, 1641–52*, ii, 422–3, Bishop MacMahon to Ormond, 1 June 1650.

14. Whitelocke, *Memorials*, 437.

15. Carte MS 27, fo. 478, Ormond to Preston, 8 May 1650; ibid., fo. 546, Clanricarde to Ormond, 22 May 1650.

16. *Diurnall of the Armies*, 10–17 June 1650, 299.

17. Whitelocke, *Memorials*, 441.

18. *Diurnall of the Armies*, 17–24 June 1650, 313, 319.

19. TT, E777 (13), *Several Proceedings*, 13–20 June 1650, 551, where the English estimated Clanricarde's strength at 4,000 men; Gilbert, ed., *Contemporary History, 1641–52*, ii, 92–4.

20. Carte MS 27, fo. 719, Clanricarde to Ormond, 18 June 1650.

21. Ibid., fo. 732, Castlehaven to Ormond, 19 June 1650.

22. Carte MS 28, fo. 18, Clanricarde to Ormond, 23 June 1650.

23. Ibid, fo. 16, Castlehaven to Ormond, 23 June 1650.

24. Ibid, fo. 18, Clanricarde to Ormond, 23 June 1650.

25. TT, E777 (26), *Perfect Weekly Account*, 10–17 July 1650, 30; Carte MS 28, fo. 49, terms of surrender for Tecroghan, 25 June 1650.

26. TT, E778 (9), *Several Proceedings*, 25 July–1 August 1650, 643–4.

27. *Diurnall of the Armies*, 10–17 June 1650, 302

28. Ibid., 24–30 June 1650, 323–34; Gilbert, ed., *Contemporary History, 1641–52*, ii, 422–3, 31 May 1650, proclamation of 'Bishop MacMahon to Gentry, etc., of the County of Londonderry'.

29. Hogan, ed., *History of the War of Ireland*, 116–17; TT, E777 (22), *Several Proceedings*, 4–11 July 1650, 580.

30. TT, E777 (22), *Several Proceedings*, 4–11 July 1650, 580–81; *Diurnall of the Armies*, 17–24 June 1650, 319; ibid., 8–15 July 1650, 354–6, for Coote's account of the battle, 29 June 1650.

31. TT, E777 (22), *Several Proceedings*, 4–11 July 1650, 581; Hogan, ed., *History of the War of Ireland*, 119–20.

32. TT, E777 (22), *Several Proceedings*, 4–11 July 1650, 581; *Diurnall of the Armies*, 8–15 July 1650, 355, for Coote's account.

33. Gilbert, ed., *Contemporary History, 1641–52*, ii, 417–18, Bishop MacMahon to Ormond, 19 May 1650.

34. TT, E777 (22), *Several Proceedings*, 4–11 July 1650, 582; TT, E607 (14), *A Declaration of the Irish Army in Ulster: sent to Parliament in a Letter from William Basil* (account of Scarriffhollis), London, 12 July 1650, 22–3; Hogan, ed., *History of the War of Ireland*, 123.

35. Carte MS 28, fo. 146, Clanricarde to Ormond, 7 July 1650; Murphy, *Cromwell in Ireland*, 354–5; Gardiner, *C & P*, ii, 105–7; Gilbert, *Contemporary History, 1641–52*, ii, 84–5; Gentles, *New Model Army*, 376.

36. TT, E607 (14), *A Declaration of the Irish Army in Ulster*, 22–3, estimates the Irish army's strength at 4,000 infantrymen and 400 cavalrymen, and the English army's at 2,000 infantry and 800 cavalry.

37. TT, E777 (22), *Several Proceedings*, 4–11 July 1650, 582; *Diurnall of the Armies*, 5–15 July 1650, 356.

38. TT, E607 (14), *A Declaration of the Irish Army in Ulster*, 22–3; TT, E777 (24), *Every Day's Intelligence*, 5–12 July 1650, 12–13.

39. TT, E777 (22), *Several Proceedings*, 4–11 July 1650, 582; *Diurnall of the Armies*, 1–8 July 1650, 352; Murphy, *Cromwell in Ireland*, 355; TT, E607 (14), *A Declaration of the Irish Army in Ulster*, 22–3.

40. Hogan, ed., *History of the War of Ireland*, 128.

41. Murphy, *Cromwell in Ireland*, 358, quoting from Gilbert, ed., *Contemporary History, 1641–52*, ii, 88.

42. TT, E607 (14), *A Declaration of the Irish Army in Ulster*, 23.

43. Carte MS 28, fo. 123, Lord Dillon to Ormond, 4 July 1650; ibid., fo. 125, letter to Ormond from some Ulster army survivors, 4 July 1650, telling Ormond that they can raise another army, but lack weapons and ammunition with which to arm it; TT, E777 (22) *Several Proceedings*, 4–11 July 1650, 582–3, for list of officers killed by the English; Casway, *O'Neill*, 266–7.

44. Carte MS 28, fo. 122, Clanricarde to Ormond, 5 July 1650; ibid., fo. 140, Clanricarde to a 'Reverend Father', 6 July 1650.

45. Ibid., fo. 144, Clanricarde to Ormond, 8 July 1650.

46. Ibid, fo. 127, Clanricarde to Ormond, 5 July 1650; ibid., fo. 209, Mayor of Limerick to Ormond, 19 July 1650, accepting O'Neill; ibid., fo. 193, Clanricarde to Ormond, 17 July 1650; ibid., fo. 195, Clanricarde's agreement to appoint Lynch to the Galway position, 18 July 1650.

47. Ibid., fos 205–6, Ormond to Master Long, 17 July 1650, telling Long that he had heard of the king's treaty with the Scots; ibid., fo. 129, Jeffrey Brown to Ormond, 5 July 1650, concerning the money.

48. Carte, *Ormond*, iii, 559.

49. TT, E778 (13), *Perfect Weekly Account*, 31 July–7 Aug. 1650, 548, for the shipment of Colonel Lidcott's regiment; *Diurnall of the Armies*, 17–24 June 1650, 313, for the shipment of Colonels Daniel's and Coles's regiments; Ludlow, *Memoirs*, 321–3.

50. Gardiner, *C & P*, ii, 106–7; Carte MS 27, fo. 627, Council of Waterford to Ormond, 5 June 1650.

51. Carte MS 28, fo. 112, Sir John Lyvett to Ormond, 2 July 1650.

52. Ibid., fo. 232, Inchiquin to Ormond, 24 July 1650; ibid., fo. 284, Ormond to ——, 6 Aug. 1650.

53. TT, E778 (23), *Several Proceedings*, 22–29 Aug. 1650, 709–10, Ireton's account of the final Waterford campaign; *Diurnall of the Armies*, 26 Aug.–2 Sept. 1650, 451–6, another copy of Ireton's account.

54. Ludlow, *Memoirs*, 324.

55. *Diurnall of the Armies*, 26 Aug.–2 Sept. 1650, 453.

56. TT, E778 (23), *Several Proceedings*, 22–29 Aug. 1650, 708–9.

57. Carte MS 28, fos 292–3, Preston to Ormond, 10 Aug. 1650.

58. *Diurnall of the Armies*, 26 Aug.–2 Sept. 1650, 455–6.

59. Ibid., 455.

60. *Aphorismical Discovery*, ii, 98–100.

61. Carte MS 28, fo. 228, Archbishop John Burke of Tuam to Ormond, 24 July 1650; Edmund Borlase, *The History of the Execrable Irish Rebellion*, London: Henry Brome, 1680, 256.

62. Carte MS 28, fo. 290, Archbishops to Ormond, 10 Aug. 1650; Carte, *Ormond*, iii, 561–2.

63. Carte MS 28, fo. 300, declaration of the four archbishops at Jamestown, 12 Aug. 1650; ibid., fo. 303, Prelates to Ormond, 13 Aug. 1650.

64. TT, E777 (24), *Every Day's Intelligence*, 5–12 July 1650, 14–15; TT, E778 (15), ibid., 2–9 Aug. 1650, 43; TT, E778 (21), *Several Proceedings*, 15–22 Aug. 1650, 698, noting that a breach had been made in the defences.

65. TT, E778 (21), *Several Proceedings*, 15–22 Aug. 1650, 698; Carte MS 28, fo. 331, a letter from Ulster to Clanricarde, describing O'Neill's gallant defence of Charlemont.

66. Carte MS 28, fo. 345, Clanricarde to Ormond, 19 Aug. 1650.

67. Ibid., fo. 349, Clanricarde to Ormond, 19 Aug. 1650.

68. Carte, *Ormond*, iii, 562–3; Carte MS 28, fo. 457, Bishop Walter Lynch of Clonfert to Ormond, 15 Sept. 1650, telling Ormond that the bishops were publishing the excommunication threat to his soldiers; *Aphorismical Discovery*, ii, 100–7, copy of the proclamation of the clergy at Jamestown, 12 Aug. 1650, including the dreaded threat of excommunication; the final threat was not issued until 23 August, and was not published until 15 September; Carte MS 28, fo. 220, Duke of York to Ormond, 21 July 1650.

69. Carte MS 28, fo. 448, Bishop Lynch to Archbishops, 13 Sept. 1650, asking them to withhold final censure; ibid., fos 495–6, Council of Galway to Lord Dillon, 23 Sept. 1650, telling him that they were telling soldiers to ignore the excommunication threat.

Chapter 8: The Advance on Limerick, 1650–51 (pp 181–200)

1. TT, E613 (13), *Mecurius Anglicus communicating the Moderate Intelligence*, 24 Sept.–1 Oct. 1650, 7.

2. Gentles, *New Model Army*, 55–60.

3. Ibid., 266–314.

4. *Diurnall of the Armies*, 23–30 Sept. 1650, 536.

5. Gardiner, *C & P*, ii, 111 n. 2.

6. TT, E618 (4), *Mercurius Politicus*, 21–28 Nov. 1650, 411–12; TT, E615 (10), *Mercurius Politicus*, 24–31 Oct. 1650, 333–4.

7. Gardiner, *C & P*, ii, 108–9 n. 3, 110 n. 2; *Aphorismical Discovery*, ii, 108–11, incorrectly claiming that Dillon and Ormond really planned to surrender Athlone. Dillon's and Ormond's correspondence make it clear that they were deceiving the English (Gilbert, ed., *Contemporary History, 1641–52*, iii, 171, Dillon to Ormond, 6 Aug. 1650).

8. TT, E615 (10), *Mercurius Politicus*, 24–31 Oct. 1650, 350; *Diurnall of the Armies*, 23–30 Sept. 1650, 553.

9. TT, E618 (4), *Mercurius Politicus*, 21–28 Nov. 1650, 411.

10. A term applied to the French tactics employed against the civilian population of Algeria in the 1960s and the title of a book about that war by Alaister Horne.

11. TT, E615 (10), *Mercurius Politicus*, 24–31 Oct. 1650, 350; Gardiner, *C & P*, ii, 111.

12. TT, E618 (4), *Mercurius Politicus*, 21–28 Nov. 1650, 413.

13. Ibid.

14. *Diurnall of the Armies*, 7–14 Oct. 1650, 479.

15. *CSPD, 1650*, 252.

16. Carte MS 28, fo. 531, Ireton to Mayor and Aldermen of Limerick, 6 Oct. 1650.

17. Gardiner, *C & P*, ii, 111.

18. Carte MS 28, fo. 586, Castlehaven to Ormond, 19 Oct. 1650.

19. Ohlmeyer, *Civil War and Restoration*, 235–6.
20. Carte MS 28, fo. 529, Clanricarde and others to the bishops, 6 Oct. 1650.
21. Patrick Little, '"Blood and Friendship": The Earl of Essex's Protection of the Earl of Clanricarde's Interests, 1641–6', *English Historical Review*, cxii (1997), 927–41.
22. Carte MS 28, fo. 549, Ormond to Castlehaven, 8 Oct. 1650.
23. Ibid., where Ormond credits him with 5,000 foot and 1,000 horse; TT, E618 (3), *A Letter from William Basil . . . concerning a Great Victory*, 26 Nov. 1650, 4, estimated his strength at 3,000 foot and about 300 horse.
24. TT, E615 (10), *Mercurius Politicus*, 24–31 Oct. 1650, 350.
25. TT, E618 (3), *A Letter from William Basil*, 4.
26. Ibid., 4–5; TT, E781 (6), *Perfect Passages of Every Day's Intelligence*, 22–29 Nov. 1650, 124–6.
27. TT, E618 (3), *A Letter from William Basil*, 3–8; TT, E618 (4), *Mercurius Politicus*, 21–28 Nov. 1650, 418–20, gives a similar account.
28. TT, 618 (3), *A letter from William Basil*, 5; *Diurnall of the Armies*, 25 Nov.–2 Dec. 1650, 658–61; Whitelocke, *Memorials*, 472.
29. Carte MS 28, fo. 614, Clanricarde to Ormond, 2 Nov. 1650.
30. Ibid., fo. 619, Clanricarde to Ormond, 6 Nov. 1650.
31. Borlase, *Irish Rebellion*, 269.
32. Carte MS 28, fo. 671, Ormond to General Assembly, 19 Nov. 1650.
33. TT, E781 (26), *Every Day's Intelligence*, 3–10 Jan. 1651, 173.
34. Ibid.
35. TT, E781 (20), *Several Proceedings*, 26 Dec. 1650–2 Jan. 1651, 1000.
36. Gentles, *New Model Army*, 392–9.
37. Gardiner, *C & P*, ii, 112–13. There are only three biographies of Ormond. The monumental six-volume work of Thomas Carte, *The Life of James, First Duke of Ormond*, is still the best. J. C. Beckett's, *The Cavalier Duke* presents a short review of his life. Lady Burghclere's 1912 account, *The Life of James, First Duke of Ormonde, 1610–1688*, is completely inadequate because of its poor documentation. T. C. Barnard is currently working on a volume dealing with the first and second Dukes of Ormond.
38. Robert Dunlop, ed., *Ireland under the Commonwealth*, 2 vols, Manchester: Manchester University Press, 1913, i, 7–8, letter from English Commissioners in Ireland to Council of State, 1 July 1651.
39. Ibid., 7, Commissioners to Parliament, 1 July 1651; Carte MS 29, fo. 928, list of major English garrisons, winter 1650–51.
40. Dunlop, ed., *Ireland under the Commonwealth*, i, 7–8, Commissioners to Council of State, 1 July 1651.
41. TT, E607 (18), *Mercurius Politicus*, 11–18 July 1650, 96; TT, E608 (1), *An Abstract from Newcastle*, July 1650, 6.
42. Bodl., Rawlinson MS A223, fos 100–3. The English government spent £42,000 for the construction of ten new frigates in 1650, and the annual expenditure for the navy alone was £780,000 from 13 May 1649 to 31 December 1650. (PRO, E351/2289, declared account of the Navy Treasurer.) The army cost at least £1 million per year in 1649–50 (ibid., E351/302, 304–7, declared accounts of the army's Treasurers-at-War). For the Assessment increase see Firth and Rait, eds, *Acts and Ordinances of the Interregnum*, iii, p. lxxxii (26 Nov. 1650); ii, 456.
43. PRO, SP25/118, fos 137–46.
44. TT, E629 (3), *Weekly Intelligencer*, 13–20 May 1651, 167.

45. *CSPD, 1650*, 570–608.
46. Firth and Rait, eds, *Acts and Ordinances*, iii, p. lxxxiv; ii, 513.
47. *CSPD, 1651*, 155–60, 168, 171.
48. Dunlop, ed., *Ireland under the Commonwealth*, i, 81, Commissioners to Council of State, 28 Oct. 1651, where they note that of the 2,000 men who died of disease at the siege of Limerick, most were new recruits.
49. *CSPD, 1651*, 536–88.
50. Bottigheimer, *English Money and Irish Land*, 135; Dunlop, ed., *Ireland under the Commonwealth*, i, p. cxxix.
51. Gillespie, 'Irish Economy at War, 1641–1652', 177–8; TT, E614 (10), *Weekly Intelligencer*, 8–15 Oct. 1650, 20, reports that between 600 and 800 people were dying each week in Dublin.
52. TT, E780 (20), *Several Proceedings*, 3–10 Oct. 1650, 797.
53. PRO, SP63/281, fos 31–44.
54. *CSPD, 1651*, 536–88.
55. Ibid.
56. PRO, SP25/118, pp 19–27, 55–77; Wheeler, 'Logistics and Supply in Cromwell's Conquest of Ireland', 48, Table 1.
57. *CSPD, 1650*, 570–608.
58. *CSPD, 1651*, 536–88.
59. *CSPD, 1651–52*, 544–77.
60. Ibid.
61. *CSPD, 1650*, 570–608; *CSPD, 1651*, 536–88.
62. Jane Ohlmeyer, 'Ireland Independent: Confederate Foreign Policy and International Relations during the Mid-Seventeenth Century' in Ohlmeyer, ed., *Ireland from Independence to Occupation*, 189–211.
63. Ibid., 107–8.
64. Ibid., 106.
65. *Diurnall of the Armies*, 6–13 Jan. 1651, 757.
66. Ludlow, *Memoirs*, 337.
67. *Diurnall of the Armies*, 4–11 Nov. 1650, 615.
68. TT, E622 (10), *Weekly Intelligencer*, 21–28 Jan. 1651, 37.
69. *Diurnall of the Armies*, 6–13 Jan. 1651, 759.
70. TT, E626 (12), *Weekly Intelligencer*, 18–25 Mar. 1651, 97; TT, E781 (32), *Several Proceedings*, 16–23 Jan. 1651, 1043.
71. TT, E781 (37), *Every Day's Intelligence*, 24–31 Jan. 1651, 195; Whitelocke, *Memorials*, 480.
72. TT, E781 (8), *Several Proceedings*, 28 Nov.–5 Dec. 1650, 938.
73. TT, E781 (33), *The Faithful Scout*, 17–24 Jan. 1651, 30.
74. Ibid.
75. TT, E626 (11), *A Letter from Colonel Hewson, from Finagh in Ireland*, 14 Mar. 1651, 3–4; TT, E626 (12), *Weekly Intelligencer*, 18–25 Mar. 1651, 97–8; *Aphorismical Discovery*, ii, 131–7.
76. TT, E626 (11), *A Letter from Colonel Hewson*, 4.
77. Ibid., 5.
78. Ibid., 6–8.
79. Borlase, *Irish Rebellion*, 281–2. Borlase published Clanricarde's proclamation of 2 January 1651 against the tories.
80. Whitelocke, *Memorials*, 483.

Chapter 9: The Conquest of Connacht and the Collapse of the Catholic Cause, 1651–3 (pp 201–223)

1. Carte MS 28, fo. 660, Clanricarde to Ormond, 26 Nov. 1650.
2. Dunlop, *Ireland under the Commonwealth*, i, p. cxxix; T. C. Barnard, *Cromwellian Ireland: English Government and Reform in Ireland, 1649–1660*, Oxford: Oxford University Press, 1975, 10.
3. TT, E784 (8), *Every Day's Intelligence*, 7–14 Feb. 1651, 215.
4. TT, E784 (11), *Several Proceedings*, 13–20 Feb. 1651, 1104–7, Ireton to Council of State, 8 Feb. 1651; Borlase, *Irish Rebellion*, 281–2; Carte MS 29, fo. 928, intelligence of Ireton's council of war in Waterford, May 1651.
5. Dunlop, ed., *Ireland under the Commonwealth*, i, p. cxxviii; TT, E784 (4), *Every Day's Intelligence*, 31 Jan.–7 Feb. 1651, 107, for Clanricarde's proclamation ordering tories to return to the organised units in Connacht and to cease their depredations; TT, E784 (3), *Several Proceedings*, 30 Jan.–6 Feb. 1651, 1076, published the same proclamation.
6. TT, E785 (13), *Every Day's Intelligence*, 18–25 Apr. 1651, copy of a captured letter from Clanricarde to Castlehaven, Apr. 1651.
7. Carte MS 29, fo. 443, letter from Perth, 6 May 1651; Gardiner, *C & P*, ii, 24–5.
8. Gentles, *New Model Army*, 402–11.
9. Carte MS 29, fo. 9, 'Declaration of the General Assembly', 7 Dec. 1650; ibid., fo. 33, Assembly's pledge to support Clanricarde, 24 Dec. 1650; *Diurnall of the Armies*, 6–13 Jan. 1651, 758–9; TT, E784 (3), *Several Proceedings*, 30 Jan.–6 Feb. 1651, 1075, Assembly's proclamation of 23 Dec. 1650.
10. *Aphorismical Discovery*, ii, 118–19.
11. TT, E785 (12), *Several Passages*, 17–24 Apr. 1651, 1255, a captured letter from Archbishop Thomas Walsh of Cashel to Monsieur Tirell, in the Abbey of Arras, 31 Jan. 1651.
12. Carte MS 29, fos 358–80, an entry book or ledger of the negotiations in Ireland; ibid., fo. 361, for Taaffe's negotiations; ibid., fo. 364, for Clanricarde's acceptance of a tentative deal with Duke Charles.
13. TT, E785 (12), *Several Passages*, 17–24 Apr. 1651, 1256–7, Colonel Plunkett, in Brussels, to Archbishop Thomas Fleming of Dublin, 3 Jan. 1651.
14. Carte MS 29, fo. 492, Ormond to Digby, 29 May 1651.
15. Borlase, *Irish Rebellion*, 287–9, for the terms of the agreement made with the Duke of Lorraine on 22 July 1651; ibid., 290–92, Clanricarde to Lorraine, 20 Oct. 1651, repudiating the agreement because the Irish delegates had exceeded their mandate.
16. TT, E785 (17), *Every Day's Intelligence*, 25 Apr.–2 May 1651, 295, for Admiral Blake's capture of the Scilly Isles, thus cutting sea communications from the continent to Ireland; TT, E786 (1), ibid., 6–13 June 1651, 334. Admiral Popham led a squadron into Dunkirk Road, preventing the embarkation of troops or supplies for Ireland.
17. Carte MS 29, fo. 492, Ormond to Digby, 29 May 1651.
18. *Diurnall of the Armies*, 10–17 Feb. 1651, 827.
19. TT, E785 (14), *The Faithful Scout*, 18–25 Apr. 1651, 138, reporting that the Spanish agent was given permission by the English to recruit 2,000 Irish soldiers in Connacht and to transport them to Spain; Whitelocke, *Memorials* 483; Stradling, *Spanish Monarchy and Irish Mercenaries*; S. R. Gardiner, 'The Transplantation to Connaught', *English Historical Review*, xiv (1899), 700.

Gardiner cites Petty's estimate that as many as 32,000 Irish soldiers were voluntarily shipped to the continent to serve in the armies of the Catholic powers.

20. Carte MS 29, fo. 463, Clanricarde to Ormond, 19 May 1651.
21. Gardiner, *C & P*, ii, 113.
22. *Aphorismical Discovery*, ii, 158–9.
23. Ludlow, *Memoirs*, i, 341–2.
24. Dunlop, ed., *Ireland under the Commonwealth*, i, 1–4, for the instructions for the commissioners, passed in parliament on 4 Oct. 1650.
25. Barnard, *Cromwellian Ireland*, 17; Gardiner, *C & P*, i, 265; ii, 117.
26. J. C. Beckett, *The Making of Modern Ireland, 1603–1923*, London: Faber & Faber, 1966, 105–6; J. P. Prendergast, *The Cromwellian Settlement of Ireland*, repr., London: Constable, 1996, xxxiv, states that there were eventually fifteen precincts.
27. Ludlow, *Memoirs*, i, 337.
28. Ibid., 337–8.
29. Beckett, *Making of Modern Ireland*, 110–12.
30. Ludlow, *Memoirs*, i, 343; Gilbert, ed., *Contemporary History*, iii, 226–7, 'Diaries of the Proceedings of the Forces in Ireland . . . from 20 July 1650 to 5 November 1651'; Gardiner, *C & P*, ii, 119.
31. TT, E638 (16), *Perfect Account*, 30 July–6 Aug. 1651, 237; Borlase, *Irish Rebellion*, 283; Whitelocke, *Memorials*, 486; Ludlow, *Memoirs*, i, 343.
32. Dunlop, ed., *Ireland under the Commonwealth*, i, 22–3, Commissioners to Sir Henry Vane, 2 Aug. 1651.
33. Ludlow, *Memoirs*, 346–8.
34. TT, E632 (6), *Perfect Account*, 4–11 June 1651, 173; Gilbert, ed., *Contemporary History*, iii, 232–3, 'Diaries of the Proceedings of the Forces in Ireland'.
35. TT, E786 (4), *Several Passages*, 12–19 June 1651, 1380.
36. *Aphorismical Discovery*, ii, 168; Borlase, *Irish Rebellion*, 284.
37. TT, E786 (8), *Several Passages*, 19–26 June 1651, 1394, letter from Waterford, 14 June 1651.
38. Ludlow, *Memoirs*, i, 346; TT, E632 (9), *A Bloody Fight in Ireland*, June 1651, 6.
39. Gilbert, ed., *Contemporary History*, iii, 230–31, 'Diaries of the Proceedings of the Forces in Ireland'; Ludlow, *Memoirs*, i, 346.
40. Ludlow, *Memoirs*, i, 346–8; Gardiner, *C & P*, ii, 119–20.
41. Ludlow, *Memoirs*, i, 347–8.
42. *Aphorismical Discovery*, ii, 160–61; Dunlop, ed., *Ireland under the Commonwealth*, 5 n. 1.
43. *Aphorismical Discovery*, ii, 161.
44. TT, E638 (15), *The Armies Intelligencer*, 29 July–5 Aug. 1651, 4; TT, E638 (16) *Perfect Account*, 30 July–6 Aug. 1651, 237.
45. TT, E632 (9), *A Bloody Fight in Ireland*, 6; Borlase, *Irish Rebellion*, 284.
46. *Aphorismical Discovery*, ii, 161–2.
47. Ludlow, *Memoirs*, i, 348–9; TT, E638 (13), *Sad News from Ireland*, 4 July 1651, 5.
48. *Aphorismical Discovery*, ii, 170.
49. Ludlow, *Memoirs*, i, 349–50.
50. TT, E786 (8), *Several Passages*, 19–26 June 1651, 1394, letter from Waterford, 14 June 1651.
51. Gentles, *New Model Army*, 378.
52. Ibid., 379, 544 n. 159.
53. TT, E640 (10), *A Letter from the Lord Broghill to the Honourable William Lenthall, Speaker of the Parliament of England*, 28 July 1651, 2.

54. Ibid., 3–4; Whitelocke, *Memorials*, 490; Borlase, *Irish Rebellion*, 283.
55. TT, E786 (8), *Several Passages*, 19–26 June 1651, 1395, letter from Waterford, 14 June 1651.
56. Gentles, *New Model Army*, 544 n. 163.
57. TT, E786 (22), *Several Proceedings*, 17–24 July 1651, 1456–7, proclamation of the commissioners, 28 Apr. 1651.
58. Ibid., 1455–6, proclamation, 22 Apr. 1651; ibid., 1457–8, proclamation offering incentives to farmers to grow hay, 28 Apr. 1651.
59. *Diurnall of the Armies*, 28 Apr.–5 May 1651, 998–1000.
60. Ibid., 1000.
61. Ibid., 1001.
62. TT, E786 (33), *Every Day's Intelligence*, 18–25 July 1651, 379–80.
63. TT, E786 (22), *Several Proceedings*, 17–24 July 1651, 1458–60.
64. *Diurnall of the Armies*, 5–12 Aug. 1651, 1218–19, for Hewson; TT, E786 (30), *The Faithful Scout*, 1–8 Aug. 1651, 368; TT, E785 (14), ibid., 18–25 Apr. 1651, 138; TT, E786 (4), *Several Proceedings*, 12–19 June 1651, 1383–4, for actions in Leinster, Ulster and Munster.
65. TT, E638 (8), *Perfect Account of the Daily Intelligence from the Armies*, 23–30 July 1651, 226, listing the towns captured by the English.
66. TT, E786 (8), *Several Proceedings*, 19–26 June 1651, 1393.
67. Ibid., 1395, for the navy's logistical contribution; TT, E786 (29), *Several Proceedings*, 31 July–7 Aug. 1651, 1486, Ireton to Lenthall, 15 July 1651, reporting his surfeit of troops; *Diurnall of the Armies*, 23–30 June 1651, 1121, for a count of the number of pressed men (4,795) and veterans (4,350) sent to Ireland since March.
68. TT, E786 (29), *Several Proceedings*, 31 July–7 Aug. 1651, 1486–7, Ireton to Lenthall, 15 July 1651.
69. Ibid., 1487.
70. Ibid.
71. For the date of the assault see TT, E638 (15), *The Armies Intelligencer*, 29 July–5 Aug. 1651, 4, letter from Limerick, 4 July 1651; *Diurnall of the Armies*, 28 July–4 Aug. 1651, 1210.
72. TT, E786 (29), *Several Proceedings*, 31 July–7 Aug. 1651, 1487, Ireton to Lenthall, 15 July 1651.
73. Ibid., 1488.
74. Ibid.; TT, E638 (13), *Sad News from Ireland*, 4 July 1651, 2–4.
75. TT, E638 (15), *The Armies Intelligencer*, 29 July–5 Aug. 1651, 4; *Diurnall of the Armies*, 28 July–4 Aug. 1651, 1210.
76. TT, E638 (15), *The Armies Intelligencer*, 29 July–5 Aug. 1651, 5, letter from Waterford, 17 July 1651; Burke, 'The New Model Army and the Problems of Siege Warfare', 22.
77. TT, E640 (10), *A Letter from the Lord Broghill*, 4–5.
78. Ibid., 3–4; TT, E640 (9), *Mercurius Politicus*, 7–14 Aug. 1651, 995–6; Carlton, *Going to the Wars*, 142–5, for a discussion of the effects of a rout.
79. Gilbert, ed., *Contemporary History*, iii, 240–44, 'Diaries of the Proceedings of the Forces in Ireland'.
80. TT, E638 (15), *The Armies Intelligencer*, 29 July–5 Aug. 1651, 5.
81. Burke, 'The New Model Army and the Problems of Siege Warfare', 22–3, 25–7; Gilbert, ed., *Contemporary History*, iii, 240, 'Diaries of the Proceedings of the Forces in Ireland'.
82. Gentles, *New Model Army*, 378–9.

83. TT, E786 (9), *Every Day's Intelligence*, 20–27 June 1651, 348; TT, E638 (14), *Weekly Intelligence of the Commonwealth*, 29 July–5 Aug. 1651, 249; TT, E640 (4), *Weekly Intelligence*, 5–11 Aug. 1651, 243–4; Gilbert, ed., *Contemporary History*, iii, 248, 'Diaries of the Proceedings of the Forces in Ireland'; TT, E786 (16), *Every Day's Intelligence*, 4–11 July 1651, 367.

84. Gilbert, ed., *Contemporary History*, iii, 245, 'Diaries of the Proceedings of the Forces in Ireland'; 245; Ludlow, *Memoirs*, i, 367.

85. Dunlop, ed., *Ireland under the Commonwealth*, i, 20, Commissioners to Council of State, 2 Aug. 1651; ibid., 28, Commissioners to Council of State, 21 Aug. 1651; ibid., 30, Commissioners to Council of State, 27 Aug. 1651.

86. *Aphorismical Discovery*, iii, 19–20.

87. Ludlow, *Memoirs*, i, 370.

88. Burke, 'The New Model Army and the Problems of Siege Warfare', 23–4; Borlase, *Irish Rebellion*, 293–6.

89. Borlase, *Irish Rebellion*, 296–9, for the terms.

90. Ludlow, *Memoirs*, i, 374–5.

91. Ibid., 382.

92. Ibid., 376–7.

93. Ibid., 377–80.

94. *Aphorismical Discovery*, iii, 7–8, Clanricarde to Earl of Westmeath, 16 Oct. 1651; ibid., 4, Clanricarde to Bishop Oliver Darcy of Dromore, 16 Oct. 1651.

95. Ibid., 16.

96. Ludlow, *Memoirs*, i, 396–7, quoting from Clanricarde to Ludlow, Mar. 1652.

97. Ibid., 398–9, Ludlow to Clanricarde, Mar. 1652.

98. Gilbert, ed., *Contemporary History*, iii, 293–6, for O'Dwyer's and Fitzpatrick's surrenders; ibid., 304–5, for Daly's surrender of Roscommon.

99. Borlase, *Irish Rebellion*, 301–2.

100. Gilbert, ed., *Contemporary History*, iii, 324–7, for Muskerry's terms; ibid., 294–6, for O'Dwyer's terms; ibid., 296–335, for the articles of surrender for nineteen separate surrenders of Irish forces.

101. Gardiner, 'Transplantation to Connaught', 700. Gardiner cites William Petty's estimate.

102. Petty, cited by Raymond Gillespie, 'Irish Economy at War, 1641–1652', 160.

Chapter 10: Ireland: Aftermath and Settlement (pp 224–239)

1. Dunlop, ed., *Ireland under the Commonwealth*, 239, Commissioners for Ireland to Council of State, 22 July 1652.

2. Sir William Petty, *The Political Anatomy of Ireland, 1672*, London: D. Brown, 1691, 17–21. Petty remains our best source for evidence concerning the size and losses of population, but there is considerable disagreement about the accuracy of his estimates. Foster, *Modern Ireland*, 130, estimates the 1641 population at 2 million; Ohlmeyer, *Ireland from Independence to Occupation*, 13, provides an estimate of 2.1 million; Pádraig Lenihan, 'War and Population' (paper generously given to me by Professor Lenihan in November 1998), argues convincingly that Petty's estimates of total population were somewhat on the high side; L. M. Cullen, 'Economic Trends, 1660–91' in *NHI*, iii, 389, estimates the population to have been 2.1 million in 1641 and 1.7 million in 1672. The figure for 1672 is Petty's. All sources agree as to the large magnitude of the population losses sustained in the period 1641–52.

3. Petty, *Political Anatomy of Ireland*, 18–20.
4. Gillespie, 'Irish Economy at War, 1641–1652', 177–80.
5. Ibid., 175–8.
6. Petty, *Political Anatomy of Ireland*, 18; Sir John Temple, *The Irish Rebellion*, London: R. White for Samuel Gellibrand, 1646.
7. Foster, *Modern Ireland*, 85–6; Ohlmeyer, 'The Wars of Religion, 1603–1660'. Ohlmeyer cites Petty's estimates of losses as well, but concludes that they are no more than 'inspired guesses' (ibid., 185). Nicholas Canny, 'What Really Happened in 1641?', 24–42, discusses the depositions taken from the victims of the initial uprising. He points out that the thirty-two volumes of depositions taken in 1641–3, while biased against Catholics, are still our best source for understanding the magnitude and nature of the uprising. The depositions taken after 1650 are extremely suspect.
8. Gardiner, *History of England*, x, 68–9. Gardiner's sources are based on the depositions of 1641–3.
9. Lenihan, 'War and Population'; Ohlmeyer, 'Wars of Religion', 163, 185; Mac Cuarta, ed., *Ulster 1641: Aspects of the Rising*, provides the best recent study of this controversial period. For an estimate of the number of Protestants in Ireland in 1641 see Petty, *Political Anatomy of Ireland*, 18; and see Ohlmeyer, *Antrim*, 110 n. 58, where she cites Ormond's estimate for the Protestant population as no more than 125,000 (Carte MS 2, fo. 238).
10. Stradling, *Spanish Monarchy and Irish Mercenaries*, 163–8; Joyce Lee Malcolm, 'All the King's Men: The Impact of the Crown's Irish Soldiers on the English Civil War', *Irish Historical Studies*, xxii (1979), 239–64.
11. Bottigheimer, *English Money and Irish Land*, 1–14.
12. Ibid., 44–55; J. R. MacCormack, 'The Irish Adventurers and the English Civil War', *Irish Historical Studies*, v (1956), 21–58.
13. Bottigheimer, *English Money and Irish Land*, 54–75, and Appendix A, List of Original Investors.
14. Ibid., 55–6; Dunlop, ed., *Ireland under the Commonwealth*, i, 248–9; Gardiner, *C & P*, iv, 104, noted that the army cost over £523,000 per year, while the revenue of Ireland was estimated to be £197,000 by the Commissioners for Ireland.
15. Gardiner, 'Transplantation to Connaught'; T. C. Barnard, 'Planters and Policies in Cromwellian Ireland', *Past and Present*, no. 61 (1973), 30–69; Prendergast, *Cromwellian Settlement of Ireland*; Barnard, *Cromwellian Ireland*; T. C. Barnard, 'Settling and Unsettling Ireland: The Cromwellian and Williamite Revolutions' in Ohlmeyer, ed., *Ireland from Independence to Occupation*, 265–91.
16. Gardiner, *C & P*, iv, 87; Dunlop, ed., *Ireland under the Commonwealth*, 244–5. Gardiner provides a detailed analysis of the August 1652 act in his 'Transplantation to Connaught', 702–6.
17. Bottigheimer, *English Money and Irish Land*, 140.
18. Barnard, 'Settling and Unsettling Ireland', 269; Barnard, 'Planters and Policy in Cromwellian Ireland', 31–2.
19. Gardiner, 'Transplantation to Connaught', 733–4; Gardiner, *C & P*, iv, 116–19; Barnard, 'Planters and Policy in Cromwellian Ireland', 32–3, 68–9.
20. Barnard, 'Planters and Policy in Cromwellian Ireland', 39; Gillespie, 'Irish Economy at War, 1641–1652', 178–9.
21. Gardiner, *C & P*, iv, 96–118.
22. Barnard, 'Planters and Policies in Cromwellian Ireland', 44–9, 53–6, 60–67.

23. John D. Grainger, *Cromwell against the Scots: The Last Anglo-Scottish War, 1650–1652*, East Linton: Tuckwell Press, 1997; Roger Hainsworth, *Swordsmen in Power: War and Politics under the English Republic, 1649–1660*, Stroud: Sutton Publishing, 1997, 80–106.

24. Jane Ohlmeyer, 'Introduction: A Failed Revolution' and 'Ireland Independent: Confederate Foreign Policy and International Relations during the Mid-Seventeenth Century' in Ohlmeyer, ed., *Ireland from Independence to Occupation*.

25. James S. Wheeler, 'Four Armies in Ireland' in Ohlmeyer, ed., *Ireland from Independence to Occupation*, 50–51.

Bibliography

Primary Sources

Abbott, W. C., ed., *The Writings and Speeches of Oliver Cromwell*, 3 vols, Oxford: Clarendon Press, 1989

Borlase, Edmund, *The History of the Execrable Irish Rebellion*, London: Henry Brome, 1680

Calendar of State Papers, Domestic, Charles I, 1625–1649, 23 vols, London: HMSO, 1891

Calendar of State Papers, Domestic, Interregnum, 1649–1660, 13 vols, London: HMSO, 1875–86

Calendar of State Papers, Domestic, Ireland, 1633–1647, ed. R. P. Mahaffy. London: HMSO, 1908

Calendar of State Papers, Domestic, Ireland. 1647–1660, ed. R. P. Mahaffy. London: HMSO, 1908

Carte Manuscripts (30 vols, Bodleian Library, Oxford)

Carte, Thomas, *The Life of James, First Duke of Ormond . . . with an Appendix of Letters Serving to Verify the Most Material Facts in the Said History*, vols v–vi, Oxford: Oxford University Press, 1851

Cary, Henry, ed., *Memorials of the Great Civil War in England from 1641 to 1652*, 2 vols, London: Henry Colburn, 1842

Castlehaven, James Tuchet, Earl of, *The Earl of Castlehaven's Review: or his Memoirs of his Engagement and Carriage in the Irish Wars*, London: Charles Brome, 1684

Clanricarde, Ulick Burke, Marquis of, *Memoirs and Letters of Ulick, Marquis of Clanricarde*, London: J. Hughes, 1757

Clarke, Sir William, *Manuscripts, 1640–1664*, ed. G. E. Aylmer, Hassocks: Harvester Press, Microform Edition, 1979, MS 2/1, 'Letters and Other Papers dealing with the Army . . . 1640–1660'

Corish, Patrick J., ed., 'The Unpublished Letters of Owen Roe O'Neill', *Analecta Hibernica*, xxix (1980), 222–48

Dunlop, Robert, ed. *Ireland under the Commonwealth: being a Selection of Documents relating to the Government of Ireland, 1651–9*, 2 vols, Manchester: Manchester University Press, 1913

Dyve, Sir Lewis, *A Letter from Sir Lewis Dyve to the Lord Marquis of Newcastle, giving to his Lordship an Account of the Whole Conduct of the King's Affairs in Ireland . . . to 1650*, The Hague: Samuel Brown, 1650 (British Library, TT, E616 (7))

Firth, C. H., and Rait, R. S., eds, *Acts and Ordinances of the Interregnum, 1642–1660*, 3 vols, London: HMSO, 1911

Gilbert, Sir John T., ed., *A Contemporary History of Affairs in Ireland, from A.D. 1641 to 1652, with an Appendix of Original Letters and Documents*, 3 vols, Dublin: Irish Archaeological and Celtic Society, 1879–80

Hogan, E. D., ed., *The History of the War of Ireland from 1641 to 1653, by a British Officer of the Regiment of Sir John Clotworthy*, Dublin: McGlashan & Gill, 1873

Holles, Denzil, *The Memoirs of Denzil Holles*, London: Tim Goodwin, 1699

Journals of the House of Commons [England]

Ludlow, Edmund, *Memoirs of Edmund Ludlow, Lieutenant-General of the Horse, Commander-in-Chief of the Forces in Ireland, One of the Council of State, and a Member of the Parliament which began on November 3, 1640*, 2 vols, Vevay, 1698

Petty, Sir William, *The Political Anatomy of Ireland, 1672*, London: D. Brown, 1691

State Papers, SP 25/118, 'A Particular of the Charges of Raising and Paying the Eight Regiments of Foot, the Six Regiments of Horse, and the One Regiment of Dragoons . . . designed to go with the Lord Lieutenant . . . April 1649 to March 1650', London [1650] (Public Record Office, London)

____ SP 63/281, 'Account of Money transmitted out of England upon the Army in Ireland, 1649–1656', London [1656–7] (Public Record Office, London)

Temple, Sir John, *The Irish Rebellion*, London: R. White for Samuel Gellibrand, 1646

Thomason Tracts (British Library, London)

Whitelocke, Bulstrode, *Memorials of the English Affairs, or an Historical Account*, 4 vols, London: Nathaniel Ponder, 1682

Secondary Sources

Aylmer, Gerald, *The State's Servants: The Civil Service of the English Republic, 1649–1660*, London: Routledge & Kegan Paul, 1973

Bagwell, Richard, *Ireland under the Stuarts and the Interregnum*, 3 vols, London: Holland Press, 1909–16

Bardon, Jonathan, *A History of Ulster*, Belfast: Blackstaff Press, 1992

Barnard, T. C., *Cromwellian Ireland: English Government and Reform in Ireland, 1649–1660*, Oxford: Oxford University Press, 1975

____ 'Irish Images of Oliver Cromwell' in Richardson, ed., *Images of Oliver Cromwell*

____ 'Planters and Policies in Cromwellian Ireland', *Past and Present*, no. 61 (1973), 30–69

____ 'Settling and Unsettling Ireland: The Cromwellian Williamite Revolutions' in Ohlmeyer, ed., *Ireland from Independence to Occupation*

____ 'The Uses of 23 October 1641 and Irish Protestant Celebrations', *English Historical Review*, cvi (1991), 888–920

Bartlett, Thomas, and Jeffery, Keith, eds, *A Military History of Ireland*, Cambridge: Cambridge University Press, 1996

Baumber, M. L., 'The Navy and Civil War in Ireland, 1641–1643', *Mariner's Mirror*, lvii (Nov. 1971), 385–97

Beckett, J. C., *The Cavalier Duke: A Life of James Butler, 1st Duke of Ormond*, Belfast: Pretani Press, 1990

____ 'The Confederation of Kilkenny Reviewed' in his *Confrontations in Irish History*, London: Faber & Faber, 1972

____ *The Making of Modern Ireland, 1603–1923*, London: Faber & Faber, 1966

Bennett, Martyn, *The Civil Wars in Britain and Ireland, 1638–1651*, Oxford: Blackwell, 1997

Bottigheimer, Karl S., *English Money and Irish Land: The 'Adventurers' in the Cromwellian Settlement of Ireland*, Oxford: Clarendon Press, 1971

Bryan, Dan, 'Ballyshannon Fort, Co. Kildare, 1642–1650', *Irish Sword*, iv (1959–60), 93–8

Burghclere, Lady, *The Life of James, First Duke of Ormonde, 1610–1688*, 2 vols, London: John Murray, 1912

Burke, James, 'The New Model Army and the Problems of Siege Warfare', *Irish Historical Studies*, xxvii (1990), 1–29

Burke, William, *History of Clonmel*, Kilkenny: Roberts Books, 1983

Canny, Nicholas, *From Reformation to Restoration: Ireland 1534–1660*, Dublin: Helicon, 1987

____ 'What Really Happened in 1641?' in Ohlmeyer, ed., *Ireland from Independence to Occupation*

Capp, Bernard, 'George Wharton, "Bellum Hybernicale", and the Cause of Irish Freedom', *English Historical Review*, cxii (1997), 671–7

Carlin, Norah, 'The Levellers and the Conquest of Ireland in 1649', *Historical Journal*, xxx (1987), 269–88

Carlton, Charles, *Going to the Wars: The Experience of the British Civil Wars, 1638–1651*, London: Routledge, 1992

Carte, Thomas, *The Life of James, First Duke of Ormond* [1735–6], 2nd ed., 6 vols, Oxford: Oxford University Press, 1851

Carty, James, ed., *Ireland from the Flight of the Earls to Grattan's Parliament (1607–1782): A Documentary Record*, Dublin: C. J. Fallon, 1965

Casway, Jerrold, 'George Monck and the Controversial Catholic Truce of 1649', *Studia Hibernica*, xvi (1976), 54–72

____ *Owen Roe O'Neill and the Struggle for Catholic Ireland*, Philadelphia: University of Pennsylvania Press, 1984

Clohosay, T. J., 'Cromwell's Siege of Kilkenny', *Old Kilkenny Review*, viii (1955), 36–47

Corish, Patrick J., 'Bishop Nicholas French and the Second Ormond Peace, 1648–9', *Irish Historical Studies*, vi (1948), 83–100

____ 'The Crisis in Ireland in 1648: The Nuncio and the Supreme Council: Conclusions', *Irish Theological Quarterly*, xxii (July 1955), 230–57

____ 'Rinuccini's Censure of 27 May 1648', *Irish Theological Quarterly*, xviii (Oct. 1951), 322–37

____ 'The Rising of 1641 and the Catholic Confederacy, 1641–5' in *NHI*, iii

____ 'Ormond, Rinuccini, and the Confederates, 1645–9' in *NHI*, iii

____ 'The Cromwellian Conquest, 1649–53' in *NHI*, iii

Cregan, Donal F., 'The Confederation of Kilkenny: Its Personnel and History' (Ph.D. thesis, National University of Ireland, 1947)

Dineen, Patrick F., 'The Siege of Clonmel' in O'Connell and Carmody, eds, *Tercentenary of the Siege of Clonmel*

Durston, Chris, '"Let Ireland Be Quiet": Opposition in England to the Cromwellian Conquest of Ireland', *History Workshop Journal*, xxi (1986), 105–12

Elkin, Robert, 'The Interaction between the Irish Rebellion and the English Civil War' (Ph.D. thesis, University of Illinois, Urbana, 1961)

Esson, D. M. R., *The Curse of Cromwell: A History of the Ironside Conquest of Ireland, 1649–53*, Totowa, NJ: Rowman & Littlefield, 1971

Firth, C. H., *Cromwell's Army* [1902], repr., intro. John Adair, London: Greenhill Books, 1992

Fissel, Mark C., ed., *War and Government in Britain, 1598–1650*, Manchester: Manchester University Press, 1991

Fitzpatrick, Brendan, *Seventeenth-Century Ireland: The Wars of Religion*, Dublin: Gill & Macmillan, 1988

Foster, R. F., *Modern Ireland, 1600–1972*, London: Penguin, 1988

Frank, Joseph, *The Beginnings of the English Newspapers, 1620–1660*, Cambridge, Mass.: Harvard University Press, 1961

Gardiner, Samuel R., *Cromwell's Place in History* [1897], repr., Freeport, NY: Books for Libraries, 1969

_____ *History of England, 1603–1642* [1863–81], 2nd ed., 10 vols, London: Longmans, Green & Co., 1883–4

_____ *History of the Great Civil War, 1642–1649* [1886–91], repr., 4 vols, New York: AMS, 1965

_____, *History of the Commonwealth and Protectorate, 1649–1656* [1894–1901], repr., 4 vols, New York: AMS, 1965

_____ 'The Transplantation to Connaught', *English Historical Review*, xiv (1899), 700–34

Gentles, Ian, 'The Arrears of Pay of the Parliamentary Army at the End of the First Civil War', *Bulletin of the Institute of Historical Research*, xlviii (1975), 52–63

_____ *The New Model Army in England, Ireland, and Scotland, 1645–1653*, Oxford: Blackwell, 1992

Gillespie, Raymond, 'The Irish Economy at War, 1641–1652' in Ohlmeyer, ed., *Ireland from Independence to Occupation*

Grainger, John D. *Cromwell against the Scots: The Last Anglo-Scottish War, 1650–1652*, East Linton: Tuckwell Press, 1997

Habakkuk, H. J., 'The Parliamentary Army and the Crown Lands', *Welsh History Review*, iii (1960), 403–60

_____ 'Public Finance and the Sale of Confiscated Property during the Interregnum', *Economic History Review*, xv (1962) 70–88

Hainsworth, Roger, *Swordsmen in Power: War and Politics under the English Republic, 1649–1660*, Stroud: Sutton Publishing, 1997

Hallick, Clive, 'Owen Roe O'Neill's Ulster Army of the Confederacy, May–August 1646', *Irish Sword*, xviii (1991–2), 220–26

Hayes-McCoy, G. A., ed., *Ulster and Other Irish Maps, c. 1600*, Dublin: Irish Manuscripts Commission, 1964

Hazlett, Hugh, 'A History of the Military Forces Operating in Ireland, 1641–1649' (Ph.D. thesis, Queen's University, Belfast, 1938)

_____ 'The Recruitment and Organisation of the Scottish Army in Ulster, 1642–9' in H. A. Cronne, T. W. Moody and D. B. Quinn, eds, *Essays in British and Irish History in honour of James Eadie Todd*, London: Frederick Muller, 1949

Hogan, John, *Kilkenny*, Kilkenny: P. M. Egan, 1884

Howell, Roger, 'Images of Oliver Cromwell' in Richardson, ed., *Images of Oliver Cromwell*

Joad, Raymond, 'An Eye-witness to King Cromwell', *History Today*, xlvii (July 1997), 35–41

_____ *The Invention of the Newspaper: English Newsbooks, 1641–1649*, Oxford: Clarendon Press, 1996

Keane, John E., 'The Cromwellian Siege of Kilkenny', *Old Kilkenny Review*, xvi (1964), 75–82

Kearney, Hugh, *Strafford in Ireland, 1633–41: A Study in Absolutism*, Cambridge: Cambridge University Press, 1959; repr., 1989

Kenyon, John, and Ohlmeyer, Jane, eds, *The British and Irish Civil Wars: A Military History of Scotland, Ireland, and England, 1638–1660*, Oxford: Oxford University Press, 1998

Kerr, Archibald, *An Ironside of Ireland: The Remarkable Career of Lieutenant-General Michael Jones, Governor of Dublin and Commander of the Parliamentary Forces in Leinster, 1647–1649*, London: Heath Cranton, 1923

Lenihan, Pádraig, '"Celtic" Warfare in the 1640s' in Young, ed., *Celtic Dimensions of the British Civil Wars*

Lindley, Keith, 'The Impact of the 1641 Rebellion upon England and Wales, 1641–5', *Irish Historical Studies*, xviii (1972), 143–75

Little, Patrick, '"Blood and Friendship": The Earl of Essex's Protection of the Earl of Clanricarde's Interests, 1641–6', *English Historical Review*, cxii (1997), 927–41

Lowe, John, 'Charles I and the Confederation of Kilkenny, 1643–9', *Irish Historical Studies*, xiv (1964), 1–19

_____ 'The Earl of Antrim and Irish Aid to Montrose', *Irish Sword*, iv (1959–60), 190–98

_____ 'Some Aspects of the War in Ireland, 1641–1649', *Irish Sword*, iv (1959–60), 81–7

McCarthy, William, 'The Royalist Collapse in Munster, 1650–52', *Irish Sword*, vi (1964), 171–9

MacCormack, J. R., 'The Irish Adventurers and the English Civil War', *Irish Historical Studies*, v (1956), 21–58

MacCraith, L. M., *The Suir: from its Source to the Sea*, Clonmel: Clonmel Chronicle, 1912

Mac Cuarta, Brian, ed., *Ulster 1641: Aspects of the Rising*, Belfast: Institute of Irish Studies, 1993

McElligott, Jason, *Cromwell: Our Chief of Enemies*, Dundalk: Dundalgan Press, 1994

McKenny, Kevin J., 'The Landed Interest, Political Ideology, and Military Campaigns of the Northwest Ulster Settlers and their Lagan Army, 1641–1685' (Ph.D. thesis, State University of New York, Stony Brook, 1994)

Malcolm, Joyce Lee, 'All the King's Men: The Impact of the Crown's Irish Soldiers on the English Civil War', *Irish Historical Studies*, xxii (1979), 239–64

Meagher, John, *Annals, Antiquities, and Records of Carrick-on-Suir*, Dublin: James Duffy, 1881

Moody, T. W., Martin, F. X., and Byrne, F. J., eds, *A New History of Ireland*, iii: *Early Modern Ireland, 1534–1691*, Oxford: Clarendon Press, 1976

Morrill, John, ed., *Oliver Cromwell and the English Revolution*, London: Longman, 1990

Murphy, Denis, *Cromwell in Ireland: A History of Cromwell's Irish Campaign* [1883], new ed., Dublin: M. H. Gill, 1897

Murphy, John A, 'Inchiquin's Changes of Religion', *Journal of the Cork Historical and Archaeological Society*, lxxii (1967), 58–68

O'Brien, Barry, ed., *Studies in Irish History, 1603–1649*, Dublin: Browne & Nolan, 1906

O'Brien, Ivor, *Murragh the Burner: A Life of Murragh, Sixth Baron and First Earl of Inchiquin, 1614–74*, Whitegate, Ireland: Ballinakella Press, 1991

O'Connell, P., and Carmody, W. C., eds, *Tercentenary of the Siege of Clonmel, 1650–1950*, Clonmel: Nationalist Newspaper Co., 1950

Ohlmeyer, Jane, *Civil War and Restoration in the Three Stuart Kingdoms: The Career of Randal MacDonnell, Marquis of Antrim, 1609–1683*, Cambridge: Cambridge University Press, 1993

____ 'The Dunkirk of Ireland: Wexford Privateers during the 1640s', *Journal of the Wexford Historical Society*, x (1988–9), 23–49

____ 'Introduction: A Failed Revolution' in Ohlmeyer, ed., *Ireland from Independence to Occupation*

____ ed., *Ireland from Independence to Occupation, 1641–1660*, Cambridge: Cambridge University Press, 1995

____ 'Ireland Independent: Confederate Foreign Policy and International Relations during the Mid-Seventeenth Century' in Ohlmeyer, ed., *Ireland from Independence to Occupation*

____ 'Irish Privateers during the Civil War, 1642–50', *Mariner's Mirror*, lxxvi (May 1990), 119–33

____ 'The Wars of Religion, 1603–1660' in Bartlett and Jeffery, eds, *Military History of Ireland*

Percival-Maxwell, Michael, 'Ireland and the Monarchy in the Early Stuart Multiple Kingdom', *Historical Journal*, xxxiv (1991), 275–95

____ 'Ireland and Scotland, 1638–1648' in John Morrill, ed., *The Scottish National Covenant in its British Context*, Edinburgh: Edinburgh University Press, 1990

Perry, Nicholas, 'The Infantry of the Confederate Army of Leinster', *Irish Sword*, lxi (winter 1983), 233–5

Powell, J. R., *The English Navy in the Civil Wars*, London: Archon Books, 1962

Prendergast, John P., *The Cromwellian Settlement of Ireland* [1865], repr., London: Constable, 1996

Quinn, David B., 'The Munster Plantation: Problems and Opportunities', *Journal of the Cork Historical and Archaeological Society*, lxxi (1966), 19–40

Ramsey, Robert, *Henry Ireton*, London: Longmans, Green & Co., 1949

Ranger, Terence O., 'Richard Boyle and the Making of an Irish Fortune, 1588–1614', *Irish Historical Studies*, x (1957), 257–97

Reilly, Tom, *Cromwell at Drogheda*, Drogheda: Broin Print, 1993

Richardson, R. C., ed., *Images of Oliver Cromwell*, Manchester: Manchester University Press, 1993

Ross, W. G., *Military Engineering during the Great Civil War, 1642–9*, London: Ken Trotman, 1984

Russell, Conrad, 'The British Background to the Irish Rebellion of 1641', *Historical Research*, lxi (June 1988), 166–82

____ 'The British Problem and the English Civil War', *History*, lxxii (Oct. 1987), 395–415

____ *The Causes of the English Civil War*, Oxford: Clarendon Press, 1990

____ *The Fall of the British Monarchies, 1637–1641*, Oxford: Clarendon Press, 1991

Ryder, Ian, *An English Army for Ireland*, London: Partizan Press, 1987

Shagan, Ethan Howard, 'Constructing Discord: Ideology, Propaganda, and English Responses to the Irish Rebellion of 1641', *Journal of British Studies*, xxxvi (Jan. 1997), 4–34

Simms, J. G., 'Cromwell at Drogheda', *Irish Sword*, xi (1974), 386–93

____ 'Cromwell's Siege of Waterford, 1649' in his *War and Politics in Ireland, 1649–1730*, ed. D. W. Hayton and Gerard O'Brien, London: Hambledon Press, 1986

Smith, Charles, *The Ancient and Present State of the County and City of Waterford*, Dublin: A. Reilly, 1746

Stevenson, David, *Scottish Covenanters and Irish Confederates: Scottish–Irish Relations in the Mid-Seventeenth Century*, Belfast: Ulster Historical Foundation, 1981

Stradling, Robert A., *The Spanish Monarchy and Irish Mercenaries: The Wild Geese in Spain, 1618–1668*, Dublin: Irish Academic Press, 1994

Tyrrell, Alma Brooke, 'Michael Jones, Governor of Dublin', *Dublin Historical Record*, xxiv (Dec. 1970), 159–71

van Creveld, Martin, *Supplying War: Logistics from Wallenstein to Patton*, Cambridge: Cambridge University Press, 1977

Wedgwood, C. V., *The King's War, 1641–1647*, New York: Book of the Month Club, 1991

_____ *The Life of Oliver Cromwell*, New York: Collier Books, 1966

Wheeler, James S., 'Four Armies in Ireland' in Ohlmeyer, ed., *Ireland from Independence to Occupation*

_____ 'Logistics and Supply in Cromwell's Conquest of Ireland' in Fissel, ed., *War and Government in Britain, 1598–1650*

Williams, J. B. 'The Regicides in Ireland', *Irish Ecclesiastical Record*, 5th ser., ii (1913), 503–14

Woolrych, Austin, 'Cromwell as a Soldier' in Morrill, ed., *Oliver Cromwell and the English Revolution*

Young, John R., ed., *Celtic Dimensions of the British Civil Wars*, Edinburgh: John Donald, 1997

Index